IMPROVISATION, HYPERMEDIA

AND THE ARTS

SINCE 1945

Hazel Smith
School of English, University of New South Wales, Australia

and

Roger T. Dean
austraLYSIS, Sydney, Australia

harwood academic publishers
Australia • Canada • China • France • Germany • India
Japan • Luxembourg • Malaysia • The Netherlands • Russia
Singapore • Switzerland • Thailand • United Kingdom

Amsteldijk 166
1st Floor
1079 LH Amsterdam
The Netherlands

British Library Cataloguing in Publication Data

Smith, Hazel
  Improvisation, hypermedia and the arts since 1945. –
  (Performing arts studies; v. 4)
  1. Improvisation (Acting) – History – 20th century
  2. Improvisation (Music) – History – 20th century
  I. Title   II. Dean, R. T. (Roger Thornton)
  792'.028'0904

  ISBN   3-7186-5888-7

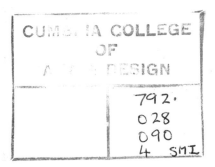
Cover photograph: cris cheek in performance in *Institutional Dim* (1993). Photo:
Jim Harold.

IMPROVISATION, HYPERMEDIA

AND THE ARTS

SINCE 1945

Performing Arts Studies

A series of books edited by Christopher Bodman, London, UK

CONTENTS

4. Improvisation in Monomedia. 1: Sound and Word

5. Improvisation in Monomedia. 2: Visual and Body

INTRODUCTION TO THE SERIES

Performing Arts Studies aims to provide stimulating resource books of a both practical and philosophical nature for teachers and students of the performing arts: music, dance, theatre, film, radio, video, oral poetry, performance art and multimedia forms.

International and multicultural in scope and content, *Performing Arts Studies* seeks to represent the best and most innovative contemporary directions in performing arts education, and will focus particularly on the work of practising artists who are also involved in teaching.

Christopher Bodman

LIST OF FIGURES

ACKNOWLEDGEMENTS

We would like to make especial acknowledgement here of some of the people and institutions who have aided the research embodied in this work. Firstly, our interviewees and those who responded to our questionnaire: these people are listed in Appendix 4 of the book. Secondly, we received particular help from our friend Rory Spence (University of Tasmania). Practical support was generously provided by Bruce Ames (University of California at Berkeley) and John Chapman (INSERM U321, Paris). Additional help was provided by several others, including Mary Chan (University of New South Wales), Dave Curtis (Arts Council of England, Film Section), Jepke Goudsmit and Graham Jones, Rob Jordan (University of New South Wales), Lloyd Swanton, and Greg White (Macquarie University). We would also like to thank David Murray (University of Nottingham) for past help in research on American poetry.

Several institutions were invaluable in their kind provision of library and archival facilities: the American Poetry Archive, at San Francisco State University; the Australian Broadcasting Corporation; the British Library; New York Public Library (Theatre on Film and Tape Collection; and the Robbins Dance Collection); University of California at Berkeley, and at Santa Cruz; University of New South Wales; and the University of Sydney.

We reference all our sources of quotations, and make due acknowledgement of the illustrations, as they occur. Here we would like to mention with thanks the special permissions received from: cris cheek; Bob Cobbing; Andy Goldsworthy; Jeff Keen; Kinetic Energy; Jackson Mac Low; and the Museum of Modern Art, New York (Rivers/O'Hara collaboration).

Hazel Smith
Roger Dean

Section I

THE NATURE OF IMPROVISATION

Improvised performances need to be undertaken by someone who has thoroughly considered beforehand those elements mentioned earlier (language, voice, gesture), and above all the actor must be careful not to speak when his partner is holding forth, so as to avoid that confusion so tedious to those who are listening, as so disagreeable to the one speaking. (Cecchini, 1629. Quoted in (Richards and Richards, 1990) p. 201)

1

INTRODUCTION

During my first years in New York (c. 1967) I fell into a free theatre workshop run by Joyce Aaron, a member of the Open Theatre. One day she asked us to do an exercise where we stood up and told a personal story as far as we could. If we blanked out or ran out of personal memories we were to jam, like a jazz musician, on a particular word or phrase until a new passage came. To my surprise, when it was my turn I experienced a memory film, a series of rather mundane events that had occurred during the previous week. I had no trouble editing or selecting which material to use as I spoke. The images all came into my mind in vivid frames and I was able to describe it all in perfect detail. When I sat down, Joyce said, 'Very interesting. Who wrote that monologue for you?'
Spalding Gray, preface to "Swimming to Cambodia" ((Gray, 1987) p. 7–8).

Purposes of this Book

A very simple definition of artistic improvising is that it is the simultaneous conception and performance of a work (Dean, 1989; Dean, 1992). But it can be an important objective of improvisation to break prior constraints, including definitions. Improvisation is not a discrete, singular concept and necessarily changes with time. The simple definition will therefore need considerable elaboration, and this will be amongst our aims in Chapter 2. At present we need to note that the concept and relevance of improvisation can extend beyond the *performing* arts, in which the whole work unfolds in the presence of an audience. For improvisation may take place in private or in public. Private improvisation may result in a work which is a single "fixed" object to be viewed in a non-performance context (e.g. a painting). Or it may result in an event which is "fixed" for performance (e.g. some plays and films).

Our purpose in this book is to dissect developments in improvisation in the arts since 1945, with a particular emphasis on process and technique. The approach is analytical and theoretical but is also relevant to practitioners and their audience. Our key argument is that improvisation has been of great importance and value in the contemporary arts, particularly because of its potential to develop new forms (often by breaking definitions). This does not mean that the resulting works have necessarily been formalist, but that they have been notable for their exploration of the relationship between creative process, structure and content. We will therefore also argue that improvised works challenge traditional notions of the self, textuality and representation, and that they are often dense, complex and multiple. Some of the forms which have arisen through improvisation have remained improvisatory, while others have become the basis of compositional processes. We view composition as a means of creating art works as fully as possible prior to their exposure to their audience. Compositions may still need performance (e.g. a symphony, or a ballet). This concept of composition is, of course, continuous with that of improvisation, but remains useful.

To varying degrees, improvisation is a part of much popular culture (the stand-up comic; theatresports; rock; hip-hop, graffiti art, rap). But as Richard Middleton (Middleton, 1990) has discussed in detail in the case of music, popular culture is often characterised by "closed" forms and procedures. Some improvisors have, however, reacted against "closed" forms. Such reactions are often considered part of the formation of an avant-garde or experimental vanguard of an art form. Consequently, improvisation usually contributes to these vanguards.

The concept of the "avant-garde" has been developed by critics and practitioners in variegated and inconsistent ways (see discussions of the term in (Perloff, 1991; Radano, 1993)). Our emphases in using this term are as follows. Firstly, that the avant-garde does react against closed forms, as just mentioned; though it has sometimes existed in a symbiotic relationship with popular culture. Secondly, that it attempts also to create new forms, which later avant-gardes can overthrow. Finally, that an avant-garde often institutionalises its separation from the rest of its artistic community, for example by formation of self-sustaining and sometimes exclusive organisations or concentrated communities of artists. Later we will also discuss the concept of a postmodern avant-garde.

Amongst our subsidiary arguments is the idea that improvisation offers more scope for performers than they may have in composed forms: this permits change in the composer/performer/audience relationship. Improvisation also provides a tool for collaboration between several individuals, be they creators, performers or audience/participants. It has been stressed by several improvisors (e.g. (Rose, 1994)) that an audience can often recognise that improvisation is taking place. This knowledge (even if obtained simply by reading a note) encourages an enthusiastic response which is otherwise sometimes lacking. An audience sympathetic to the risk-taking of performers is a supportive one.

Improvisation may even permit the destruction of the audience/creator separation which has existed particularly in Western society, but often somewhat less so in other societies. Hypermedia and interactive technologies will facilitate this. But improvisation has extreme relevance beyond the arts, for example in education and psychotherapy. We have discussed some of these issues briefly in the body of the book, and given outlines of their importance in Appendix 2.

Improvisation has not only encouraged collusion by the audience with the artist, but also collaboration between artists. In some spheres, such as musical composition, collaboration between creators has been quite unusual and perhaps relatively unsuccessful. This may be simply because of a lack of experience in collaboration, or it may also reflect particular difficulties of such work because of the relatively "fixed" aesthetic viewpoints of the participants, and the hesitation to mould these to each others'. Collaboration between artists working in different media may overcome these problems, and improvisation has often been a means of achieving this.

It is also our view that improvisation, and process analysis in general, should be more widely used as critical concepts. In fact, analysis of the creative process is generally neglected in studies of artistic works. The discussion of improvisation can be a useful way of characterising certain types of creative process which balance ideas of control and lack of control, without resorting to naive views of either spontaneity or absolute composition. However, improvisation and the broader creative processes of which it is part, are never de-contextualised, value free concepts. The term improvisation has been used by different people to support a range of artistic and cultural values at different times, while the act of improvising has often been performed by people who would not describe their actions as such. It is one of the purposes of this book to show how improvising and ideas about it have changed with time, and how they are affected by different art movements and cultural situations. We have included some artists who would not normally be described as improvisors but whose techniques seem to us to be strongly connected with improvisatory ones. We also examine some of the controversies surrounding improvised works, or works which are presented as being improvised, and the kind of assumptions surrounding these disputes. In some cases artists have made extravagant claims for the improvised nature of the work, because they thought this would attract attention. In other cases critics have seriously undervalued the improvised nature of the process, and have asserted that the work was not improvised, because composition would have greater artistic or academic status.

In fact there has been a long-standing prejudice against improvisation. Promoters of artistic events have often identified improvisation with a financially non-viable experimental art. Similarly, there has been a tendency amongst critics and the academic community at large to undervalue these kind of works because, particularly when improvisation takes place in performance, they are non-repeatable, unfixed and transient. The critic often presumes that such events are incomplete preparations for a later finished performance, and does not appreciate the quite distinct nature of an improvised work. This wildly mistaken presumption has been widely discussed (for example, in (Marowitz, 1978)).

A further problem improvisation poses which critics are reluctant to face, is that there is often no script or score, no object which can lend itself easily to critical analysis. Even where there is a text it will be incomplete: either a score used as a basis for improvising or a provisional transcription. Likewise, recordings or films of improvisations present problems to an academic community still very rooted in texts and the myth of their finality. Keir Elam points out that semiotic performance analysis, as conducted in the later 60s and 70s, was "an 'avant-garde' and methodologically anti-traditionalist endeavour" which tended to look to the avant-garde for its "ideal models of theatricality" (Fitzpatrick, 1989) p. 4). Yet it still favoured theatre that was textual because it offered an object for analysis.

This emphasis on textuality should have been, and to some extent has been, eased by more recent theoretical debates which have opened up the concept of the text. Post-colonial theory has produced a greater awareness of the marginalisation of oral texts (Ashcroft, Griffiths *et al.*, 1989), and structuralist/post structuralist theory has generated the realisation that no text is a fixed and static product, since it is always subject to the reader's activity. These ideas have a direct bearing on improvised work. However, because improvised work is not widely understood or available and is sometimes misread as a nostalgia for spontaneity, it has not been seen to fit so easily with contemporary theory as, for example, L=A=N=G=U=A=G=E poetry (Andrews and Bernstein, 1984), which is now more widely discussed in the academic community. We will argue that improvised works have often challenged the dominant norms of representation and subjectivity more fully.

The critical appreciation of improvisation also requires different types of analytical skills from those normally developed in the academic community: the ability to analyse sounds or events on an aural or visual basis, or to mediate between event and transcription. These are skills which academics may be reluctant, or find it difficult, to acquire. Moreover, many members of the cultural establishment are rooted in the idea of creativity as a teleological progression towards a final work underpinned by labour and revision, a conception which improvisation tends to unsettle. For young aspiring artists the ephemerality of improvisation produces problems of its own; they need commodities to show and sell. All these perceived and partly imagined difficulties have resulted in a strong pressure towards composition amongst artists and a prejudice against improvisation amongst critics. It is possible, however, that the change towards a more computer-orientated society will ameliorate this situation, since hypertext and virtual texts will tend to change substantially the basis of all textuality.

In developing our arguments about improvisation we will necessarily be highly selective in our illustration of works, though we aim to discuss a very wide spectrum of the relevant ideas. Our emphasis will be on works from Europe, North America and Australia, and this includes works of the Afro-American diaspora, such as jazz. Because of our focus on the period since 1945, we will not discuss in detail traditional improvised forms such as Indian music, though we may make occasional reference to them.

We seek to illustrate possibility as well as fulfilment and achievement, by unravelling the nature of the improvised procedures, their elements and output. We do not aim (nor would it be possible) to provide a comprehensive chronological survey, or to catalogue "important" works: rather we choose examples to illustrate potentialities, and to reflect the broad internationalism of the improvising endeavour. Every person with a substantial experience of improvised arts is likely to find some of their favourite practitioners omitted; however, we suspect that, in compensation, they will find practitioners included with whom they were previously unfamiliar. Our approach will be both synchronic and diachronic, since we wish not only to analyse improvising techniques, but also to show that improvisation was particularly influential in the sixties, and has diversified and transformed since then into a variety of forms of creativity, including performance art and hypermedia.

Like the practice of improvisation itself, we will largely eschew conventional categories of the arts (such as "theatre", "music" etc) in favour of their analytical separation into component elements. By discarding these categories we can show more logically the relationship between improvisation and any particular medium. We will discuss individual media ("monomedia"), their assembly into bimedia and polymedia, and the semiotic con- and divergences which result. (The current term "multimedia" is most often used to refer to the juxtaposition of several media, which are still kept quite separate from each other, though the usage of the term is highly variable. In contrast our term, polymedia, is entirely general. We will use it as both a singular and plural form, for simplicity, and by analogy with the current usage of the word multimedia.) Similarly, we will discuss the environments in which improvisation takes and has taken place, distinguishing real, constructed and virtual spaces. We will emphasise the importance of technological change, and computerisation in particular, for this has permitted the development of spaces in which improvisation can not only be non-linear (as was true of much improvising before 1945), but also multi-dimensional and interactive. By this we mean that both creator and audience can influence the progress of a work such that discontinuities become continuous, and multiple layers change their juxtaposition with each other, and may remain silent or be expressed. While it has always been possible for these ideas to be used by an improvisor, hypermedia make this explicit and more readily available and appreciated.

Our methodologies in devising this book have been both multi-dimensional and interactive. Besides surveying on-line available literature on the subject, and reviewing it, we have also searched many areas such as performance or orality, which impinge on improvisation. We have also sought and analysed a range of improvised examples of the various mono-, bi- and polymedia forms we have distinguished. Videos, films and recordings (usually non-commercial and only available in libraries and archives) have been our objects of study, but also live performances, written texts which are "transcriptions" of improvisations, and scores which may be the basis for an improvisation or a combination of the preceding. Our research is inevitably biased towards work which is available in transcribed or recorded form, but we have also obtained a considerable amount of material which is not readily available.

Study of the creative process inevitably throws up methodological problems, since it is not always obvious how a particular work of art has been created. To this end we have not only read numerous accounts of the process by improvising artists but have also prepared a questionnaire, which has been circulated to practitioners, theoreticians and critics (see Appendix 4). We have also interviewed improvising representatives of each of the monomedia, using the questionnaire as a basis for conversation. Some of these interviews have been published or quoted elsewhere (Dean, 1992; Dean, 1992; Smith, Dean *et al.*, 1993), but pertinent elements of them are included here. Methodological issues are discussed further in Chapter 2.

Improvisation, or at least the concept of improvisation as it is loosely used, is associated with many fields. In searching the literature on the subject on-line, it is necessary to exclude many of these fields to obtain the material one needs. Key amongst the exclusions, appropriately perhaps, is the concept of "improvement": if one searches for "improv#" (where # indicates that any completion of the word is acceptable), then improving ideas abound. The most useful single search term is "improvis#", which has to be supplemented by "impro" and "improv" (terms quite often used in theatre discourse).

The range of topics unearthed by the search "improvis#" in Current Contents (all online editions 070189- 032394, including the Arts and

Humanities Citation Index) is quite remarkable: it ranges from barnacles (*Balanus improvisus*) and shrimps, to cardiology, forensics, incendiary devices, psychotherapy, vaginoplasty and war. Of the 176 items revealed, 34 have no relevance to the arts. "Impro" produced no hits, while "Improv" gave only articles about the Lotus Corp business software application of that name.

The impression gained is that artistic improvisation is gradually becoming a serious and more common area of academic attention, though the small numbers of publications do not permit a clear assessment of the change. From reviewing published major research books specifically on artistic improvisation in the current era, it is clear that the area is still a minor one: the majority of such books since 1960 are listed here: (Spolin, 1963; Hodgson and Richards, 1966; Schuller, 1968; Moreno, 1973; Jost, 1974; Johnstone, 1979). Some of the few other books focussing on improvisation retain an idealistic, romantic approach, and do not attempt to make the concept very precise. For example, in "Free Play", Nachmanovitch suggests that "for art to appear, we have to disappear", and by this he advocates a meditational or shamanistic approach (Nachmanovitch, 1990). While encouraging interest in improvisation, this does not provide analytical frameworks for assessing its impact.

It is interesting to compare the searches based on academic literature with those based on more popular magazines or newspapers. The example of Radano's detailed study of sound-improvisor Anthony Braxton (Radano, 1993) reveals how little impression can be gained, even from popular magazines, of audience response and involvement. To the contrary, most of the ideas he is able to discuss usefully are those of critics, often professional, and hence representing a narrow community of opinion. In the case of jazz critics, as complained by LeRoi Jones (a.k.a. Amiri Baraka (Baker, 1990)), this community of opinion is often not highly knowledgeable.

Our searches of the popular literature (as undertaken in April 1994) indicate that the term improvisation is becoming more widely used in print, and hence perhaps that the appreciation of its relevance is widening. We will argue that this widening is essential, not only for the development and appreciation of the arts, but also because of the possibility through improvisation of enhancing "audience" participation in the arts. We will also indicate that improvisation is of fundamental importance and of future potential in psychological development generally, and in education specifically.

Before commencing our analysis, we will outline very briefly the backgrounds of improvisation, and the societal and cultural context of our period. We emphasise here that, in agreement with Radano, we do not propose a "vision of stylistic continuity and order" (Radano, 1993), but rather one of heterogeneous evolution in time. The reader should be aware that the analytical separations we will undertake will necessarily give some impression of forming streams of stylistic continuity, and we intend this, but it is important that the multiplicity of contemporaneous endeavour be kept in mind throughout.

A Summary of Improvisation before 1945

Artistic improvisation has differed vastly in importance in different places and times. So while it has been central in Indian music for many centuries, its importance in Western music has oscillated markedly. It was essential to the troubadours and the medieval period; important in the Baroque era, particularly as a mode of decoration or enlargement of preformed harmonic structures; and with the exception of the organ tradition declined thereafter until the advent of jazz (e.g. (Dean, 1992) (Moore, 1992)). Subsequently, as we will discuss in more detail later, its influence and application in sound has broadened. Improvisation, though common in earlier forms, may often have been used in quite constrained ways. Its influence and significance are therefore probably rather different from those of post 1945 improvisation. While the importance of improvisation also varies considerably between different traditional art forms, it seems fairly general that in non-western culture its impact has been almost unbroken, while in western culture it has been intermittent. A few simple examples must suffice, and the reader is referred to previous literature for more detailed description and analysis.

The Homeric tradition of oral story-telling involved an elaborate form of formulaic improvisation (Ong, 1982), and though the tradition was broken, it was the antecedent of many forms in theatre and other verbal performance (such as the work of Antin and Gray, to be discussed in Chapter 4). Its relationship with the improvising forms within jazz has also been discussed (Smith, 1983). The medieval jongleurs or minstrels from 1100 to 1500 performed their romances from memory, but studies by Quinn and Hall (Quinn and Hall, 1982) suggest that improvisation was used as a back-up procedure if memory failed. Elements of each performance were improvised in the sense that the jongleur chose from certain pre-determined rhyme words to construct the romance's couplets. Minstrels ceased to operate in the Elizabethan era, but entertainers such as Lockwood, who travelled England between 1542 and 1572, gave extempore performances which included songs, mime, dances and anecdotes, and encouraged the audience to participate (Wiles, 1987).

Improvisation may have played some part in early Roman theatre, particularly in comedies. Similarly, in the middle ages there were travelling entertainers: mimes, singers, acrobats and puppeteers, who probably worked in a partially improvised fashion. Medieval outdoor theatre stages were often erected in fields and gardens, in the streets and in market squares. Improvisation continued to some degree in Elizabethan performances, as part of the carnivalesque, popular aspect of the theatre. This alternative aspect of the Elizabethan theatre resulted from the influence of popular festivities: these festivities often included scenarios, stories and characterisations which were indeterminate and also gave license to socially repressed behaviours (Bristol, 1985). Richard Tarleton, the famous Elizabethan clown active in the late sixteenth century, often improvised at the end of a play and engaged in contests with the members of the audience who would throw up rhymes which he was expected to better, but he would also sometimes add improvised speeches in the course of the play (Wiles, 1987). Similarly, the Elizabethan performer Will Kemp often added to his parts, and was one of the principal exponents of jigs which were performed at the end of plays, such as Shakespeare's. These jigs included extempore dance, music and acting (Baskervill, 1929; Wiles, 1987). This practice is mentioned in Shakespeare's "Hamlet" (Act 3 scene ii) where Hamlet says "...let those that play your clowns speak no more than is set down for them...".

The development of body movement forms in Asia and Oceania seems to have involved improvisation, but this was then subsumed into a rote-learned tradition, becoming rather less important (see for example recent studies of Polynesian dance: (Kaeppler, 1987)). In Western culture the commedia dell'arte, from the mid sixteenth to the early eighteenth century, amalgamated the streams which could retrospectively be viewed as theatre and dance, and used improvisation in both (Duchartre, 1928; Cairns, 1988; Fisher, 1992). Improvising enabled the commedia to accommodate a wide range of entertainers including buffoons, tumblers and dancers. It was also a way of adapting to different dialects in different places: this would have been virtually impossible through scripted drama. The commedia, which was highly stylised and non-naturalistic, was improvised but within certain limits: a subject was known beforehand and rehearsed in advance, some material was prepared for insertion by players at appropriate moments, and they could also fall back on standard routines such as the comic lazzi. This meant, according to contemporary commentators, that actors sometimes settled too easily for stock dialogue and familiar situations, but it did mean that freeplay was possible in performance (Duchartre, 1928; Richards and Richards, 1990). Improvisation declined with the development of the plush and decorous theatre space in the 18th century and with the rise of the director, who tended to impose and teach rather than allow for the creativity of the performer (Frost and Yarrow, 1990).

A major intermission followed before the emergence of Surrealism, Dada and Futurism in the early twentieth century. Dada performances at the Cabaret Voltaire in Zurich during the first world war often involved improvisation, and so did the other two related movements. All three also courted concepts of chance and indeterminacy which can abut on improvisatory modes. For example, around 1916 Jean Arp allowed pieces of paper to fall to the ground and then pasted them together in whatever order resulted. Collaboration and multi-media work were also important in this early 20th century avant-garde and these often led to or stemmed from improvisatory practices. Most significantly, Surrealist practices were linked to the notion of automatism, as shown in André Breton's definition in the 1924 Surrealist manifesto:

> *SURREALISM, n.-Pure psychic automatism, by which it is intended to express, verbally, in writing or by other means, the real functioning of thought. The dictation of thought, in the absence of all control exercised by reason, and outside all aesthetic or moral preoccupations. ((Rosemont, 1978) p. 122).*

This technique was adopted by Breton and other poets and painters such as Max Ernst. Automatism was also at the root of games such as the "Exquisite Corpses", where sheets of folded paper were passed round a group of people who each contributed a phrase or part of a drawing without knowing what the whole would be. Automatism for the Surrealists was linked to Freudian psychoanalysis: they believed in the role of the unconscious as a source of creative activity. This also concurred with the Surrealists' Marxist politics, since freeing of the unconscious was a way of transgressing social control. Automatism was a form of improvisation, though its practitioners tended to describe it in a somewhat romantic and idealistic way, as a direct route to the unconscious. In addition, automatism clearly attempted to minimise the control and interactivity of which improvisation is capable. Surrealist procedures had a wide influence on early twentieth century writing, one example being "Kora in Hell: Improvisations" by William Carlos Williams (Williams, 1920). This work has been discussed by (Fredman, 1990).

A Brief Quick-time Movie of Improvisation since 1945

We present here a highly compressed synopsis of key improvising achievements, to pave the way for the more detailed discussion of their processes, forms and contents. The diagram (Figure 1) attempts to indicate the convergences of some of the various flows. Later in the book we will break up the conventionally conceived media of the arts, e.g theatre, into their constituent components. Here we will refer to those conventions to introduce the unfamiliar reader to their improvising domains.

We must start our brief survey with jazz, since it is probably the most familiar idiom of improvisation since 1945. Furthermore, the bebop era of jazz was approaching its peak in 1945; it had brought emancipation of technique, fluency, velocity, and harmonies had been extended by the addition of upper components to conventional chords. There were soon some early dalliances with improvising which neglected all the major conventions of jazz. These conventions included the reliance on formulaic referent structures (the 32 bar popular song for example); the reliance on continuously expressed and unchanging pulse and metre; and the avoidance of harmonic complexity, substantial modulation from one key to another, or atonality. Lennie Tristano was one such iconoclast in the 50s. In the early 60s he was followed by Don Ellis and Paul Bley, who also elaborated complex compositional superstructures in their improvisations.

More important was the free jazz movement, which by an elemental reliance on motivic (and often metonymic) improvisation, gradually broke down all the conventions just mentioned. Pioneers were Ornette Coleman, John Coltrane, and Cecil Taylor. A European and Japanese free improvising movement was concurrent, and had quite different features, as well as many in common. It lead into a type of continuous-sound improvisation, exemplified in the work of Evan Parker, and to the unemphatic work of Derek Bailey and others. Currently, computers are important in two main ways. Firstly, in computer interactive work, in which software components of the computer are used to affect the progress of an improvisation and vice versa. Secondly, in the multi-layering of improvisation, which can be achieved by means of performance into computers followed by the digital repetition and modification of that material. The use of the international "ether" of digital sampled sounds is transforming sound improvisation further. For example, there is a multi-user dungeon (MUD) available on the internet in which one can interactively create one's own techno work.

A counterpart to the free jazz movement of the sixties was the first generation of Abstract Expressionist painters, such as Jackson Pollock, who began their excursions into abstraction in the late forties but reached their peak during the fifties. While the concept of improvisation in a non-performing art requires detailed discussion (Chapter 2), it is worth noting the film (Namuth, 1951) of Pollock working in real time on a painting, eventually "losing contact" as he put it, but clearly using improvisatory processes. The Scottish artist Alan Davie also produced many works by brief improvisations in this period, and other artists have elements in common (e.g. Yves Klein and his works involving fire; A.R. Penck in some of his simple linear work; Bruce McLean). A contemporary equivalent of this process is the construction or modification of video images in realtime, and this is increasingly the domain of improvisors (e.g. Nam June Paik in the 60s and 70s; Don Ritter presently).

In the sixties many artists began to develop their work in association with environmental elements. Improvisation extended this movement in the work of Robert Smithson, David Nash, and others. Richard Long plans and improvises walks and constructions in the open environment, and may not even leave clear indications that his work is there to be seen. His record can be photographs instead, though often an object remains. More recently — with work which began in the seventies and has continued into the nineties — Bruce McLean, Andy Goldsworthy and others have exploited the ephemerality of natural objects to improvise art works, both for museum display and for environmental decay, preceded by photographic record.

Human body works are equally part of the natural environment, and throughout the era of "performance art" an improvised element has been present and sometimes central. Other work by Bruce McLean in the 60s and 70s, together with some by Stuart Brisley and Yvonne Rainer, involved long improvised movement patterns and a body form which was distorted in some ways. Similarly Mike Parr mutilated himself in performance in the 70s and subsequently, while Stelarc in the 80s still "hung" himself repeatedly. The concept of creating a new body by these processes is an ultimate extension of the concept of enlarging one's mind-set by improvisation. In the eighties and nineties performance art has diversified in a number of directions. The performances of British poet, cris cheek, for example, have a complex verbal basis and mark a partial return to theatricality and fragmented narrative.

In other media, as in music, one of the key features of improvisation has been the possibility of co-creation by several individuals. In dance this has been particularly important in "contact improvisation", which involves improvised movement through body contact, and has been led by Steve Paxton since about 1972. Offshoots of his work included the US group Pilobolus (since 1973), and there is an undoubted if ambivalent relation between contact improvisation and the important developments in dance fostered by Merce Cunningham (1940s to the present).

Improvisation in film has sometimes comprised direct physical superimposition on the film (e.g. British film-maker Jeff Keen, since the 60s). But in addition Keen and other film-makers (e.g. Godard, Cassavetes) use the actors' event improvisations or contact improvisation. Some film-makers (since 1964), such as the Canadian music-text-visual improvisor Michael Snow, use fixed cameras to record whatever happens in a defined space: sometimes permitting a convergence of improvisation in life and art. Theatre has also shown the influence of these ideas of body, contact, co-creation and environment. For example, some exercises in Viola Spolin's pioneering book on theatre improvisation (Spolin, 1963) involve contact work, and this has influenced a whole school of actors. Improvisation by co-creation in performance has been limited, though it was an element of the work of groups and directors in America and Europe such as the Living Theatre, Compass, Kiss, and Theatre Machine (1950s–1970s). These gave rise to the international theatresports movement, and to some improvisatory TV programs, both professional and competitive. More common has been improvisation in rehearsal, developing a work which was then essentially fixed — to the degree a musical score is fixed — for performance. A notable exponent of this approach has been Mike Leigh (mainly from 1970s to the present), and many of his works have also resulted in films.

The difficulty of verbal improvisation was often a limiting factor in theatrical improvisors' efforts, and perhaps part of their reason for concentration on improvisation in rehearsal. However, some specialist verbal improvisors have made fascinating contributions: for example, the Americans David Antin, in his "talk-pieces" (since mid 1960s), Spalding Gray in his highly entertaining monologues (mainly since 1980s) and Steve Benson (since 1970s). The "text-sound" or sound poetry movement, which explored the interface between language and sound often involved extensive improvisation in both fields. Notable exponents are Bob Cobbing (UK; mainly since 1950s) and Jackson Mac Low (US; mainly since 1950s).

Thus improvisation, as Figure 1 indicates, has been highly active and vastly important since 1945. But developments in improvisation should be set in the context of other related artistic developments initiated by John Cage, a highly innovative musician, poet, and visual artist. He was probably the period's single most complex and diverse practitioner; his first works appeared in the 30s, and he continued to compose until his death in the 1990s. Cage himself was not very interested in improvisation, but rather in chance determination as a compositional method, and the incorporation of environmental events into artistic events. Nevertheless, these processes bear a close relationship to improvisation, and are similarly oppositional to mainstream composition, and to the concept of authorial power.

Cage's techniques and approaches were enormously influential and this had an oblique and interactive effect on improvisation. Sally Banes does not address the matter of Cage's relationship to improvisation but summarises Cage's achievement as follows:

> *Cage's influence on the various arts — in the use of chance methods, a Zen attentiveness to everyday life, an interest in the non-dramatic theatricality of all the arts, and a distinctly dadaesque humour — is ubiquitous. ((Banes, 1993) p. 29).*

She also lists numerous artists and movements which reflect Cage's influence and these include: Allan Kaprow and Happenings; Dick Higgins and Fluxus;

Robert Rauschenberg and sculpture and painting; Jackson Mac Low and poetry; the Living Theatre and Off Off Broadway; Stan Brakhage and film; Merce Cunningham and dance; David Tudor and Robert Dunn and new music. Many of these artists were not primarily improvisors but their processes were often complemented by, and used in conjunction with, improvisation.

We reserve for later (particularly Chapter 10) discussion of the interactive opportunities offered by computers. Although our objective is not to provide either an extensive or a comprehensive list of improvisors and their products, the reference list supplements the materials discussed in the body of the chapters to facilitate the reader's involvement in the field. Many sound works on disc are referenced, but a large improvisation discography is not provided, since one is available in a previous publication (Dean, 1992).

Social and Cultural Context of Improvisation after 1945

The relationship between developments in improvisation and the social and cultural context are complex, for the cultural context is unstable and variable, and the relationship between the two is inevitably interactive. In addition, we are dealing with improvisation in a number of different locations all of which had highly specific social contexts. The following is an attempt to point towards certain relevant social and cultural forces which were in fact highly volatile and specific, and whose influence was often felt long before, and long after, it was most explicit or overt.

In the whole period from 1945 postmodernism has gradually asserted itself, but has often overlapped with continuing modernist values and ideals. Postmodernism has been described in many different ways, some of which are mutually contradictory, but is usually regarded as a social and cultural, rather than purely artistic, phenomenon. Jameson, for example, argues that postmodernism is a stage in the development of capitalist culture resulting in the occlusion of the historical past; the collapse of a sense of political purpose in a multi-directional hyperspace; a breakdown of the distinction between high art and popular culture; the loss of the defamiliarising aspect of modernist art; the large-scale commodification of culture; and the fragmentation of the unified subject (Jameson, 1984). On the other hand Laclau and Mouffe argue that postmodernism requires a rethinking of socialism in terms of a plurality of identities generated by differences in gender and race and sexual orientation, as much as the Marxist notion of class (discussed in (Best and Kellner, 1991)).

Attempts to characterise postmodernism in art have centred on a number of problems about its nature and how it can be distinguished from modernism. In 1980 Ihab Hassan (Hassan, 1980) proposed that postmodernist work had certain characteristics which contrasted strongly with modernist art. He drew up a lengthy list of dichotomies to illustrate this, so that modernism was identified with characteristics such as romanticism/ symbolism, form (conjunctive, closed), purpose, design, hierarchy, mastery/ logos, art object/finished work, while postmodernism was to be identified with characteristics such as pataphysics/dadaism, antiform (disjunctive, open) play, chance, anarchy, exhaustion/silence, process/performance, happening, participation. The categories he draws up have a certain force, though as Margaret Rose points out they can be easily deconstructed to show that postmodernist works have modernist characteristics (Rose, 1991).

Charles Jencks, however, argues that postmodernism is not a substitute for modernism but co-exists with it: it is "double-coded". Nevertheless, the distinction between modernism and postmodernism is still maintained. Postmodernism is seen by Jencks as a reaction against the alienating effects of modernism: it is popular, pluralist, piecemeal, pro-metaphor, pro-historical reference, pro-humour, and pro-symbolic ((Jencks, 1986) p. 213) also discussed in ((Rose, 1991) p. 113–116).

A central issue in the postmodern debate is whether postmodern art occurs within a certain period (1945 to the present), or whether art is postmodern because it bears certain characteristics irrespective of period. For Hassan the characteristics of postmodernity appear as early as 1890. Lyotard uses the term modern to "designate any science that legitimates itself with reference to a metadiscourse... making an explicit appeal to some grand narrative, such as the dialectics of the Spirit, the hermeneutics of meaning, the emancipation of the rational or working subject, or the creation of wealth" ((Lyotard, 1984) p. xxiii). In contradistinction, he characterises postmodernity as "incredulity toward metanarratives" ((Lyotard, 1984) p. xxiv). Postmodern theories also range from the optimistic (Jencks sees postmodern as regenerative), to the apocalyptic theories of Jean Baudrillard in which the real is reduced to simulacra (Poster, 1988).

Most of these definitions of postmodern culture are more geared towards the product than the process and therefore do not address the matter of improvisation directly. However, Hassan's early attempts at characterising postmodernism propose improvisation and process as component characteristics. More recently Nicholas Kaye has suggested that since "the postmodern might best be conceived of as something that happens" and "because a 'performance' vacillates between presence and absence, between displacement and reinstatement", then performance can be viewed as a "primary postmodern mode" ((Kaye, 1994) p. 22–23). This is obviously relevant to improvisation which lies at one extreme of performance.

In this book, while acknowledging that there is a considerable overlap between modernist and postmodernist endeavour, we take the view that postmodernism involves: a pluralist rather than absolutist view of politics and history; a critique of modern forms of rationality; a radical critique of representation, of the unified self and of a universal truth; a merging of popular culture and high art; a tendency towards quotation and pastiche; and the greater incorporation of technology into art. While some theorists such as Jameson (Jameson, 1984) or Bürger (Bürger, 1984) saw postmodernism as the end of the avant-garde, we agree with Nicholas Zurbrugg that there is a "postmodern avant-garde" which emphasises performance, multi-media work and technology (Zurbrugg, 1988).

As mentioned above, an avant-garde may establish itself partly by institutionalising a separation between itself and the rest of society. We point out also that an audience or society at large may identify artistic endeavours as separated, impenetrable, or extreme, and in so doing also create a concept (positive or more often negative) of an avant-garde group. These groups may not coincide with those which might actively identify themselves as avant-garde, but are probably a likely feature of the interaction between the arts and society. In this sense the existence of an avant-garde — whether or not so called — is perhaps inevitable.

Although improvisation is part of the postmodern avant-garde outlined above, it is also part of postmodernism in the wider sense, because it is a technique in both popular culture and high art and involves some interchange between the two. It can also be viewed as a reaction against the modernist ideals of permanence, transcendence and artistic autonomy perpetuated by modernist art, and by critics such as Clement Greenberg and Michael Fried (Greenberg, 1966; Fried, 1968), ideals which still permeated this period. In practice, however, improvisors have often maintained a complex mixture of modernist and postmodernist ideals.

During our period improvisation has developed from live performance event, to improvisation as computerised interactive procedure, though improvisation as live performance event still occurs in parallel, or in combination, with computerised interaction. This movement, from live improvisation to interactive computerisation, developed partly in response to the changing social and artistic ethos of the era after 1945. This ethos changed from one in which improvising artists were, in general, more influenced by a radical socialism, to one in which they were more influenced by postmodern political relativism and extreme technological change.

Radical socialism, which attracted many improvisors, was a gradually emerging effect of the aftermath of the second world war, and became particularly strong during the sixties. Western society was still deeply shaken by the horrors of world war, but wars still proliferated worldwide and continuously (from Korea and Vietnam, to the Middle East and Africa). Nevertheless, the cold war and the fear of communism dominated international relations, and social and economic inequalities were still pervasive. These factors precipitated a counter-cultural movement in Europe, Australia and America in the sixties and early seventies. The counter movements, sometimes known as the "beat generation" or "flower power", severely questioned social conventions relating to sex, drugs, education and western religion, and the economic self-preservation of the privileged. In the quest for values which were anti-materialistic and pacifist these movements turned to non-western philosophy and art. The counter-cultural movements were strongest in America, resulting in demonstrations against the Vietnam war, and a profound questioning of the ethics of war. In England, while the old world of class conventions was still pervasive, the Labour movement grew in influence. The Labour party won the 1964 and 1966 elections and new strands of Marxist thought infiltrated from the continent.

Many artists in the sixties were politically aware and active, and we will see in ensuing chapters how the interest in the use of improvisation as a process was often (though not always) linked with ideas about politics and the need for social change and spiritual wholeness. This produced an ideology of improvisation, which was often superimposed upon the activity itself. The gestalt theory of Paul Goodman, the work of Freud, Reich and Marx, and an interest in the values and altered states of consciousness suggested by Eastern religions were all integral to this ideology (see for example (Banes, 1993)). Particularly important was the Freudian concept of the unconscious as a store of dreams and associations not normally accessible to the conscious mind: improvisation, like automatism earlier, was seen as a way of accessing the unconscious. Zen Buddhism was also important in its assertion of ever present time; repetition as the basis for discipline; and poetry and irrationality as a way of accessing the unconscious. It stressed "the illuminated commonplace", and meditation and the development of intuition as a means of enlightenment rather than scripture (Tucker, 1993) (Marsh, 1993).

Collective work, so central to much improvised art, seemed an ideal vehicle for artists such as the Living Theatre, who were dedicated to Marxist ideals of political equality and co-operation. Improvised performances often took place under severe economic restraints and in alternative venues, since they were regarded with suspicion by the establishment. Improvisation was also a way of opposing censorship: it posed a particular problem to the censor because of the difficulty of ascertaining what would happen from performance to performance. Technically, improvisation on stage was illegal in Britain until 1968. In 1958 Joan Littlewood's Theatre Workshop was prosecuted because their play "You Won't Always Be On Top" departed from the script approved by the censor, and included a new scene in which a mock opening ceremony was performed in a public lavatory by an actor who imitated Winston Churchill. Similarly, the Living Theatre were persecuted by the police and imprisoned because their events included performer and spectator nudity (as well as for supposed tax offences). Improvisation, in the form of scriptless performance, has sometimes been a very important means of evading the censor in extreme political situations where any explicitly political script would have been immediately banned. It has been used to this end by Athol Fugard in South Africa, in Poland by the Teatr Osmego Dnia in the seventies, and in South America (Boal, 1979) (Unruh, 1989). Improvisation was also seen as a way of opposing commodification in an object-orientated market, as in many cases there was no lasting record of a particular performance.

During the fifties and sixties jazz improvisation was widely influential on artists from other disciplines. Jazz clubs such as The Five Spot in New York formed social environments in which artists could meet and exchange ideas (see "The Day Lady Died" by Frank O'Hara (Allen, 1979)). Improvisation was attractive to experimental artists from the late forties onwards because it allowed ideas and structures to develop which were not pre-conceived. It was part of a wider movement in which artists sought to overcome pre-world war traditions and the predictability which accompanied them. Playwrights attempted to break out of the dead end of plot and character; and out of the social ethos of the drawing room drama in which the lower social classes were usually depicted as servants. Experimental poets such as the Beats, Black Mountain and New York poets in the USA, re-evaluated the role of rhyme, metre, metaphor and symbol, and the concept of the poem as a written text and unified whole. Dancers reconsidered the beautification and symbolisation of the body and returned to its materiality.

The pre-war experiments of the Surrealists, Dadaists and Futurists became models, rather than contemporary mainstream art. This climate of experimentation included an increased emphasis on art as process. For example, Charles Olson's idea that "one perception should lead directly to another" (Olson, 1973), Frank O'Hara's idea that "you just go on your nerve", ((Allen, 1979) p. 498) and Jackson Pollock's concept of being "in my painting" were all related to improvisation. This attraction to art as process also precipitated the growth of performance art, Fluxus, and Happenings. These were not primarily improvised: sometimes they were "fixed", or contained only a small improvised element, or were arrived at by preparatory improvisation, but in their tendency to turn art into event they shared some common ground with improvised work. This interest in process was part of a larger reaction against the nineteenth century ideal of the creative process as it was symbolised in the concepts of genius, individuality, permanency and privacy. Many of the artists of the fifties, sixties and seventies were attracted to types of creativity which transgressed that ideal and which were also central to improvisation: e.g. creativity through collaboration, creativity in public, creativity for the moment, creativity in popular culture.

The growth of post-colonial politics and culture had a major impact on improvisation during this period. Improvisation and post-colonialism are arguably linked, since in some cases composition can be argued to be a colonialist form imposed on cultures which had been more improvisation-orientated pre-settlement. During the early part of the period the influence of colonialism and western imperialism was still strong. For example, particularly during American domination after the second world war, Japanese musicians moved away from their own classical music — which involved improvisation — towards a Westernised form of composition, as represented by composers such as Takemitsu. Similarly, the affluent classes in colonial India cultivated Western concerts, and progressively neglected their own music. However, from the sixties onwards, post-colonial politics and culture, linked with advances in social anthropology, produced greater world-wide awareness of ethnic art (e.g. (Rothenberg and Rothenberg, 1983)). Some of these ethnic arts used improvisatory procedures, e.g. Indian music, and opened up alternative ideas about the creative process.

In America the civil rights movement had a major impact in the sixties, drawing attention to the economic repression of Afro-Americans and racial discrimination against them. This was linked with a shift towards Africanization in American culture in the sixties and seventies, most notably in the rise of the twist and rock and roll as popular culture, but also in sport, cinema and television. The values of Afro-American music, including its emphasis on improvisation, were embraced by the white avant-garde, though sometimes as part of a naive, even racist ideology, that mythologised blacks as more spontaneous, more rhythmic, and closer to nature (Dean, 1992; Banes, 1993).

Feminism emerged as a major force in the 1970s, not only through campaigns for equal rights and pay, but also through the work of feminist theorists, who argued that the role of women and the concept of femininity were constructed round patriarchal values which oppressed women. In the eighties the feminist movement was increasingly divided about whether its focus should be the equality of gender roles, or the celebration of woman's essential difference from man and her unique qualities and power, with some shift towards the latter perspective (Barrett and Phillips, 1992). This issue of equality versus difference was negotiated in different types of improvised work: gender equality was emphasised in the neutralising of gender roles in contact improvisation, while certain forms of feminist performance art (e.g. the work of Carolee Schneemann) challenged male representations of women's bodies by offering anti-patriarchal alternatives (Forte, 1990; Novack, 1990; Adair, 1992). Nevertheless, in some spheres of improvisation there is still a notable lack of women, an issue we address intermittently throughout the book.

In the eighties and nineties improvisation has in some respects become more integrated into the social fabric at large. This is now a culture in which everything is progressively commodified, and yet, paradoxically, in which so much is also dispensable, ephemeral or "virtual". Even war has been commodified, as graphically demonstrated during the Gulf War of 1992, but only by transmuting it into a condition of virtual unreality, where its existence beyond the television screen is almost in doubt. Improvisation is of growing importance in popular culture, theatresports and television games. It is also a more general requirement of a performance-orientated society in which politicians, performers on TV talk shows etc. all have to be able to improvise (Perloff, 1991; Smith, 1993). As such it is part of what Walter Ong has called secondary rather than primary orality, and is characteristic of an electronic society (Ong, 1982). However, improvisation of these sorts usually takes place within very constrained limits and is sometimes superficial: the improvised element is slight, and the emphasis is on adaptability and dispensability rather than creativity. Improvisors may sometimes have taken forms from popular culture, but this relationship has generally been parodic and ironic. The situation is complex and paradoxical, for our society has become increasingly conservative, and under Thatcher and Reagan (in the UK and the US) economic restraints against any kind of experimental art were particularly severe.

The work of some improvisors impinges on a more commercial sphere (such as Spalding Gray's film and book "The Monster in the Box" (Gray, 1990)) and improvisation has sometimes been incorporated into the mainstream, such as the Royal Shakespeare Company's film and stage version of Dickens' Nicholas Nickleby (1982). But economic deprivation is still the norm for improvising musicians who often have a "day job" to support themselves or resort (where possible) to social security (in the UK) (Bailey, 1980; Association of Improvising Musicians, 1984; Baker, 1990; Jackman, 1992). Thus commodification is not all-conquering! In fact the current social ethos is still in some respects very discouraging to improvisation. We are conditioned to avoid taking risks, to "play safe", to avoid failure, and to produce commodities. In many ways, primary and secondary education "is about reducing improvisation" (Rose, 1994). Mostly we are encouraged to be well prepared for any public task and to keep any element of unpredictability to an absolute minimum. So it is not surprising that improvisation is still relatively rare in some creative spheres, such as theatrical performance as opposed to rehearsal, and that many creators have not developed improvising techniques, despite their increasing inclusion in some branches of education (e.g. the drama school).

The ideological position of improvisors during the eighties and nineties is therefore the result of a complex mix of influences. The ideology of the politically motivated, anti-materialistic sixties has continued to be influential, but overlaps with, and has been partly superseded by, the political pluralism of the eighties and nineties, with its greater stress on racial and sexual difference and environmentalism. Important here is the appropriation of improvisation by feminist theatre groups who see the collectivism of improvisation as ideologically acceptable; the attraction for dancers of dance forms influenced by contact improvisation because they challenge traditional gender roles; and the incorporation of improvisation into spheres other than art, such as psychotherapy. Likewise, environmental artists may not call themselves improvisors, but their concept of art as changing and transient like nature, suggests that the Green movement has brought its own type of improvisatory process. The greater awareness and acceptance of multi-culturalism and racial difference (particularly in the more post-colonial societies such as Australia and Canada) has also resulted in the greater integration of different kinds of creative processes, including improvisatory ones, but without some of the racial essentialism of the sixties.

The agendas then have changed since the sixties, or perhaps there are less agendas altogether. This changing ethos is demonstrated in different attitudes toward commodification: although many improvisations still take place without record, improvisation has itself been progressively commodified in the form of films videos, recordings and now cd-roms. This has met with little resistance from its practitioners, anxious to make their way in the economically stringent present. Similarly the power of improvisation to stop war seems less probable, and the Gulf War did not have the same strong effect as Vietnam in stimulating a burst of related improvisatory art. Currently the rise of computerisation is having a major impact on social structure and human interaction. Particularly important is the more widespread use of the personal computer, the development of user-friendly software, and the rise of computer networks and information highways. These developments are producing massive savings in human time and energy and are also bridging gaps in time and space, creating a global, post cold war culture. But they are doing this by reducing live human interaction. For example, video conferencing can now substitute for the board meeting, and education is gradually changing to interactive learning, by becoming student-machine, rather than teacher-student, orientated. Artistically there is a corresponding change of emphasis from live performance to studio events, which combine electronics and live performance. This is what Nicholas Zurbrugg has called a combination of real time and reel time ((Zurbrugg, 1982) p. 120). Hence improvisation now often takes the form of interacting with a computer program rather than collaborating in live performance with another artist.

These changes will direct the future developments of improvisation, and we speculate further on them in later chapters, notably Chapter 10 concerning computers.

2

IMPROV(IS)ING THE DEFINITIONS

What is Improvisation?

> *But what exactly is improvisation? In principle, it is a coincidence between the production and transmission of a text — the text being composed* within *the performance, as opposed to those that were composed* for *the performance. In fact, improvisation is never total: the text, produced on the spot, is so by virtue of cultural norms, even re-established rules. What is, for the improvisor, the weight of these norms? What constraints perhaps result from them? ((Zumthor, 1990) p. 181)*
>
> *Improvisation: the skill of using bodies, space, all human resources, to generate a coherent physical expression of an idea, a situation, a character (even, perhaps, a text); to do this spontaneously, in response to the immediate stimuli of one's environment, and to do it à* l'improviste: *as though taken by surprise, without preconceptions. ((Frost and Yarrow, 1990) p. 1)*

Most statements about improvisation stress its exploitation of the present moment and the concomitant excitement and fluidity this generates. Improvisors rarely commence with a detailed awareness of what will happen; and in many cases they are actively striving for the event to be novel, to them as well as to the audience, even at fundamental levels. The improvisor engages with process and change rather than permanence, though some improvising traditions seek to conserve central conventions. Improvisation is concerned with processes rather than products, it is social rather than solipsistic. The possibilities which improvisation offers for relating to the world and others in a highly attentive and flexible way should not be underestimated.

Despite this, naive romantic notions of spontaneity, simplicity and lack of expertise, are no more appropriate to improvisation than to any other creative process. As the previous chapter suggested, an ideology has grown round improvisation often shrouding it in notions of intuition, mysticism, and unconscious activity. This ideology was particularly influential in the sixties, and important because it indicated that for the participants, improvisation was more than a formal device, it was a mode of existence. However, these ideas do not capture the particular character of improvisation on a detailed technical level.

In order to discuss adequately the influence and role of improvisation in the arts, therefore, it is necessary first to define it in a useable and more specific way. No single definition of improvisation can be satisfactory because there are many different kinds of improvisation. Moreover, there is no absolute opposition between improvisation and composition, only a gradient of creative endeavour from pure improvisation to complete composition. (Though the term composition is particularly used in relation to music, it is applicable to all types of artistic work.) All improvisations have in common the fact that they are a particular type of procedure which requires skill and practice. This is often obscured in discussions which suggest that improvisation is an unprepared sequence of events which are entirely spontaneous.

In its purest form an improvisation involves the simultaneous conception and performance of a work of art. Such an improvisation is a public performance which takes place without any pre-written score or script. It is in the nature of improvisation that it will be always be different from the last improvisation, and that it will not necessarily be saved in a reproducible form.

Pure improvisation, therefore, takes place at the intersection of performance and creativity, and there are two consequences of this: 1) it takes place within a defined time frame; 2) it occurs continuously through time, at speed, and does not involve revision. The improvisor makes a succession of choices in performance which cannot be erased, so everything (s)he does within the performance must be incorporated into the whole. This involves an attentiveness to the present moment, so that creativity is a response to the here and now, though the choices made by the improvisor are inevitably influenced by past experience of improvising. It is because these choices are different with every performance that no two improvisations are the same.

The concept of the time frame in improvisation is different from the three types of time which Richard Schechner outlines as the major varieties of performance time: event time, set time, and symbolic time. Event time is defined as that in which "the activity itself has a set sequence and all the steps of that sequence must be completed no matter how long (or short) the elapsed clock time". Set time is that "where an arbitrary pattern is imposed on events — they begin and end at certain moments whether or not they have been 'completed'. Here there is an agonistic contest between the activity and the clock." Symbolic time operates "when the span of the activity represents another (longer or shorter) span of clock time. Or where time is considered differently, as in Christian notions of 'the end of time', the Aboriginal 'dreamtime' or Zen's goal of the 'ever present'" ((Schechner, 1988) p. 6–7).

Improvisation does not take usually place in set time because no exact time limit is established before the improvisation starts. Some improvisations may take place in event time (those in which a score or set of instructions set out a sequence of events which have to be completed). But many free improvisations do not, since any sequence of events can occur. Improvisations can take place in symbolic time (for example, a repetitive improvisation might imply its permanent continuation after its termination), but this is not common. Pure improvisation therefore usually occupies a unique type of performance time which we might call "improvisatory time". It occurs in real time and normally acknowledges the concept of an approximate time frame (the players usually have to stop their entire performance at a certain time). But within this limit the performers may generate several improvised pieces of different lengths, and the exact length of the piece is self-generating — that is, it is a consequence of the structure of the improvisation itself.

The improvisation may be solo but is quite likely to involve other performers whose choices are continuously modifying and transforming each other. The public nature of the improvisation means that the audience can potentially influence it, and the whole improvisation takes place within an environment, features of which may be incorporated into it.

It is necessary to be clear that not all performance is improvisation, yet the two have much in common, and the performance situation is the one in which improvisation in its "purest" sense can take place. To illustrate the similarities: most performances involve variability, some elements of freedom or imprecision e.g. the interpretation of dynamics and speed and phrasing in music, or the delivery of lines and accompanying gestures in theatre. Performance requires the presence of an audience and offers a range of semiotic systems such as kinesics, proxemics, lighting, costume, props, music, sound language, make up, in which to operate (Elam, 1980). Performance is not synonymous with improvisation because a performance may often be a realisation of a fully written script or musical score. But improvisation can be the most radical use of the performance situation, since it allows the parameters of audience interaction and performance variation their maximum play.

All the features of "pure" improvisation listed above, except the roles of the audience, can equally occur in private, and we distinguish some such improvisation as "applied". A related though not identical distinction has been made by Frost and Yarrow (Frost and Yarrow, 1990). This terminology is apt, because usually an applied improvisation is a step towards producing a work which will eventually be displayed to audiences, perhaps on a canvas. An applied improvisation might alternatively be used towards the formation of a subsequent live performance which is no longer improvised, or to produce a recorded work such as a techno pop song. Musicians who produce fully notated scores for performers often also use applied improvisation in developing them.

Improvised performances which take place for the purposes of making a sound recording, film or video, but occur without an audience, are a special case. They involve pure improvisation but do not allow for the possibility of audience interaction; in other respects, however, the camera replaces the audience to a degree. The process of the improvisation and its progression through time is still available to the audience, even if the reception of the work is delayed. In this respect such recording processes remain distinct from applied improvisations.

In detecting the occurrence of improvisation (whether pure or applied), it is also necessary to take account of the fact that virtually every aspect of creativity can operate in ways which form continuity between improvisation and composition. Or to put it another way, an improvisation is a component of many creative procedures which would never in their entirety be viewed as improvisations. But different kinds of creative process differ in their weighting of improvised-composed elements. A work may involve improvisation in relation to one of its constituent creative processes, or in relation to several. The analysis of the role of the improvisatory components, whether vast or not, is our objective. This is much more important than any attempt to decide whether a work as a whole deserves the description "improvised" (or "composed"). If such a decision is needed, it could probably most logically be based on an aggregation of the improvised-composed balance of all the component creative processes: a difficult and arbitrary endeavour. In general we do not need to attack this relatively unimportant question. We will show that even in the case of many non-performing arts, where often many of the creative processes veer towards the compositional, the analysis of the impact of the improvisatory processes is valuable.

We can now appreciate that many works have used pure or applied improvisation, but these processes have been adopted in different ways in different arts. For example, many theatrical works have been composed through applied improvisation ("workshopping" in private) and are almost entirely fixed by the time the play reaches public performance. Here improvisation is crucial in the evolution of the play, allows for collaboration between creators, and resituates the role of the playwright. A novel which is written in private but at speed in whole or in part, or a painting which is completed in one quick session, are further examples of applied improvisation. Here the artist or writer often creates a kind of private performance situation, for as Schechner says, alluding to Erving Goffman's

"The Presentation of Self in Everyday Life", "...performing is a mode of behaviour that may characterise any activity. This performance is a 'quality' that can occur in any situation rather than a fenced-off genre" ((Schechner, 1988) p. 30). At the furthest edges of improvisation are works of art which, while created in private and discontinuously, arise through procedures of exploration and transformation, and a readiness to accept any possible outcome, which seem to distinguish their creative processes as loosely improvisatory. Many of the artists in our survey saw their work as partially improvised, even if they did not regard themselves as improvisors.

Finally, computerisation is altering our definition of improvisation quite radically. Computerised improvising does not always involve a public event and therefore cannot be simultaneously performed and received. However, it does foreground an element implicit in the performance event: that of interactiveness. For example, in hypermedia the improvisor collaborates not with other performers or the audience but with the computer program, making choices which may never be entirely fixed or reproducible (see Chapter 10).

The Process of Improvising

Whereas critical theory has vastly opened up the analysis and understanding of *reception* of works of art, analysis of the creative *process* has tended to be undervalued in criticism and theory. We wish to connect the process of creativity in improvisation with the work created and its reception: and to emphasise exactly the process-product interchanges which have been neglected by critics. Our emphasis is inescapable in the case of improvisation, since the process of creation is normally synchronous with that of production.

An important element in improvising is the balance between using procedural formulae and pre-existent material, and creating new material, new combinations of material and new procedures. Improvisations are not entirely self-generating and most improvisors have a bank of "personal cliches" to which they resort. The newness of the improvisation depends on how wide a range of personal cliches the improvisor has, and the extent to which (s)he can recombine and transform these in performance. On the other hand, the improvisor is usually willing to use whatever materials are available: for example, environmental improvisors might use any aspect of the environment in which they work, and do not necessarily depend on prior knowledge or expectation of it.

Another useful distinction often made in discussion of improvisation is between referent and non-referent work. A referent improvisation is one which is based on a pre-arranged structure, procedure, theme or objective which dictates some features of the work. For example, the *structure* referent might be the harmonic and metrical structure of a blues, used as a basis by the jazz improvisor; or it might be a pre-arranged succession of events, whether narrative or not, as articulated in several of the improvised performances of theatre groups such as Kiss (Burnett, 1982). Improvisations might be based on pre-arranged *procedures* of performing (e.g. use the technique of pizzicato string playing; or progress through previously unspecified event types 1......n). A *thematic* referent would take a particular subject as its starting point: it might be that of death (as in "Terminal" by the Open Theatre). A work would have an *objective* as stipulated referent when it sought to achieve that objective during its progress: for example, Stockhausen asks his performers in some improvised pieces to achieve particular sonic states. Thus the referent rarely suggests more than the simplest outline of the macro-level of the improvisation, and the improvisor has virtually complete control of the micro-level, which then permits control of the macro-level.

Gioia's characterisation (Gioia, 1988) of referent based jazz pieces as using a "blueprint" (which would almost completely determine the output), thus seems too greatly simplified. He contrasts this with the looser forms of jazz which involve "retrospective" determination of structure, and these correspond roughly to the non-referent works we will now consider. Gioia's restricted and negative view of such "retrospective" interpretation is used to support his conclusion, quite mistargetted from our perspective, that jazz is an "imperfect art". Perfection is not frequently a necessary or relevant concept in improvisation. When it is relevant, "perfection" is just as accessible by retrospective determination of structure as by prospective. In the case of a painting, such retrospective determination might involve erasure; in the case of a kinetic performance it would involve reconstruction.

A totally non-referent work would be one in which no pre-arranged organisation or concept existed specific to that work. Nevertheless, each improvisor would necessarily have preformed ideas, which might influence the improvisation, yet not be unique to that work. Thus again there is a continuity between the two categories, referent and non-referent, rather that a disjunction, and it is probably difficult to achieve the extreme of non-referentiality. This could, perhaps, occur during trance or shamanistic performance, though frequently these would be highly referential in relating to conventional ritual procedures. Some of the relevant concepts of creativity are discussed later in the chapter.

The axis of referentiality is interesting when one considers group performance. It is quite common for several co-improvisors to initiate a work with independent improvising-referent frames. The postmodern trend towards multiplicity of meaning, and self-deconstruction within works, is thus quite explicit within much group improvising, and we will indicate that the enhancement of such multiple approaches to meaning in a work is in part a consequence of the influence of improvisation. As Frost and Yarrow say "Improvisation underlies and underlines the fact that meaning is created in performance as the collision or negotiation of different sets of meaning: that, for instance, which appears to reside in the 'text' and that which individual performers perceive and/or mediate; that which the audience expects and that which they receive; and so on" ((Frost and Yarrow, 1990) p. 165).

Even more importantly, group improvisation gives rise to the possibility of inter(personal)activity. In such processes mediation between multiple referent frames can occur, whether by formation of continuity or magnification of discontinuity (Marowitz, 1978). Similarly, in non-referent improvising, there are inevitably features of each individual performer's output which can be noted by others, and incorporated or dismissed by them. Thus a multiplicity of semiotic frames can be continually merging and disrupting during a "free" (i.e. non-referent) improvisation.

Another dimension of interpersonal reactivity may be provided by the presence of an audience. Performer-audience interactions are very varied. They are often very limited, and sometimes the apparent feedback from the audience may be misleading: an improvisor may feel that communication is not occurring when in fact it is. Some improvisors may deliberately choose to disregard reactions of the audience (for example, some who find themselves viewed by their habitual audience as avant-garde or difficult). However, the audience may influence the discourse, and the role of the audience may be magnified, so as to break the distinction between audience and performer. Beyond this, the process of improvisation in private (mainly "applied" improvisation in our discussion above) and in public ("pure" improvisation) need not differ much.

A further distinction is needed between private applied improvisation and some forms of rehearsal involving improvisation. "Rehearsal" is a common feature of the preparation of theatrical and musical performance groups, and usually involves repetition of elements of a future performance which are already largely fixed. What is rehearsed by improvisation, however, is more problematic and varied. In the case of musical groups it is often the referent material, if any, and its efficient presentation and utilisation. But what of "rehearsal" by "free-improvisation" groups? This often occurs, though some improvisors prefer to avoid it and have even refused to participate in any performances which involved a referent known to them (e.g. musical notated scores (Bailey, 1980)). A process of mutual familiarisation takes place in these free improvisors' rehearsals, and in our experience it seems to largely involve recognition of standard frames and personal clichés of the individual players, of standard modes of response they may have to certain (sound) fields, and the development and exploitation of these and novel responses. This opinion is also shared by other improvisors in other arts (e.g. (Marowitz, 1978)).

Thus the use of improvisation in rehearsal may be simply to mutually familiarise the participants. Applied improvisation is nevertheless common in theatre and film production, where it is used to develop the material which will eventually become the whole substance of a final performed work. In Chapter 8 we will discuss an important example of this, the work of playwright and film-maker Mike Leigh. While this process seems less common in contemporary music, it was normal in rhythmic musics such as those of the Indonesian Gamelan, and of significance in 60s repetitive music developments such as those of Terry Riley. A later example is the work of the Necks, whose repetitive but modulating rhythmic patterns sometimes derive partly from applied improvisation which produces a referent, even though they are always developed further during performance (Necks, 1989; Buck, 1992).

It may also be useful to distinguish two extreme psychological stances the improvisor might seek: the sensory and the non-sensory. In taking a sensory stance, the improvisor would attempt to internalise and interpret all the materials provided in the improvisation, whether by him- or herself or by others, and to generate further materials related to those provided. In taking a non-sensory stance, the individual would not only make no response to external material, but would attempt to avoid even perceiving it. Nevertheless, (s)he would of necessity generate continuing material. To what degree the non-sensory position is possible, and whether a similar desensitisation to one's own output can be organised, are subjective and debatable matters, though there is no doubt that some improvisors on occasion cultivate these approaches. The sensory vs. non-sensory axis is again continuous and not disjunctive.

The sensory improvisor may create material which is either primarily introverted or extroverted. In other words, the generated material may be intended primarily to affect the semiotic field of the individual generating it (the introvert attitude), or to affect the fields of the other participants (the extrovert attitude). An extreme case of the extrovert stance is contact improvisation, whose central objective is mutual sensory and physical adaptation through direct body contact (Chapter 5). Some improvisors, such as pioneering guitarist Derek Bailey, often apparently veer heavily towards the introvert stance (Bailey, 1980). The terms introvert/extrovert can also refer to an individual's stance towards the audience, but as noted above, the audience/performer distinction need only be one of degree (de Haan, 1991).

Equally important in the process of improvising is the use of associative or non-associative techniques. For example, in verbal improvising this associative/non associative axis might be seen in terms of metonymy where, at one extreme, the improvisor works by close association from a particular word. At a remove from this extreme is the creation of new metonymies in which the basis of association becomes more and more remote, and at the other extreme is a virtually non-associative process. (An improvisor might start at one pole and move through to the other). These ideas are relevant to the process of an individual improvisor, and to that of a whole group. But individuals tend most often to develop their material by a transformative process, which necessarily entails that they generate self-associative tracks. These may at the same time be associative or non-associative with the other contributions within the improvising group.

There are a variety of such transformative processes. Repetition, which has been very important in Minimal music, dance and other art forms, is simply transformation with respect only to time or phase. Even more important in improvisation is the continuum between expansion and contraction of materials, which can operate not only in time, but also with respect to pitch, word, movement etc. The improvising process often makes the improvisor concentrate on small elements because (s)he cannot see the overall whole. This means that a multiplicity of elements is likely to build up, especially where a number of different improvisors are interacting with each others' small units. The total effect is likely to be very different from that which develops when a creator starts out with a whole in mind. The improvising process therefore often tends to be synecdochal (by which we refer to concentrating on parts) rather than totalising (concentrating upon the whole).

It may be useful to schematise several types of improvisatory process here, and to give examples of outputs which approximate these schema. Clearly, the permutations of the parameters discussed already are numerous, and we have therefore arbitrarily selected a limited number of extreme cases (Figure 2a & b).

Creativity, Orality, Textuality and Improvisation

The idea of improvisation is related to that of creativity as working process. This idea of creativity as process includes that of *finding* the art work by an explorative process rather than working towards a pre-conceived goal. To give oneself over to the process is to be prepared to open oneself up to the unknown. Creativity as process also involves allowing the work of art to become self-generating, so that words, for example, suggest other words by sound or sense. Creativity as process is not identical to improvising because it may involve privacy, revision and discontinuity, but it bears a relation to it. Rothenberg (Rothenberg, 1990) asserts that finding the meaning of a poem while writing it is usual for most writers, though he also argues that artists are generally largely unaware of the nature of their creative process.

For Rothenberg, creativity is "the production of something that is *both* new and truly valuable" (p. 5); a stance with clear conservative and modernist overtones, which are reflected throughout his nevertheless interesting book. He has also distinguished "Janusian" and "homospatial" creative processes, and these are highly pertinent to improvisation. The Janusian process involves the generation of simultaneous opposites:

> In the Janusian process, multiple opposites or antitheses are conceived simultaneously, either as existing side by side or as equally operative, valid, or true. In an apparent defiance of logic or of physical possibility, the creative person consciously formulates the simultaneous operation of antithetical elements or factors and develops those formulations into integrated entities and creations. ((Rothenberg, 1990), page 15).

He goes on to say that this process "seldom appears in the final product". ((Rothenberg, 1990), p. 15). However, in improvisation, and probably in avant-garde and postmodern work generally, this is not true. Indeed, such continuing juxtaposition of multiple antitheses is highly productive.

The homospatial process may occur at a subsequent stage in the generation of a work, and involves "conceiving two or more discrete entities occupying the same space, a conception leading to the articulation of new identities" (p. 25). Again, in experimental work including some improvisation, this homospatial process may be ever present. One can detect these Janusian and homospatial features in improvisatory texts (e.g. Frank O'Hara), music (e.g. John Coltrane), film (e.g. Jeff Keen), and elsewhere, as we will discuss later.

Several authors (e.g. (Rothenberg, 1990 ; Weisberg, 1993)) resituate the idea of the relationship between unconscious and conscious processes after Freud. Previous theorists have tended to emphasise the role played by the unconscious in creative work, and improvisors have often talked about improvising as a means of accessing the unconscious. However, as Rothenberg points out, this tends to suggest that creative work is always the result of pre-existing features, while "a meaningful definition of creativity should include the idea of human beings producing truly new ideas, theories, artistic styles and forms, or inventions" ((Rothenberg, 1990) page 52). He argues that the notion of a largely passive unconscious could not account for artistic form, though it may play a part in artistic work. This view can be useful in helping us to appreciate improvisation as a largely conscious procedure which may, because of speed and lack of revision, also access ideas from the unconscious.

In psychological terms, a performer may control some processes at the analytical level, and other more rapid processes solely at a motoric level (as discussed by (Pressing, 1988)).

This access to unconscious elements corresponds to a process of extending oneself, which is implicit in many improvisors' approaches. For some it can reach towards the state of becoming one with the world. In this respect it can be seen as shamanistic, though not necessarily with the overtone of becoming curative often associated with the latter. Several authors (Tucker, 1992; Levy, 1993) have suggested that the shamanistic spirit is common to many contemporary artists, be they painters, writers, musicians, and its importance in improvised theatre has also been considered ((Frost and Yarrow, 1990); p. 4–5). In particular, Tucker views the free jazz movement as strongly shamanistic (Tucker, 1992).

Shamanism was particularly important in traditional oral cultures and continues to be in some. Since improvisation tends to take place in non-written forms, it too is linked to orality and is generally more likely in an oral culture. Literacy has produced a dependency on written forms and the notion of a fixed text (Ong, 1982; Zumthor, 1990). In an oral culture, in contrast, no absolutely fixed version of a story exists, and each telling of the story will be adapted to respond to a unique situation. "In oral tradition, there will be as many minor variants of a myth as there are repetitions of it, and the number of repetitions can be increased indefinitely" ((Ong, 1982) p. 42). Also important here is the more public aspect of orality: "primary orality fosters personality structures that in certain ways are more communal and externalised, and less introspective than those common among literates" (Ong, 1982). It is now impossible to return to a state of primary orality (that which preceded textuality), yet improvisors often exploit both orality and textuality, for example by means of a textual referent for their improvisation, or by recording their improvisation in a subsequent text. But orality has not been uniformly esteemed in our current literate culture. As Ong argues, Derrida's stress on textuality and his critique of phonocentrism tend to undervalue orality, and this may contribute to the underestimation of improvisation (see Chapter 1).

However, improvisation can be seen to be consistent with the theories of Derrida, Barthes and Foucault in challenging the notion of the creator as sole and immediate focus of meaning (Derrida, 1972; Barthes, 1977; Rabinow, 1984). The emphasis in much improvisation on collaboration, or on the projection of multiple selves, radically interrogates traditional notions of subjectivity. Collaboration, for example, involves the merging of the self with another, so that it may be impossible to tell who has done what, and the more closely the collaborators work together the more their contributions will be assimilated (Smith, 1988). Similarly, the resituating of the subject, which Barthes' concept of "the death of the author" and the Derridean questioning of the notion of presence involve, has lead us to question generally the idea of the artist as the origin of meaning. Rather the artist is the site at which systems of meaning intersect. This helps us to understand that the source of an improvisation is not solely the personality of the creator: personality is an artificial and largely social construct. In addition there may be no such thing as completely spontaneous acts, since our actions move within semiotic systems and so are to some extent pre-conditioned.

Theories of Improvisation and Their Sociopolitical Basis

Even the preceding brief sections have shown how complex is the background to improvisation. Yet many other important factors would be relevant were one to attempt a thorough theory of improvisation, such as the psychological and political significance of improvisation.

Why does improvisation exist? Logical, irrational and intuitive processes are probably necessary components of the human mind. We propose that their interaction produces an infinity of possibilities, and amongst these will inevitably be some which qualify as improvisation. This argument is close to that concerning the interaction of the conscious and the unconscious, discussed above. The development of a separate concept "improvisation" is, of course, the result of a social convergence in the discourse of language. Once recognised, such a convergence can enhance the development of the phenomenon of improvisation itself.

One of the aims of this book is to understand how artistic improvisation creates and projects its products: here we point to the difficulties of a purely psychological understanding of these issues. We have described and categorised many improvising procedures above. The question is one of explanation: during an improvisation, what is the psychology of the individual participant, and what dictates the flow of the event? Besides training and experience, we need to take into account the mind-set of the performer(s) at the time of performance (and note that we are using performer here without the implication of performance in public). In some respects improvisation offers a means of extending the self, as we have mentioned above. As Frost and Yarrow argue, "Under the influence of the improvisatory, self may thus begin to define itself: it is liberated both psychologically and semiotically." They indicate that improvisation also permits "the acquisition of extra sign-potential" enhancing the languages available to the performer ((Frost and Yarrow, 1990)), page 161). However, we cannot assume that the performer *always* wishes to "extend" him or herself, or the world at large, or that this is the only factor.

The notion of self-extension, especially in improvisations which engage more than one person, has to be modified by that of group interaction. Pressing has suggested that flow is directed by the recognition and use of transition points established in real (ongoing) time during performance (in (Sloboda, 1988)). In this view, an improvising group convenes at several successive points in making clear changes in the nature of its improvisation. Here the group psychology would somehow be determining the individual psychology (except where the output of one individual dominated the whole at the transition point). A difficulty with such an argument is that groups may not make uniform transitions (Nettl, 1974; Dean, 1992), and this is consistent with the tendency to synecdochal rather than totalising construction in improvisation which we mentioned above. Creativity-based theories of improvisation have been discussed previously, following the ideas of Johnson-Laird and others. These computational and generative theories indicate how the development of individual improvisations can establish in each case a unique grammar, syntax and semiotic field (Dean and Smith, 1991; Dean, 1992). Their mutual interaction could be the basis of group flow. In this case, the exchange and interaction of semiotic fields between the improvisors would be a gradual and continuous process, not normally characterised by transition points.

There are as yet no wide-ranging sociological or anthropological theories of improvisation which deal with improvisation throughout different art forms. However, critics in specific areas have attempted to address the relevance of improvisation at more than a purely technical level. Discussing theatre in particular, Frost and Yarrow see improvisation as an ordered, progressive and flexible way of relating to the world:

> *Habit is the great enemy of evolution. Is the kind of thing that happens in improvisation similar to the processes, by which, for instance, a biological structure evolves to new levels of order? It might well be, for improvisation is about order, and about adaption, and about truthfully responding to changing circumstances, and about generating meaning out of contextual accidents. It is about failing, and about not minding failure. It is about trying again, and about enjoying the process without straining to get a known result. It is about creation. ((Frost and Yarrow, 1990) p. 3).*

So improvisation can have implications both for self-development and for social organisation, and the process of improvisation has often been directed against artistic and social control. This argument needs modification since there is often a gap between theory and practice, and within any improvisatory milieu there are "mainstream" and "alternative" improvisors. This is particularly the case in jazz where some improvisors and critics strive to preserve conventions, and even to repress those who wish to break out of them (Dean, 1992; Berliner, 1994). It is also necessary to distinguish between the process and its products. The subject matter of an improvisation can be of any kind. It can be conservative, and in some music, for example, it might be sufficiently abstract for there to be no objectively perceivable political content.

Nevertheless, there seems to be a general consensus among critics that improvisation is intrinsically anti-hegemonic. Frost and Yarrow argue:

> There's nothing left or right wing about improvisation per se, but as a challenge to the dominant cultural assumptions about what is "the basis of the actor's art", and an attack on received notions of "the artist", the adoption of impro as a method of play creation becomes a political act in itself. It de-emphasises the individual writer, and privileges the creative ensemble — the workshop, with all its connotations of crafts and working-class skills. ((Frost and Yarrow, 1990) p. 148).

Bruce Johnson, discussing the relationship of jazz to the cultural hegemony, similarly suggests that improvisation in jazz is highly resistant to commodification (Johnson, 1993). He further argues that modernist critical discourse (which he characterises as the discourse of high art) tends to reduce the art work to a commodity, so jazz can only fit into that discourse by becoming "radically deformed". For Johnson jazz is "primarily a performance art, with a crucial somatic component" and can only be captured on recordings "by excluding one of the most central attributes of jazz: its element of non-repetitiveness." (Of course, what Johnson really means here is "non-reproducibility", since he is well aware of the internal repetitiveness of most jazz forms, both rhythmically and harmonically.) According to Johnson, the resistance of jazz to commodification has resulted in its trivialisation in modernist discourse which needs fixed, closed texts as the basis of discussion. In any case modernist discourse is inappropriate for the discussion of jazz: it tends to either recuperate jazz as high art or dismiss it as popular culture, and relies too heavily on the notion of artistic autonomy. A discourse of jazz needs to confront the conditions of the consumption and production of the work of art, including the idea that it does not emanate from "some kind of romantically transcendental undistracted act of creation" (Johnson, 1993).

Johnson makes a valuable contribution in his discussion of the resistance of jazz to commodification and need for a new discourse about improvisation. As he notes, his article is a "provisional" step and thus many of the ideas need much further discussion. For example, one of his two central premises, that jazz is particularly resistant to commodification in comparison with classical music, deserves further consideration. Since the era of the phonogram, closely congruent with that of jazz, it has been possible to record elements of the music for subsequent digestion. Johnson claims that in spite of recording, jazz can still resist commodification far more than other musics. This is to imply that jazz recordings are less complete than recordings of other musics. We can agree with Johnson that there are elements of musical experience for both audience and performer which are specific to the moment of performance, and not present in the recordings. However, do any of these elements distinguish jazz from other musics? Because, some elements specific to the moment of performance *are* reflected in the recordings, for example aspects of the real-time interaction between musicians.

Johnson's argument — that commodification of jazz is more difficult than commodification of other musics — depends on the idea that more is lacking from jazz recordings than from those of other musics, and clearly this is highly debatable. Quite possibly the array of recordings of key jazz figures such as Coltrane, Davis, Coleman (though selected from a much wider range of performances they have given) provide no more limited an impression of their output than do the scores and recordings of Beethoven, also selected (partly by the composer himself) from a much wider range of efforts.

Johnson has yet to undertake the generation of a satisfactory alternative discourse, beyond implying that the discourse of popular music is a preferable environment for the discussion of jazz than the discourse of modernism. He does posit the idea that this discourse should take greater account of the physicality of jazz, but there seems to us no reason to suggest that jazz is any more physical than any other form of music-making: its emphasis on rhythm and pulse does not separate it from many other musics, and does not necessarily entail ideas of physicality. Furthermore, the idea that jazz is a music of the body runs the danger of being essentialist. And of course any music (jazz or other) stored in the form of print or cd can only be processed by a body and a mind. Johnson emphasises the importance of orality for analysing jazz, and this process had previously been commenced by several authors (e.g. (Smith, 1983)), discussed in (Dean, 1992)). We continue this approach more broadly in this book.

The possible ways in which the production and consumption of improvisation affects any particular work are yet to be analysed by Johnson, and his statement that "jazz in the concert hall is not making the same statement as jazz on a record or in a studio or in a pub" remains merely assertion, though this issue has been studied by Jackman (Jackman, 1992). In general, Johnson's work concentrates on the social and political context of jazz and the discourse about it, rather than detailed technical analysis of particular works and the processes that produced them: we believe that a discourse of improvisation must include such analysis. But we concur with Johnson that increased discussion of the process rather than the product is essential for understanding improvisation in general, including the particular case of jazz, and this is one of the central objectives of this book.

Frost and Yarrow (Frost and Yarrow, 1990), concerned with improvisation in the theatre, make some important points about the relationship between censorship and improvisation. They discuss how improvised work has often been marginalised and repressed by the establishment because it did not result in a finished script which could be passed and edited by the censor. At the same time, they point out that improvisation has sometimes been used as a way of outmanoeuvring the censor and allowing political dissent to be disseminated: this has been crucial in extreme political situations where any criticism of the government in a written script would be banned (p. 146–151). (We discuss further the way improvisation has responded to censorship in Chapter 8.) Frost and Yarrow also chart the historical loss of community in the theatre, and the way the interactive audience had been totally suppressed by the nineteenth century. They see improvisation as a return to a more socially engaging experience which is "more disturbing, more immediate, and also more powerful and rewarding" ((Frost and Yarrow, 1990) p. 174).

Cynthia Novack (Novack, 1990) produces a highly convincing account of the social genesis and significance of the body/movement activity, contact improvisation, in America, particularly the way it attempted to overturn social hierarchies and subvert traditional gender roles. However, her account focuses solely on contact improvisation, in which the reversal of gender roles is central and overt, but neither improvisation nor feminism in other art forms are part of her brief. There have been some documentary studies of women in jazz, but these have not produced a comprehensive theory (Wilmer, 1977; Placksin, 1982). Much scope remains for analysis here and we include some discussion of gender and improvisation in this book.

The changes in improvisation in the arts in different periods is a difficult area of enquiry, and attempts to engage with this have not been wholly successful. One quite recent study (Moore, 1992) attempts to address the "decline of improvisation in Western Art music" during the late 19th and early 20th century. Moore mentions that in some improvising traditions (such as that of Persian music) those improvisors who challenge conventions may be chastised by their peers who wish rather to avoid change. Of course such a response is common, as when Ornette Coleman first appeared in New York in the late 1950s, and was met with ridicule because of his innovative style. As Mike Snow has pointed out (Snow, 1994), the acceptance of the new jazz of Coleman and Cecil Taylor was immediate by the painters of the time (including some of the Abstract Expressionists) but extremely reluctant by many musicians.

Moore is concerned with changes in the importance and extent of a kind of musical improvisation which is fixed, conventional and formulaic, and with the reasons for its decline. For him, such improvisation is "a performance and event based musical act deriving its structure and characteristic style from a combination of longstanding culture models and individual interpretations of them" which he says become "internalised" in the performer. Moore indicates that the "internalised" act should be consistent with "stipulated and communally coherent aesthetic parameters", and he recognises the distinct and separate nature of free improvisation. "Stipulated" improvisation, a limited category of referent improvisation, is important in most spheres, if transiently, and we discuss it quite extensively here, for example, in jazz and in the films of Mike Leigh. But we argue that improvisation is only fully exploited if it permits the breaking, remoulding and rebreaking of such "parameters", and indeed only if the possibility exists of reformulating the parameters on each occasion. Moore is not able to provide a powerful rationale for the decline of the conventional almost "fixed" improvisation style he addresses, and the difficulty of the task is apparent from the article: but it would be much more difficult to define factors acting on more variable entities, transforming improvisatory styles.

In contrast to Moore, we are more interested in patterns of change in improvisation. One outcome of this has been a previous suggestion, by one of us, that improvised music could perhaps be interpreted in the light of the modernist/postmodernist "divide", as three almost sequential postmodernist trends ((Dean, 1992) p. xxii–xxiii):

> *First, the movement of Third Stream, in the 1950s and early 60s, in which classical compositional techniques and orchestration... were allied with... jazz improvisors. ...Also part of this first wave are the groups which emphasised oriental influences... These activities are postmodern... particularly in their use of older techniques in a new amalgam, which is overtly referential toward the old...*
>
> *The second postmodernist wave, chronologically, would be the work of some of the European (for example AMM ...) and American (for example Pauline Oliveros ...) free improvising ensembles which... elevated the status of environmental contributions to an improvisation performance. ...This can be construed as postmodernist in that it avoids the elevated ideal of the self-driven creator producing an autonomous work, and emphasises instead... the interaction between performer, environment and listener.*
>
> *The third postmodernist wave is that of the recreators, prevalent in the 1970s and 1980s, and of the jazz funk movement. The recreators produced a slightly updated version of the hard bop style of the late 1950s...*

The third wave could reflect a consumerist pressure, in that the work was more viable economically. Rap, which is characterised by simple rhythmic patterns (evaded occasionally by "breaks" and ruptures), subsequently became aligned with this wave, even if it originated in social outrage amongst Afro-Americans in South Bronx, New York (Rose, 1994).

In a further development of our ideas about this, we now propose that the second of these waves corresponds to a postmodern avant-garde like that discussed by Zurbrugg. The music of this second wave was most commonly described as avant-garde. However, it also fulfils several of the criteria Zurbrugg proposes for a postmodern avant-garde, as well as other more general postmodernist criteria. Zurbrugg mentions particularly technology, performance and multimedia as contributing to his postmodern avant-garde. The free improvisors of our second wave enlarged the input from their surroundings, be it audience and loft or railway-shed, or external environment. They also shared an emphasis on technology, in that they often interacted with their environment partly by making, modifying and using recordings of it. In addition, they exploited unusual acoustic spaces as important contributors to some performances. They quite often used vocal as well as conventional instrumental sound, and though they were not usually concerned with multimedia so far as to include controlled independent visual objects, they expanded the sound medium considerably. Their emphasis on the use of their specific environments also enhanced the role of performance, since little of the event could be viewed separately from the specific location. Whether Zurbrugg's criteria for a postmodern avant-garde are essential or paramount is, of course, a matter of debate. However, we note that our second wave of avant-gardists fulfil other more general criteria of postmodernism which we established in Chapter 1.

A brief discussion of one specific case of the postmodern avant-garde may help to clarify this: the Association of Creative Musicians (AACM) in Chicago, and Anthony Braxton in particular (mentioned but not extensively covered in our previous work (Dean, 1992)). While the work of these musicians is commonly considered to be avant-garde, it can also be reassessed in terms of the criteria of the postmodern we developed in Chapter 1. Many of these criteria are fulfilled by the work of AACM (and particularly that of Roscoe Mitchell), and Braxton (see (Radano, 1993) for further documentation). For example, Braxton's multiple superimposition forms (termed "collage" by Radano), in which several pre-existent Braxton compositional structures are combined in real-time performance, can be viewed as determined by process, performance and participation. The performers can introduce or determine the choices of constituent works, and at the same time chance may have an influence. On the recording (Braxton, 1989) the works which are superimposed are not only by Braxton, but also by Briton Tony Oxley. Thus Braxton's texts are erased to such an extent that they become quotations and sometimes almost pastiches. Similarly the performances of "All the things you are", a jazz "standard" on several Braxton recordings (e.g. (Circle, 1970; Braxton, 1989)) involve both quotation and erasure of the original texts, and a merging of popular culture and high art. Braxton has also worked quite extensively with technologically innovative collaborators, using synthesisers, samplers and computers. The resultant Braxton works certainly challenge the concept of the lone creator.

More difficult is the question of whether Braxton's works embody "incredulity towards meta-narrative", Lyotard's summation of the postmodern which we also discussed earlier. Braxton is well known for his almost metaphysical verbal texts, which themselves are clearly a kind of meta-narrative relating to his music. However, their dense obscurity (recognised by (Lock, 1988) and (Radano, 1993) as well as ourselves), indicates that they have no clear implications for the interpretation of the music. In the diversity of his works and their questioning stance towards common musical processes, we see little reason to doubt that such "incredulity" towards metanarrative *is* important.

Braxton's work, and much of AACM's, thus fulfil the concept of the postmodern avant-garde. A postmodern avant-garde is sometimes thought to be a contradiction in terms; but if postmodernism is a consequence of the socio-economic structure, then it is inevitable that the countercurrents discussed by Raymond Williams ("the counter-hegemony" (Williams, 1977)) would accompany it, and the postmodern avant-garde is one.

Though concomitant with wider trends in the improvising arts, the "black revolution" in jazz — the creation of "free jazz" in the 1960s in America (see Chapter 4) — has received unique sociological treatment, as previously discussed (Dean, 1992). Was free jazz a music of revolt against a repressive white culture? And if so how was it concurrent in Europe, US and even Japan? The argument proposed (Dean, 1992) was that the interpretation of free jazz as a music of revolt was perhaps too simplistic, even a little romantic (and concordant ideas of Mackey and others are outlined in Chapter 4). It was proposed that more fundamental interpretations within the discourse of sound art itself might be equally important. However, no discussion was offered of the relationship between semiotic change (the development of new signs, such as new sound complexes and musical approaches) and the perception of such change. In other words, it was solely argued that semiotic change (that is the formal development of black free jazz) was unlikely to be primarily a reflection of the black musicians' response to their social condition. What remains more likely in our view is that the performers and the audience constructed an arbitrary association between the musical characteristics and their aspirations to elevate their Afro-American heritage: in this way the musical developments became signs of the revolt movement. These constructed relationships may well have catalysed increasing use of these new sound-complexes by the musicians.

Such catalysis by the audience would have been quite limited in the US though, since the employment opportunities there for black jazz musicians were virtually negligible. For conventional Afro-American jazz musicians to aspire to a jazz career might be to seek a route of escape from the limitations and depression of a social milieu (see for example (Berliner, 1994)), though with only a small chance of success. And as Amiri Baraka had to complain stridently even in 1986, the "wages" for most jazz musicians were "laughable" ((Baker, 1990) p. 65). When one considers specifically the Afro-American innovators of the music, they "might literally starve to death" (to quote Baraka again: (Baker, 1990) p. 63). In the case of a later innovator, Anthony Braxton, a quite detailed documentation of the economic hardship of trying to establish a creative niche in the US, and the somewhat greater opportunity in Europe, has been provided (Radano, 1993).

Catalysis by the artists themselves of the political importance of their work was probably far more powerful. The African spiritual aspirations of key figures such as John Coltrane are well documented (e.g. (Kofsky, 1970)) and ideas from African music were potent and valuable forces upon the nature of his music (as in many works such as Africa Brass; and A Love Supreme). There is no stylistic disparity between these works, and those such as "Alabama", which are overt vehicles of political complaint (in this case about Southern racism in 1963). Later Afro-American innovators, such as the Chicago musicians in the late 60s and early 70s, recognising the lack of audience support or response, formed their own institutions (notably the Association for the Advancement of Creative Musicians) so as to provide a vehicle for the catalysis of development of their music. The London Musicians' Collective, and its important journal, Musics, served the same purpose particularly in the early 80s. As Radano points out, such institutionalised separation of a group from their milieu and also from their peers is a common self-sustaining feature of an avant-garde (Radano, 1993).

Sociological theories about music are always challengeable, because music generally has a less overt relationship with its social context than other art forms, for example those in which language plays a part. The referential aspect of language means that any word has obvious potential meaning, and however complex and multiple it may be that meaning is socially constructed. Similarly the body is part of a complex sign system with social and political connotations. How overt these connotations are depends on how much any particular work sets out to be abstract or representational, though it is almost impossible for any work containing visual, verbal or bodily signs to be completely abstract.

Thus improvisation is necessarily linked with ideology, but to varying degrees in different art forms, as has also been discussed in Chapter 1. We are concerned in this book to understand these factors in relation to the improvisatory process and its artistic impact.

Methodologies and the Taxonomy of Improvisatory Media

To pursue our analytic purposes to the best, we have found it desirable to break down the components of our discussion into the smallest relevant constituent units. Thus it is not helpful to commence with a complex polymedia form such as theatre; rather we prefer to consider its constituent elements in isolation, revealing that there are many works produced using single elements. We have termed these elements "monomedia": for example, sound, word, visual object etc. Then we proceed to discuss combinations of two media (e.g. text-sound as a member of the bimedia category "sound/ word"), and only finally to consider polymedia (such as film, theatre etc).

We alluded in the Introductory chapter to the practicalities which limit our methodologies: for example we cannot investigate past improvised works of which no embodiment remains. And we have to accept that audio-visual recordings of past real-time improvised works are far from complete representations of them, often largely lacking, for example, the audience/ environment interplay. Yet such recordings are very valuable, and we have sought to use them extensively. Of course, in many cases, as in the films of Cassavetes or Leigh, or in some recorded soundworks, the final work results not only from whatever improvisation is recorded, but also from the subsequent cutting and editing process.

We may view these recordings as "transcriptions" of the event itself. As such they succumb to many (if not all) of the limitations of the transcription of the events into some form of notation, be it literary text, musical score, Laban notation, or psychotherapeutic notation (Keeney, 1991). For example, transcriptions often present polymedia as if they were monomedia (e.g. theatre as words). In addition, they usually present discontinuous items (e.g. musical notes) as representing a continuity (e.g. sound). Transcriptions rarely claim to define any of the putative "transitions" discussed above. The mode of description of the individual component events is of course also problematic: for example in dance, valuable notation systems such as that of Laban, are often focussed on describing movements of individuals, while a major thrust of the improvising may be toward co-creation, and in body work, towards merging of bodies. Novack described this Laban notation problem as Eurocentric, by illustrating a body clump (four improvisors performing within the contact tradition she views as American) whose description could not be given adequately in Laban

(Novack, 1988). Musical transcription tends to simplify grossly the rhythmic structures involved in improvised work (Hartman, 1991; Dean, 1992).

The ideas of improvisors themselves are very interesting sources for the analysis and understanding of improvisation. We considered carefully the design of a questionnaire for improvisors, and how it might be used. We predicted (correctly) that the response rate and the detail of response were likely to be limited, even from our close contacts in the field. Thus any attempt at a statistical survey was unlikely to succeed. Furthermore, a statistical approach could only have validity if all responders understood the questions in the same way, in other words, if the concepts behind the questions were made very explicit. In contrast, we were more interested to obtain the ideas of the improvisors as to the nature of improvisation, their understanding of its potential and meaning, and so on: this entailed our avoiding being explicit about our own conceptions. A statistical approach was therefore not applied, and our questions were intended to be very broad ranging and somewhat provocative. Our uses of the responses occur throughout the text, and the responses are summarised in more detail in Appendix 4.

There is no ready and generalisable solution to the conundra of analysing improvisation which we have outlined above, and each individual discussion needs to take account of this. We will not always have space to reiterate these issues in the body of the text, and hence the reader is requested to keep these issues very much in mind throughout. Even more with an improvised work than with a composed one, we suggest, the possibility of finite interpretation is not to be expected, or even desirable.

Section II

ELEMENTS OF IMPROVISATION

All that is needed is some preparation to effect greater smoothness and harmony, to ensure as far as possible that all is consonant with a well-organised performance. If all does not then turn out as expected, this will be the more readily excusable, for scripted performances too are not always successful... (Perrucci on improvisation, 1699. Quoted in (Richards and Richards, 1990) p. 203).

3

ENVIRONMENTS FOR IMPROVISATION

One of the important influences on an improvised performance, and its impacts, is the environment in which it occurs. This is not only true for those improvisations which overtly engage with environmental input (in a Cageian sense), but also of most others, through actions on both improvisors and audience. The environment may be a limiting factor, modifying what would otherwise be "free" improvisation. Similarly, the environment is a major factor on the proxemic situation for the audience i.e. their relation to space and each other. The environment may be sociopetal (meaning that it pulls people together) or sociofugal (reviewed in (Elam, 1980)). This proxemic axis indicates whether the circumstances bind the audience into the performance, or the contrary. The environment of the performance may dictate whether it is possible or not for an audience member or a performer to experience all of the events it comprises: a dispersed exterior performance may prevent this. The environment also provides a certain cultural ethos which may affect both the production and the reception of the improvisation (Jackman, 1992).

We distinguish four space-types in which improvisation occurs, and present them in order of increasing artificiality. In later sections of the book we discuss improvisation within the process of determining spaces for living and for the arts, as well as proposing in Appendix 1 possible future real spaces for improvised performance.

Real Space

Rather than accept a conventional constructed theatrical, club or concert-hall environment for performance, many improvisors have chosen to work in real spaces, entrained only by the limited possibilities of movement during the passage of the piece. A verbal-movement piece might well only occupy part of a day, and hence be restricted to a moderate space as in the case of street theatre. But environmental artists Richard Long and Andy Goldsworthy can traverse large areas of space in producing their visual or conceptual works, many of which involve improvisation. In either case, the audience (present later) may be able to view the whole space, but may well not necessarily see the whole work. Thus some of these works are sociofugal, unlike most in the constructed space-type.

Real spaces are not self-limiting in the same way as constructed spaces, and allow more fluidity of movement; they also open up possibilities of working within rural environments as well as urban ones, drawing the artists closer to nature and environmental changes in weather and lighting. Improvising in urban spaces allows artists to draw on buildings and detritus (e.g. the visual artist David Hammons (Hammons, 1994)) as part of their improvisations, and to interact with the general public. It also permits the subversion of normal forms of city life including pedestrian and traffic movements. Improvising of this kind connects with a long tradition of alternative forms of outdoor entertainment such as carnival, which are by nature socially transgressive, indeterminate, and involve many different art forms, as mentioned in Chapter 1.

The real space entrained by a transworld radio improvisation is immense; but the space is not fully expressed for the observer. Lesser limitations apply with transworld television or video works, but it is probably only in virtual and hypermedia spaces that the full breadth of such possibilities will be utilised.

Constructed Space

Most performance (improvised or otherwise) takes place in man-made spaces, such as the hall, often with stage and even proscenium arch. These spaces constrain the performance considerably, but they also offer the audience the opportunity to inspect all the elements of the piece, and in this limited sense are often sociopetal. However, they also create sociofugal barriers between audience and performer. Special performance devices, such as performers moving around the space, or multiple simultaneous events, are needed to overcome the sociofugal aspect.

Besides the large scale form of the building itself, other smaller scale influences (e.g. stage design) are at work. Thus the history of theatre and stage architecture and design is full of devices to change the performer-audience relationship, though few if any of these were specifically designed with improvisation in mind. Notable are the concept of the "Totaltheater" of Walter Gropius (1927), and "stressed skin" movable structures such as the Polytopes of Iannis Xenakis. Numerous constructed performing spaces, such as gardens, boats, and special architectural objects without housing functions, have been conceived independent of any ideas of improvisation; indeed many of these were not intended for performance at all (though Richard Schechner's Performing Garage in New York was at least specifically adapted for the purpose). Most kinds of building have been subverted into venues for improvised performance at least occasionally. The history of performing spaces is conveniently summarised in an issue of the Architectural Review (Sharp, 1989).

Often the constructed venues for improvisation are not the conventional or mainstream ones: they may be cafes, community centres, bookshops or pubs, such as the King's Head in London, which has long served as a theatrical fringe venue (Craig, 1980) or the Five Spot in New York, once the centre for jazz performances, but also a meeting place for artists of all disciplines. In the theatre improvisation has tended to be part of an alternative movement which has taken place not in the big theatres of the West End or Broadway, but in fringe theatres or off-off-Broadway. Improvisation has sometimes taken place within these environments because of the economic constraints within alternative forms of dance, theatre or music. But they were sometimes also chosen because they were not identified with the establishment and helped to create a different social ethos. Theatrical performance in a pub, for instance, creates an environment which is less elitist than mainstream theatre, and suggests participation by a wider range of social class. Sometimes these venues were maintained by the group concerned at peppercorn rents (a railway building used by the London Musicians' Collective, for example).

Music making in a pub has similar connotations, and in some respects is more relaxed for members of the audience than a classical music concert, because they can walk around, buy drinks, even talk, as is the norm in India at classical music concerts. They can choose to drift in and out of such performances, allowing for realistic fluctuations in attention. It is also relaxing for the performer, who can readily mingle with the audience and behave in a way more closely related to his normal behaviour than the classical musician can: this may have an advantageous effect psychologically on his/her performance. In addition environmental sound is less separate from performed sound in such an environment and can, on occasion, be incorporated into the music. Tickets may also be cheaper than in concert-halls, allowing students, the unemployed etc. to attend. However, it is easy to romanticise the advantages of such environments, for the disadvantages are quite severe. Noise from the audience may abut on, and even obscure the music, forming a distraction for listeners and players alike. The music can become subordinate to social activity and improvisors may be discouraged from performing at their best by signs of inattention to their work. This can be a reason for even a conventional improvisor (as well as the experimental improvisors mentioned in Chapter 1) to cultivate an attitude of indifference towards overt audience reactions.

Virtual Reality

Virtual reality is that which can be represented, apparently in three or more dimensions, on a computer screen and by means of an image generation program whose positions reflect information about the virtual space. Thus one can walk through a virtual reality using a computer mouse, and gain an impression of how that space would seem were it a real space. Of course this process can sometimes be used to represent real spaces, but that is not our main concern here. (Note that a confusing plethora of terms are used in the literature of this area, and virtual space is one, sometimes given a restricted usage, distinct from virtual reality, which usage we will generally avoid: c.f. Chapter 10). As Jon Rose has pointed out (Rose, 1994), in a sense radio can be used as a "virtual reality for sound", but this is probably a use which will not be made widely available, since commercial pressure will favour virtual realities including visual elements.

A virtual reality whose bounds are not predetermined, but which are generated by the computer program, offers an essentially unrestricted environment for improvisors to use. It could also be influenced by time-dependent, interactive and random factors (e.g. a random number generator within the program). The difficulty, of course, is the preconception that the improvisor or the audience might have as to what constitutes a space, and what physical objects should define a virtual space, especially as their behaviour need not be bound by any physical limitations i.e. they do not have to follow physical laws. The utility of these spaces will expand as these preconceptions broaden and video and interactive video works exploit them more fully. Indeed, as familiarity with virtual reality grows, these works will increasingly be seen as such.

Virtual reality creates several different kinds of social environment which can be moulded to the needs of the occasion, and which have different social consequences. On the one hand, the participant in a virtual reality is normally alone in it, or at least unaware of others. But the activities of others within the same virtual space can be made visible to each user, perhaps as symbols or icons: this is the case in a "multi-user dungeon" (MUD) on the Internet. In addition, virtual reality can conjure a shared space for several clearly represented (visible) bodies which actually exist at the time in quite different spaces, even long distances apart. This is discussed further in Chapter 10, and it is already well recognised that the concept of interaction between bodies, and the possible feeling of infringement of one's body space, can be powerful in such virtual spaces.

Hyperspaces

In a virtual space, it is still normal to move linearly from one area to another; and for the contained space to be apparently three dimensional. These are not necessary features of such "cyberspace" however. Hyperspaces, like hypermedia programs, offer not only non-linear progression, but also multi-dimensional articulation through text, image and sound. A multi-dimensional articulation is one in which any point, whether distant or close, can be reached directly from any other in a single step. While hyperspaces rarely fulfil this ideal as yet, the possibility exists and will be readily available in the future. Such hyperspaces are a sub-category which we have chosen to distinguish from the parent group, virtual reality.

Thus the application of hyperspaces for improvised performance is overwhelmingly attractive. Instead of the space dictating limitations of the improvisation, the improvisation will be able to dictate the nature, disposition of, and the access to, the space. Each "transition" (c.f. Chapter 2) in an improvisation could be associated with a corresponding transition of the event space(s) in which it occurs.

We will return to these present and future possibilities in Chapter 10.

4

IMPROVISATION IN MONOMEDIA.
1: SOUND AND WORD

In the remainder of this Section (Chapters 4–5) we begin the analysis of the contribution made by improvised works to different art forms, by discussing individual media separately for the purposes of clarity. In the next Section (Chapters 6–8) we gradually combine them. Some of the interesting uses of any particular medium have occurred within the monomedia (and appear in this Section), others within bi- and polymedia, and hence will be discussed later. We commence with sound and verbal monomedia; a polymedia such as theatre, which uses words, will be discussed in a later chapter.

We distinguish non-verbal from verbal sound, because of their differing degree of referentiality (Dean and Smith, 1991; Dean, 1992). Note that this usage of the term "referentiality", which is concerned with the meanings of signs and their relationship to reality is quite different, and rather more specific, than that of "referent" used to describe certain approaches to improvising in any medium (Chapter 2).

We have previously offered a detailed analytical survey of sound improvisation since 1960 (Dean, 1992), and for further details of some of the topics covered here, the reader is referred to that volume, which also provides lengthy discographies, complementing the more limited referencing of recordings which we give in this volume.

Sound Improvising

Brief historical survey of sound improvisation before 1945

Although it may be surprising to a Westerner, improvisation is at the centre of rather more musical traditions in the world than composition. Much of the music from Africa which is newly appreciated in the West as "World Music" (see for example, (Frith, 1989)), involves sophisticated improvisation springing from traditional African music. Thus the music we often now hear from Mali, Zaire, and Senegal has such origins. Similarly, the indigenous musics of many Asian countries (for example, India, Indonesia, Japan) are improvisatory. Quite often the music is produced by applied improvising, in which after development by improvisation in rehearsal, the performance may be largely but not entirely fixed.

In a society such as that of Bali, such musical forms are well specified because of their very clear social roles, accompanying particular village and domestic ceremonies which occur daily. But when one listens to a gamelan in Bali today, performing in a village for a traditional ceremony, one can hear flexibility, elements of pure improvisation, errors and their compensation, and possibly some influence of Western music. The influences seem to be two fold. First, some elements of Western popular music are having an impact. This is bound to be the case since every village bought its own communal TV more than a decade ago, and now many houses possess them. Second, one hears signs of a reciprocal influence of Western repetitive music (such as that of Reich, Riley described in (Schaefer, 1990)) on the way in which the gong sections of a gamelan superimpose their rhythmic patterns: there seems to be more phasing in and out than used to be the case. While this impression requires more detailed study, there is no doubt that, conversely, Balinese music style has influenced Western composition, since McPhee's classic studies (e.g. (McPhee, 1949)), culminating in works by Reich, Riley, Glass and others.

It is actually only in Western music that there has ever been any significant period in which improvisation was *not* central. For in the West its importance has oscillated. In the medieval period it was common in the performances of the Troubadours. Then, in the period of Classical composition, composers like J. S. Bach, Mozart and Beethoven were accomplished keyboard improvisors, and expressions of awe at their prowess abound in the journals of their period. The descriptions mostly imply that they undertook improvisations which were closely based around standard forms in which they composed (such as the Fugue, or the Sonata), and that they followed essentially the same harmonic and melodic technique. Thus their improvisations were strongly referent based. A late example of such stylistically entrained improvisations are those recorded by Elgar in 1927: piano pieces, close to the slightly superficial and charming style of some of his piano compositions. But by this time, church organ improvising was almost the only continuing improvisatory form in Western music, and it was not until the strong development of jazz, and particularly the arrival of Bebop around 1945, that Western art music began again to take advantage of the possibilities of pure improvisation.

In all periods, composers in most art forms, including music, have often used a limited degree of applied improvising in forming their works:

> ...*because composing is not a performance activity I feel it is valid to differentiate between "spontaneous composition" and improvisation. In cases when the term "improvisation" is*

applied to non-performance art forms (e.g. in Kandinsky's "Improvisation" series) I think what is being referred to is more what I would conceive of as spontaneous composition. (Hall, 1994).

New Zealand composer-improvisor Neville Hall is here referring to what we describe as "applied improvisation" in the work of the composer. Besides this, it is also well known that composers from all periods of this century have been attracted to jazz, and allowed its influence to dominate some of their works (for example, Ravel, Milhaud, Stravinsky, Antheil).

But since pure improvisation is so important in music since 1945, we will not further discuss applied improvisation in sound. Indeed, music is probably the Western art form which uses improvisation the most, and probably the one most people would associate with improvisation.

Recent introductions to some of the long-standing non-Western improvising traditions, such as those of India, the Middle East and Japan, are widely available (for example see (Nettl, 1974); Racy in (Nettl, 1991) on Arabic work; (Bailey, 1980) and the TV film series based on it by Marre; and information and references in (Dean, 1989; Dean and Smith, 1991)). A helpful introduction to most forms of sound improvising can be obtained through a number of articles in the current edition of the Grove Dictionary of Music, and some in the Grove Dictionary of Jazz.

Jazz since 1945 and its influence on sound improvising in general

When you hear music, after it's over, it's gone in the air, you can never recapture it again. (Eric Dolphy speaking on (Dolphy, 1964)).

Jazz is probably the most well known form of improvisation. Jazz is an Afro-American music largely developed by Black Americans, but particularly since 1945 — the period of Bebop — diffused throughout the world. It is a music which emphasises repetition, particularly in rhythm. Jazz rhythm usually involves a fixed and strongly stated pulse, and superimposes on it the phenomenon of "swing". Swing involves, besides special accentuation of sounds, a "continuity — the forward-propelling directionality — with which the individual notes are linked together" (Schuller, 1968). A different kind of swing was still a part of the freer improvisation which from the 60s onwards broke down all the previous conventions of jazz. Swing is thus a complex concept, which Gunther Schuller has well characterised, and which one of us has discussed in detail previously in two books (Dean, 1989; Dean, 1992) specifically dealing with improvisation in music :

swing not only involves enhancing the disparity of accentuation of pulses within metre, but also the slight displacement of sounds in relation to the relatively constant pulse interval, and the alternating distraction from and re-emphasis of the normal positions in time of the pulses. This concept of swing can be applied even when the pulses do not remain constant in length for more than a very short time (or limited number of repetitions); and this is important in free jazz, and to a lesser extent in free improvising in general. ((Dean, 1992), p. 10)

The cutting edge of jazz in 1945 was the music of Bebop, pioneered by Charlie (Bird) Parker (saxophone), Dizzy Gillespie (trumpet), Thelonious Monk (piano) and Charlie Mingus (bass). It represented a revolution against the previous conventions of jazz, and its fervour influenced the Beat generation, including the poets (such as Kerouac and Ginsberg) we will discuss later. The music often employed popular song themes and structures as the basis for improvisation, commonly using their 32 bar form in repeating cycles. It thus remained very tonal, based on a fixed pitch centres, and conventional scale patterns. Strong modulation (to new tonal centres) was rarely used, pulses were often very fast, but rhythmic approaches were rather unvarying. Bebop retained the strained pitches of blues, close to the African origins of jazz, but it is much simpler than much African traditional music in its rhythmic structures. Each pulse in bebop was usually subdivided into two by the soloists (resulting in 8 notes per 4 beat bar), and the rhythm section (piano, bass and drums) had a special responsibility for maintaining it. The wind players were responsible for the melody statement called "the head" (presumably because it was memorised), and were the primary improvisors who took "solos" accompanied by the rhythm section. But Bebop introduced many new complexities into the music :

Harmonically, the beboppers were particularly concerned with the higher intervals of chords, adding sevenths, ninths and elevenths on top of simple chords, using flattened fifths, and exploiting these in the improvisation of the soloists... Motivically, Parker's improvisations were complex, and could be quite consistent in their derivation. On the other hand, the motivic material used for the improvisation was often disguised or neglected : hence the term 'silent theme' characterises improvisations on harmonic sequences derived from well-known standard themes (popular items), but with little reference to the original theme, and often no serious replacement of it. ((Dean, 1992) p. 6–7)

It is interesting that jazz up to and including bebop, in common with popular songs, exploited the repetitious form of the 32 bar structure (or the 12 bar structure in the case of blues). For such an emphasis on "repetition" seemed particularly important in some of the changes in composed music, and in composed and improvised dance in the 1960s. The dance work of Anna Halprin is an example mentioned by Sayre (Sayre, 1989), and is discussed later in this book. Her piece "The Bells" comprised seven movements permuted for eight minutes, though not correlated with repetitious sound accompaniment. Jazz, and many traditional improvising forms in India, Bali and elsewhere, thus anticipated and contributed to this enhanced importance of repetition. Sayre does not mention these antecedents, and this may be indicative of a more widespread lack of appreciation of them, which we are seeking to overcome here.

The subsequent "free jazz" movement of the 60s was a very heterogeneous process, in which essentially all the conventions of previous jazz (including the emphasis on repetitive structures) were broken down and shown not to be essential for the continuation of a dynamic music. The musics of key Black musicians John Coltrane, Ornette Coleman and Cecil Taylor, were all very different. On the relatively rare occasions when they played together, they had considerable difficulties in adapting to each other (e.g. Coltrane playing with Taylor on record: (Taylor, 1958)). This was in spite of considerable mutual admiration (see for example (Litweiler, 1992) for description of the relationship between Coltrane and Coleman). Yet all three contributed importantly to this process and sustained and fed off each other. The rhythm section players were no longer confined to fixed pulses or roles and the harmonic patterns could be inconstant. Or the improvisation could be based almost entirely on associative metonymic continuity of motivic improvisation, with little constraint upon the resulting harmonic relations, as particularly in the work of Ornette Coleman.

The key figures achieved this opening up of possibilities in quite different ways, but all aspired to represent the power of a specifically black experience. Nevertheless, they worked with white musicians, and their audience was probably mainly white. The fact that the audience was predominantly white has been rehearsed repeatedly by Amiri Baraka, and is confirmed for the 70s and early 80s by the US data collected and analysed in 1982 with support of the National Endowment for the Arts. This data was summarised in (Baker, 1990) as showing that the jazz audience was "mostly urban, young, white, well educated...". It was striking also that in this survey, while 54% of respondents indicated that they "participated" in jazz in some way, only 43% admitted to "liking" it.

The musical achievements of these Afro-American musicians in the early 60s were represented as the "black revolution" in jazz, both by the way in which some of the performances were promoted and by subsequent analysts, such as Kofsky, whose 1970 book is well known if debated (Kofsky, 1970). This presentation was itself an ideological attempt to associate their music narrowly with the black political revolution, in spite of their predominantly white audience. LeRoi Jones (later known as Amiri Baraka) was one of the greatest enthusiasts of this music, but he made more of its continuities with 40s and 50s black music than of any new socially revolutionary import:

It was a lateral and reciprocal identification the young white American intellectual, artist, and Bohemian of the forties and fifties made with the Negro, attempting, with varying degrees of success, to reap some emotional benefit from the similarity of their positions in American society. In many aspects, this attempt was made even more natural and informal because the Negro music of the forties and again of the sixties… was among the most expressive art to come out of America…

But the reciprocity of this relationship became actively decisive during the fifties when scores of young Negroes and, of course, young Negro musicians began to address themselves to the formal canons of Western nonconformity, as formally understood refusals of the hollowness of American life, especially in its address to the Negro. The young Negro intellectuals and artists in most cases are fleeing the same "classic" bourgeois situations as their white counterparts… ((Jones, 1966) p. 231).

The political and psychological stances of the innovators such as Coleman, Coltrane and Taylor were diverse, and as discussed extensively in the literature (see also analysis in (Dean, 1992) and outline in Chapter 2) they cannot be uniformly or monothematically associated with the ongoing black political revolution of the time. Coltrane, for example, was primarily committed to a mystical and meditative Eastern religious approach, rather than to political activism. Coltrane in performance, similarly, appeared trance-like rather than extrovert, proactive or revolutionary (as shown on the several films of his concert and studio work). Nevertheless, he was sensitive to the Afro-American background and to the racial tribulations of the period, such as the 1963 events in Alabama.

A later Afro-American intellectual, the academic and poet Nathaniel Mackey, has helpfully analysed the complexity of the political relationships of the black artists in this period, arguing that the attempt to separate the black from the white artistic traditions was far from ideal:

…Amiri Baraka was important to me at a time when he was very much involved with a literary scene that was predominantly white, that was in many instances otherwise white were it not for him …The separateness of the black literary tradition has to do with the segregation of black people, the subtle and not so subtle apartheid which is the history of this county and continues to be part of the social fabric and the assumptions that govern a great deal of social life, most of social life, in this country. I don't feel an obligation to assert a sense of a separate black literary tradition. The tendencies and the inclinations that do that are so pervasive and so dominant that in many ways it goes without saying that it is separate, but the thing that needs to be emphasised is that that separation is a consequence of social practices that we're supposed to be against. (Mackey in (Foster, 1994) p. 71–2).

That Mackey also has music in mind is clear from the succeeding passages in which he emanates great enthusiasm for the work of Taylor, Archie Shepp, Marion Brown, Bill Dixon, and the later Anthony Braxton. He emphasises the intellectuality of their work, and how it challenged the stereotypes which society in general, and critics in particular, tried to use to understand black music. For example:

> *...Cecil Taylor doesn't seem to be embarrassed by {his} echoes of Bartok or Messiaen. But then you have neo-conservative critics like Stanley Crouch come along and accuse him of just retreading Messiaen and the like. That sort of mind is more comfortable with cut and dried definitions and discriminations, but Cecil's bigger than that, and that's one of the things we should be instructed by in his music. ((Foster, 1994) p. 79).*

A corollary of Mackey's emphasis on the intellectuality of the free jazz pioneers and their emphasis on preparation by private "woodshedding", is that he queries the white emphasis on the black musician as an "embodiment of instaneity, instinct, pure feeling, in some unmediated way uncomplicated by reflection and intellect" (p. 77). As he mentions (p. 78):

> *...Marion Brown {alto saxophonist} said about the new music of the sixties... that he sensed that many of the people who were bothered by the music and were reacting against it were bothered by the level of abstraction of the music and the way in which that level of abstraction being engaged in by black musicians diverged from and called into question certain notions regarding black people's relationship to abstraction, the idea that black people, if not in fact incapable of abstraction, tend to shy away from it in the direction of the immediate, the physical, the athletic, the performative.*

Similarly, Gioia (Gioia, 1988) has debunked the "primitivist myth" about jazz, but he unfortunately goes on to elide improvisation with "spontaneity", and to contrive a series of romanticised stereotypes in his attempt to characterise the jazz musician in general. For example (p. 56), he says that jazz musicians "lack the patience and decorum" necessary for concert and classical performance, a remark clearly far from appropriate to the elegant, if intense, devotion of John Coltrane. As we have already shown more generally in the introductory chapters to this book (in agreement with Mackey), improvisation is usually much more cultivated, formulated, sophisticated, and even intellectual than the term "spontaneous" or the idea of "instaneity" permit. Berliner has also exposed this misconception of "spontaneity" in jazz (Berliner, 1994).

Parallels to US free jazz emerged soon in Europe (from around 1967), particularly in the work of such as Brotzman, Dauner, and Schlippenbach in Germany, Willem Breuker in the Netherlands, and AMM, Evan Parker and Derek Bailey in the UK. There is no doubt that these musicians were influenced by the American movement, but their political stances were less specifically bound up with racial difference and more with other forms of social repression. For example, Eddie Prevost, of pioneering free improvisation group AMM, was concerned with state dehumanisation:

> *The high rise block for instance — a very structured way of organising people. Even the Welfare State {in the UK} which was a marvellous thing when it began, began from an organisational, paternalistic point of view, rather than looking at people as separate entities. People were seen en masse. And I think a lot of improvisation was a kind of response to that dehumanising aspect of life. (In (Childs, Hobbs et al., 1982/3)).*

Free jazz gained its name by asserting that any of the conventions of jazz could be done away with, but usually by retaining some, so that a clear continuity with the rest of jazz was preserved. Certainly, ever since the 60s, jazz has continued as a very broad entity, exploiting all the conventions and all the disregard of convention implied by the coexistence of free jazz and the mainstream of modern jazz which emerged from bebop.

On the other hand, free jazz in the US was quite distinct from that in Europe, although the two interacted. Many US free jazz players in the middle 60s onwards worked more in Europe than in the US, since their music was far from successful commercially in the US. They frequently played with the avant-garde of Continental European improvisors, such as Alan Silva (bass), and many became based in Paris (see for example, (Radano, 1993)). But the European musicians were far more commonly influenced than the Americans by the developments in contemporary composed music. These included electronics and its sound world, and the overpowering of total serialism by approaches relating to texture and sound-structure (as in the music of Ligeti or Xenakis). The European improvisors often had direct experience of this music, as in the cases of Vinko Globokar (trombone) and Michel Portal (clarinets). This resulted in far greater interest in unfettered exploration of sound, timbre and texture, and the evolution of novel instrumental techniques which in turn influenced composition very markedly, as in the work of Ferneyhough, Dillon, Barrett and many others (Dean and Smith, 1991).

Cornelius Cardew has described this exploration by improvisors, particularly in relation to AMM (AMM, 1968; AMM, 1982; AMM, 1987), as follows:

> *Informal "sound" has a power over emotional responses that formal "music" does not, in that it acts subliminally rather than on a cultural level. This is a possible definition of the area in which AMM is experimental. We are searching for sounds and for the responses that attach to them, rather than thinking them up, preparing them and producing them. The search is conducted in the medium of sound and the musician himself is at the heart of the experiment. (Cardew, 1971)*

This quotation underlines again the difficulty of interpreting any improvised music which possesses a large degree of exploration and "informality" (like free jazz), in terms of simple politico-cultural themes. It is significant that this statement comes from a strong socialist (Cardew), and concerns a committed socialist group (AMM). It shows that even such committed musicians may realise the difficulty of relating their political positions to musical exploration, and that Cardew did not see the music as the expression of a particular political point of view. As he said elsewhere, if with typical complexity and ambiguity, the "free improvising" musician "uses the world as a directive" which is "unwritten" (Cardew, 1976). The extended quotation above also reveals clear differences in attitude and approach between the US and European free improvisors at this innovative period in the 60s and early 70s, such as a greater openness in the latter. The European improvised music of this period hence became known often as "free music" rather than "free jazz", which term was restricted to that music which retained more recognisable connections with the conventions of jazz.

Perhaps what was most shared by the Black free jazz and the European free music improvisors was the emphasis on group collaboration. To quote Evan Parker:

> *What makes (free music) relevant is that it's a group activity. You have to look for this other organism, which is the group mind. You block access to that group mind if (your own) personality is too strong. (Quoted in (Lewis, 1972)).*

These two features of sound improvisation, the exploration for new sounds and textures, and the use of collaborative group work, are central topics in the more recent developments which we will discuss later in this Chapter. For detailed coverage of free jazz and free music on a more technical level, the reader is referred to (Jost, 1974) (Dean, 1992) (Radano, 1993). While it should be apparent from the nature of improvisation, perhaps it deserves stressing again that analytical linearities in our descriptions of changes in sound art are not to be equated simply with any value-bearing concept of "progress". Changes are not concerted, nor uni-directional, and always relate to a multiplicity of influences, only a few of which we can properly hold in focus at any one point.

On the nature and importance of contemporary improvised music

> *Improvised music is a music of self definition. (Prevost in (Small, Durant et al., 1984)).*

Sound presents a particular problem for semiotic analysis: what discrete element could constitute the smallest sign? The separable notes of a classical sonata might be candidates, though probably some assembly of them would be more useful. But the problem remains how to analyse the signs within absolutely continuous sound systems, such as the timbral streams of Evan

Parker, or the computer music transformational stream, which we will discuss further later in this chapter? Clearly, higher level features, for example those which are superimposed on the continuities of timbral streams, have to be chosen. Meyer has argued in a sophisticated way that music builds up expectations which are fulfilled or "frustrated" (see for example (Meyer, 1956)). Thus a soundwork may (through its own progression) build up high level predictions in the mind of the listener as to what will follow. In a conventional jazz form, for example, there will be expectation of pulse continuity, accentuation, and meter. This can be "frustrated" when a suspension or submergence of the pulse or a complex syncopation occurs, and according to Meyer this may be important for the affect of the piece. More generally, expectations which pertain to recognition of repetition, and the attendant development of intensity, are equally likely to be valuable. This problem has been discussed in detail previously (Dean and Smith, 1991; Dean, 1992).

Listeners to a recording (CD, radio) of a previous (or even simultaneous) sound improvisation may feel themselves to be in the position of an audience member, but in fact, as most performers have agreed, the recording does not embody all features of the performance. Instead, it forms a separate object from the performance, with its own advantages and attractions, but without the process of the performer-audience interaction. For example, the extra-musical behaviour of an improvisor may be part of the information which leads the audience to their "expectations" of subsequent events. Thus the expectations of the CD listener may well be different. It is important to consider this when assessing sound recordings, especially as they form the major source of evidence on improvised sound. It is misleading to feel that recordings are an infinitely better source of information about past sound improvisation than the material we have available about unrecorded theatrical improvisations. In each case we can only gain a limited impression.

Even though the frequency of sound improvisation performance has oscillated vastly in past Western culture, throughout the period since 1945 sound is probably the medium which has engaged the largest number of artists in improvisation. We need to ask why this might be. One factor is probably the immediacy of sound production on traditional musical instruments, and now on digital ones: there is no impediment to production, as there is, for example, in making a visual image by painting techniques. The latter usually requires gradual construction before anything interpretable by an audience emerges. Sound production also occurs over time, but all the component elements remain separable (because sequential) parts and they need to be appreciated as such, unlike those of a painting, which eventually can be appreciated in a single viewing, and in an order dictated by the viewer. That one can immediately "perform" a work in public, if improvising, is probably an additional attraction. It is also a feature which makes it possible to undertake the performances fairly economically, since the substantial periods of group rehearsal needed for performance of comparably elaborate compositions can be avoided.

While verbal improvising has been relatively unusual in the period since 1945, we will point out later that its potential is just as great as that of sound improvising, and that the constraints we have just mentioned can be over-ridden. We also note that verbal improvising was probably more common in earlier oral cultures (see Chapter 1 for brief comment). Indeed it shares its origins in oral cultures with jazz, which developed from the blues, the worksong, and the African origins of its creators ((Smith, 1983); summarised by Smith in (Nettl, 1991)).

Techniques specific to improvised sound and their development in the 1960s and 70s

Are there particular features special to sound improvising? Certainly there are many conventions, and indeed jazz often seeks to identify itself as such by emphasising them. Amongst the main jazz conventions are the reliance on formulaic referents for improvising, and the cultivation of individual tone or sound, in a reproducible form. Most jazz improvising still uses formulaic structures such as the twelve bar blues and the 32-bar "standard" tune, with fixed quite simple harmonic patterns which repeat, and improvisation primarily of intensification. Very little improvising related to the jazz tradition escapes from the convention of the dominance of rhythmic repetitiveness, though on occasion this becomes a rather looser concept of pulse, as mentioned above.

Do the uses of sound in improvisation in our period differ from compositional usages? Perhaps the most obvious distinction is in the degree of collaboration between creators' inputs. In improvisation the creator/ performers can contribute diverse inputs in a relation of equality (and we will discuss some specific examples in detail below). In sound composition, while there may be several performers, the role of creator is largely disposed with the composer. The creative input of the performers, though difficult to assess in terms of subjective impact, is restricted, as judged by the limited distinctions between different performances. Separate performances of most compositions maintain many common features (e.g. sequence of notes, timings, dynamics). The audience role can also be greater in improvised sound, though this is not commonly exploited.

One might think that intensification, and emphasis on rhythmic impulse would also be central features of sound improvising, hardly shared with composition. This is true of jazz, and therefore perhaps, in terms of frequency, of sound improvisation in general. But the features are by no means common to the whole range of sound improvising, which is extremely diverse. In fact another equally important development in improvisation (generated by the "revolutionary" tendency to extend the world and oneself by means of improvisation (c.f. Chapter 2)) has been the development of microtonal inflection of instrumental playing (for example in the work of John Coltrane). Similarly important in improvisation has been the "exploration", mentioned above by Cardew, of so called "extended techniques" on instruments, particularly within European free music. These were so named in the 60s, and often resulted from the instrumentalists conceiving ways of reinterpreting their instruments (e.g. using the bass as percussion; playing between the stopping finger and the nut above on a string instrument, instead of between the finger and the bridge below; harmonics on the piano, viewing it as a string instrument instead of as a keyboard percussive one; wind multiphonics). Philip Corner played the piano with his feet in some 60s events (see (Banes, 1993), p. 211). Much of this emphasis relates to the 60s excitement with the "wisdom of the body" (Banes, 1993):

> *Improvisation… not only in jazz, but in the other arts, was prized by the 60s avant-garde for two reasons. It symbolised (perhaps even embodied) freedom. But it also relied on the wisdom of the body — on the heat of kinetic intuition in the moment — in contrast to pre-determined, rational decision-making ((Banes, 1993), p. 211).*

As Corner also mentioned ((Banes, 1993) p. 211), in relation to his piece "Big Trombone" from that time, "I wanted to create in my own terms something that had an unimpeded, uninhibited rush of physical energy". The context makes clear that these are features he attributes to jazz, and to Afro-Americans. The influence of physical involvement with the instrument is evident widely in later improvisation, as in the work of Jim Denley, with flute, voice, and flax, an instrument combining flute parts with saxophone parts (Denley, 1991–2) (Denley, 1992). It is also apparent in composition, as Richard Barrett indicates of his work:

> *…important is the intimate relationship of both {improvisation and composition} to a tactile conception of all aspects of sound, the praxis of sound, as it is handled, stretched, torn, breathed, caressed, scraped into music. Of relevance here perhaps is my concern in composition to derive materials as directly and deeply as possible from a perception of the physical nature of the instrument and its relationship to the player, such that it might be said that, viewed from this angle, my compositional methodologies are those of an improvising performer "seduced" into composition by a desire to work with a greater diversity of instrumental resources than one lifetime would afford the necessary command and fluency. (Barrett, 1994)*

The development of new instruments, such as Nam June-Paik's TV-cello (a cello with a TV body: (Paik and Godfrey, 1973)) for Charlotte Moorman, can also be viewed as a means of extending the world, though they move further away from the wisdom of the (human) body, instead creating alternative (instrumental) bodies. Such constructed instruments are discussed in great detail by Ernie Althoff (Althoff and Dean, 1991) and Hugh Davies (Davies, 1987), and have general utility. Some are at the interface of construction and digital software/hardware (e.g. see (Nunn, 1988)) which we consider further in the next section, and to which we return in Chapter 10.

Synthesisers and digital sound and the development of "continuous stream" improvising

Digital instruments, which in theory can produce any sound, and hence seem to have the potential to be the ultimate instrument for musical performance, were developing at the same time as instrumental extended techniques in improvised music (1960s–70s). The two developments overlap in their contribution to what can be called "continuous stream" sound work. By this we mean those works which involve absolutely continuous sounds (rather than a discontinuous succession of attacks, as on the piano). These are usually works in which several continuous strands co-exist, merging into a single texture. The overall texture is the centre of the musical discourse, and it evolves by gradual changes in the individual (if merged) strands. These textures and strands are often contrasted successively or simultaneously with other distinct elements. In this sub-section we will outline this development, characteristic of the period since 1970.

We need first to summarise some of the nature and development of synthesisers, particularly digital, since these now predominate for good technical reasons. The development of digital sound synthesis and reproduction is undercutting the specificity of musical instruments. For a computer can generate a highly respectable trumpet sound, given enough computer memory and processing power. Computer memory soon becomes limiting when computers are used for sound reproduction work, because of the immense memory demands which would be entailed by recording long complex sounds (1 minute of sound requires roughly 10Mb of memory). Therefore, present portable computers cannot imitate instruments fully; nor perhaps should this be their objective. They have their own unique uses.

One of these is the capacity to generate continuously varying sounds, and if these originate from sound synthesis, rather than sound recording, the sounds can be very long. In contrast, human generated sound, on instruments or using the voice, is mainly presented in discontinuous short units (the "note" of the classical music score). This is sometimes conditioned by the nature of the instrument, as with the separate keys of the piano or vibraphone; sometimes by stopping to breathe (as with voice, trumpet or clarinet). However, this is not a necessary feature since some instruments (for example the organ) can be sustained continuously, or almost continuously (as with string instruments, where each change of bowing direction is necessarily associated with some discontinuities, even if not brief silence). Furthermore, circular breathing, using both nose and mouth, permits continuous air supply to a wind instrument, and has been traditional in the performance of the didgeridoo (the Australian Aboriginal instrument), in vocal techniques in Afghanistan, and elsewhere. Circular breathing has also become a conventional technique within contemporary music since the 1970s, composed (as in works of Kagel, Globokar, and many others) and improvised (notably in the work of British saxophonist Evan Parker).

Parker, through his interest in timbral variation in long-sustained saxophone sounds, became a major innovator. Together with Derek Bailey (guitar), he was a major force in free music from the late 60s onwards. His tenor saxophone playing was initially inspired by the most free explorations of John Coltrane, and particularly his incantatory late works such as "Expression" and "Interstellar Space" (released only after Coltrane's death in 1967: (Coltrane, 1967; Coltrane, 1967)). Parker co-founded with Bailey the seminal free music label, Incus. He was, and still is, a member of most of the key free improvising groups in Britain (such as the London Jazz Composer's Orchestra, and the Tony Oxley group), and of several multinational groups, such as the Quartet of German pianist Alex von Schlippenbach. Parker was initially often a source of "high-energy" in an improvising group. In this role, his output would be intense and densely packed with action, but not necessarily all at a high dynamic level. Parker's work soon revealed another kind of continuity: instead of using a rapid succession of discrete events, tonguings or other articulations, he developed timbral change within a single sustained sound. As mentioned already, Coltrane often made microtonal changes to notes, re-articulating them successively with this objective, and it seems that the greatest effect of this process is the change in timbre, rather than simply the minute change in pitch. Parker, using circular breathing and usually not rearticulating the sounds, took this further and further, until his sustained sound-stream would evolve over a whole solo performance, often lasting about 45 minutes. Fine examples of such work are on his recording "Monoceros" (Parker, 1978). His work is quite remarkable and a major contribution to improvised music. When collaborating with others, he can assist with a group texture — or as he himself puts it — with a "laminal" sound. He shares this with the electro-acoustic group AMM, and as their sustaining force, Eddie Prevost says:

> *What is certainly perplexing, though, is that really, ...there have been few manifestations of the kind of group which use, to use Evan Parker's term, a "laminal" approach; layered textures. In the European free jazz side there's still been this emphasis on individual statements in juxtaposition to each other. (In (Childs, Hobbs et al., 1982/3)).*

In this, Prevost refers primarily to *successive* "individual statements", in which there is a hierarchy of role amongst a group of free improvisors at any instant, even though they may be co-equal overall. He probably also had in mind, though, the multiplicity of *simultaneous* event which was developed within free music.

The emphasis on long-sustained sounds brings to mind the shamanistic repetitive ritual, also of long duration. It is interesting that protracted circular breathing, though clearly providing enough oxygen for survival, may nevertheless be associated with reduced supply of oxygen compared with that in normal circumstances. Possibly such "hypoxia", because of its well known metabolic effects (Dean and Wilcox, 1993), may be relevant to changes in the psychological state of the improvisor. Jon Rose similarly mentioned the need for a degree of "athleticism" to undertake free improvising, and has engaged in one violin performance which lasted for twelve hours continuously ("Sound Barriers" 1980; (Rose, 1994)).

Evan Parker can sustain a continuous sound-stream improvisation for at least forty-five minutes, but on digital instruments sounds can be made absolutely continuous for the whole duration of a work of any length. Even the now classic Yamaha DX7 synthesiser (introduced in the early eighties) can generate continuously varying sounds lasting several minutes, and up to sixteen of them simultaneously, creating a complex evolving sound. With more recent advances in availability of computing power, this capacity has expanded vastly, and is more than sufficient for the duration of any piece which might be presented in concert. The limitations of digital synthesisers as improvising vehicles are primarily a consequence of the limited responsiveness of their keyboard interface, in comparison with that of the piano, or more extremely, that of wind and string instruments. This is gradually being overcome by their technical advance (e.g. increased control devices for timbral modification are inbuilt: (Pressing, 1992)); and by increasing exploitation of the universal "ether" of sampled complex sounds now available for performance by electronic keyboard.

Digital instruments or modification processes also facilitate the dissociation between input (pressing a key for example) and output (the sound of middle c on the piano for example). The key attack may produce unexpected outputs, pitch relationships may not be as they seem on the keyboard and so on. Such dissociation is an important device and attitude in free improvisation and has been discussed before in some detail (Dean, 1989;

Dean and Smith, 1991; Dean, 1992). It can be obtained to a degree on a conventional musical instrument (e.g. playing near the bridge on a string instrument) but it is certainly much facilitated by electronic processing.

Processes in sound improvisation

A range of processes are important in the progression of a sound improvisation, and we will now discuss some of the most important. One such process is the use of repeating procedures (not simply repeating chord sequences as in conventional jazz) as part of the generation of a work. John Coltrane's piece "Ascension" (Coltrane, 1965) illustrates this. It had a simple repeating procedure of soloist-group improvisation-soloist, spearheaded by the leader's exaltation to the performers to achieve a new spiritual plane. "Free Jazz" by Ornette Coleman and his group was analogous (Coleman, 1960). Similarly, Terry Riley's incantatory Indian-inspired repetitive improvising involved elaborating very simple procedures. Alongside Riley, American and European composed "minimal" music (such as that of Glass, Reich) acquired the same characteristics.

Besides using repetitive processes, sound improvisors also have the opportunity — unique in music — to think ahead to procedures (and therefore states and structures) they would like to initiate, and to seek means to do so. Even if they improvise alone, this is not simple; but if they improvise with others they have to pursue very subtle strategies to manoeuvre their fellow improvisors into this state. Often they are more interested in reaching a procedural amalgam in which part is conceived by themselves earlier in the performance, part by others: this is a more readily attainable, and often more diverse, multi-meaningful approach. Examples occur on austraLYSIS' double CD recording "The Next Room" (austraLYSIS, 1994). In the work "Solid as an Age" an improvised rhythmic and harmonic structure was recorded silently into a synthesiser, while other keyboard sounds from the same player were audible, and then the recorded material was sounded repetitively to influence the procedures of the other two improvisors. Cognitive studies are beginning to confirm that "expert" improvisors can formulate and apply flexibly overall improvisatory strategies during performance (Hargreaves, Cork *et al.*, 1991). It is not necessary to assume (as Berliner does in a valuable study of the mainstream of jazz improvisation up to about 1960) that "operations of improvisation involving more than one person require the instant assimilation of ideas across the band's membership" ((Berliner, 1994), p. 497). Assimilation can be retrospective, external, or irrelevant.

A different kind of process is that in which the interactions between different musicians, in generating a sound piece which has no pre-existent material, are controlled by a score. Sound improvisation has pioneered this, and we can refer to them as interactive process improvisations. We will discuss an example in detail shortly. This kind of interactive process control is very different from the control over process which is exerted by a notated score from which players perform. In performing such scores the players have little opportunity to influence future outputs from their fellow players, even though they may mildly influence the simultaneous sound generation, in placing and dynamic. An example of this kind is shown in Chapter 1, and several are discussed in (Dean, 1989).

Intermediate between completely notated composition and interactive process improvisation, are improvisations based on referents which contain precise musical material. Particularly in the US, the results are often termed "comprovisation": for example this usage is common amongst the members of the Rova saxophone quartet, though its precise time of origin is not clear (Ochs, 1994). Butch Morris (bassist, composer) now refers to the process of directing improvisors through what are sometimes comprovisations, as "conduction".

We should consider more specifically some of the processes which can be controlled in sound improvisation (Dean, 1989). One issue is how the materials of any combination of improvisors interrelate. In a sensory (and generative) stance, the sound improvisor will assimilate the material of one or more of the other improvisors, and generate further material not only subsequent to it, but also perhaps with a conceived relation to it. As we indicated, the generated material may be introverted, in the sense that it is primarily of relevance to the producer. Or it may be extroverted, in the sense that it is intended to further influence the output of another improvisor, or of the group as a whole. The technical procedures for this require the improvisor to imagine gradients of relationship on which to place any particular generated response. Infinite numbers of such gradients are possible, and usually they will not be known to the other improvisors: indeed they may be subconscious to the user. A simple example is thinking of a gradient of dynamic intensity, without regard to any other feature such as pitch, timbre, texture. A complex example might be thinking of a gradient of "green-ness" of sounds. This could be done by distinguishing components of sounds as "green" by virtue of their similarity to sounds of living organisms, their dependence on materials derived from dead organisms, or their proximity to the nature of rural rather than urban environments. These two examples are chosen to illustrate that one can focus on primarily music-technical levels, or on extra-musical levels. In the latter case, one has to superimpose metonymic or arbitrary connections between the extra-musical level (green-ness) and musical components with which one can actually work. Lysis' recording "Superimpositions" (Lysis,

1987), is largely concerned with such controls of interaction, and the "Heteronomies" presented there are based on referent scores which contain no musical material, but request particular kinds of interaction conceived on gradients from positive to negative (as in Figure 2.1). Thus on any gradient which an improvisor has chosen, one extreme can be associated arbitrarily with positive interaction and the other with negative interaction. Alternatively, the positively interactive extreme of such a gradient can be taken to be that which has most similarity with the sensory material.

An important corollary of such interactions and controlling them, is the possibility of bringing about substantial transition points in the improvisation of a group, where many parameters change at once. This possibility is as important in free improvising (with no referent) as it is when a score is used to control interaction. It can be the primary determinant of structure in an improvisation, as in Coltrane's "Ascension". The following score for improvisors by David Toop is an example of such attempted control:

> *lizard music: a figure, phrase,*
> *cycle sound etc is played*
> *specifically to create a feeling*
> *of stasis. at various points*
> *throughout the piece all players*
> *change simultaneously to another*
> *statement as if the previous one*
> *had not happened. no statements*
> *are pre-arranged between the*
> *players. satisfactory systems*
> *of simultaneous change are*
> *investigated. lizards are studied.*

> *May 1972*
> *(In (Cobbing and Griffiths, 1992) p. 148).*

Clearly this score requires multiple faculties in the improvisors. At once they have to recognise that one of their fellows has made a change sufficient to require all players to change (unless a cueing system is used), and also to generate "another statement as if the previous one had not happened". The idea of a sound-gradient is intrinsic in this, since a direct repetition of a previous sound complex would certainly give the impression of continuity, rather than the requested discontinuity, so a contrast with previous sounds is implied. On the other hand, the impossibility of the task is also apparent: any sound can be conceived as having a relation to a previous one, and thus cannot necessarily abnegate the existence of the previous sound, as requested. As Toop and his close associate, Bow Gamelan member Paul Burwell, have discussed, complex but arbitrary individual assumptions are likely to be involved in performances of sectionalised music such as this (Burwell and Toop, 1976).

Conversely, textural improvisation and sound-streams such as those of Evan Parker reveal that it is not necessary to have such obvious sectional transition points. Structure then resides at a much deeper, more detailed level within the sound world. To appreciate this is to begin to grasp how the important structures in improvised sound are at least as complex as those in composed music (see (Dean, 1992) for further analysis).

As we have outlined, interactive process improvisations may involve sound artists in controlling how they generate and how they modify their sound material, and equally how they relate it to that of their fellow performers. An example of an interactive procedural improvisation score has already been shown in Figure 2a, and here we will analyse another interesting example, John Zorn's "Cobra". Note that both the devices in Figure 2a and in the Zorn score could be used to control improvisation in other media, but were conceived for sound performance. The relationship between the piece and the swirling improvisatory elements of the Cobra group of painters (see later) is evident when one listens to recordings of it (Zorn, 1985).

Interactive process sound improvising

John Zorn is an American saxophonist and composer who has worked in jazz and in free improvisation (for example with Derek Bailey's Company). He is also active in postmodern music which is much more commercial, and in film music. Figure 3 shows a segment of the Zorn score "Cobra" (reproduced from the CD sleeve), which is in toto a one page set of symbols and several pages of instruction/explanation for any number of players (recordings: (Zorn, 1985)). The essence is that each improvisor can offer procedural cues by means of hand signals, which are then transmitted (or denied) to the rest of the group by a "prompter" who does not generate a sound input. These commands can indicate, for example, the formation of a new performing sub-group (and the cessation of playing by the others), or gradual cross-fading of the performing groups. They can also indicate transient formation of duos and other groupings, which temporarily relate primarily to each other by various musical procedures (e.g. exchange, contrast). These particular commands do not have any necessary influence on the nature of the sound, dynamic, or activity. But another batch of cues issued through the prompter concern these components. In addition, a clever set of commands (the "memory commands") require all the players at a particular instant to remember precisely what they are playing ("record"), and then to be able on demand to reproduce it ("playback").

These commands and procedures characterise the so called "normal Cobra" level of the piece. A tendency in performances (such as those in Sydney 1994 organised by guitarist Oren Ambarchi) is for commands to succeed each other very rapidly, so that the sound work is a series of abrupt transitions with no detailed exploration of any particular event. This can be very interesting, but the contrast of longer evaluation of a particular command is also available, since the prompter may decline all offered commands for a period of time. Another tendency is for the players to issue memory "record" commands at points at which entertaining genre playing is occurring. Genre, a term used by Zorn himself in the notes, implies a sound structure which the audience will probably recognise as closely allied to some familiar style.

Another layer of process possibilities, the "squad" commands, permits avoidance of both these latter features, and provides many other opportunities for the improvisors to control the function of the whole group. Thus an individual may wave a headband at the prompter, be accepted, don the headband, and then become a "guerrilla". In this condition the guerrilla may do anything until another performer (the "spy") successfully requests the prompter to "kill" him or her. The guerrilla may also form a potentially more permanent "squad" by recruiting two other players to join, also donning headbands. Such a squad may control the function of other musicians, may play alone or with a group "drone" accompaniment, and thus may investigate particular areas of sound at length. In some command states the squad cannot be stopped, while in others it can be "challenged" and unless the challenger is identified, then the squad loses guerrilla control, and the whole group returns to the "system" command status of normal Cobra. In "squad" mode as in normal Cobra, there can be a tendency for performers to challenge the squad very rapidly, which somewhat goes against the objective of having a squad facility. But within squad mode, the guerrillas can choose to establish unchallengeable states if they wish, and thus both the frequent abrupt transitions and the emphasis on genre can be avoided.

Within the squad mode a command which emphasises genre re-creation is available; this is clearly a post-modern procedural element. In this "fencing" command, a succession of players each have to generate different genres, and each individual may be called on to generate several, representing quite a challenge. The potentially militant theatricality of such performances, with commands and headbands, is quite in keeping with Zorn's own proclivity for wearing army-like dress. While Cobra has usually been performed by sound improvisors, it would be accessible and interesting to improvisors in other media, particularly those involving verbal elements.

It is interesting to contrast the potential for generation of hierarchy, and squad control in Cobra, with Zorn's own egalitarian views, and to consider them both as models of political control. Zorn expresses his egalitarian position as follows, envisaging himself as the "prompter":

> *In Cobra the players are making all the decisions. Or ninety percent of them — I'm also part of the band, so I can make decisions too. It's a typical misunderstanding to see me as the conductor, the boss. But everyone in the band is gesticulating at me wildly, waving hands, waving hats, and the audience should be able to see what's going on. But audiences are so used to the notion of an autonomous musical mind that's in control of everything that they're often blind. They bought the line, which is so disgusting. (Zorn, 1991)*

Zorn refers to the piece as "democratic", presumably envisaging the guerrilla squads as other than terrorists, and concludes:

> *I do insist on asking why everything is put into boxes. And how can we break those boxes apart? That's a racial, cultural, social, musical question that is urgent and broadly resonant…*
> *Decision making, that kind of activity of a person — a person's being conscious — is the opposite of escapism. My pieces are opposed to escape. (Zorn, 1991).*

Like improvisation in general, Zorn's piece embodies the need for both self-dependence and social responsibility. The political aspect of the music is here more to the fore than in many modernist works, such as much of the 60s free jazz, so "Cobra" emphasises the political possibilities of improvisation. But it is striking that in spite of Zorn's democratic intent, the piece permits even a totalitarian guerrilla operation to dominate. Presumably Zorn is sufficiently sceptical about society to feel that such domination by force will remain a possibility for some time to come.

Collaboration and the development of new forms by sound improvisation

We have emphasised that improvisation permits collaboration between creators rather more readily and frequently than composition does (though collaboration in performance is always an important part of music-making), and we have discussed some of the processes involved. Perhaps even more important in relation to the development of new forms and novel products, is the possibility of collaboration between creators from different media. While this will be most relevant in later chapters on bi- and poly-media, we can note here the great impact of collaborative sound improvising on sound forms, and summarise some of the achievements to which we have alluded above.

It is perhaps appropriate first to consider why collaboration is so central within sound improvising. Most probably the reason is the very simple one, that many instruments are not readily self-sufficient in music, and most lack some of its possible dimensions. For example, pitch and harmony are not readily available to the player of untuned percussion, while a guitarist or bass-player finds it difficult to create the same depth of percussive impact as the percussionist. For these reasons, musical groups form, and performance in groups is far more common than solo performance. This is just as true in improvisation as in composed works, and hence collaborative improvisation was bound to occur. In this it differs from all the other mono-media we discuss, for in all the others the individual can be perfectly self-sufficient, and indeed, sometimes collaboration is particularly difficult.

Compositions for improvisors offer another form of inter-personal collaboration, though one which is not so immediate. A plethora of scores, procedural, graphic, ideational, partly notated, exist for use by improvisors. Sometimes, as discussed elsewhere (Dean, 1989; Dean and Smith, 1991; Dean, 1992) these can be highly stimulating, and lead to the same kind of instrumental exploration we have outlined above. From the improvisor's point of view such compositions can be a more straightforward, if less taxing, approach to the "stretching" of instrumental sound which Barrett mentions seeking in his compositions, and which is also characteristic of Ferneyhough, Dillon, Dench and others (Dean and Smith, 1991). From the composer's point of view, the difficulty of such a collaboration is that of finding appropriately sympathetic and experienced improvisors, who also need to know more about composition than many do:

> It's seldom that I have the opportunity to write for performers who are really equipped to cross the line from interpretation to improvisation. I've been experimenting with notations that extend the role of interpretation, in an effort to involve the performer more in the creative act, but this is a very different thing from allowing a performer to improvise. As a performer I am interested in presenting both compositions (i.e. performing from detailed notation) and improvisations, as well as works that involve elements of both interpretation and improvisation. I find that the various creative processes yield different results, all of which can be interesting. (Hall, 1994).

We can now outline some of the formal and structural developments attained by largely collaborative sound improvising since the 60s. On a rhythmic level, as demonstrated previously (Dean, 1992), improvisors in sound have gradually elaborated control, complexity, and finally multi-layering, so that improvising groups might superimpose multiple pulse rates, meters, and rhythmic "feels". Improvised movement between these states also allows more complex transitions. The pulse components, instead of bearing simple whole number relations (as in the music of American composer Elliott Carter), may bear any of the infinity of relations (as in that of Conlon Nancarrow): a pulse 5.7983/4 times as fast as a previous one might occur. Furthermore, it is practical for an improvising sound group to maintain for significant lengths of time several independent pulse fields, before (perhaps) all mutually gravitating to one (for example works by Circle discussed in (Dean, 1992)). These advances, which depend on real-time collaboration, parallel those in composition, but are rather different, and in many ways more open, even granted the inevitable imprecision when an interpretive performer negotiates a 7/5 times pulse shift.

On a harmonic level, jazz was somewhat simpler than concurrent composition in sound, until as the period developed it became more diverse and complex, through the collaborative efforts of its practitioners. But throughout it emphasised microtones, which were lacking from most Western composition. This emphasis also expanded, so that true microtonal improvising, especially using synthesisers, became quite potent and readily available. These developments of new forms necessarily overlapped with the initiation of motivic change in improvisation: here Ornette Coleman and others spearheaded an enhancement of the importance of metonymic progression, which had its counterparts in the through-composed songs of Schubert and many other works, but which was again handled very differently in improvisation.

Perhaps the most interesting output of formal innovation from improvised sound was that alluded to already, in which discrete events in sound were replaced by continuous ones, as in the work of Parker, Mangelsdorff, and subsequently Braxton and many other wind players. This work often sought to magnify the timbral variations possible within the sound-world of an individual instrument, and to focus the musical event play on this.

The idea of continuity in sound abuts that of exploiting environmental sound in art works. While this was not particularly an improvisors' idea, many sound-artists since 1945 have exploited environmental sounds as the basis for improvisation, or as a tape counterpart to improvisation. For example, Pauline Oliveros, in one of her "Sonic Meditations" (Oliveros, 1962) asks the performers to prepare a tape of a defined environment for a chosen period; and then to improvise with it using their normal instruments. This trend has been enlarged as the Green movement has developed and imbued greater awareness of environmental issues (Oliveros discusses this broadly in several articles and interviews such as that in (CCMC, 1985)). There is also a clear parallel between Oliveros' piece and the 60s–70s Structural Film procedure in which a camera gazes unblinkingly at whatever actions occur within a fixed space: for example in Mike Snow's "Wavelength" and "Back and Forth" (<—>) which we discuss later. In both the sound and the film works, the "material" of the environment becomes the material of the resultant work (Gidal, 1975).

Australian Rik Rue, on the other hand, prepares multiple tapes of environmental and other sounds, which he then manipulates in performance by means of a four track analogue tape, together with digital tapes, so that he can project a huge range of combinations of sounds (Rue, 1991). There may be some random element in the choice when he quickly picks up a new cassette to play from the four track, but quite often he would be able to predict which segment of the tape would emerge next. The rapid access on DAT and prerecorded custom CDs, together with the random access function on the latter, permit the improvisor to use the whole range of possible control, from nil to complete. Rue has also produced sound tapes with which others improvise; for example "3 Nocturnal Windows" (austraLYSIS, 1994). In this work the two instrumentalists improvise in relation to the environments on the tape, acting often but not always as "intruders". One (using a sampler) performs with sounds mainly taken from the environments, which may be sonically manipulated (pitch, waveform) as well as performed freely. The piece suggests the Australian Bush, including the crackling of a camp fire, and these "found" sounds are used as musical motives. In this way, Rue and other improvisors use environmental sound to question the apparent autonomy and non-referentiality of music, emphasising the connection of musical sound with that of environmental sound, and the fact that both may be absolutely continuous in time. This approach also brings music into a more direct relationship with political, social and environmental discourse.

We turn finally in this sub-section to collaboration with electronic machines, and their contribution to sound continuity and other innovations. Composition, for a long period, only exploited such continuity of sound production in electronic music, (with the exceptions in the 70s of Globokar & Kagel who were much in contact with improvisation). However, improvisation developed it even for conventional instruments. As well as being evident in the work of individuals, this same emphasis on continuity of sound was encouraged in group improvisations by the scores of Stockhausen for improvisors, which were often interpreted by electroacoustic groups. Such continuity has been the root of the process we referred to as textural sound improvising.

Digital instruments often permit the live use of sequencing techniques, so that an instrument can be performed upon, and then recreate that performance, with or without modification. Such uses of sequencing permit each individual to self-collaborate, as well as collaborate with others, and thus permit even the small sound-improvisation group to create multiple layers of rhythmic, harmonic, motivic and textural play. The two 60-minute improvisations on our own recent double-CD "The Next Room" (austraLYSIS, 1994) illustrate this quite extensively. The first is somewhat modernist in its instrumental, microtonal and sampled sound diversity and timbral exploration. The second creates a repetitive rhythmic and harmonic pattern, postmodernist in its relation to 60s jazz, on top of which is multiple rhythmic, harmonic and textural field improvising, instrumental and electronic. The computer music group The Hub adopt other approaches to such complexity, involving networking their performing stations, and often cultivate a sound-mass which is more prone to merge into an apparent single field. Their data is exchanged currently mainly at the level of MIDI signals (see chapter 10) and the exchanges are algorithmically controlled (Brown, 1994). According to Chris Brown such algorithms may sometimes tend to generate "set pieces", which can then be regenerated, at least in outline.

The use of computers in sound improvising still introduces the element of stress, and overtness of improvising effort, to which we referred earlier. As David Wessel (Wessel, 1994) mentions, this springs from the complexity of the physical set up needed with most present equipment, but can be a positive inducement to both performer and audience. With future virtual (radio) and computer-controlled connections between equipment, rather than current tangles of wires, this stress may disappear (c.f. Miditap, discussed in Chapter 10). Wessel also points out that the complexity of the software, such as MAX (see Appendix 3), often requires the performer to expend much mental energy on remembering the status of instruments or modules, and hence what they will do when driven next. This stress is for him productive too, but also permits an element of "non-reproducibility" (rather than randomness; to quote Chris Brown again). This is positive for an improvisor, being another facet of the dissociation between action and output mentioned earlier.

There is no doubt that sound improvisation has vastly enlarged the performers' roles: they have become the creators. Whether it has changed the performer-audience relationship, unless the audience is actually invited to participate in sound generation as in Cardew's "The Great Learning" (Cardew, 1968–1970 (3rd edition 1984)), is more difficult to gauge. Confrontation of the audience is common in duo- and polymedia (see later) involving sound, but instrumentalists (and microprocessor players) tend to be somewhat immobilised, if not earthbound, by their instrument. Thus a key impact of pure sound improvisation on the audience has been to permit the detection of risk and effort, as mentioned by Jon Rose. On the other hand,

Michael Snow (Snow, 1994) describes improvised music as a "social occasion", indicating that social exchange takes place, and that the performers become at times the audience of other performers: as he sees it, the "social occasion becomes the subject". This position emphasises the possibility of merging the performer-audience roles, but in a different way.

If audience members detect the risk and effort of an improvisor, they probably also recognise that sound-generating instruments are not simply machines to be switched on and run; they are not immediately accessible to use by the audience. Rather they are generators whose input has to be controlled precisely, and whose output is infinitely flexible. This flexibility is rarely fully exploited in composed music, but rather more commonly so in improvised. Computer technology has helped, recently permitting interactive performance. This has in turn allowed improvising musicians to control a huge array of sound sources, by means of signals derived from their own playing; in other words, by a transmutation of their improvised sound input. Other modes of interaction are possible, and shared by composers: for example algorithmic composition. The distinction is in the nature of the interaction, whether between instrument, sound input and computer (as in the improvisatory interaction), or between composer's mind, computer keyboard input, and computer. The forms which result have differed, and this is an expanding area at present, to which topic we will return in Chapter 10.

Sexual and social politics in sound improvising

> *Improvisation has a unique position... in that it is much less amenable to stultifying commodification, less easy to assimilate into the strategies with which the ruling ideology turns artistic activity from an expression of (the possibility of) the emancipation of thought and practice into a cosmeticised middle-class pastime, than even the most "oppositional" composition-oriented work. This does not imply that improvised music therefore constitutes a model of a "perfect society", ...since it will always, under the present circumstances, reflect also the contradictions and tensions endemic to the society in which it is situated... (Barrett, 1994)*

Women are generally vastly under-represented in improvised music. For example, Roger Dean has improvised with more than 100 other improvisors, from Australia, UK, Europe, Asia, USA, and South Africa. Yet amongst these have been only ten women. Such a ratio (or less) is the common experience of male improvisors (Wilmer, 1977; Placksin, 1982), and they often recognise that their own assimilation of the issue of discrimination against women in music was belated (e.g. RD; (Rose, 1994)).

The discrimination against women in most forms of music is quite clear. Sandy Evans, a woman and a leading Australian jazz musician (Evans, 1994), has been amongst those active in trying to overcome this tendency, and this is encapsulated in the ironic and forceful title of one of her earlier influential groups "Women and Children First", active in the early 1980s. While this name presumably referred to the priority women and children received in situations such as the sinking of the Titanic, there are other obvious connotations. Several of her compositions reflect related ideas also. The name of the English group FIG (Feminist Improvising Group) also emanated these pressures.

One facet of the discrimination or discouragement women have suffered in relation to improvised music is their irregular frequency amongst performers of different instruments. There are relatively few female improvising trumpeters, a gradually increasing number of female saxophonists, such as the leading mainstream player Kathy Stobart in the UK, but rather more singers and pianists. Amongst female pianist-improvisors one can readily think of: Gerri Allen, Joanne Brackeen, Marilyn Crispell, Connie Crothers, Marian McPartland, Mary Lou Williams (from North America); Irene Schweizer (from Europe); and from Australia, Judy Bailey. Is the piano feminine? It may be notable that amongst this list are only a few Afro-American pianists. Perhaps amongst Afro-American jazz musicians there is a greater diversity of instrumental affiliation than there is amongst (white or black) classical musicians. For example, as early as the fifties, Melba Liston was a notable female jazz trombonist, yet it would have been unusual to find a female classical trombonist. However, the discrimination against women continues in the newer Afrodiasporic forms such as rap (Rose, 1994).

Another aspect of the male-centred nature of sound art development must be that aesthetic values are being dictated by the (mainly male) patrons of the forms. These values are largely object and form based: as Neville Hall suggested criteria based on process might be more valuable and appropriate. As he continues: "whether these revised criteria would be more "female" is difficult to say" (Hall, 1994).

It is difficult to translate the undoubted patriarchal history of patronage for music, and of musical creators, into an assessment of the femininity or otherwise of sound works. Some authors fight to do this, for example relying on the idea that the first subject of a sonata form composition is the thrusting masculine one, while the second is the softer, more feminine and incomplete one (e.g. (Sayre, 1989)). Such studies are complex, and at present in their early, highly debatable stages, as are studies of the psychological sound-art propensities of the sexes (Dean, 1992). Parallel issues are at an even less advanced stage of analysis in relation to gayness and improvisation.

Gay improvisors may be quite divided about these issues. But British jazz composer Graham Collier (discussed in detail in (Dean, 1992)) sees little connection between his sexual orientation and his music:

> *I am what I am and that shows in the way I work but I don't think being gay has a particular relevance apart from my general niceness... Certainly I'm against the macho view of jazz... (Collier, 1994)*

He continues by mentioning that many heterosexual men by now reject this macho view, which can probably be approximated to the "physical, athletic" jazz performer of the 60s discussed above by Mackey. Collier's partner, John Gill, has presented much interesting information to show that gay musicians are very important in 20th century music, and he makes considerable reference to improvisors (Gill, 1995). He indicates that they have suffered particular difficulties in pursuing their activities because of their sexual orientation, which has also often been a tabu subject for critics. However, Gill does not attempt to analyse the relationship between gayness and the nature of the musical outputs.

What of the other political issues which abut improvised sound? One interesting fact is that, on occasion, sound improvisation can be an object of censorship, while at other times overtly political works can slip by unnoticed thanks to bureaucratic inattention. Jon Rose has experienced censorship in Germany on three occasions, but never in Australia; conversely he produced a piece in protest against the Berlin Olympic Games without even attracting a reprimand (Rose, 1994).

From the point of view of an individual, improvisation permits a free choice of presented socio-political position, as discussed in conversation between Rik Rue and Roger Dean (Rue, 1991):

> *RD: Could it be that improvisation is a way of evading admitting to your core personality?*
> *RR: Possibly, but I find that a very restricted point of view.*
> *RD: Some improvisors are extremely flexible!*
> *RR: Yes, flexibility is possibly the greatest gift to have because you might need to be white or black.*
> *RD: An improvisor can be both.*
> *RR: An improvisor can be both. Sound as organised sound is quite restrictive as an artform, so it depends on what society one lives in and how one can integrate with it. Improvisation seems like evolution of music. It is like dropping a pod in the right sort of fertilisation pattern for a plant. It is quite natural. I think it has got scientific in a particular kind of way. It's as if one's response to a comment could be re-addressed.*

So an individual sound improvisor may be able to align with any psychological or political stance, to use any parts of "the world" as "directive", as Cardew puts it. The stance need not be one to which he or she adheres intellectually or emotionally, but may be "fictional", just as it can be in literature. Improvisation can thus be a vehicle for expressing any view, even though it is frequently oppositional.

The issues are necessarily even more complex when one considers a group or society. Trombonist and educator Simone de Haan believes that we need to "get away from that image of the professional musician as the only possibility of being creative as a musician. Somehow music has to become more a part of our lives again" (de Haan, 1991). He recognises that this could remove commercial and arts bureaucratic pressures, but would replace them in the short term by educational bureaucratic ones.

> *The general emphasis in music education from the professional entrepreneur's perspective is to take the standard concerts out to the schools. Instead, it should be to create projects where, through providing appropriate models and ongoing workshops, students may become more involved in composing and playing their own music. Until these types of activity become more commonplace in our educational environments, we won't see music develop to the degree where it is a central activity, integral to our daily lives.*

de Haan, as an experienced and committed improvisor, includes improvisation as an important component of "students… playing their own music". Advances towards this may be facilitated by the development of computer sound, as we will discuss later.

Improvisation has been seen as a means to avoid commodification, but there is no denying the virtually immediate commodification and exploitation of even improvised music, once recorded. Doc Rosenberg, a pioneer of the relative violin and other "Australian musical dynasties", created pungently and seriously by Rose and Linz takes a blindfold test from Downbeat June 1968 ((Rose and Linz, 1992) p. 98). He opines:

> *1. Brandford Marsalis. Shopping Mall Blues.*
> *Hey that's Brandford — you can't fool me with that. I picked up on that immediately he played that ascending fourths figure — also the sound of his horn. Yep, they all sound like that. Actually it could have been any one of about 100,000 tenor saxophone players with a college education and a mid-period Coltrane aesthetic. How did I know it was him? Because this is Downbeat which is mainly just advertising for Columbia, and Marsalis records for Columbia, and Columbia are giving him maximum hype at the moment. Quite simple really. And I see you got my cheque there, so I'll give it 5 stars.*

It is fascinating to fantasise how improvised music could appear in Downbeat now that CBS is run by Japanese Sony.

Verbal Improvising

This section discusses verbal improvisors and their contribution to oral and literary discourse. Sound poetry and phonetic work will be regarded as bi-media, and so their improvising practitioners will be considered in a subsequent chapter. Since linguistic signifiers can be both sounds or visual marks, improvising with words can take both oral and written forms. Oral improvisation lends itself most clearly to the pure improvisatory process, since it can take place in a performance situation. However, it is also possible to characterise a range of writing processes as having a close relationship to improvising, e.g. writing in private at speed and without revision, so that we may see these techniques as instances of applied improvisation. A writer may also mediate between written and oral forms of improvising by talking into a tape recorder and then transcribing what he says: this technique has been used, for example, by American Beat, Allen Ginsberg and British poet, cris cheek.

Both applied and pure verbal improvising can use a large range of linguistic techniques. It can conform to the conventional syntax of writing, where the relationship between signifier (the outward form of the word) and signified (the concept) is controlled strongly. Alternatively, it can exploit the syntactical flexibility of speech, or attempt to break free of syntax altogether and create chains of signifiers which do not close meaning off into a recognisable signified. Improvisation can take place through association, at the level of word, phrase or sentence, and this association can be promoted by either sound or sense or a mixture of the two. As mentioned earlier such metonymic improvising can give rise to new metonymies or to extreme dissociation (that is the improvisor keeps changing direction rather than continuing in the same direction). The improvisor may use variation, or permutation of phrases or sentences, or repetition whereby s(he) returns to a particular word or phrase and uses it as a springboard for others. Narratives may also be generated by starting with a theme-referent, or more radically narratives may generate themselves from purely linguistic starting points. This can be achieved through techniques of association and transformation (letting a concept generated in one sentence form the basis for the next), and through the technique of reincorporation suggested by Keith Johnstone (Johnstone, 1979), where a concept which has dropped out of the story is brought back in again at a later stage.

Writers improvising

Applied verbal improvising consists of writing at speed, using a transformative process whereby words suggest other words. Writing is conventionally tied to the idea of revision, that is, continuous improvement towards an ideal version. In improvised writing speed, lack of revision and verbal self-generation are used as a means of inducing translogical ideas.

This section offers an analysis of applied improvising, concentrating mainly on three American writers in the fifties and sixties, Jack Kerouac, Allen Ginsberg and Frank O'Hara, whose particular historical and artistic context made improvisation especially attractive to them. Ginsberg and Kerouac were part of the Beat movement, characterised by a rejection of many of the materialistic values of contemporary America; a belief in sexual liberation and the spiritual values of eastern religions; an involvement in the "fast" world of drugs; and in the case of Ginsberg a deep aversion to the Vietnam war. Their attraction to improvised procedures was also the result of deep reverence for jazz both as a music and creative process.

Frank O'Hara, writing at the same time as Kerouac and Ginsberg, belonged to the New York School of Poets (well documented recently by Geoff Ward (Ward, 1993)) which also included John Ashbery and Kenneth Koch. The New York School was more influenced by painting (Abstract Expressionism in particular) than poetry, and also by European surrealism. O'Hara's poetry came from a somewhat different ideological position from that of the Beats, less influenced by eastern philosophy and jazz (though improvisation as a process in jazz music obviously had an impact on O'Hara). It is more postmodern in its political relativism and denial of unifying truths. Most of all it is a poetry which celebrates the present moment, and it is this absolute attention to the present which probably attracted O'Hara to improvisation (Smith, 1988).

Kerouac, Ginsberg and O'Hara all produced work which related to the ideas of Black Mountain poet Charles Olson, embodied in his essay "Projective Verse":

> *And I think it can be boiled down to one statement (first pounded into my head by Edward Dahlberg): ONE PERCEPTION MUST IMMEDIATELY AND DIRECTLY LEAD TO A FURTHER PERCEPTION. It means exactly what it says, is a matter of, at all points (even, I should say, of our management of daily reality as of the daily work) get on with it, keep moving, keep in, speed, the nerves, their speed, the perceptions, theirs, the acts, the split second acts, the whole business, keep it moving as fast as you can, citizen. And if you also set up as a poet, USE USE USE the process at all points, in any given poem, always, always one perception must must must MOVE, INSTANTER, ON ANOTHER. (reprinted in (Olson, 1973) p. 149).*

The approach that Olson advocates here is improvisatory and strongly metonymic. In fact, the Beats, New York poets and Black Mountain poets all shared a strong reaction against the new critical orthodoxy of critic Allen Tate and the related work of poets Howard Nemerov, Robert Lowell, Richard

Wilbur and Louise Bogan. This was characterised by traditional meters, metaphor as analogy, the concept of the poem as an organic whole, and of poetry as a moral order. The reaction was also directed against the writing processes which produced these orthodox poems: the reliance on set forms, and the idea of revision as essential to the well-crafted poem.

The most vehement reaction against this kind of writing process can be found in the work of Kerouac, who totally avoided revision ((Weinreich, 1987) and desired to discover form rather than imitate it. In "The Essentials of Spontaneous Prose" Kerouac advocated a freewheeling approach to writing rather than one of selectivity: "free deviation (association) of mind into limitless blow-on-subject seas of thought" (quoted in (Weinreich, 1987) p. 2). The emphasis was on speed and the adoption of a state in which the conscious censoring mind would not interfere. "If possible write 'without consciousness' in semitrance (as Yeats' later trance writing) allowing subconscious to admit in its own uninhibited interesting necessary and so 'modern' language what conscious art would censor, and write excitedly, swiftly, with writing-or-typing-cramps, in accordance (as from centre to periphery) with laws of orgasm, Reich's 'beclouding of consciousness'. *Come from within, out-to relaxed and said*" (quoted in (Tytell, 1986) p. 142).

It is revealing that although he is here evoking a technical procedure, Kerouac's language stems from sixties philosophy and ideology. The ethos is of jazz improvisation, Zen Buddhism (the concept of the trance), Freudian psychoanalysis and the ideas of sexual liberation propounded by Wilhelm Reich. However, the influences upon it reach back to the surrealist experiments earlier in the century, particularly Breton's notion of automatic writing (see Chapter 1). Rather than being maximally powerful and in control, the writer gives up control as he submits to the unconscious; he is both in the present moment and yet out of it. The idea that the conscious would somehow censor the unconscious is crucial here, and is influenced by Freudian psychology.

Kerouac's description of his psychological state is somewhat idealised: in a useful study of his processes Weinreich demonstrates how his method is a mixture of spontaneity and control, the basis of the improvised method. It is also important to realise the degree to which Kerouac's "spontaneous bop prosody" was influenced by the jazz music which was contemporaneous with him, rather than the more general concept of improvisation. He frequently compared the writer's role to that of the horn player "Jazz and bop', in the sense of a, say, a tenor man drawing breath, and when he does, his sentence, his statement's been made...". In addition, he mentions the fact that the jazz musician "has to stop where the chorus page stops" ((Weinreich, 1987) p. 9). He is referring here to the bebop musician's penchant for improvising on popular songs with repeating harmonic structure (the chorus) often of 32 bars, and implying that his work often follows a similar pattern. This would be in addition to the idea of phrase coinciding with breath, since a breath would usually not suffice for a chorus. The two approaches can be merged, as they are by the bebop musician.

The influence of jazz on Kerouac is undeniable, and impressive at a technical and musical level: it is also graphically displayed in his performances, which show the influence of jazz phrasing and timing. But his enthusiasm for it was symptomatic of a nostalgia for a black culture, typical of the period and forged largely by white stereotyping. Referring to Kerouac's "romantic racism", Nathaniel Mackey says:

> *The sensibility of Kerouac is that of a refugee or would-be refugee from the white centre who is seeking some alternative to himself, a self he sees as too hung-up in convention and tradition — the ratiocinative, the reflective, the intellectual — while in black music he sees a model of spontaneity and of gut feeling... an over-simplified "understanding" of what the music is about and where it's coming from. ((Foster, 1994) p. 79).*

Kerouac was influential on Allen Ginsberg who describes a similar technique for writing "Howl" (Ginsberg, 1956) in 1955–6. Ginsberg, sending Kerouac what he called the "100 per cent original draft. There is no pre-existent version", wrote in a letter, "I realise how right you are, that was the first time I sat down to *blow*" (quoted in (Tytell, 1986) p. 217). Here Ginsberg draws an analogy with jazz musicians blowing (that is, improvising on their instrument). O'Hara, in contrast, is not a self-declared improvisor, and was probably more influenced by painting than jazz. However, in an interview with Edward Lucie Smith (in (O'Hara, 1983) p. 21) he said "I don't believe in reworking — too much. And what really makes me happy is when something just falls into place as if it were a conversation or something". There is much anecdotal evidence to support the idea of his writing at speed and lack of revision (Berkson and LeSueur, 1980). O'Hara's writing method is also apparent in a film where he discusses a script with film-maker Alfred Leslie: he continues to type while he discusses the script, and while on the telephone to a friend (Moore, 1966). In O'Hara's work, improvisation is linked to "just go{ing} on your nerve", to a commitment to change and transition.

Applied improvising: processes

Although some ideologies of improvisation seem to suggest that improvised poems come straight from the unconscious, and while this is a view perpetuated by some of its practitioners, in fact verbal improvising consists of detailed strategies and techniques. Applied verbal improvisors usually have some means of inducing improvisation, such as using particular types of materials or aids, or adapting the place or time-frame in which they write. Kerouac typed "On the Road" on a continuous role of paper as if it were one long paragraph, and as a means to keep writing without stopping. When finished it consisted of one sentence which covered over two hundred pages of print. John Clellon Holmes recalls Kerouac in the process of writing: "how the typewriter clattered without pause" ((Weinreich, 1987) p. 41). Allen Ginsberg sometimes wrote by speaking into a tape-recorder which he clicked on and off as ideas came to him: the way that the phrases are arranged on the page is strongly influenced by the way they were vocalised, though words spoken in different breaths were sometimes run together on the same line with interesting effect (Ginsberg, 1971).

O'Hara, who also said in the interview with Lucie Smith that he was attracted to writing because one could write relatively fast ((O'Hara, 1983) p. 21), sometimes wrote poems quickly in response to challenges from friends:

> *One Saturday noon I was having coffee with Frank and Joe LeSueur… Joe and I began to twit him about his ability to write a poem any time, any place. Frank gave us a look — both hot and cold — got up, went into his bedroom and wrote "Sleeping on the Wing", a beauty, in a matter of minutes. ((Berkson and LeSueur, 1980), p. 82–83).*

He liked to write under the pressure of the moment. In "Adieu to Norman, Bon Jour to Joan and Jean-Paul" ((Allen, 1979) p. 328), which was written in the hour before a lunch with Norman Bluhm, he speculates whether he will "finish this in time to meet Norman for lunch". Sometimes he created a time frame, such as his lunch break, within which to write his poems.

O'Hara' manuscripts show evidence of a minimum of revision (Smith, 1988) and much anecdotal evidence has been compiled about O'Hara's ability to write poems rapidly even in situations considered unsuitable for creativity, such as a crowded room. Grace Hartigan has related how O'Hara wrote poems in bars (Hartigan, 1986). Kenneth Koch has spoken about the way O'Hara would dash off a poem in the middle of a group of people at a party, or whip up several poems in quick succession (Koch, 1986). Koch succinctly sums up the improvisational intent of O'Hara's work when he says "The speed and accidental aspect of his writing are not carelessness but are essential to what the poems are about: the will to catch what is really there and still taking place." Bill Berkson, a friend and collaborator of O'Hara, makes a similar point when he says that for O'Hara "composition was a matter of performance, of staying on the boards. The trick was to maintain a voice, to give it enough force, or gusto, so that the lyric occasion might absorb all contradictions and interruptions-subject to both the poet's will and his fancy" ((Berkson and LeSueur, 1980), p. 162).

Writers who improvise tend to work with linguistic techniques like those mentioned earlier, which help them to keep generating material without knowing what it will be. From Kerouac's writing about how to write, and from his style, one can deduce many aspects of his technique: the way in which sound association created by assonance and alliteration, and the creation of rhythmic propulsion, each lead the sense; the use of repetition of a word or phrase as a base from which to generate new images; the use of what Kerouac called "the jewel centre", a privileged image from which meaning can flow; the mixture of recycling and reinvention from novel to novel; and the long image laden, metonymically driven, grammatically loose sentences, often packed with adjectives and nouns without the subject — verb — object construction we might expect. The following (one of the shorter sentences) is a typical example from "Visions of Cody" ((Kerouac, 1992) p. 74–75):

> *Old Bull balloon who usually went around wearing a poker-wrinkled but respectable suit with a watch chain, straw hat, Racing Form, cigar and suppurated red nose (and of course the pink flask) and was now fallen so low, for you could never say that he could prosper while other men fell, that his usually supposititious half-clown appearance with the bulbous puff of beaten flesh for a face, and the twisted mouth, his utter lovelessness in the world alone among foolish people who didn't see a soul in a man, hounded old reprobate clown and drunkard of eternity, was now deteriorated down to tragic realities and shabbiness in a bread line, all the rich history of his soul crunching underfoot among the forlorn pebbles.*

We can see here the accumulation of antithetical images: "drunkard of eternity" and "the rich history of his soul crunching underfoot among the forlorn pebbles"; and sentences which are circular rather than progressive.

Similarly, Ginsberg uses sound as a way of sustaining the improvisation, what he has called the "tone leading of vowels" (Ginsberg, 1971) and the long breath. "Howl" emphasises the long line, dense with antithetical images and held together with a repeating structure ((Ginsberg, 1956) p. 9) :

> *I saw the best minds of my generation destroyed by madness, starving hysterical naked,*
> *dragging themselves through the negro streets at dawn looking for an angry fix,*
> *angelheaded hipsters burning for the ancient heavenly connection to the starry dynamo in the machinery of night,*
> *who poverty and tatters and hollow-eyed and high sat up smoking in the supernatural darkness of cold-water flats floating across the tops of cities contemplating jazz…*

These antithetical images force into words the paradoxes of American life in the fifties, in which it is a bohemian, marginalised and oppressed culture which is visionary. Thus Ginsberg's style is in may ways a poetic equivalent of Kerouac's prose style.

O'Hara allows events which are happening while he is writing to tumble into the poem. For example, if he is listening to music on the radio he will mention it or, as in "On Rachmaninoff's Birthday #158", use it as a stimulus for self-expression "I better hurry up and finish this/before your 3rd goes off the radio/or I won't know what I'm feeling" ((Allen, 1979) p. 418–419). Similarly, Alfred Leslie explains as he talks on camera to O'Hara that one of the aspects of the proposed scenario is that "it's nobody else's business what people do when they are alone" and when O'Hara reads back the script it contains Leslie's sentence (Moore, 1966). His poems sometimes emphasise the immediacy of the speaking voice as in "Anxiety":

> *I'm having a real day of it.*
> *There was something I had to do. But what?*
> *There are no alternatives, just*
> *The one something. ((Allen, 1979) p. 268).*

But his strategies are also "word-centred" and metonymic:

> *Perhaps it is to avoid some great sadness,*
> *as in a Restoration tragedy the hero cries "Sleep!*
> *O for a long sound sleep and so forget and so forget it!"*
> *that one flies, soaring above the shoreless city,*
> *veering upward from the pavement as a pigeon*
> *does when a car honks or a door slams, the door*
> *of dreams, life perpetuated in parti-colored loves*
> *and beautiful lies all in different languages. ((Allen, 1979) p. 235).*

sometimes in such a virtuosic way that they lead to new metonymies or even complete discontinuities.

> *Yippee! she is shooting in the harbour! he is jumping*
> *up to the maelstrom! She is leaning over the giant's*
> *cart of tears which like a lava cone let fall to fly*
> *from the cross-eyed tantrum-tousled ninth grader's*
> *splayed fist is freezing on the cement! ((Allen, 1979) p. 108).*

O'Hara was less influenced by incantation and song than Kerouac and Ginsberg: his poetry is a fascinating attempt to bring together speech-orientated and writing-orientated kinds of improvisation; a colloquial yet campy speaking voice; and a tradition of literary linguistic experimentation extending from Gertrude Stein. He captures the rhythms of speech but also pivots on words, playing on their multiple meanings and exploiting their syntactic ambiguity. And there is an even greater tendency than in Ginsberg and Kerouac's writing towards antithesis, that is, towards existing within many sets of dynamic and changing oppositions. In fact all these writers, particularly O'Hara, seem to be graphic examples of the kind of Janusian strategies outlined by Rothenberg, where antithetical concepts are generated simultaneously.

Writers were particularly attracted to improvisation in the fifties and sixties, but many writers still use related techniques. For example, the American poet Clark Coolidge, a poet who has been active in jazz has said:

> *When I realised I could write, it was when I put jazz playing together with Kerouac's work, reading Kerouac and realizing he was improvising… when I read Kerouac, I thought this guy doesn't know where he's going, he's improvising, he's winging it. And that was the big discovery that enabled me to be any sort of writer at all. (Coolidge, in (Foster, 1994) p. 25)*

Coolidge, who has most recently been described as a forerunner of the American L=A=N=G=U=A=G=E poetry movement, has identified himself with this kind of writing process. His description of the importance of improvisation shows how it was a reaction against stultifying ideas such as:

> *the whole pedantic notion that you know what you're going to say and then you find the right word for it. That there's only one, and you find it and put it down. If you don't get it, you go and search and you can't go on until you do find it. ((Foster, 1994) p. 25).*

Coolidge's work also exemplifies some of the other aids to applied improvisation which the poet may choose to use. A volume by him is due to appear shortly, related to the music of the Rova quartet (Ochs, 1994). Apparently, the Rova work resulted from a request from them that Coolidge write sleeve notes for a CD. He agreed, and asked for a set of their previous recordings to which he would listen while writing the new notes. This initiated a train of poetic improvising in the company of Rova music, the products of which will be revealed soon. Similarly, the British writer, Paul Buck, often improvises poems with a minimum of revision ((Buck, 1980); see (Fisher, 1977–80)). Buck has a particular sympathy with avant-garde music, and he has written series of poems in response to (and often simultaneously with listening to) music by Frances-Marie Uitti (cello), Lysis and others.

For many writers, improvisation is probably now a technique available in a palette of compositional procedures (including some revision) rather than one to which they rigidly adhere. In the broadest sense it can be seen to be influential on many experimental poets who are interested in allowing language to lead the way, rather than letting any pre-conceived sense dictate its direction. It is used by cris cheek (cheek, 1994), Carla

Harryman (Harryman, 1994), and many others, though often in conjunction with other techniques (Smith, Dean *et al.*, 1993).

Similarly, applied improvisation may be a way of producing a playscript which is then performed. Playwright Richard Foreman describes his writing process in the following way:

> *Sleep. I take naps during the day. To 'clear' my mind, so that I can 'begin again'-start a new day, as it were, whose writing comes from a new place... I 'fire' bursts of writing... then, to avoid being dragged into the river of that 'discourse which has just gotten under way,' I need to move back to the firing area. I SLEEP, I NEGATE THE DRIFT of the writing burst I've just fired, its tendency to live its own life and write its own development. I wake up cleansed, and fire again! ((Kaye, 1994) p. 51).*

Improvisation is sometimes the basis for collaborations between writers. O'Hara collaborated in the 50s and 60s with several writers including Bill Berkson and Kenneth Koch. In the collaboration with Koch on the dadaesque poem "The Mirror Naturally Stripped" (1956) the two men wrote lines in alternation. In retrospect, Koch was unable to remember who had written what, and the poem is a seamless text written provocatively in the first person (Koch, 1986).

A more recent instance of such a collaboration is that between Steve Benson and David Bromige ((Beckett, 1994) p. 45–50). Both talked into a microcassette as a continuation of a conversation that they had been having. They then transcribed it with slight editing (mostly done by Bromige). It was typed up into three columns rather than two, to problematise the notion of who was speaking when, with some matching (e.g. of rhymes) across the columns (Bromige, 1994). Similarly, Paul Buck and Ulli Freer have collaborated, sitting together and pushing a piece of paper backwards and forwards (Buck, 1994).

Oral verbal improvising: its basis and practitioners

Oral verbal improvisation is pure improvisation based on the idea of creation in performance. It is currently uncommon because it presents all the difficulties and challenges posed by language itself. Language is a discrete system of identifiable units, words, and so the improvisor must always find and articulate the next word, and simultaneously negotiate the possibilities of meaning it presents. For this reason most oral improvising is in some way referent-based. This referent may be a particular procedure, such as using a pool of words or phrases, written texts or theme, as a springboard for the improvisation. Alternatively the present day improvisor may use devices such as a tape recorder, which allow self-collaboration (through multitracking), or collaboration with the machine (by simple pre-recording of referent material).

It is worth noting again that oral verbal improvisation was more central in primary oral cultures, and their immediate successors, where literacy was restricted to a small proportion of the population (for example, discussions in (Quinn and Hall, 1982; Poole, 1985)). Interestingly, several improvising traditions from primary oral cultures are still in operation. Those of Iran seem particularly fascinating to an outsider, and have received some detailed study (Beeman, 1981). An improvised story-telling tradition there has been documented extensively by Sbait (Sbait, 1993), and his article gives transcriptions of subtle improvised verbal responses by a pair of performers.

In western culture there has been a renewed interest in oral verbal improvising from the sixties to the present day, even though the number of practitioners is small. This has coincided with a tendency for all the arts to become more performance orientated. We concentrate here on the work of the Americans David Antin, Spalding Gray, Steve Benson. Equally relevant is the exceptionally inventive verbal improvising of British poet, cris cheek, but since his performances also involve visual and gestural elements they will be discussed mainly in the polymedia section (Chapter 8).

David Antin is a "talk poet" who mixes philosophical discussion, poetic metaphor, storytelling, anecdote, and humour. Antin's work is very much an improvisation of ideas: his monologues suggest the lecturing technique of the university academic (until recently Antin was part of this milieu). As Charles Altieri points out, Antin eclipses the critic by explicating his own ideas, and the talks are a kind of intellectual round up of topical events and stimulating philosophical issues with relevant personal material (Altieri, 1986). At the same time, they are full of anecdotes and resemble the routines of the stand up comic, and they also spin poetic metaphors which bind the talks together. They therefore mix styles from both high art and popular culture. Improvising in Antin's work is not overtly linked to a wider political agenda, but since his work constantly exposes the way that language is used to manipulate power structures, the improvising seems a means of rebutting this stranglehold. Antin's work is also implicitly oppositional in its rebuttal of the literary establishment and its maintenance of standard written forms. He feels closer to jazz improvisation, in particular the work of John Coltrane, than he does to conventional poetry (Smith, Dean *et al.*, 1993).

Benson's work developed mainly in the late seventies and eighties and explores many different performance strategies, including monologue-improvisations upon pre-written or pre-recorded texts which are spoken or played simultaneously, and texts improvised in response to pieces of music. Buddhism, the L=A=N=G=U=A=G=E poetry movement of which he is considered part, and contemporary philosophical and literary theory, are all important influences on his work. However, Benson resists elucidating the exact relationship between his Buddhist beliefs and his concept of the self (Johnson and Paulenich, 1991). He also writes for the page and his books include orally improvised and written work (though it is still often improvised into a tape recorder, or written with a minimum of revision). Benson's improvisations and texts are not overtly linked to a political stance: in fact they rarely mention public and historical events, and references to specific times and locales are few and are not usually followed through. Nevertheless, his work investigates the relation of the self to a society which encourages alienation and conformity.

Spalding Gray's autobiographical, more theatrically-based monologues came out of his experimental work with the Wooster Group in the seventies, and the will to self-discovery, stemming from the suicide of his mother. But they are also influenced by popular culture. His film, "Monster in the Box" (Gray, 1990) based on personal ruminations and anecdotes, reveals his relation to popular culture, and engages ironically with stand-up comedy and voyeuristic tv confessional programs.

The potentialities of oral verbal improvising

Oral verbal improvising creates a sense of occasion and a communal social event: it also makes the act of creation visible. The degree to which the audience can influence the progress of the improvisation is of significance here. David Antin claims that he "tunes" to his audience, adapting his talk to their responses. This a complex issue since his talks do not usually involve active audience participation, and therefore allow only limited interchange. Feedback from the audience normally consists only of facial expression or noise level, and must often be misleading. But Antin actively attempts to engage in eye contact and thus to control and energise the audience, especially with any of his acquaintances who are present (as we observed in a performance (Antin, 1992)).

But the audience can also be engaged more actively, so that they become co-creators of the text. For one performance in San Francisco in 1987, Steve Benson prepared a page of text of words, phrases, sentences and distributed copies to the audience. Benson then read from the page, but progressively made adjustments and derivations partly in response to audience interventions (Benson, 1994). At the same time the audience can be problematic, since the improvisor may feel uneasy with it or may misread it, or there may be little response. As Benson says in the transcription of his performance "About the Subject", "...the audience..., which I had no sense of communication with or of really wanting to please. I felt sceptical as if I were talking to myself, not trusting myself and not sure either whether I was listening" ((Benson, 1988) p. 177).

One excitement of improvising is that it allows the performer to explore the present moment. David Antin has often talked about the recreativeness which dominates many poetry readings: simply reading a poem is like "returning to the scene of the crime you try to re-enact it and the more you try to bring it back to life the deader it becomes" ((Antin, 1984) p. 148). The medium of the talk excites him because of the sense of occasion, and the opportunity to be creative afresh each time. Likewise, Steve Benson asserts that improvising seems a more meaningful way to respond to the occasion of the poetry reading than merely reading poems. He hopes that "if I keep stimulating myself to present thoughts without conclusions there will be a usefully interesting field of thought impressions, language impressions" (Benson, 1994).

So improvisation poses a particular challenge of going with the flow of the talk and yet not sinking in the effluent. Benson's performances often involve cogitation about avoiding being trapped by a focus or theme, about how to keep in the process. His talks (which are also an investigation of the process they engage) confirm that the improvisors should not have a goal, for improvisation is "how to begin on purpose some duration/having locked the keys in the car" ((Benson, 1988) p. 192). The verbal improvisor does not necessarily follow through a single idea but can allow several different streams of thought to develop simultaneously. If he does the multiple meanings can change with the flow, a special feature of such oral verbal improvisation.

Oral improvising: the speaking subject and the problem of gender

Oral improvising might seem to be a naive return to the centrality of the speaking subject in art, but in fact it can also pose a particularly strong challenge to this notion by directly confronting it. It can do this in a graphic way by introducing the bodily presence of the creator but at the same time problematising the whole notion of "personality". The improvisor is not an actor, nor simply himself, rather s/he generates and assembles material. The improvisor cannot simply project, glorify, or theatricalise his or her personality. Nor can (s)he use words or bodily gestures in an unmediated way, in fact (s)he may consciously try to avoid it, by projecting several competing or contradictory selves, or by creating complex relationships between the linguistic first person and the voice which speaks, both of which may change or be multiple. Antin sometimes introduces his own experience into the talk and may draw attention to his own physical features, such as his baldness (Antin, 1992). However, the talks are not confessional in character and the fictional non/fictional status of the incidents he relates are always in doubt. Antin sometimes adopts stances (within the same talk) which in many respects are totally at odds with each other. In "The Currency of the Country", he is the learned intellectual who is familiar with the term post-industrial society, the arts and Unesco. But he is also the naive spectator who, by showing his confusion about the same term, exposes the way we accept beliefs that we do not really understand, and also the means by which the educated and powerful use language to mystify and ultimately to exploit. Nevertheless, Antin does not adopt alternative persona (through voice or gestural change). This is why the expression stance (which implies a change of position) is appropriate, rather than mask (which implies concealment). Nor does Antin theatricalise the talk through extensive use of gesture. His "talk" does relate to the talk and experience of Antin the live person, but this is subordinate to the less specific impression of a mind in the process of thought.

Antin is interested in the process of thinking: "And the closest I can get to thinking is talking" (Smith, Dean *et al.*, 1993). The talks are an arena for shared thinking; the tenor of the talks is "cool" rather than expressive, reflective rather than confessional. Moreover, the self must mediate itself through language and there is never a complete "fit" between thinking and talking. "When i am talking what I say is never quite what I intend to say" (Smith, Dean *et al.*, 1993). This complex sense of self is also explored thematically by Antin in the talks: in "what am i doing here" he suggests the impossibility of encapsulating oneself as a consistent person " the only way that I can conceive of myself as a personality is by an act of memory" ((Antin, 1976) p. 10; spacing retained from the original). Though memory is the basis for many of the anecdotes in the talk, Antin undercuts his own representations, by demonstrating that memory is unreliable. He does this by making overt the difficulty of recall, and by posing different versions of the same incident.

Benson's texts involve a much more fundamental deconstruction of the self than the talks of Antin, and his work originated "in an insecurity about the nature and actuality of my existence" ((Johnson and Paulenich, 1991) p. 20). In "Berg's Chamber Concerto", ((Benson, 1988) pp. 158–164) improvised in response to that piece of music, the questions "did you cry for help" and "can you make out the words I am saying" seem to be directed at an internal self rather than another person. Benson adopts different physical voices which appear to emanate from the same person, but move between normal sounding and histrionic or hyper-sounding. In interview he said that he never knows whether the self which emerges will be "upbeat and lyrical or severe and depressive" (Benson, 1994). In fact his piece "About the Subject", performed in 1983 and based on a pun on the word "subject", suggests that any concept of identity conceals an essential absence which has to be confronted. The piece takes the form of a dialogue on many different levels, while at the same time subverting the notion of dialogue as reciprocal. So the "you" Benson addresses throughout could be both part of himself or someone else, while the identities of "you" and of "I" are each not necessarily the same from beginning to end. Nevertheless, it is in improvisation that the self can renew itself, though this is paradoxical because improvisation is itself fleeting and impermanent: "Art offers you the opportunity to create a separate, expendable construction (of yourself) to contrast with the less definite, less stable, and unfailingly present one..." ((Benson, 1988) p. 176). Improvisation is also a way to resist the social straightjacketing of the subject : the constant emphasis in his work on the idea of searching, probing, refocusing, can be interpreted as a reaction against the rigidity of modern American life. This "fixes" personality in the workforce, the media and advertising, and yet alienates the individual.

At the other end of the scale Spalding Gray does tend to theatricalise his experience and uses blatantly autobiographical material. But there is a large degree of ironising here and a discontinuity in the storytelling which make the use of the first person sophisticated and self-conscious. Gray's monologues may be the nearest approach to "confessional" improvising, but they are still a far cry from Donahue and Oprah. Gray holds his audience's attention by exposing obsessive and irrational aspects of behaviour, or by disregarding social tabus that usually remain undisclosed.

> *Shortly after that masturbation took hand. I'm not saying that it was Julie's fault — actually I had discovered it while I was going out with her. Thurston Beckingham had told me that if you took a piece of animal fur and rubbed your dick real fast it would feel good. That's all, just rub it and it would feel good. I didn't have any animal fur around the house and I wasn't the type of kid to go out and buy some just to do that. But there were a lot of Davy Crockett hats in the neighbourhood. ((Gray, 1987) p. 124).*

Gray became interested in monologues because they offered an escape from what he felt to be the pretence of acting. He wanted to investigate himself, but this self was always separate and problematic: "I wanted to explore myself as other. I wanted to investigate my actions. I no longer wanted to pretend to be a character outside myself. The streets where I encountered this other were in my body and mind. The 'other' was the other in me, the constant witness, the constant consciousness of self." His monologues, nevertheless, adopt the stance of what Krzysztof Wodiczko calls the "bewildered man-child trying to understand the 'real' world" (Wodiczko, 1985). The following is a typical example:

> When I was in therapy about two years ago, one day I noticed that I hadn't had any children. And I like children at a distance. I wondered if I'd like them up close. I wondered why I didn't have any. I wondered if it was a mistake, or if I'd done it on purpose, or what. And I noticed that my therapist didn't have any children either. He had pictures of cats on the wall. Framed. ((Gray, 1987) p. 39).

Verbal oral improvising is an area where women seem to be conspicuous by their absence. Although many women are active in text-sound improvising (see Chapter 6), the genre of the verbal monologue seems either to have been unattractive or inaccessible to women. One can only speculate on the reasons for this, but such monologues might be identified with aspects of male discourse — of taking centre stage, of holding forth, and of projecting a confident veneer — which women could only take up parodically or ironically. Although both Gray and Antin participate in this male discourse, they do so with varying degrees of ironic, self-awareness. Gray's monologues might seem to reinforce conventional humour about male sexuality but have a kind of "feminine" sensitivity. Antin sometimes tells stories which, though narrated by him, also imply the female point of view (such as the story about Candy who goes out with a man who has cherries tattooed on his penis). But the gender position of the speaker is most fully deconstructed by Benson. His verbal improvisations are highly androgynous, and his deconstruction of self inevitably means that no strong gender identity is asserted. In fact at times he constructs himself as feminine, for example in the cross-dressing allusion, in "About the Subject", to putting on layers of tights ((Benson, 1988) p. 174).

Oral verbal improvising: the process and its effects

Because of the difficulty of oral verbal improvising, it is very limited even in contexts in which it might be expected, such as the Afrodiasporic form, rap (Rose, 1994). Those who do improvise verbally often prepare themselves in some way for their performances, though this varies from individual to individual and from performance to performance. None of the improvisors discussed here always prepare for their events, and when they do they only want to prepare to an extent which does not undermine the unpredictability of the performance. Usually preparation takes place at the macro rather than the micro level and the use of a referent, or series of referents, is common. This may involve some prior reading or thinking round a particular topic, a technique sometimes adopted by Antin (Smith, Dean *et al.*, 1993). Gray usually uses an outline of his talk as the basis for his monologue, but the detail is improvised. Benson employs a wide range of referents, including written texts of his own, which he either intersperses with passages of improvising or uses as "prompts" for improvisations. At certain points in "About the Subject" (Benson, 1983) he used words on small pieces of paper as prompts for improvisations. In this performance he also interspersed written and improvised texts. This creates a change of pace and dramatic tension: the written passages are tauter, making us think not only about the relationship between writing and speech, but also about the tension between formed thoughts and thoughts in the making. On other occasions the "referent" for Benson may be a particular objective or technical challenge.

Spalding Gray's monologues "India and After (America)", performed in 1979, are more dictated by what we called, in Chapter 2, an objective referent. An assistant sat behind a desk with a dictionary and stopwatch, chose a word at random, and allotted Gray a specific number of minutes in which to relate a part of his narrative associating from that word. His stories dealt with the trip to India, the first few months back in the States, and the traumas he had endured. Gray used this device because he felt that he was "too close to the material" (it was very recent). In the normal monologue form the material also came out too continuously and was therefore boring. This procedure helped to break it up and shape the formal element.

In "Word", an improvisation performed several times by Hazel Smith (1994: London, UK; Sebastopol, USA), the referent consists of a list of words, some generated by applied improvising. These words do not share a logical connection. The words consist of nouns, verbs and adjectives but not conjunctions; these are added at will during the performance to make largely, but not entirely, syntactical phrases. The words in the list are combined freely; sometimes one word functions as a pivot for several related phrases, sometimes words are permuted. Most of the added words are conjunctions, but on occasion other words may also be used. There is a temptation to read the words in a linear way: however, the challenge is to combine words from different parts of the list and to keep the meaning as fluid as possible. Although the words can take the meaning in many different directions, some of them refer to textual processes. So the piece often becomes self-referential, about the process of textuality itself.

Another way of setting up an improvisation is to use basic technology as part of the performance. Steve Benson has often used a tape recorder, which may play verbal passages (improvised or written) or music. Sometimes these are used as back up for performances, or he may try to respond to a tape while he is improvising. In either case his orientation to the tape becomes of major importance, and Benson likes this to be exploratory as possible. Using such a tape for performances in Milwaukee and Ann Arbor in 1986, he found it was "less interesting to try to speak only in the gaps between taped lines or only simultaneous with the taped lines than to speak with an exploratory interest, looking towards possible kinds of orientation without assuming any" (Benson, 1988). Benson may improvise into a tape recorder, rewind and replay the tape, and then perform another improvisation in response to what he hears (the audience may or may not here the rewound version in tandem ((Benson, 1988) p. 18). This is a simpler version of a technique (using sequencers rather than tape recorders) used in live musical improvisation, and discussed earlier in this chapter.

Alternatively the technology may become the medium for a studio based improvisation, such as Steve Benson's 3 track "I was an absent alien" (Private recording, 1992). This demonstrates some of the possibilities even a basic technology can offer. Each take was recorded while listening to the previous recordings through headphones. In the mixing that followed, the volume for each track was modified according to a pattern determined in advance of recording (Benson, 1994). This results in dense polyphony. Sometimes all the voices seem fairly equal, sometimes one voice predominates and appears to be accompanied by the others. The self becomes multiple, and the resulting selves fade in and out in changing relationships to each other. This multiplicity of self expresses itself also at a semantic level. Each line is fluid in meaning and this is increased because each horizontal line is itself disjunct. The piece creates both vertical and horizontal semantic relationships, and we are pushed and pulled between hearing the three voices as interacting, or following one line. For example, at the beginning of the piece one voice says "tides linger across the blonde beach" while the other says "a route through the back roads where only no-one knows", but we can hear these lines in a number of different combinations such as "tides a route through" or "the back roads the blonde beach". This creates a fast moving mosaic of intersecting and rapidly shifting meanings which extends the dialoguing implicit in Benson's performance work.

Oral verbal improvisors also sometimes use props. This takes them nearer to the realm of the theatre, but the use of the props is sufficiently subsidiary for us still to count the improvisation as monomedia. In his San Francisco State University improvisation (Benson, 1983) Benson used pieces of cloth, plastic and string and constantly changed his clothing. One of the challenges Benson chose here was to keep the relationship between words and materials fluid (Benson, 1994).

Recycling, looping and related techniques also have an important effect on the structure of the performances. David Antin sometimes recycles material from talk to talk, and he also uses recycling as a means of generating the talk: often looping back to a topic, theme or image, or making a topic re-emerge in a different way. For example, in "what am i doing here?", the topic of the talk comes back in the guise of the self in a preliterate society.

Antin's talks move between discursive sections, with stories sandwiched between them on a fairly symmetrical basis. During the discursive sections Antin pivots dexterously from one topic to another. So in "what am I doing here" he moves within the first few seconds through the following topics: the function of poetry readings; poetry readings as genre; writing and the future; ways of defining a poet; poetry and talking; poetry as a lie; history and memory and so on (Figure 4).

The transitions are sometimes smooth, sometimes disjunctive, but Antin continuously knots, unknots and reknots images, creating a multi-stranded texture which weaves the different sections seamlessly together. This technique also allows Antin to pursue a large number of different topics and make links between them, and to be discursively philosophical in a way which poetry has often disallowed. The ideas which Antin explores are not necessarily unusual in themselves, but the connections he weaves between them are often stimulating. In "what am I doing here", for example, he explores: poetry's entrapment in conventional definitions; the impossibility of truthful representation and of maintaining a consistent self; the inconsistency of memory; the elusiveness of social responsibility; and the subordination of the individual to social forces which are often arbitrarily manipulated. By moving between them, Antin makes us see how all these areas of experience and discourse interconnect, in the way that they evade any fundamental truth, and continually exceed the systems which we generate to contain them.

Steve Benson sometimes structures his talks through the alternation of written and improvised texts. But changes in direction, mixed with a looping pursuit of certain ideas means that his pieces foreground repetition with variation rather than logical progression. In Gray's talks there is a balance between the recurrence of central ideas and a rather discontinuous (though associative) link between ideas. This is one of the sources of amusement in the monologues. Grays claims that this discontinuity is an effect of memory: "memory fragments and creates its own frames", since remembering is not usually a linear experience.

Verbal improvisors also employ a range of linguistic strategies to generate and develop material. Steve Benson often negates what he has just said, or tries to change the syntax and disrupt the stream, to keep the meaning open (Benson, 1994). In general, Antin's talks are more conventionally syntactical than Benson's; he is compelled by the transmission of ideas and this requires a grammatical framework. He is less stimulated by the idea of linguistic experimentation: "I am not interested in transforming

English grammar, but I am interested in the full range of English and its varieties of speech-registers and its ways of movement from here to there" (Smith, Dean *et al.*, 1993). However, as Stephen Fredman points out, Antin's sentences are paratactic rather than hypotactic, that is, he is usually opening out the sentence rather than closing it off ((Fredman, 1990) p. 140). Antin's talks also hinge on metaphors which are explored in multiple ways, like the metaphor of driving in "what am i doing here?". Gray's sentences are more hypotactic than Antin's, and are the most conventionally grammatical amongst those discussed above.

Transcriptions and recordings of oral improvising

We have already pointed out the difficult issue of recorded improvisations. Verbal improvising throws up quite particular questions in this context, about how such improvisations should be recorded and the kind of relationship they create between the oral and the written. For as Ong points out, in our culture orality can never be uncontaminated by writing (Ong, 1982). The oral improvisors discussed here all mediate between the oral and the written, finding that some adjustment or change of position is necessary to produce a written document. Spalding Gray, for example, found that to produce written versions of his monologues he needed to rework transcripts of performances: this helped to preserve the "original breath and rhythm of my voice". Using the transcripts directly produced problems: "When I tried to do this I found I no longer had my own voice." ((Gray, 1987) p. 10).

    Mediation between the oral and written is implicit in the title that Antin gives to his work, "talk poetry", and the talks mix spoken forms such as story-telling, and written forms such as metaphorical cohesion and logical argument. Although there is no written record of many of Antin's talks, some of them have been published in the volumes "Talking at the Boundaries" and "Tuning". However, in interview Antin pointed out that the texts are not transcripts of the talks but analogues of them. Tapes are usually made of his performances, often by Antin himself using a walkman recorder (Smith, Dean *et al.*, 1993). On one occasion while performing and recording himself, he ironically referred to "making the text" as he paused to reverse and reinsert the cassette tape after about 30 minutes of talk (Antin, 1992), and the length of the tape dictated the end of the talk. When writing up the talks Antin uses a tape of the talk to recreate its contour, but he does not transcribe it word for word. This is a process of "rethinking" in which he sometimes inserts extra stories which he feels the time frame of the performance could not absorb (Smith, Dean et al., 1993). The written text then is not secondary to the aural one but runs parallel to it, and critic Charles Hartman (Hartman, 1991) makes an important point when he suggests that Antin's texts and talks have a symbiotic relationship (we hear the spoken text in the written text and the text of the talk makes good reading). In fact, Antin considers a written text a more effective means of circulating the talks than a tape recording, since a tape recording "contains stuff that people don't hear and it doesn't contain things they do pick up" (Smith, Dean *et al.*, 1993). Though the tape recording may not be so different from the live event as he thinks, his attitude underpins the mediation between the aural and written which his work involves.

Antin's transcriptions of his performances are therefore a good read, free standing in themselves (you do not have to have heard the improvisations to enjoy them) but they do not attempt to make the written version into a completely new entity. Some of Steve Benson's transcriptions do. In his piece "Back" (see Figure 5) the original referent text and the subsequent improvisation form two versions which run down different sides of the page, and sometimes merge in the middle, producing a new hybrid text which has a kind of echoing or delay effect. Here Benson is making us interrogate the status of either written or spoken text. Neither is final: both are part of an ongoing process in which written text and improvised performance can evolve and interweave to produce further texts.

5

IMPROVISATION IN MONOMEDIA.
2: VISUAL AND BODY

I've seen people make themselves up in an afternoon, become instant holy men, just make themselves up. I saw Richard Schechner do it in Central Park. It was a lovely May day, back in the days when the Hare Krishnas used to chant from the Bowery up to Central Park, and they'd be so high by the time they reached the park that they'd look as if they were floating six inches off the pavement. They'd all come floating down the steps of Bethesda Fountain and a crowd of about two hundred people would gather around. Well, on one beautiful May Sunday, this spectacle stirred Richard's competitive juices and he took off all his clothes except for his Jockey underwear and asked me to hold them for him while he took out his Indian prayer rug, laid it by the fountain and stood on his head. This outrageous new spectacle immediately drew the crowds away from the Hares to him. ...All I could see were the soles of Richard's feet sticking up through the crowd, and I could see some of the people dropping little chunks of Italian Ices down through the holes in his underwear.

After about twenty minutes of this, Richard came down and ran over to me and said, 'Quickly, give me my clothes. Let's get out of here.' And as he was getting dressed I looked over to see that he had about twenty-five new converts ready to follow him anywhere. Some of them were asking, 'When will you return?' As Richard answered over his shoulder, 'I shall return,' others asked, 'Where are you going?' And Richard said, 'I am walking east.'

I think they would have followed him right into the East River without a doubt in their heads.

Spalding Gray, from "Swimming to Cambodia, Part Two" ((Gray, 1987) p. 93).

Visual Monomedia: Improvisation in Painting and other Two Dimensional Work

While painting is not essentially a performance medium, there are many ways in which improvisation does contribute to it. Firstly, painters can, if they wish, introduce a quasi-performance dimension into the process, rather like the applied improvising of the writers in the previous chapter, so that the painting is completed at speed and without erasure. A few painters have extended this idea by painting in public thereby becoming pure improvisors. Secondly, they can introduce elements which produce unpredictable results e.g. rolling or throwing paint onto the canvas. Thirdly, they can start without knowing what the painting will be, and build it up gesture by gesture, a technique used by abstract artists. This is very different from the compositional process of painting a still life, or working with a definite subject in mind.

During such gestural construction the artists may use association, antithesis, balance, permutation, and contrast, of colour, shape, density etc. This process involves a dialogue within the medium, so that each gesture becomes a "response" to the "call" of a previous one. As the preceding points suggest, improvisation is linked in painting with thematic and formal freedom, and is therefore more likely to result in abstracted than figurative and realistic work. It is easier to achieve abstraction (if desired) in painting than in, for example, poetry, because paintings are not composed of discrete signifying units like words. In a painting it is difficult to decide what a single unit is (whether it is a brushstroke or a block of paint consisting of several brushstrokes etc), and so signification can be more indeterminate (discussed in (Smith, 1989)). Because of this, improvisation was particularly useful in the substantial development of abstract painting after 1945.

Improvisation in painting since 1945

Improvisatory techniques were one way in which painters after World War II could break out of traditional mimetic modes of painting. They also aided the re-thinking of painting as an easel-based activity, and the resulting painting as a framed and decorative object which hangs on the wall. The Surrealists were one source of these developments, particularly their appropriation of the Freudian concept of the unconscious in automatism, which was seen as painting directly from the unconscious. Surrealism had a major impact upon the European movement Cobra which began in the late thirties, and consisted mainly of painters from Belgium, France, Denmark and Sweden and Holland, such as Asger Jorn and Karel Appel. Cobra was particularly active immediately after the Second World War and broke up in 1951. It was driven by a Marxist philosophy: a belief that capitalist society had stifled the creativity of the proletariat. Although they shared their belief in Marxism with the Surrealists, these artists partially rejected surrealism because it "was an art of ideas and as such also infected by the disease of past class culture" (Cobra Manifesto (Stokvis, 1987) p. 29). They proselytised for a democratic art in which the people as a whole would be engaged.

Cobra strived for an art which articulated the present moment, in which "the creative act is more important than that which it creates" (Cobra Manifesto (Stokvis, 1987) p. 30). Like the surrealists they believed in the power of the unconscious mind to access creativity, and celebrated spontaneity in childhood experience, primitive culture and their own work. Their ideals connect with the idea of improvisation, but were cloaked in a romantic description which privileged the irrational over the intellectual (as we discussed in Chapters 2 and 4).

Cobra constitutes a transitional phase between Surrealism and Abstract Expressionism. The latter movement, which began in America in the late 1940s, included the painters Pollock, de Kooning, Kline, Newman, Rothko and later Helen Frankenthaler. These painters revolted against several types of painting prevalent in America at that time, such as social realism, regionalism and geometric abstraction. Instead of perpetuating these styles they explored new techniques and approaches to express what they felt to be psychological and mythic truths. They were particularly influenced by the surrealists, many of whom, such as Ernst, Breton, Dali, and Matta, had fled to America after Paris fell to the Nazis in 1940. The Abstract Expressionists saw exciting possibilities in the pursuit of irrationality in Surrealism, and also in automatism as a technique, especially as it was being developed by Matta. He wanted to explore abstract automatism (whereas Breton was biased against abstraction, and abstract automatism had hardly been explored in the surrealist movement previously). Automatism could not be an end in itself for the Abstract Expressionists, but they wished to use it in conjunction with other techniques. They were also influenced by related techniques in other art forms, particularly jazz, of which Pollock was an ardent enthusiast (see for example (Mandeles, 1981)).

Abstract Expressionism, sometimes known as action painting, had counterparts elsewhere such as the work of Alan Davie, Peter Lanyon and William Scott in England. Davie, in particular, adopted improvisatory techniques: born in 1920 he is also a musician, who has recorded with many free improvising musicians such as Frank Perry, Daniel Humair (another painter), Lysis and Tony Oxley. Davie, who was strongly affected by Surrealism, Jungian analysis and Zen Buddhism, saw art as a crucial aspect of the struggle of humanity to free itself from the restrictions of the ego, and as a means of tapping the collective unconscious (Tucker, 1993). In 1958 he rejected the tag "Action Painter", though he seemed to conflate the ideas of action, event and process with self-expression when he said that "there is no question of the picture expressing the activity of its production or even the emotions of the artist at the time" (Davie, 1958). Central to his artistic outlook is the concept of intuition; of regaining the childlike, unselfconscious mind which he also sees as intrinsic to Zen thought; and of escaping from a dualistically trained mind and the supremacy of the intellect. These beliefs are not synonymous with improvisatory techniques, but as we have seen they were held by many improvisors.

Since the demise of Abstract Expressionism, painting has continued to absorb improvisational techniques, for example in some of the works of (East) German A. R. Penck and Norwegian Frans Widerberg. Improvisation has also been incorporated into performance and environmental art in the work of artists such as the Scot Bruce McLean (also a painter, and active from the 60s to the present).

Improvisatory processes in painting since 1945

Painters adopt an improvisatory approach when they start off with no preconceived notion of what the painting is going to be like. In Cobra there was an emphasis on finding the painting in the process. According to their manifesto they sought an art which is "spontaneously directed by its own intuition" ((Stokvis, 1987) p. 29) and which gives "the greatest possible latitude to the unconscious" ((Stokvis, 1987) p. 29). In 1939, Asger Jorn one of its key painters wrote, "Creating a work is a continuous process and one whose result is unknown... when I see my finished work, I am always filled with the most tremendous astonishment" ((Lambert, 1984) p. 31). Jorn also said of the way he conceived "The Blue Picture": "The composition comes of its own accord. I started to paint from one side, adding one form after the other until the picture was full... I was extraordinarily surprised that a painting could be made in that way, going from one form to another and carrying on without worrying about the picture as a unified whole. Perhaps it has something rather cubist about it here and there, but it is exactly the opposite of the Cubist method of composition" ((Lambert, 1984) p. 33). This description epitomises the synecdochal process mentioned earlier. In Cobra the results of these processes are quite figurative, but the subject matter is often mythic, almost grotesque, and with a high level of abstraction anticipating Abstract Expressionism.

In the latter, this wish to start without a pre-conceived notion was linked to a desire to rethink the premises of much previous art and an urge (partly created by an interest in psychological analysis) to portray the unconscious mind. These painters wished to break out of the straightjacket of earlier representational painting and looked to new kinds of processes to confront what they called "a crisis of subject matter" ((Sandler, 1970) p. 31). This resulted in a much freer approach to painting, which withdrew from the idea of capturing a likeness or painting from a pre-conceived sketch. Instead the painter played with the elements of the medium, such as colour and shape.

When they spoke about their processes the Abstract Expressionists particularly stressed the fact that they did not know when they started what direction the painting would take. For Robert Motherwell starting work was "the feeling, not that 'I'm going to paint something I know', but through the act of painting I'm going to find out exactly how I feel" ((Ross, 1990) p. 111). The common lack of prior sketches (see Kline's remarks in ((Ross, 1990)

p. 93)), the painting as event rather than object, and the attraction to taking risks during the creative process were also prominent themes. They stressed the relevance of these exploratory processes to a modern world. Pollock said "I don't work from drawings... and color sketches into a final painting... My opinion is that new needs need new techniques. And the modern artists have found new ways and new means of making their statements. It seems to me that the modern painter cannot express this age, the airplane, the atom bomb, the radio, in the old forms of the Renaissance or of any other past culture. Each age finds its own technique" ((Ross, 1990) p. 140–145).

The result is highly abstract painting which shows continuity with the pioneering freedom of the "Improvisations" of Kandinsky at the beginning of the century. Pollock's paintings such as "Autumn Rhythm" (1950) and "One" (1950) are high energy constructs which have no beginning or end and no central focus, but which project "time and energy in motion" as he called it. This is similar to the frenetic energy of much Bebop improvising and also free jazz. In a Pollock, energy may relate to manifestations of time and motion in nature, such as the rhythm of the sea, or to psychological dynamism or turmoil. In other words, the painting is not without potential reference (nor could it be), but the reference is not specific. The painting is also self-referential: that is it refers to its own processes.

Because of its emphasis on painting as activity and duration, some Abstract Expressionist painting was sometimes known as "action painting", a term introduced by Harold Rosenberg. Rosenberg characterised the movement in a famous statement, that at a certain moment "the canvas began to appear to one American painter after another as an arena in which to act — rather than as a space in which to reproduce, re-design, analyze or 'express' an object, actual or imagined. What was to go on the canvas was not a picture but an event" ((Anfam, 1990) p. 9–10). Similarly, Rosenberg argued that the value of Abstract Expressionism, and of art generally, lay in process rather than product: this annoyed some artists because, although they had sometimes expressed related views, they felt that he was downgrading their work ((Mackie, 1989) p. 75–104). It is relevant to this ideal of painting as process that these artists (again in common with many others) were often unsure when the artwork was finished. Robert Motherwell said: "The {French painters} have a real 'finish' in that the picture is a real object, a beautifully made object. We are involved in 'process' and what is a 'finished' object is not so certain" ((Mackie, 1989) p. 76). Barnett Newman saw painting as a continuing, unresolving activity, "I think the idea of a 'finished' picture is a fiction. I think a man spends his whole life-time painting one picture or working on one piece of sculpture" ((Mackie, 1989) p. 76). As Mackie points out "The work of art, then, has 'duration' because in one sense it is not really an object but an occasion for exercising creativity; and since the creativity continues on beyond the work, into another work and so on, it becomes natural to see the art work as simply an object bearing the signs of that activity" ((Mackie, 1989) p. 88).

Improvisation could not be pursued solely through conventional brushwork, but rather required the use of unusual tools and strategies. The Abstract Expressionists used techniques such as working with the canvas on the floor (a technique already used traditionally in Indian sand painting), throwing, dripping or rolling paint on to it. It was necessary sometimes to use tools other than the paintbrush. For example, Pollock resorted to sticks or hardened paint brushes which functioned as sticks, a basting syringe and a tin of paint to pour onto the canvas. Sometimes the paint was thrown or dripped on the canvas in such a way that the result of the action could not be completely controlled. The idea of putting the canvas on the floor also changed the painter's relationship with it: and in Pollock's case he sometimes spread rolls of cotton duck on the floor. According to Lee Krasner, Pollock would then sometimes paint his small black and white paintings side by side, and would decide afterwards where to frame each picture.

Details of the way the artist interacted with the canvas can be seen in Hans Namuth's pictures and film of Pollock painting (Namuth and Falkenberg, 1951). Namuth's pictures of Pollock painting "Autumn Rhythm" show how he "quickly and expertly flipped, flung, twirled, thrust and splattered his pigment, manipulating mundane hardware-store materials with a masterful combination of abandon and grace" ((Landau, 1989) p. 196). The pictures disclose "a man totally immersed in his work, alternately hunching over, leaning sideways, leaping in the air, shifting one foot forward, then the other, crossing his legs, stepping back from and stepping into the canvas". ((Landau, 1989) p. 196). The film (which is more able to catch the action) shows Pollock transforming the painting as he works: it reveals how the density increases and creates new layers of depth. Techniques of rolling and soaking paint into horizontal canvases were utilised, and probably developed further, by Helen Frankenthaler and Kenneth Noland (as shown in (Antonio, 1972)).

The subject of speed and lack of revision in the processes of Abstract Expressionists is shrouded in controversy. Establishing such matters when the process is private is, of course, complex. Mackie, Leja and many other critics have pointed out that a mythology has grown up around the processes of Abstract Expressionist painters which has obscured what really happened. They argue that the paintings were not all made in wild quick flourishes, that a range of procedures were involved, and that the paintings sometimes arose as the result of slow deliberation. It is well known that Rothko and Newman sometimes did plan their images beforehand ((Mackie, 1989) p. 77, (Leja, 1993) p. 127–41). In the last decade critics such as Serge Guilbaut and Eva Cockcroft have suggested the ideological basis of many of these action painting myths: that they supported the idea of the genius painter who quickly dashes off a painting, and that they were also exploited by the State to glorify the impression of American freedom as a component of the cold war (Frascina, 1985). Leja also points out that while Jackson Pollock maintained that he was painting from his unconscious, he really was *representing* his unconscious ((Leja, 1993) p. 127): and this was far from "automatic".

The involvement of conscious control does not undermine the pertinence of applied improvisation in some of the work of these painters. In fact the idea of improvisation as a procedure which combines freedom and control is just what these accounts of action painting lack: they either neglect to consider the concept of improvisation, or use an undefined and romantic view of it. There is a tendency in such accounts to see the creative act as either/or: e.g. if the painter made sketches then (s)he could not be spontaneous. The accounts also rely on a flimsy concept of spontaneity, at the same time as deriding it. We have been at pains to point out that spontaneity is not a usefully precise concept, and that improvisation is not the same as automatism. Furthermore, improvisation is a conscious process, and not an appeal to the supremacy of the unconscious in creative activity. We have stressed more the role of the translogical and the way in which conscious procedures in improvisation can induce such elements. By using the idea of improvisation, one avoids the inappropriate concept of passive unmediated creativity which the concepts of spontaneity and automatism tend to induce. In fact the painters' accounts of their processes show that sometimes they worked quickly, sometimes more slowly. Kline stated that he liked to do paintings right away but that he could not do that all the time ((Ross, 1990) p. 101). Rosenberg distinguished between de Kooning's "short and long" paintings on the basis of how long they took to do (Mackie, 1989), while the film of Pollock shows him working from start to finish.

Scottish painter Alan Davie also completed some of his paintings in the 1950's at speed (within a time frame of about twenty minutes (Davie, 1980–3)) and he would also sometimes erase one substantial painting with another. Improvisatory principles are at the root of Davie's teaching principles, as an extract from his notes on teaching shows:

> *To demonstrate the dynamic nature of the creative force, I usually begin with simple exercises in pure idealess activity: directly putting down black marks, with no end in view, purposeless and aimless. Strangely enough the student finds that to work without thought requires a great deal of mental discipline, and it is some time before he can achieve an image without the intermediary of reasoning. (preface to (Davie, 1963).*

Davie now still sometimes uses a series of "automatic" drawings (as he terms them) to initially energise a picture: he then isolates the best of the drawings, enlarges and fixes them. He usually works on several paintings at once (Davie, 1980–3), "building up their independence in unison" (Januszczak, 1983).

The attractions of working at speed, therefore, still continue into the eighties and nineties. Scottish artist Bruce McLean likes to work at speed and within a certain time limit, because it means that he has to push the work in a certain direction rather than be overwhelmed by all the possibilities that could be pursued. He says that he likes to build a situation where there is "no time left", like a performance (in which area he is also involved). Sometimes he returns to a painting which started as an improvisation, but the important factor is that the main direction of the work is established through the improvisation (Archer and Furlong, 1983). His improvising is therefore on occasion discontinuous, and this kind of technique is adopted by many painters who probably would not regard themselves as improvisors in the strictest sense. It is true, for example, of the expressionist Norwegian artist Frans Widerberg documented in Tucker (Tucker, 1992). He refers to the concept of "interrupted" improvisation and says that while larger paintings may take longer "in smaller sizes and lighter mediums like watercolour drawing there is hardly any execution, like breathing, the work creates itself, and will be there in less than fifteen minutes" (Widerberg, 1994). In Paris in 1994, Widerberg painted a number of small watercolours with a tiny pocket size tin of paints he carries. We watched him as he worked continuously: each watercolour was completed within six or seven minutes.

Erasure is relevant to the issue of speed in the work of these painters. A sound improvisor has no means of erasing (in the sense of hiding from the audience) a sound that has been produced. An applied visual improvisor may hide a previous mark, while a pure visual improvisor (painting in public) can also hide one, though it may previously have been seen by the audience. The surface of a Pollock painting, viewed closely, and the process shown in Namuth's film, indicate that there are layers of paint in many of his works which are hidden in the final entity. They may still have an impact, because of their slight effect in varying the depth of paint, but they are not directly visible as gestures. Like the improvising writer (Chapter 4), the improvising painter may therefore use at least one extra dimension of control, erasure or submerging, beyond those available to all improvisors. It is ironic that Robert Rauschenberg made some paintings by attempting to erase some canvases given to him and painted by de Kooning (for example, his "Erased de Kooning, 1953"). Rauschenberg commented that he had failed to erase them even in weeks of work (Antonio, 1972; McCabe, 1984).

Improvised paintings may sometimes arise out of collaborations. The "cobramodifications" were joint works by several members of Cobra which involved the overpainting of previous paintings. Also important were the joint experiments of William Baziotes, George Kamrowski and Jackson Pollock in improvising a painting together, resulting in "Untitled 1940–1941" (McCabe, 1984). Painting can be improvised when it involves collaboration with found objects, for example in some of the work of Robert Rauschenberg, where the artist finds the material as he proceeds. And the artist may use these found materials by means of techniques of which the outcome is partially unknown, e.g. the transfer techniques used by Rauschenberg and also by other artists such as Australian Bill Brennan. Somewhat like brass-rubbing, the transfer techniques involved rubbing over a pre-existent image (usually a colour graphic from a magazine) so as to transfer colour selectively to another sheet.

The act of painting is also on occasion "performed" in public. For example, Canadian artist Nancy Love routinely undertook complete works (in the 1970s–80s: (Snow, 1994)) at the same time as listening to improvisations of the Canadian Contemporary Musicians' Collective (CCMC) in their venues in Toronto ("The Music Gallery" in its various forms: (CCMC, 1985)). The Japanese Gutai painters, in their merging of painting with proto-"Happenings", sometimes improvised whole works in public. Similarly, Allen Fisher, British poet-painter, painted live on occasion (see Chapter 7).

Two dimensional visual work also includes photography. In motion film production, as we discuss elsewhere particularly in relation to Michael Snow, Peter Gidal and Jeff Keen, manipulation of the developing of film can use improvisatory components, though normally it is very restricted (often mechanical) in means. But the event of taking a single *still* picture with a camera is nearly always a very brief one. Thus many of the graded distinctions between improvisation and composition which we have characterised in Chapter 2 are almost irrelevant. Indeed, few of the practitioners of photography seem to lay stress on any concept of improvisation which is clearly distinguishable from composition (Hudson, 1990).

A component of improvisation can of course exist at many levels in the photographic process, notably in the dark room, as we discuss later. But if the object to be photographed is a constructed one, then the process of construction offers improvisatory scope. Australian photographer Peter Lyssiotis produces all the images for the series of improvised music released on the label Tall Poppies. He is particularly appropriate to undertake this task, since his multilayered images are constructed by taking pre-existent images (often commercial), "shuffling" them around on a horizontal surface, and then photographing them (Lyssiotis, 1994). The images are not "stuck together (or onto a background)", but remain loose, "so that each negative tends to be little different from its predecessor as the bits and pieces move fractionally". Lyssiotis, who produces books of photographs and texts, and collaborates with other writers, such as Anna Couani, (Couani and Lyssiotis, 1989) says "the same image... is used in three of my books — each time serving a different function". In "Outside of a Dog", a work in preparation at the time of our writing (to be published appropriately by "Masterthief Enterprises"), Lyssiotis writes, entirely within the spirit of improvisation:

> *I cut out pictures from magazines, put them beside each other and push them around a bit. Whoever said that the pen is mightier than the sword forgot the scissors. (p. 2)*

and later,

> *I'm never sure if I've hit a vein, or missed. Sometimes I get to know the next day, sometimes, the next year. (p. 5)*

and in summary,

> *And let's not revere the camera either, the technology. We see out of two eyes, whereas the camera has only one. All photographs are deformations of the reality that we can imagine with our eyes. I refuse to accept the magnificent bribe which camera technology offers. Instead, I continue to rely on my eyes, my hands and my scissors. I think best in paper. (p. 10)*

Lyssiotis clearly has reservations about direct photography of "reality". And since we do not envisage that new insight will be gleaned by considering possible improvisation within such direct photography, we have chosen not to discuss photography in further detail in this Chapter, though it is considered in Chapter 8. However, it does recur in the next section of the chapter as a dependent component of the improvisatory process in the work of some environmental artists.

Improvisatory Elements in Environmental Visual Art and other Three-Dimensional Forms

> *...make something which experiences, reacts to its environment, changes, is nonstable...*
> *...make something indeterminate, which always looks different, the shape of which cannot be predicted precisely...*
> *...make something which cannot "perform" without the assistance of its environment...*
> *...make something which reacts to light and temperature changes, is subject to air currents and depends in its functioning on the forces of gravity...*

...make something which the "spectator" handles, with which he plays and thus animates it...
...make something which lives in time and makes the spectator experience time
...articulate something Natural
Hans Haacke's notes in January 1965 ((Vowinckel, 1981), p. 26)

Unconnected Sentences on Gardening.
A garden is not an object but a process.
Flowers in a garden are an acceptable eccentricity. (Ian Hamilton Finlay in (Beardsley, 1989)
p. 133)

Elements of improvisation are detectable in the work of environmental artists who use natural objects as the basis of their art. Environmental art, which first began as a movement around the 60s, is known by a variety of different names such as nature sculpture, or earthworks. These works can be appreciated in the context of the Green movement and increased concern about environmentalism, since the sixties; they also renegotiated the terms of 19th century landscape art, in which the artist maintained a unity between self and nature but only interacted with the landscape by painting it mimetically. Such art contrasted with the English landscape garden tradition of the same period, in which the artists worked directly on nature. Similarly, in recent environmental art the artist makes art by working on nature rather than producing an imitation or impression of it.

The movement, which is international, has included the work of such artists as Robert Smithson, David Nash, Richard Long, Bruce McLean, and Andy Goldsworthy. These artists make constructions with natural or man-made materials in the environment (sometimes producing patterns quite similar to those of nature itself), or pass through the environment, marking it with objects or photographing it. Their work is part of a postmodernist tendency towards "a process of dematerialization, or de-emphasis on material aspects (uniqueness, permanence, decorative attractiveness)" ((Lippard, 1973) p. 5). It also results in partial decommodification of the art object: as Lippard asserts (p. 8) "The people who buy a work of art they can't hang up or have in their garden are less interested in possession. They are patrons rather than collectors". The quotation above from Haacke succinctly formulates many of the possibilities of environmental art and the way it can interact with the environment. It is useful to note how he stresses change, performance, indeterminacy, time-dependence and the possibility of spectator interaction.

Environmental artists improvise in ways that are distinct from those which can take place with new technologies. Goldsworthy's "improvising" is in sharp contrast to the technological bent of many other contemporary artists, and is much more closely related to the processes of growth and decay, change and regeneration within nature itself. Improvising with nature is a way of hooking into that change. However, Goldsworthy does stress that he is not anti-technology, and will use basic technologies if they are necessary for his work.

Collaboration with nature

When artists work with materials as they find them in the environment, rather than deciding to build something specific in a particular place; or when they interact or "collaborate" with the environment; they are improvising. Andy Goldsworthy says:

> For me, looking, touching, material, place and form are all inseparable from the resulting work. It is difficult to say where one stops and another begins. Place is found by walking, direction determined by weather and season. I take the opportunities each day offers: if it is snowing, I work with snow, at leaf-fall it will be with leaves; a blown-over tree becomes the source of twigs and branches. (Goldsworthy, 1990)

Goldsworthy's artworks are usually site-specific, so that he uses maple leaves in Japan, or snow at the North Pole.

Similarly Sieglinde Karl (biography in (Anderson, 1988; Smith, Karl *et al.*, 1990)) is an Australian artist whose work evolved from the sphere of contemporary jewellery (often working with natural forms and/or materials) but now ranges from bodyworks to installation and environmental work. She has engaged in a series of "Offerings" made on the spot in various locations around Tasmania and recorded in photographs. The first was at Sundown Point, North West Tasmania, 1992, and the second at Little Musselroe Bay, North East Tasmania, 1993. These works are concerned with the specific associations of these landscapes and Karl says:

> These works are made after a prolonged stay in a place when an intimate feeling for that particular landscape has been reached and a starting point emerges. The work process is usually about 4–5 hours, with no preconceived idea — the forms emerge through play, observation and contemplation.
>
> The natural materials used are from the site and therefore represent some of its particular characteristics. The operculums {lids covering apertures of shells} from the "Sundown Point Offering" are plentiful at this place because of the abundance of Aboriginal middens (Karl, 1994).

Karl's outlook is coloured by Jungian analysis, Aboriginal history and a concept of "the sacred". Here the title of the work has religious but paradoxical implications: an offering which symbolises the everlasting, but which is transient.

Change and transience in environmental art

Artists can also improvise with the changing vicissitudes of the environment. Andy Goldsworthy says: "I have become aware of how nature is in a state of change and how that change is the key to understanding... Often I can only follow a particular train of thought while a particular weather condition persists. When a change comes, the idea must alter or it will, and often does, fail" (Goldsworthy, 1990). A particularly cold winter in the UK enabled Goldsworthy to work with ice and icicles in the small pools at Glemarin Falls on the River Scaur in Dumfriesshire, making sculptural formations out of them.

Goldsworthy sees art as learning rather than saying, and the process is more important to him than the product (Goldsworthy, 1994). In environmental art the artist changes, interferes with or adds to nature in some way, but the art object is often not lasting, since nature, through a continuous process of growth, destroys it. Goldsworthy feels that the work is often at its best when threatened by imminent destruction or erosion, so that the sense of fragility and transience is part of the meaning of the work. This suggests that design can be made, but must inevitably fade and pass away, to be found again.

Erosion and transience characterise both natural and mental processes. This was poetically expressed by Robert Smithson (1967) in metaphors of dissolving and exchange between the two spheres:

> *The earth's surface and the figment of the mind have a way of disintegrating into discrete regions of art. Various agents, both fictional and real, somehow trade places with each other — one cannot avoid muddy thinking when it comes to earth projects, or what I call "abstract geology". One's mind and the earth are in a constant state of erosion, mental rivers wear away abstract banks, brain waves undermine cliffs of thought, ideas decompose into stones of unknowing, and conceptual crystallizations break apart into deposits of gritty reason... To organise this mess of corrosion into patterns, grids and subdivisions is an aesthetic process that has scarcely been touched. (Quoted in (Vowinckel, 1981), p. 72).*

Notice here also the way Smithson uses the idea of working outwards from this dynamic transformational process into an organisational process.

In her exhibition "Transience, Place, Memories" (1988), Sieglinde Karl made garlands (which she called wreaths) from natural plant materials. These wreaths have a variety of connotations, from Ancient Greek and Roman civilisations, to bridal and war ceremonies, to Balinese dances. A viewer could choose a wreath to wear while visiting the exhibition. The wreaths withered, although photographic documentation of the event remains. In the video, "Environmental Art" (AREA, 1990) we see a number of artists experimenting with an extreme aspect of transience through the use of fire. David Nash built a construction from wood near the White House (Washington) and then set fire to it, making a "woodstove". At the same time a thunderstorm erupted and the art work was enveloped in mist. The result was a spectacular work which ended in ashes. Robert Smithson's "Spiral Jetty" (made at Great Salt Lake, Utah, 1970) was inspired by the pink colour of the water (caused by algae), and by a legend that proposed that the Great Salt Lake was connected to the ocean by an underground channel. At times it is covered with water, and sometimes when the water lowers, salt crystals (also shaped in the form of spirals) sparkle on the rocks. Smithson is concerned with entropy: the spiral itself is falling inwards.

Keeping up with environmental conditions sometimes requires creating at speed. Working with ice, for example, means using the ice when it is not so frozen solid that it cannot be moulded.

> *I worked in the shadow of the gorge where the sun only reached for a dangerous half-hour each day. In this cold shade I tentatively began to stick ice to ice to icicle to rock — making works in pairs — going from one to the other — giving time for each new piece of ice to freeze.*
>
> *As the cold intensified my work became more ambitious and demanding — one work a day, with the ice sticking in just a few minutes. What had taken days in previous winters was now being made in a single day. I cannot explain the feelings of that short time — working with the cold, hot with excitement. (Goldsworthy, 1990).*

Consequences of environmental improvising

Environmental artists effect an exchange between art and nature, but in a way which problematises as well as asserts that relationship. In Goldsworthy's work, for example, the works make patterns out of natural materials, but those patterns often highlight designs within nature itself. In this way the nature-art dichotomy is challenged, often returning us to look more sharply again at nature as design. The works are part of the setting and yet a focus of attention. The relationship between art and culture is often complex: Sieglinde Karl's "offerings" recycle shells from aboriginal middens into new "artworks" in the environment, but the shells can look like Graeco-Roman mosaics.

Environmental work breaks down 19th century concepts of art as everlasting, static and autonomous, ideals which still permeated some aspects of modernism. It takes art not only out of the picture frame but also out of the gallery and resituates it as transient, outdoor and site specific.

Reception and documentation of environmental improvisation

While the concept of transcription (so important with regard to performance events) does not operate in the same way here, transient environmental art works are often recorded as photographs. The photographs may document the artwork undergoing changes, for example how it looks in different lights, or they may document the artist interacting with the artwork in a way which could not be sustained: e.g. Andy Goldsworthy throwing sticks in the air (Figure 6).

In a public interview Goldsworthy (Goldsworthy, 1994) joked that he originally had to take photos to show his tutors what he was doing, and that it was "still a bit like that". In other words, the documentation is a means of justifying the activity and making some concessions to artistic durability. However, he says that the photos also leave a visual trail for him, a lasting memento of a transient moment of art. Sometimes the documentation becomes the work: ice melting on a piece of paper leaves a trace, which Goldsworthy has also often used as the basis of paper-works. Environmental events are sometimes partially captured on video and film (AREA, 1990).

With several of the transient works, there is a special moment at the point of extreme activity or decay. In the case of some ice or stone works it is the point of collapse; when sticks and stones are thrown in the air or on water, it is the point of maximum ascendence or impact. If the artist initiates these moments, then it is feasible to capture them in photography, but it is generally unlikely that audience will be present. If nature controls them, then it is likely that both photographer and audience will be lacking. Clearly, the artist has to choose a stance towards these issues, often dictated primarily by practicality. The artist also has to realise that spectators, coming upon the work in nature, may choose to interact with it in positive or negative ways. They may then experience the work in a special way, but sometimes choose to destroy it.

Body Improvising

> *I do go into somewhat of trance because when I perform I want to be different than acting… I'm really interested in being a medium… I put myself in a state, for some reason it's important, so that things come in and out of me, I'm almost like a vehicle. Karen Finley (Finley and Schechner, 1988).*
> *…an Eleatic paradox… How can the infinitesimally small be together infinitely great?… patterns and structure at any level of complexity {can be} repeated by self-referencing either inwardly or outwardly, upwardly or downwardly, partly or wholly… Now, apply this process to the human body… Alex Reichel (program for (de Quincey, 1992–3)).*

Our purpose here is to isolate improvising which uses the body alone, so as to form a basis for later discussions of the body in broader contexts, such as polymedia. As most sociologists have argued, society is never disembodied. Dance, discomovement, sport, hip-hop and particularly breaking, are body functions which contribute to the articulation of society. Indeed, the mind is only externalised in real-time through the body, unless words or some secondary medium are active. Thus we here consider separately body improvising itself.

The body forms a pre-linguistic basis for identity, and may have the same degree of flexibility as identity itself. It also has culturally entrained "grammars" of gait and of other aspects of movement. Using Meyer's formulation ((Meyer, 1965); see Chapter 4), sound is largely non-referential (and indeed is often syntactical and formal), while body works are mainly referential (and also formal). The referentiality is inescapable because of the association between the body and everyday social exchange. The mind uses the body as one of its vehicles for daily contact with other minds (and as illustrated in the amusing quotation about Richard Schechner at the head of the chapter, it can also be a means for controlling others). Conversely, the body can be used as a means of expanding the self by performing a process which seems to alter the mind of the performer. Several aspects of performance can be viewed as producing such inwardly directed catharsis. For example, physical self-abuse, masochism, gender questioning and sometimes shamanism can be part of such efforts. In many kinds of body performance, improvisation has no stated or emphasised role. Thus two major books on performance (Sayre, 1989; Marsh, 1993) do not mention the word in their indices, and hardly in their texts. However, this does not mean that improvisation is unimportant; rather, that it is neglected in critical discourse in favour of other aspects of performance.

The ways in which the body was experienced and presented loosened in the nineteen-sixties, as Sally Banes points out, and avant-garde artists tended to celebrate the body for what it really was, rather than for the way it was socially viewed. They challenged the traditional representation of a beautiful pure body which has been socially constrained: in particular, feminists interrogated the idea of the female body as the passive site of male observation. For some artists this resulted in emphasising aspects of bodily experience which had been socially repressed, the Bakhtinian effervescent, grotesque and carnivalesque body which blends easily with other objects and bodies, and indulges in extravagant eating, drinking, sexual activity and licentious behaviour. For others it meant treating the body more as an object in itself, to emphasise what Yvonne Rainer called its "unenhanced physicality" ((Banes, 1993) p. 190). The body was also seen as the site of heightened consciousness, which might be attained through the Zen technique of concentrated awareness, or through the use of drugs. Improvising seemed important here because it was a way out of stereotypical notions of the body, both as pure and beautiful, and as a container for the self, and also because it offered a way of balancing the spontaneous and rational.

We can approach the role of body improvising by considering the tabulation offered by dance-movement-performance artist Rainer (1966): (Rainer, 1974). Rainer expressed her "rage at the impoverishment of ideas, narcissism and disguised sexual exhibitionism of most dancing...". She proposed that the body artist should downplay elements of dance she viewed as characteristic of conventional art, and make substitutions:

downplay or eliminate	*substitute*
phrasing	energy equality and "found" movement
development and climax	equality of parts
variation: rhythm, shape, dynamics	repetition of discrete events
character	neutral performance
performance	task or task-like activity
variety: phrases and spatial field	singular action, event or tone
the virtuosic movement feat and the fully extended body	human scale

It might seem that blandness of performance is all that could ensue from these suggestions. But body improvisation could capitalise on singularity and human scale, and by so doing avoid the professional, trained and conventional features of dance. Rainer's objectives were political as well as formal, particularly with regard to the changing role of women in dance which until the 1950's had been very male-dominated, both in terms of the separation of dance roles and professional opportunities. She objected to John Cage's ideas that methods of nonhierarchical, indeterminate organisation could "awaken us to this excellent life": on the contrary they should alert us "to the ways in which we have been led to believe that this life is so excellent, just, and right" ((Sayre, 1989) p. 88–89).

Much body work was inspired by the Japanese theatres of Noh and Butoh, in which minute body movements could be critical vehicles; by the Futurist and Dada events, some of which comprised unorthodox body presentations with little other event; and by the conventional ballet and dance streams.

Some key participants in the field of body work since 1945 can be mentioned briefly, and we will refer to artists with varying degrees of commitment to improvisation, so as to provide a frame for the discussion of improvised components. Some of the seminal works of Merce Cunningham (since the 1940s) are important to this field in that they were largely independent of the music which accompanied them, and some performances were without music or speech. These works also share with contact improvisation (see below) a lack of intentionality, or more particularly, a wish to avoid presenting a preconceived meaning. In some cases they were intended as "indeterminate" in senses also related to the work and ideas of John Cage, mentioned in Chapter 1.

More directly related to improvisation were the European influences of Mary Wigman, transmitted in the US since the 1950s through Alwin Nikolais and Murray Louis (Nikolais and Louis, 1988): improvisation was an important part of the essential training of this school. On the other hand Anna Halprin, who was particularly influential in the 60s, on the West Coast of the US, was concerned with applying improvisation as a central performance technique (Halprin and McCarty, 1967). Like some other improvisors mentioned already, she was particularly enthused by the idea of making creative processes detectable to members of the audience, partly with the hope of their becoming less separated as "gawkers", as she put it; and partly because of the extra levels of appreciation this awareness of creation might impel.

They were followed by a period in the late 60s and 70s in which cathartic and body-abusing work was frequent. Examples include Arnulf Rainer, Stuart Brisley, Yvonne Rainer herself, Mike Parr (who cuts himself so far as to inflict multiple bleeding wounds: see Chapter 7), Bruce McLean, Hermann Nitsch, and the Judson Dance Theatre. Most of these artists were operating within Performance Art, a polymedia form which will be discussed later; and improvisation was probably central only in the cases of Rainer and Judson.

The violent aspects of these performances spring from many of the factors mentioned already in this section, and perhaps more specifically from two factors. Firstly, drug-taking which often resulted in physical self-abuse. Secondly, the violent events of the time (such as the Vietnam war, the 68 uprisings). Another possible reason for this self-wounding may have been be a reaction against modernist ideas of self-expression, what Parr called "the bullshit of modernism", by substituting self-abuse for self-fulfilment.

Important here also was the challenge to representations of the female body in the work of Robert Morris and Carolee Schneemann. Robert Morris' "Site", comprised a partial living simulacrum of Manet's Olympia (performed by Carolee Schneemann), unveiled in performance. This work turned painting into sculpture and attacked "the rationalistic notion that art is a form of work that results in a finished product" (Morris quoted in (Sayre, 1989) p. 70) but still accentuated female passivity. Carolee Schneemann's later reaction to the piece was antipathetic, because she was still being directed by men. In her autobiographical documentary of her performance works: "More than Meat Joy" she says "I WAS PERMITTED TO BE AN IMAGE, BUT NOT AN IMAGE-MAKER CREATING HER OWN SELF-IMAGE" ((Sayre, 1989) p. 74–75). However, in "Eye Body" (made slightly before Site), she publicly covered and transformed her body in confrontational ways, for example with ropes and rags. In using her own physicality as the art work she felt she challenged male expectations of the female body, and the acceptable behaviour of female artists, more fully.

Emancipation of the female body was also achieved by the separate but confluent stream of "contact" improvisation (commencing in the early 70s), which had antecedents in some of the theatre improvisation exercises of Spolin (Spolin, 1963), and in some of the artists mentioned already in this section. Steve Paxton, earlier a member of Cunningham's company, was a key initiator and the reluctant polemicist of this medium, which has arched into the work of most adventurous dance companies today. Contact improvisation directly concerns body improvising, cooperation and co-creation. It is the central topic of this section and one of the best examples of pure improvisation.

Contact improvisation and other developments in body improvisation

While American studies credit contact improvisation as a specifically US creation (e.g. (Novack, 1988)), and Steve Paxton as its major founder around 1972, as always the origins and influences are complex and interesting. Several kinds of antecedent performance involved a range of body contact in improvisation, for example some work of The Grand Union (a group which is discussed later). Their accumulating work variously called "Performance Demonstration", "Continuous Project-Altered Daily " etc. (c. 1968–70), partly used body contacting improvisation, in a "process of 'erosion' and reconstruction as the group... substitute their own materials", to quote Rainer (Rainer, 1974). She was initially director of the pieces, and by then "collaborating" with Paxton and others. The Living Theatre's work, such as the piece "Paradise Now", also exploited most forms of bodily contact.

The social antecedents to contact improvisation were the development of rock and roll dance in the 50s — an emanation of black culture into white at the time of the civil rights movement in the US — and the rise of the twist in the early 60s. As with these antecedents, it was one of the ideals of contact improvisation that it be accessible to trained and untrained alike; in this respect it was like a sport. It is not often noted however, that rock and roll dance movements were largely synchronised with the musical rhythms, whereas contact improvisation was usually done without external sound, and so could avoid such articulation. But the relevance of the rock and roll dance floor is symbolised in the middle section, "Party" of Gene Friedman's "3 Dances" (1964), in which Steve Paxton (see below) and Robert Rauschenberg perform, together with members of the public at a Museum of Modern Art (NYC) event; this film was a Judson group offshoot production.

The performing spaces for contact improvisation were usually the simplest, without props, and this also linked them with Grotowski's "poor theatre", in which an actor is nothing but one "who works in public with his body" (Grotowski, 1991). This theatrical connection also extended to the Living Theatre, Bread and Puppet, Open Theatre (and others discussed in Chapter 8), many of whose participants had experience of physical performance, risk taking, and other activities contiguous with contact improvisation in dance.

Contact improvisation, Novack suggests (Novack, 1990), is an embodiment of a particular period of political consciousness in the sixties, the outcome of a need to create new collaborative dance forms in a society devoted to individualism. It also arose in response to a preoccupation with the body in the 1960s which is evident in art dance, social dance, psychological movements and the sexual revolution, and has continued since. As she says, the essence of this trend is that an intelligent self was seen to manifest itself through a fit body. Contact improvisation also anticipated the wider view of sexuality that has characterised the eighties and nineties: dancers found it liberating to engage in physical contact that was not sexually charged and which often involved contact with people of the same rather than different sexes. Deborah Jowitt's emphasis on duo contact partners throughout the movement as "lovers" as well as "combatants", seems to us misplaced (Adshead-Lansdale and Layson, 1994).

Contact improvisation was a direct attack on many of the characteristics and values of ballet as high art and the kind of social organisation they imply. It was done without costumes, scenery or props and did not beautify the body; it conveyed a postmodern sense of self in stressing the idea of the dancer as an ordinary person and the continuity between everyday movement and dancing. It was in principle non-hierarchical in that all the dancers had equal status, and it required curved movements rather than erect posture. It eschewed symbolic content (Paxton, 1988), posing the body as a sign in itself rather than the container for an expressive self, and it did not try to convey any kind of narrative or romantic content.

Most significantly of all, contact improvisation neutered gender roles and even reversed them: in conventional ballet the woman, for example, is normally lifted by the man, symbolising her comparative frailty, and the differences between the sexes are made explicit in costumes which outline the body shape. In contact improvisation loose clothing hides the bodyshape and the exchange of weight, rather than weight per se, is important, so the differences in physical strength between the sexes are hardly significant. Sex roles can be reversed (Adair, 1992). In this sense the contact improvisation movement was one of the most radical feminist forms of improvisation. However, it is important to note that it was directed towards de-emphasising sexual difference in the interests of sexual equality. Contact improvisation did not speak for all types of feminist thinking, since it did not celebrate the essential otherness of women, the particular physicality of women's bodies, which theorists such as Hélène Cixous have seen as essential to the feminist enterprise (Cixous, 1986), and which was epitomised in the work of performance artists such as Schneeman.

Contact improvisation probably began seriously with the experiments of Paxton in 1972, involving "partners giving and taking weight" almost continuously (Novack, 1988). An enhanced bodily self-awareness (risks, strains, possibilities) was needed, and developed in parallel with a comparably enhanced awareness of the body of those partners in contact. The bodily giving and taking was thought to cultivate social and mindly freedom and exchange. Following Cunningham's idea that any movement could be used in dance, the flexibility and scope of contact improvisation was apparent. Contact improvisation's potential sensuality was attractive, since it was not circumscribed by the conventions of distance intrinsic in the twist and most rock and roll dancing. The audience was quite often infected by the feeling of sensual freedom and mutual physical availability of both performers and themselves. For example, in an improvisation c. 1964–5 Yvonne Rainer collaborating with Jill Johnston repeatedly jumped into the laps of men in the audience (Anderson, 1987).

There were some later changes in contact improvisation. By the late 70s disco dancing was common, and involved heterosexual contact between pairs of people. Contact improvisation, in contrast, was gender non-specific in its combinations. By the 80s the initiators of contact improvisation had become "professional" in both technical and economic senses, enhancing the inevitable potential separation between amateurs and themselves, and similarly between themselves and the audience. In addition, Bill T. Jones has said (1985: (Novack, 1988)) that what had earlier seemed free flowing in his own contact improvisation now seemed "messy". Such impressions were more widespread amongst dancers, and perhaps explain the relatively infrequency of contact performances per se since then. The continued influence of contact improvisation within dance and movement in general is, however, undoubted.

Amongst the body movements elicited by contact improvisation were some articulated by individuals, and many by combinations. For example, in individual movement the emphasis on very large free movements resulted in multiplicity: different parts of the body moving in different directions. They were also coordinated in ways which are not routine for practical movement, such as successive segmentation, controlled arcing, rising and falling. The procedures are the essence of what we have termed sensory improvisation. These trends within contact improvisation complemented the pre-existent dance repertoire of minute movements, inherited from Japanese and other theatres, and from Tai Chi and aikido, Asian martial arts forms. They also related to many movements from the Cunningham stable.

These and many other body movements are revealed in the films of contact improvisation. In "Magnesium" (1972), a film of eight contact improvisors, there is much repetition of actions, particularly of rapid downfall to the floor and then restanding. It is striking that the performers have developed many well coordinated and diverse ways of reaching the floor, but only a few of rising. There is no controlled sound component. (The piece is performed on a special mat, but there is continuous hardly varying sound mostly deriving from the floor noises, except for a moderate portion from external traffic and aeroplanes. This continuous monotony of sound is probably the result of recording the event with an "auto-level" function recorder, which automatically amplifies soft sections much, and loud sections little. As Paxton mentioned (1988) in NYC he had to "tune out 90% of the time").

Two-person exercises in catching the flying body are shown, and there are also body groupings. In "Peripheral Vision" (1973) there is a conversation by Paxton, which emphasises the balance/body contact and gymnastic elements, and rather than the aesthetic. Paxton emphasises "not thinking about it", since "thought is too slow". He also comments that there is an unusual "personal moment" where Nancy Stark-Smith smiles, though Paxton remains on the ground inactive. Conversely, there is also a mistake where Paxton's foot hits Stark-Smith's head! The difficulty of trio groupings is apparent and discussed, there being a tendency for them to fragment into two, leaving one person uncontacted. The emphasis on gender equality and mutual self-help results in there rarely being frontal heterosexual contact.

In group movements, the possibility of tall, transiently stable structures emerged in contact improvisation, contrasting with the held and supported jumps of classical ballet. An entertaining description of such "human pyramids", reached by a process of "gymnastics and tumbling" and "having fun", was given of the group Mangrove, performing in NYC in 1978 (Anderson, 1987). In addition, the construction of forms in which pairs of bodies heavily intertwined, soon lead into the asymmetric multiple-body masses characteristic of many later dance companies. Amongst these are Pilobolus, who have removed the improvisatory component from the performance, rather using it during construction of the work. Antecedents for this were the body-piles of the Living Theatre (as in Paradise Now 1970). A particular contact improvisation device is the "explosion" of the pile (discussed (Paxton, 1988)), whereby a group of performers rapidly moves apart. Novack has provided a photo essay of contact improvisation movements (Novack, 1988) and analysed its development in a very valuable book (Novack, 1990).

The contact improvisor Mary Fulkerson (pictured in (Adair, 1992)) carried several American dance streams to Britain when she moved there in the early 70s ((Novack, 1990); Fulkerson is seen in "Chute", a film released c. 1979, with Paxton). With the Strider company in the UK, she reversed the emphasis on the generation of the tall body masses which we have mentioned. As Jordan says, Fulkerson took Strider from "vertical to horizontal" (Jordan, 1992). Thus her "release work", a development from the main contact improvisation stream, emphasises floor and "horizontal" work. Similarly, Richard Alston's "Soft Verges" (1974) involved much contact and floor based improvisation in its first half. Even so, the 70s was the "decade in which British contemporary dance" became "independent... of the American tradition" (Jordan, 1992), and later improvisatory works (see later sections) reflect this also.

Later (mid 70s onwards) American contact improvisation became more "pedestrian" and slower moving, and movements often commenced with smaller contact areas. A good example is the 1978 film of Contact Improvisation videoed by the dancer Stephen Petronio: in addition this shows that even at slower speed, trio sections are still unstable. Again sexual connotations are avoided. Even in 1988 Paxton talked of his continued interest in pedestrian actions, available to audience and performer alike, and his wish not to use music, being "someone else's work".

Contact improvisation is an unusual example of collaboration, in which almost all group activity is divided into sub-activities each involving at least two people. Both sound and movement improvisation involve several continuous strands (of sound and movement respectively). But in contact improvisation each individual usually depends on at least one other for the maintenance of even one movement strand. In contrast, in a sound improvising group, each individual can maintain one or more sound strands without assistance. This mutual dependence in contact improvisation is both a potential and a limitation. It is difficult to assess to what degree recombining pairs or groups of contact improvisors were able to transfer the movement-strands they were cultivating from one contact combination to another. It is also often unclear to what degree participants were focussing on the movement-strands of participants other than those with whom they were in contact. Their sensory responses may often have been limited to their immediate group. Hence it is also unclear to what degree they would be able to develop the continuity of a pre-existent strand transferred to them in a new contact combination. This means that their generative potentials might be limited, in respect of mainly operating within their current contact combination. However, transferability of strands is not an essential feature of any art, even of those whose participants seek multiplicity of form or content. Thus contact improvisation offers ways of avoiding many of the conventional limitations of group dance, in which only a limited number of independent strands function, usually because of the strong emphasis on symmetry, coordination, individual control and elegance. In these respects, contact improvisation enforces the independence of strands which Merce Cunningham often demanded.

From the point of view of signification, contact improvisation's lack of overtly sexual action could be thought a limitation, since emotional and related sexual issues are frequently at the centre of artworks, and bodies are particularly efficient vehicles of these subjects. Similarly, the emphasis on sportly and gymnastic action, and the consequent almost complete avoidance of symbolism and metaphor may seem restrictive, even if historically necessary. Sometimes the pieces largely neglect the possibility of developing any artistic meanings, and remain essentially gymnastic. Clearly certain expressive possibilities are excluded or made less accessible by these features. On the other hand, the egalitarian, feminist and body-neutralising features of contact improvisation are extremely valuable in their own right, and perhaps could not readily co-exist with broader expressive aims. The aesthetic advance of the independence of movements, the multiplicity of strands, and the construction of asymmetric body piles are also immense achievements of contact improvisation.

The temporary waning of contact improvising in the mid 80s may, therefore, be succeeded by a future development in which its special potential for direct body interaction, not shared by any other approach, can be used to develop new types of signal. For example, such body contacts (and not just individual body movement as presently) might become systems for controlling interactively the function of other media, such as virtual world, hypermedia, or moving image. Such a relationship could provide a complement to the quite common approach of providing single performers with such links. To devise a way in which the impact of combinations of bodies, and their changed forms, could influence the other components of the resultant work, would be fascinating. We will return to these topics in Chapter 8.

SECTION III

COMBINING MEDIA IN IMPROVISATION

Unfortunately these days everyone fancies he can dabble in improvised playing, and the very dregs of the populace attempt it, imagining it to be easy, not realizing the peril that lies in their ignorance and presumption. (Perrucci on improvisation, 1699. Quoted in (Richards and Richards, 1990) p. 202).

6

IMPROVISATION IN BIMEDIA.
1: SOUND/WORD; SOUND/VISUAL; SOUND/BODY

Sound/Word Improvisation

We noted in the previous chapter the difficulties which arise from trying to improvise in a verbal medium. In improvisation using sound and words, the two can act as a spring board for each other (for example, the verbal improvisor can think while the musician fills in the gaps). It is also possible to improvise on the continuum which links words to sound, therefore releasing the performer from the difficulty of always having to think of a specific word.

Improvising with word and sound creates a non-hierarchical relationship between the two, since the words are not "set to" music: rather the two interact in a transformative, dynamic relationship. Sound/word improvising can therefore help to create a tension between words and sound, and a kind of semiotic exchange between them. This semiotic exchange is possible because the two systems have common characteristics, even if in different degrees. Words are made up of signifiers (sounds), as well as signifieds (concepts), so sound is intrinsic to language. The presence of music heightens this sensuous aspect of language: it pushes us to appreciate more abstract uses of language and allows us to experience them as rich and meaningful. Music, on the other hand, is a less referential system than language (it is difficult to say what the signified is), but the presence of words can inject a degree of referentiality, by suggesting relationships between particular sounds and possible meanings. The sound/word medium therefore permits exploration of what constitutes meaning in each component, allowing new types of meaning to emerge as part of their cross-over.

Improvising with words and sound often involves immediate response to the possible significations and qualities of words and sounds. Sound and structure have always been important in poetry, and sound is often played off against sense in traditional poems, but within certain constraints. The sound had to fit with the sense, even though poets must often have allowed the meaning to develop in unexpected ways because they liked the sound of a particular word. Improvising can amplify this play-off between sound and sense and can create a merging of them. While such merging also occurs in experimental non-improvised text, improvisation can produce an extreme multiplicity and simultaneity of sound-word relationships, and has provided an important influence on works which are not fundamentally improvised.

Many different types of interaction between a poet and a musician are possible in an improvising context. Sometimes the improvising is mainly done by the musicians because they are more used to improvising (although improvising skills are not common amongst musicians, they are even less common amongst writers). Sometimes musicians may improvise in response to largely composed text (as in the case of the Australian group "Machine for Making Sense" (Rue, 1991; Machine for Making Sense, 1993)). In the case of most poetry and jazz performances the speakers may adjust timings in response to the musicians but do not fundamentally improvise the text. A very few performances involve a mixture of read texts and improvised words or vocal sound. The musical improvising uses features discussed in Chapter 4, and there have been notable practitioners in the US (e.g. Kerouac with Al Cohn) and in the UK (e.g. Christopher Logue with Stan Tracey), particularly in the 60s and early 70s. We do not discuss poetry and jazz in further detail here; but the following works give entries into this area: (Wallenstein, 1979–80; Kerouac, 1990).

Where text is improvised the verbal improvisor may keep entirely to the verbal domain. But there are also many different types of phonetic improvising which overlap with vocal improvising, and many performances range between the verbal and vocal extremes. In some cases poets do not work with musicians but provide both the text and the sound themselves. Whatever the degree of semantic basis for the performance, the performer can always use his or her voice as a musical instrument, exploiting pitch, rhythm and timbre to musical effect.

All these types of activity are related to the "text-sound" movement, sometimes known as "sound poetry". The text-sound movement stemmed from the experiments of the Surrealists, Dadaists and Futurists at the beginning of the century, particularly the phonetic poetry of Hugo Ball (1916) and Kurt Schwitters' "Ursonate", but re-emerged as a strong movement during the fifties to seventies, through the work of such practitioners as Gerhard Ruhm, Bob Cobbing, Henri Chopin, and Bernard Heidsieck. Richard Kostelanetz characterises text-sound as "an intermedium located between language arts and musical arts" and says that "the term 'text-sound' characterises language whose principal means of coherence is sound, rather than syntax or semantics — where the sounds made by comprehensible words create their own coherence apart from denotative language" ((Kostelanetz, 1980) p. 14.

Kostelanetz does not use the term to cover pieces which use defined pitches, but the term is normally used more broadly in relation to verbal/text/sound interactions.

Text-sound varied from one place to another, for example in America it was closely associated with experimental music such as that of John Cage, and of minimalist/systemic composers such as Steve Reich and Terry Riley. In contrast, Henri Chopin has argued that European work is more abstract than American and that this relates to the different social ethos. Zurbrugg puts Chopin's view as follows: "it may be that this abstraction (or rejection of *words*) is somehow linked to a certain European nihilism (or rejection of organised religion), and an accompanying wish for liberation from verbal conventions" (quoted in (Kostelanetz, 1980) p. 164).

Text-sound, however, is part of a much wider context since text and sound are brought together in many different ways in contemporary culture, for example in popular songs. Zurbrugg has also pointed out the way in which

> *popular forms of radio broadcasting... have both* re-defined *certain experimental art practices, and* extended *their audiences, by associating them with more accessible categories, such as 'post-industrial' music. In something of the same way, concepts like 'sound sculpture', 'sound installations' and 'video installations' have allowed different kinds of 'sound art' to find more widespread exhibition, and more significantly still, to be* created *for more widespread exhibition ((Zurbrugg, 1989) p. 34).*

Text-sound then is the name for a historical phenomenon which was particularly important in the fifties to seventies, but has been influential and gathering momentum since under a variety of different names. Larry Wendt, for example, talks about word/sound work in the eighties and nineties as "post-sound poetry" (Wendt, 1993). Such work is represented in many types of performance art and radio art, and the various other categories Zurbrugg mentions above.

Many sound/word works are composed works which are then realised in performance. However, the level of realisation required in performance varies considerably, sometimes requiring extensive improvisation. Dick Higgins has differentiated various different classes of sound poetry, one being poems without written texts (Higgins, 1984). We concentrate here on such freely or partially improvised works.

Text-sound improvising: theory and politics

In the 50s–70s the ideological basis for text-sound improvising was not necessarily consistent from one performer to another, but tended to stress radical politics. Many text-sound artists saw improvisation as a revolt against the literary establishment and a means towards social liberation. For example, Mac Low's belief in "pacifist communal anarchism" was basically a creed of equality which the instructions such as "listen and relate", accompanying his pieces, are designed to induce. These demands on the performers can be seen to be antithetical to the competitive demands of capitalist America ((Smith, 1993) p. 23–24). Bob Cobbing's view of text-sound was similar: "a new means of communication which I believe is an old method re-established, which is more natural more direct and more honest than, for example, the present day voice of politics or religion" ((McCaffery and Nichol, 1978) p. 39). Another important influence was gestalt therapy, as in McCaffery's idea of "the energy gestalt" ((McCaffery and Nichol, 1978) p. 32). Paula Claire extravagantly imbued text-sound improvisation with mystical significance: "the incredible mesh of our own total structure which vibrates sympathetically with the whole universe" (McCaffery and Nichol, 1978) p. 21). Scepticism about such romantic terminology was expressed by several other practitioners such as Stephen Scobie (in (Kostelanetz, 1980) p. 46).

Buddhism was also an influence on some practitioners. Jackson Mac Low, whose work often involves creating structures which encourage improvisation under tightly controlled conditions, was influenced by the Buddhist concept of choiceless awareness: the notion of perceiving phenomena as far as possible without attachment and without bias. He felt that "allowing performers to make significant decisions both diminishes the role of the author-composer's ego and helps make the performers more conscious of both ego and non-ego" (Smith, 1993). This was similar to the idea of egoless composition in the work of John Cage. Mac Low had worked with Cage and in many respects they shared a common outlook.

Practitioners, when talking about text-sound improvising, consistently returned to the relationship between the mind and the body. This focus on the body has sometimes led people, even its practitioners, to view text-sound as phonocentric (i.e. privileging speech over writing), and embodying a conservative notion of the speaking subject. Talking about sound poetry McCaffery claims that in fact such work:

> has not dealt with this fundamental issue of presence and the way that that is the big ideological contamination that's gone on for 2000 years. I say that presence is a contaminant because it's a way that sound poetry connects with philosophical notions, political notions, economic notions, the whole base and super-structure within western society, western culture, western economics that is based on a sense of presence. The meaning is that thing that is there as a full plenitude. And whereas in sound poetry we kicked out meaning, we did not kick out the fullness and plentitude. We kicked out the meaning to get a closer kind of immediate presence between sound and energy and the physical body. And I think that restored a very

conservative notion of the self. What Freud and Lacan teach us we have not fully explored in sound. There's still the sense of the enunciator and the message enunciated. And that's where my reservation around sound poetry is. ((nichol, 1987) p. 14).

McCaffery here is obviously reacting against the romantic views of many text-sound improvisors, which he himself had promoted. However, improvisation does not have to go hand in hand with the concept of presence and plenitude: as we have shown improvisation is always a largely conscious negotiation between past and present experience. It is concerned with the passing rather than the lasting moment, and should not be conflated with simplistic views of personality or the immediacy of speech.

Text-sound: processes and products

Text-sound improvising sometimes uses an improvising referent. For example, Bob Cobbing may take graphic scores as the basis of his improvisations. In some scores, such as "Alphabet of Fishes" or "Worm" (Allnutt, Aguiar *et al.*, 1988; BirdYak, 1988), the semantic element is stated, but the way the words are vocalised in terms of rhythmic delivery, timbre and pitch is left free (Figure 7). The vocal delivery and the response of the musicians (Ma-Lou Bangerter, Lol Coxhill and Hugh Metcalfe) transform the emotional/ intellectual content of the referent while staying quite close to it. The semantic element is very different from that of a normal poem, for example in "Worm" the referent-words are all connected with the idea of a worm, and are set in lists rather than syntactically connected. The columns are, nevertheless, arranged rather like stanzas, with each couplet ending with the word "worm". The syntax is supplied by the vocal delivery and the interweaving musical motives and textures of the musicians. Each time the word "worm" is reached Cobbing performs a cadenza on it, and the musicians respond instrumentally, for example with frenetic glissandi or tremolando on the violin. When the words "ingratiate insinuate intrude invade" are delivered with violent urgency they take on connotations which are latent in the rather flat looking text on the page. The list of words turns into a musical-poetic and emotionally charged evocation of death and decay only hinted at in the referent text. Performances of the pieces differ, but have what Cobbing calls a "family resemblance".

Both Cobbing and Paula Claire have used objects (such as a cabbage, stone, a piece of rope, bricks or cloth) as the basis of their improvisations. In the 70s Paula Claire performed her "pattern sounds" i.e. sound improvisations on the surface patterns and textures of inanimate objects" ((McCaffery and Nichol, 1978) p. 14). The Canadian group, the Four Horsemen, which started to collaborate in 1969, sometimes used precise scores to work from "in which sound features and values are specifically described, as too are the points of entry and exit." Sometimes the text was something to work against ("anti-text": (McCaffery and Nichol, 1978) p. 34) (Figure 8). In other cases the Horsemen used what McCaffery called bricolage as the basis of improvising: each member of the group would bring texts such as his own discarded writing, or cuttings from the newspaper. The material might be used as a starting point during a performance, and then abandoned as sound patterns started to emerge ((McCaffery and Nichol, 1978) p. 34).

In the case of Jackson Mac Low's "Gathas" the performer is presented with letters based on mantras which (s)he can reassemble into structures of sounds or letters. Each score of the series of "Vocabulary" pieces offers words and musical pitch sequences derived by Mac Low from the letters of the name of a person, and the performers must construct them into musical and linguistic patterns. The instructions for these pieces set certain limits and guidelines for performance, balancing freedom and constraint, and combining a partially pre-determined structure with a superimposed improvised one which arises in performance.

In "A Notated Vocabulary for Eve Rosenthal" (Figure 9) words and notes derived from the name "Eve Rosenthal" are given to the performers, who are required to improvise on them within certain limits. The score is also visually quite stimulating, and because it is only a skeleton suggesting possibilities, each performance will be different. The performers can choose paths through the work rejecting certain possibilities of meaning, making the piece, for example, less or more political or contemporary. This has interesting historical implications, because however old the score becomes it can always be invested with contemporary specificity.

At the same time each performance will have a certain structural similarity with others, because they all emanate from the same set of instructions. This raises the issue of the deep or intrinsic structure represented by the score (the structure which all performances must share) and the superimposed structure (which arises in individual performances). The structure of the whole piece is a complex amalgam of these two structures, which can only be brought into being by the collaborative improvising of the participants. In interview, Mac Low characterised a bad performance as one which transgresses or ignores the instructions, but beyond this very important proviso he is prepared to accept whatever the performers produce (Mac Low, 1992).

Clearly "A Notated Vocabulary for Eve Rosenthal" brings music and sound together in an interactive, non-hierarchical way. The combination of linguistic and musical systems, and their interaction through the collaboration of the performers, create multi-layered structures in which several discontinuous semantic and sound streams can co-relate. This is demonstrated in the following transcription ((Smith, 1989) p. 163) of a brief passage from a live performance:

voice one:	*enter ever heaven*
voice two:	*enter rove lean*
voice one:	*enter ever revel rat*
voice two:	*enter rove lean*
voice one:	*halt strove enter oar steer sheen*

However, such transcription only reflects the verbal element. A word may provide a springboard for a sound, or a combination of words produced by one performer may be "played upon" by another, verbally or musically.

As a result the musical and linguistic systems converge. In previous work one of us has demonstrated the ways in which these works produce an exchange of semiotic systems, so that the musical elements become more referential and the linguistic elements more abstract (Smith, 1989; Smith, 1993). The words, which are spoken not sung, are brought into dynamic interplay with the music; the conjunction does not involve the hierarchical subordination of words to music we find in song. On the one hand, the words can make the music seem more referential than it would otherwise. For example, in one performance by Lysis of this piece, the florid passage on the vibraphone which followed the word "tear" seems to have more of a weeping quality because of its juxtaposition with that particular word (Lysis, 1985). In another performance by the same group, the connotation of "rupture", which can alternatively be associated with the word "tear", was exploited by a forceful flurry on the piano (Lysis, 1984). On the other hand, the music allows us to appreciate a high degree of abstraction in the language as novel and stimulating. The patterning of the words is foregrounded, but meaning is still present though in a way which emphasises semantic multiplicity. Within any combination of the words different possibilities of meaning present themselves and sometimes these contradict each other. So the sequence "art halt slave" could suggest that art can stop slavery, or conversely that art should be discontinued because it can enslave.

Like many avant-garde artists Mac Low does not see any necessity to make his work a vehicle for direct political statements; however, this does not mean that the work is not political. As we have seen, the political aspect of the work can be partly identified with its processes and the way it breaks down the hierarchical structure between performer and composer. It also displaces the traditionally and socially accepted ways of using language (the language of the symbolic order), and allows what Julia Kristeva calls the semiotic aspect of language to emerge. Furthermore, performers might choose to present a politicised text by their choice of word combinations and sound juxtapositions.

Philip Corner's "Worded Music" ((Kostelanetz, 1980) p. 67–69) also establishes a multiplicity of relationships between words and music. Words (e.g. "allegro", "indefinitely prolonged", "fortissimo") alone make up the one page score; they are irregularly placed, and all relate to different types of musical performance. But the instructions permit several ways of interpreting or manipulating the words verbally, by speaking, singing or vocalising, as well as instrumentally. For instance, the players can directly translate the words into the musical quality named; play the quote implied by the words (e.g. blue heaven, the title of a popular song); extract the rhythmic features of the words; translate the words into phonic elements; or use the word as a cue to improvise a musical or spoken commentary. Therefore the words can be approached from a literal or sonic point of view and vocal delivery can range between speaking and singing. The degree of improvisation can vary between performances: sometimes it may only comprise choosing the words or suitable musical equivalents, while sometimes the musical or spoken commentary can be predominant.

Another type of referent is a set of instructions which suggest one or several words, or a mood or idea, as the basis for sound/word improvising. One such example is Australian poet Jas H. Duke's "Stalin" (Duke, 1989; Duke, Undated (1988 or earlier)) p. 127). In this piece the word stays the same, but the mode of delivery, while suggested in outline, is open to considerable variation.

> *and from here on just repeat the word* STALIN *until you fall down exhausted. Try to convey both the terror and the betrayal of hopes and the mediocrity and the self-confidence. Uncle Jo wasn't a man to trifle with. Those that laugh at him now were shit-scared of him when he was alive. Try to get that across. You're dealing with a species of evil spirit. Try to remember that.*

So in this passage Duke (as often) is half-joking half-serious, choosing the highly emotive "Stalin" as his focus and yet referring to him as Uncle Jo. The instructions are in the same vein, suggesting the performer reiterate the word until he literally drops. This piece also raises the issue of how much the writer has himself in mind as the realiser of the text, and how much another person. In fact, Jas H. Duke (who died recently) has produced the ideal realisations of these texts, which have rarely been attempted by other people (who then largely imitated Duke).

Duke's performances of "Stalin", though varied, tended to have several features in common: mainly through a highly idiosyncratic delivery.

Sounding like a train gathering speed, he propelled himself behind his own voice to the point where he could no longer control how fast, or in what direction, he was going. Each performance consisted of changing contortions of the voice, part gasp, part laughter, part hiccup, and a tendency to vary the rhythmic meter from 3/4 to 4/4 at will. Duke indulged in huge accelerations and decelerations and swooped from low to high pitches. The improvisational element permitted the work to take on a wide range of shapes (Smith, 1991).

In the case of Roger Dean's "Be Construct" (Harbourside Brasserie, Sydney, 1990) the referent was one of Amanda Stewart's texts, heard by Dean for the first time immediately beforehand. "Be Construct" was a solo musical and verbal improvisation using voice and piano. Stewart's satirical text was couched as a pseudo-logical argument involving concepts from literary theory. Elements of the argument were used by Dean with simultaneous deconstruction: individual letters from the words which formed the argument were used both as the basis of pitch centred passages (B, C# etc.) and to illuminate associated concepts enunciated verbally by the performer ("C sharply"; "B construct", "D(ei)fy" etc.: (Smith, 1991)). Such semiotic overlaps between text and sound were later used by Dean in a short composition for piano "It Gets Complicated" (Dean, 1993), in which the pianist speaks a text with several levels of connotation, relating to science, psychology and performance. This was a clear and self-aware example of the process of improvisation later becoming the basis for fixed composition, a phenomenon which we have mentioned before.

Sound/word improvising often involves the use of very small elements of words or phonemes, and sometimes more concentration on the voice and vocal delivery than on words. Paul Dutton describes how in work with the Four Horsemen:

> *I was carried beyond phonemes into shrieking, squawking, squeaking, gargling, lip-flubbing, growling, groaning, muttering, giggling, sobbing, aspirating, drumming on my cheeks at higher or lower pitches by dropping or raising my jaw, and popping my tongue off different points of my palate at different intensities for varying pitch and volume ((Dutton, 1992) p. 10).*

These vocal techniques are evident on some of his recordings (Horsemen, 1988; CCMC, 1994). They have been taken even further by other vocal specialists such as Phil Minton (e.g.(Minton and Turner, 1993)), David Moss (Moss, 1988) and Maggie Nichols (Lask, 1982).

Bob Cobbing often uses growling sounds in conjunction with fairly flat texts, thereby creating a tension between vocal delivery and semantic content. The process tends to be associative, letting the voice lead the way so that sounds may result from physical processes or sensations. bp Nichol (Canadian improvisor and also a member of the Four Horsemen) used a variety of vocal noises including blowing into the microphone in two performances "Eight Part Suite" and "White Text Sure" (based on a visual smudge: (nichol, 1982)). According to Dutton ((Dutton, 1992) p. 15), these were improvised.

Talking of the voice as an instrument Dutton says:

> *That instrument is happiest not knowing what's coming next. I prefer to follow my nose and the sounds that come out of it, finding a little flutter of saliva happening somewhere in my throat while sustaining a pitch, and working up that flutter into a full-fledged gargle, perhaps changing the quality of it with some rapid opening and shutting of the mouth, shifting into labial percussive effects and proceeding to — well, but something's lost in the transcription.*

Most text-sound improvising is sensory-generative at least in terms of its internal dynamics. Steve McCaffery describes the relationship between the members of Four Horsemen in terms of metonymy and synecdoche:

> *As parts we become 'whole' by merely recognising our partiality, our molecular independence. The operating notion of the 'whole' is not that of a consummate aggregate of parts, but of a juxtapositional whole, the 'whole', that is, as a concept placed alongside the 'parts', entering into relationship with the parts but in no way dominating them ((McCaffery and Nichol, 1978) p. 33).*

Sometimes the concept of interaction has been extended to the audience. For example Paula Claire said: "Improvisation and participation have been essential in my work since the mid 1960's. I wish to be a catalyst, not a performer to a passive audience" ((McCaffery and Nichol, 1978) p. 21). In addition, bp Nichol would improvise in response to audience suggestions.

Text-sound and technology

Text sound improvising, from its outset, sometimes incorporated other technologies. Henri Chopin, for example, often improvised breathing sounds in non-semantic works which combine vocal improvisation with edited studio work (Chopin, 1983). However, recording and reproducing technologies are progressively allowing more manipulation in real time, as we move from analogue to digital means. These latter include sampling, a sampler being a digital recorder which records and replays excerpts of sound which can then be manipulated by keys or computer. Through the use of this technology the voice can be changed in real time, radically transforming it in rhythm, pitch and dynamic. This changes not only the sound but also its implications and specificity. For example, the voice can become both male and female, or can be manipulated to the point where it is barely recognisable as a human voice. At the same time sounds can be humanised, or made to sound verbal, so that again there is semiotic exchange between the two systems.

This exchange allows exploration at the edges of both music and language. In the radio piece "Collaboration" by Amanda Stewart and Warren Burt (1987), there are both improvised and composed sections. Stewart's own improvised sounds are at times accompanied by sampled sounds of her voice. The voice sounds are a mixture of stuttering, half-realised sounds such as croaking, and suggest a voice on the edges of both language and music. Often the sensation is one of struggle and anxiety and the surfacing of residual, suppressed and non-verbalisable meaning. Amanda Stewart says about Collaboration:

> *In two sections live voice and electronics improvise together. In this process I did a vocal improvisation and Warren recorded compressed fragments of it and arranged these sounds on the sampler so that each vocal sound was spread across three keys on the keyboard... There were a total of seventeen vocal sounds arranged in this way across a four octave keyboard. Then we improvised — me with my amplified voice in one stereo channel and Warren playing the "vocabulary" of my sounds on the sampler in the other channel. It was an exhilarating process — abstract vocal sounds colliding in fast musical play, exposing some of the complex ways in which sounds do and can group together into micro-systems. The sounds might be heard as phonemes, or cross-cultural non-verbal signs or as musical materials. There was a lot of play with musical puns, onomatopoeia, speech intonation puns (Smith, 1991).*

Stewart has also indicated the general implications for her of this work:

> *The vocal sounds might be heard as phonemes or half words, expressionist grunts or musical materials. But what's important is that oppositions like those between language/music, machine/human, subject/object, break down, making other understandings more imperative. ((Zurbrugg, 1989) p. 46).*

Recently Stewart has begun to incorporate improvisation more extensively into her work, often using pre-written texts or word listings as a trigger. She picks out and works with words, phonemes or phrases from the text; combines words from different parts of the text; or diverges from and adds to the text in ways which seem appropriate to the improvised moment. Semantic elements are juxtaposed with pitched vocalisations and non-verbal vocal noises. Multi-tracking is sometimes used as an aid to improvisation so that the live improvisation can be a response to a pre-recorded voice. Her note on ≠ 1993 explicates her use of these approaches:

> *≠ is essentially a semantically engendered piece. It is comprised of four layers of commentary and interjection. I composed a text in which the word order was set, but the performance of*

these words was to be spontaneously manipulated by the voice (without processing) in "real-time" improvisation. I recorded this first performance onto the left channel and then recorded a second text on the right channel that overhears, comments on and interjects over the first. The third and fourth layers are stereo vocal improvisation that makes occasional comments on the first. If you listen to the left and right speakers in isolation you can hear the two texts overhearing and commenting on each other and their semantic dimensions are emphasised. The texts use a diversity of references and constructions, from schizoid operatic personal pronouns like "s$_{he}$ ^{it}" to mercurial tirades, fractured words, phonemes, calls, statements, outbursts, stutters, pronouncements, mouth sounds, "concrete nouns", parallel speech... so that modes of listening are constantly switching between different fields of shape, suggestion and meaning. ((Wendt, 1993) p. 76).

In "Poet without Language" ((Smith and Dean, 1991); recorded on (Smith, 1994)) a mixture of analogue and digital technologies are used, combining compositional multi-tracking of the voice with manipulation of samples in realtime (Wallace, 1995).The musical sounds are taken from text samples which have been digitally edited, from string and percussion sounds generated as samples and as synthesised objects, and from other electronic keyboard sounds, mainly synthesised. The relationship between verbal and non-verbal sound is exploited in a wide range of ways, including the use of reversed samples, amalgamated samples, and digitally transformed sounds, so that dense rhythmic structures are sometimes built up from words and parts of words, and different parts of the words are stressed or emerge at different times. The musical sounds are also used to counterpoint textual suggestions such as those of ethnicity, which are present in the text. The text is multi-layered and multi-referential: the piece deals with questions of race, language, and concepts of the mind, but also refers to itself at the interface of language and music. It takes the form of a score allowing for considerable improvisation on the samples, but with specificity as to which sample should be used when (Figure 10).

Hazel Smith's "Simultaneity" ((Smith, 1994), also recorded on (Smith, 1994)) for solo voice and improvisor, consists of a written text which toys by sound and association with the word simultaneity. The improvisor uses a sample of the word, and both loops it and uses it in rhythmic improvising. The piece has some connection, in its rhythmic propulsion and phasing, with systemic (minimalist) music. The speaker and the improvisor are sometimes simultaneous, sometimes slightly out of phase, and the sampled word often creates sounds quite removed from its verbal connotation e.g. in one place, used at speed, it sounds like squawking birds.

The computer sound improvisation group The Hub (from the San Francisco Bay area) has undertaken some sound-text improvisation. On one of its recordings a small section is documented of "Hub Renga", a 90 minute live radio performance in which they used the computer Internet (The Hub, 1994). This permitted writer-subscribers to the Californian network called "The Well" to provide single lines of text from their home computer keyboard during the performance (see Chapter 9): these lines were read by three speakers. It had been prearranged by the performers that if certain "keywords" occurred in the speech, they would function as "triggers" which would elicit significant responses in the ongoing computer sound stream. These responses were "automatic", according to the CD sleevenote, in the sense of being programmed within the computer hub. The sound elements were entirely generated by the Hub, using its computer interactive local-network approach. The keywords were not known to the text writers and the interaction was also limited in that the verbal contributors, while hearing the piece, could only guess which elements were the results of their input. Thus they could not modify their own contribution so as to influence more precisely the ongoing process.

As Chris Brown suggested (Brown, 1994), for the performers, "sound sharing" (of words and computer sounds) is difficult, though "memory sharing" (of ideas) is rather easier. And as Perkis says "a remarkable sense of community" results, notably at one point where multiple texts arrive almost together and are spoken almost simultaneously by the three speakers (CD sleevenote). The results show the potential for exploitation of such networked interchange of polymedia components, for future improvisation.

Sound/Visual Improvisation

Improvised work combining only these two media, in the sense of making them both overt to the audience, is surprisingly limited. Rather, it nearly always occurs in polymedia forms such as film or theatre. Nevertheless, several visual artists have been very involved in sound improvising, such as Davie, Penck, and Tom Phillips. They seem usually to have made visual scores for sound improvising, and rarely to have made works which display both components.

One could make a weak case that an exception occurs when a work is on display in a gallery in which the artist then performs; for some at least of the audience a true sound-visual work may result. This has happened with works by Davie, Phillips and progenitors such as Duchamp, whose visual sound scores are well known.

Sound-visual work also encompasses some experimental film and video in which there is no (verbal) narrative. (We exclude silent movies, with verbal narrative provided as intercut, and indeed improvisation in such works seems to have been quite limited, except for that contained within slapstick performance.) These films are oppositional to the norms of mainstream Hollywood cinema in which actors play roles which are largely generated through dialogue, and are agents in "plots" which work their way through to a denouement. They are usually low budget, low tech films made in black and white in contrast to the superficial glamour of Hollywood films. An archetype of the sound-visual film is Canadian film-maker Michael Snow's "New York Eye and Ear Control" (Snow, 1964). The title of the work emphasises its bimedia nature, and Snow himself has commented on his objective of making the sound and visual elements equal players, and thus avoiding the sound becoming "subservient" to the visual image. As he says ((Snow, 1994) p. 54), sound forms

> *a counterpoint with the images — which were measured and classical—as opposed to this very spontaneous, very emotional sound...... It's a simultaneity, not just one thing accompanying another.*

This co-equality is also a means of merging and interchanging the two potentially separate semiotic streams. The sound track of this work, which was recorded before the filming, is improvised free jazz by a group of pioneers who used Snow's New York painting studio of the time for rehearsals. The filming featured Snow's long standing symbol, the Walking Woman, and is of largely predetermined action. However, there are some improvised moments, and Snow has mentioned the influence of Cassavetes' "Shadows", which we consider in Chapter 8. The non-narrative nature of the film (especially since it is also non-verbal) means that the visual component does not dominate as it might if it had to carry a narrative. The sound improvising is dense and overtly tense, consistent with the limited impression of New York the images convey. But more importantly, the sound catalyses quite unexpected impacts from some of the images: for example, the Walking Woman appears to fly. The equality of the two component media is very important to this film, and the ideas it contains were very influential, on Warhol, Morrissey and others of the period (MacDonald, 1993).

In conversation with us (Snow, 1994), Snow said that he was more interested in "putting an object in the world" than saying something about the world. He did not see his work as strongly politically motivated, though he thought "it was worth defending creative living". Again the ideological aspect of his films might be seen to be bound up with their processes, which fail to meet the expectations of commercial cinema "entertainment" and focus on aspects of everyday existence, which are usually edited, or edited out, in commercial films.

Several other Snow films involve non-narrative, so called "structural film" techniques, and are also non-verbal. Structural film concentrates on the medium of the film, and the process of film-making at the expense of narrative and other forms of visual continuity. Like improvisation itself, therefore, structural film emphasises the process as much as the product. For example <—> ("Back and Forth") is a continuously panning (i.e. back and forth) view of a classroom filmed from a fixed camera position. It involves an elaborately planned series of events, performed by friends of Snow, and even the arrival at the outside of a cop, who peers in at the window, was organised. However, a few of the other events were improvised, and throughout the actors are not playing roles so much as allowing certain events to happen. The whole places unusual demands on the viewer, requiring extreme patience because very little happens and the events are fairly banal. The film challenges normal modes of perception and the ability to pay attention when change is minimal. One possible set of readings of this work involves the construction of spatial narratives catalysed by, but essentially unconnected with, the limited narrative of the events themselves. In spite of Snow's vast improvisatory bent (see other sections on sound), his use of improvisation in other films is largely restricted to the development and editing process, and is discussed later.

The British structural film maker and critic Peter Gidal (born 1946) has offered some very relevant comments, in the light of his own works, and their tendency to record events and environments which are either improvised or not completely controlled (Gidal, 1994). Gidal is an important theorist of structural film (Gidal, 1975), and teaches at the Royal College of Art, as well as being a practitioner. Commonly the environments in his films are largely unrecognisable (as in his "Guilt" (1988), and "Denials" (1986)), though he points out that in his more recent "Flare Out" (1992) "there's less that's unrecognisable". He is often represented by his films from the 70s, such as "Room Film 73" (1973; 55 minutes) and "Silent Partner" (1977), or their immediate predecessor, "Clouds" (1969). The two 70s films contain long passages of unidentifiable images which seem to be changing textures, somewhat analogous to the continuous-stream sound improvising we discussed earlier; and, as one might expect from the title, "Clouds" takes the same form. Very occasionally a drastic transition point occurs: in one of the 70s films it is an intermittent image of an aeroplane, seeming distant, almost model-like. The aspect of unrecognisability in the films is complexified by the superimposition of image-fading, re-focussing, re-framing and a plethora of other techniques which specifically concentrate on the process of controlling the image recording and editing. Gidal:

I improvise within my filmwork. It is important as in spite of pre-planning, the films are a process of my response to the machine in relation to the real, that which the camera is aimed at. That real. There are other reals. The changes that occur moment to moment are pre-conceived and not pre-conceived, and the dialectic of those "two" systems produces a filmwork which is as unknown to me as to anyone else. This is not only at the time of inception, of first rushes, but often for years thereafter, after many viewings still. (Gidal, 1994).

He goes on to indicate that the feature of "unrecognisable" images is probably important to this "unknown" quality.

It is intriguing to ponder the reasons for the relative lack of sound-visual improvising in the 50s to 70s. One of the factors may be the conventional influence of the then perceived nature of the media. For example, visual media were usually thought suitable to produce "scores" which could then be used in the more performative sound arena. This may have been amplified by the fact that sound improvisation was much more common than visual, so that even those visual artists interested in improvisation were tempted to produce for, rather than with, sound artists (as in the cases we mentioned at the beginning of this section). The conventionally different time scales for sound performance (brief), and production of visual works (long), also created barriers.

Behind the difference in time scale also lies the issue of the efficiency with which sound and visual media can be manipulated by any machines the performers use. Here again there were differences between sound and visual work which might have tended to strengthen barriers. Thus analogue (sound) synthesisers began to be quite important from the 50s onwards. Though they had practical limitations, such as stability of tuning, they permitted in principle most kinds of sonic exploration, and hence were highly attractive to improvisers from Sun Ra to Paul Bley (Dean, 1992). At the time no comparable technology was readily available to the visual worker. By the 80s, computer visual instruments, such as the early Fairlight model, began to catch up with the parallel developments of computer sound instruments, of which the Fairlight company had also made a pioneering example. The recent vast increase in the speed of digital signal processing has reduced the barriers between the two media, and the possibility of bimedia improvisation is now convenient and evident. Even now some difficulties remain, such as the fact that to process visual images at high resolution and at the same speed as film frames is beyond the capacity of most desk-top computers, and compromises of image compression etc. are needed. Whereas sound processing at the quality of compact discs (where the sound is represented by 44.1 thousand digital samples per second) is quite within their capacity. However, by now the usage of digital media, such as cd-roms, has jumped over mono- and bi-media presentation straight into multimedia, using sound, visual, verbal, film, body representations etc. This is because the main use of cd roms is in commercial, educational and entertainment applications which seek realistic representation, and therefore focus on representation of human bodies. So even an artist interested in sound and visual improvisation is now quite likely to combine it with body work or some other component. This is the case for example with Ritter (see Chapter 8), who often includes people and their bodies in the visual stream of his works.

The lack of exploitation of the sound/visual bimedia in isolation is unfortunate. Certainly many fascinating possibilities remain there to be explored; and some software appropriate to facilitate this is available and continues to be developed (see Appendix 3). We hope that the current widespread availability of cd-rom multimedia platforms will encourage some more systematic use of this bimedium (see also Chapter 10).

Sound/Body Work

Apart from contact improvisation, discussed in Chapter 5, most bodily improvising has occurred in polymedia forms such as dance and theatre, and much will be discussed when we deal with these in Chapter 8. However, it is important to consider the relationships between the subcomponents of such polymedia; in the present case specifically sound and body work, so as to clarify achievements, restrictions and potentials. So here we consider those few works which isolate these two components from, for example, visual or verbal elements. As always, the subdivisions we use are arbitrary disjunctions within continuous forms. We will concentrate on works in which ancillary visual elements, such as set and costumes are limited, though again this distinction is one of degree.

As in the case of sound/visual improvising, a key issue is the degree to which the equality of the two component media is expressed in the forms. The conventional relationship between the two media in non-improvised sound/body forms is one in which the sound is largely subordinated to the body. This is true even though the dance might be set to pre-existent music. And the most obvious development within sound/body improvising is that in which it gradually became possible for the sound to respond to the body in real-time.

We should first analyse how sound has usually been subordinated to body work in composed sound/body artworks, so as to be able to see how their co-equality could be achieved in improvised works. In some composed (or improvised) forms, subordination occurred because the body movements generated the sounds, and there were no separate sounds (as for example, in much contact improvisation discussed already). More recently, the subordination results largely from the fact that the body work is usually performed live, and though composed has flexibility, whereas the sound is usually fixed, and often recorded. It also occurs because far more of the resources of the commercial production are spent on the body work. The fact that the choreographer or company often commissions the sound also reflects this commercial imbalance, and it can strengthen a comparable artistic imbalance. In contrast sound/body improvisation challenges all these assumptions and relationships, and can permit the body work to be influenced by many parameters (such as proximity of sound) which are usually not available. Equally, it can allow mutual responses within the two media which rarely occur in composed work: for example a sound shape might be derived from a concurrent body shape by a sensory-generative process on the part of the real time sound improvisor. This relationship, in which the body-artists can influence sound generation by other performers, is perhaps the rarest. Having noted these potentials, we can consider the degree to which they have been exploited in this bimedia; and we can bear in mind their relevance to the discussions of polymedia in Chapter 8.

In considering contact improvisation we mentioned that presentations usually took place without sound accompaniment. But several participants have commented that the improvisers were encouraged to be rather free in their use of mouth and nose sounds, so that exaggerated exhalation and protoverbal sounds were common. It seems that these have rarely been used as systematic strands in the bimedia performances, though clearly they could be. These potentials were more exploited in the polymedia work of Chaikin and others (Chapter 8).

The simplest process for relating sound and body occurs whenever the body movements are necessarily responsible for sound generation, and when this is the main sound source in the work. Such an approach does not begin to challenge the hierarchical relationship between body and sound until musicians are present and their separate musical stream is influenced by the movements. It is notable that the simplest approach springs mainly from traditional forms such as clog-dancing, and its more recent offshoot, tap-dancing. Clog-dancing is a long standing folk tradition (c.f. (Hall, 1985; Kraft, 1989)), apparently of relatively fixed forms, and the solid, quite heavy wooden clogs (shoes) are responsible for moderately paced sound generation. Livia Vanaver has indicated that contemporary exploitation of this continues in the US, with limited "rhythmic" improvisation, and that her company, "Vanaver Caravan" produces "innovative" performance largely related to traditional music (as shown on the film (Bull, Cornell *et al.*, 1988)). There is little sign that the clog dancing influences the musical rhythms, and there is no pressure towards evolution of the body/sound relation in this form because it is maintained by traditional societal applications.

A better known form in which the body dictates the sound is tap-dancing, associated in the commercial world with Fred Astaire. It is normally accompanied by jazz or another strongly rhythmic music, and it does allow the tapped movements to influence the rhythms of the musicians. The tapped rhythms, which are largely improvised, are also generated by rhythmic approaches closely relating to those of the accompanying music. The shoes are much lighter than clogs, with several specialised tapping surfaces, and can be moved with greater rapidity and multiplicity of flux. As US tap-artist Heather Cornell says, traditionally this form is improvised with strong rhythmic impulse, and she and her company Manhattan Tap exploit body sounds other than the taps, mainly body-impact sounds (Bull, Cornell *et al.*, 1988).

For example, Manhattan Tap (shown in action in (Bull, Cornell *et al.*, 1988)) improvise usually with conventional jazz accompaniment. They often perform blues, or other standard jazz forms, and take improvised solos, short "breaks" and other improvised forays based on jazz techniques. Thus a common procedure in both tap and jazz is for a group of soloists to take cyclic turns to improvise (i.e. to "trade") four bar patterns against the twelve bar pattern of the blues (and this is seen on the film). If there are other than multiples of three improvisers, then there is the necessity for a carefully controlled number of cycles of these breaks, since the performers normally accept the constraint of finishing the series of breaks at the end of a twelve bar "chorus" rather than anywhere within it. The performers thus have to have sufficient musical and rhythmic understanding for this, and tend to be more proficient rhythmically than many dancers. As Cornell says, they "create as musicians as well as dancers" (Bull, Cornell *et al.*, 1988). Most of the work in the tap area is commercial, cabaret-orientated performance, but tap can go outside this. The possible limitations of the form are the relative rhythmic simplicity (though this does not seem a necessary feature), and the inability of the dancers to generate long-lasting sounds. Tap dancing begins to undermine the dominance of body over sound, because the sonic exchanges between the bodyperformers and the soundperformers can be reciprocal, at least on the level of rhythm. A full equality of exchange can, of course, only be achieved in a more flexible, less conventionalised medium, where, for example, rhythmic sound is complemented by a wider range of other sonic approaches. This was approached in some work by free jazz percussionist John Stevens, working with tap artist Will Gaines in the UK (particularly in the early 80s).

Such sound/body equality is not common, even within the offshoots of the highly egalitarian, contact improvisation movement which tended to overturn conventional hierarchies. Contact improvisors, however, did begin in the late 70s and 80s to use more sound elements. An interesting example is the film of Steve Paxton himself, performing at St Marks and then engaged in discussion with Bill T. Jones, the other performer presented on the same "Studio Project" (Paxton and Jones, 1983). Jones' work and the discussion, will be mentioned later (Chapter 7). Paxton showed first a video of some of his earlier silent "pedestrian" work (a piece called "Flat"), mentioned in Chapter 5: as he says on the film, "Walking is an important thing". Then he performed a solo work with music by Bach, in which he articulated every possible joint, and many which seemed non-existent. This created a continuity of movement which formed a marked disjunction with the discrete note patterns of the Bach. The piece is very striking. Although the sound is not improvised and so is non-responsive, the work suggests some of the ways in which body improvising was developing in relation to sound. In particular it shows the developing emphasis on individual continuous movements, which complement that of the contact body-pile, and the earlier pedestrian movements.

There is no attempt in this, or most works by the contact improvisors, to develop a more reciprocal exchange between sound and body. Clearly direct collaboration between bodyworkers and soundworkers might facilitate this: either or both parties could work in an improvised manner. But even the American, Anna Halprin, a key figure in body improvisation since 1965, hardly exploited these possibilities. She was primarily interested in the relationship between movement in everyday activities, in nature, and in dance, and challenged many other conventions of the sound/body media. For example, some of her "scores" for improvised performance included the audience as participants, a trend in common with many other improvised media, as we have seen. "Initiations and Transformations" (1972) invited the audience to "hop and shuffle sequences" (Anderson, 1987) so that they too became body-movement sound-sources, but they could not be expected to induce sound-body reciprocity. Furthermore, her scores were improvising referents, rather than completely notated sound/body structures, so that reciprocal exchange between sound and body was not enforced. Indeed her early work might equally be considered theatre, because sound as a separate object was not always important, rather it was generated by the dancers. Later in her work, sound-generating props like radios were used, so that a chance element of sound input was involved. Eventually, she used composed sound which was prepared in advance, such as that of Morton Subotnick in "Parades and Changes" (1967). The degree of influence of the body work upon the sound generation remained limited in Halprin's work.

Several of the 60s sound-body works involved improvisation in both components, though few permitted the body to influence the separate sound generation. Rainer's "Seascapes" (presented 1963 in a Judson event) included improvised repetition of bodily actions, like some of the Halprin works, and was associated with a repetitive tape by LaMonte Young. The sounds were derived from forcefully displacing furniture in the performing space vicinity (the tape was entitled "Poem for Chairs, Tables, and Benches, Etc. or Other Sound Sources"). The generation of this tape was improvisatory, but within clear constraints like those of Young's other works (such as "X for Henry Flynt"), which require repetition of a complex action, but produce variation of the nature, impact and perception of that action.

We could mention several other sound/body works in which improvisation took place within both of the component media. In most cases it seems as if the exchanges between the two components were limited; in some it is very difficult now to judge. Examples of the later are: "Going On" (1979) by Paxton and percussionist-vocalist David Moss (Anderson, 1988), and the earlier Judson collaboration of Cecil Taylor and Fred Herko (1962), in "Concert of Dance #1", which was billed as "improvisation" ((Banes, 1993) p. 67). In view of the breadth of vision of the musicians involved in these two collaborations, it is likely that they achieved real responses to the body work, and hence that reciprocity was achieved. But documentation of these performances does not suffice to assess this adequately.

More sound components were involved in the improvisation work of US dancer/choreographers Nikolais and Louis, but the relationships between the improvisation of sound and the body movements seem quite limited, as judged particularly by those seen on (Nikolais and Louis, 1988). Similarly, in the 60s Judson piece "In their Own Time" by Sally Gross, an improvisation for 6 dancers, the music by Philip Corner from "Keyboard Dances" used rhythmic playing inside the piano, while the dancers used non-rhythmic approaches. The dancers were each allocated a 2h span of a clock, and improvised actions relevant to that time span (e.g. sleeping, standing up, etc). They could move either out of the time zones (to a chair in the middle of the performing area), or to another time zone, by moving around the circumference of the clock ((Banes, 1980) p. 267). Improvisation was thus important here, but did not develop full exchange between the media.

Processes and potentials in Sound/Body improvising

We have seen how sound in this bimedia was conventionally subordinate to movement, and how little early improvising tended to challenge that. The view that this subordination is desirable is supported even by the several books which concern the teaching of movement improvisation in general. For example Blom and Chaplin ((Blom and Chaplin, 1988) p. 89, a.o.) view music as having "its own persistent logic. It neither interacts with nor responds to the mover's individualised pursuits, but forges ahead on its own track". While this is obviously one possibility, their book does not explore others in which sound and movement are more interdependent. Subsequent passages go on to reinforce the restricted view that the music will (ironically) dominate the dancer, and do not encourage interactive improvisation. Morgenroth (Morgenroth, 1987) is more diverse and adventurous, and offers several exercises concerned with sound development by the dancers, or sound coordination. She admits the possibility of "dancing with and against the music" (p. 118).

In contrast, the possibilities for merging the sound and bodily streams, and hence for semiotic convergence to catalyse multi-referentiality (as discussed already), are also fascinating. Indian traditional dancing, perhaps particularly that of Southern India, involves dancer-musical relations which are improvised yet precise. Firstly, the dancer is almost as familiar as the musicians with the rhythmic structures they use, their repetitive yet developing nature, and with the overall form of the musical performances. Secondly, the dancer coordinates the rhythms of the body movements to a degree only attempted in recent American dance which uses repetitive or jazz-driven rhythms. One thinks here of the work of Lar Lubovich, Trisha Brown or Molissa Fenley (such as the latter's "Hemispheres" (1983) including music by Anthony Davis performed by Episteme). However, most of American rhythmic bodily movement has used composed or pre-recorded sound, and most of the movements have also been choreographed.

Yet in Indian dance the movements may be traditional and largely choreographed, but scope remains for improvisatory transitions in the dancer's rhythms to influence the musicians, and apparently vice versa. Thus the dancer may lead a pulse transition, of the kind discussed in Chapter 4 in relation to sound improvising itself. We have seen such subtle interactions in dance performances presented internationally, and also in those given in Westernised Hotels in Bombay and New Delhi. Thus they are probably widespread in the profession. It is not our aim to discuss these effects in detail here, nor have we the experience of the field to do so, but they form an important pointer to the possibilities for the body to control sound improvisation.

We can conclude by discussing some of the few Western works which have directly sought to exploit the potentials of reciprocal improvised interaction between the bodyartists and the soundartists. Rhythmic interaction is probably the most clearcut form of interaction in body/sound work, in that its precise nature can be shared to whatever degree desired. In contrast, musical transformation of a movement shape cannot attain great precision, or be so multidimensional as the original movement. A constraint with regard to rhythm is that most dancers have only a limited analytical understanding of it, and most do not read notated music, though it is quite common for them to undertake exercises in keeping and understanding pulses, and in maintaining varied meters against a single constant pulse, or using non-metrical patterns (Morgenroth, 1987). This constraint does not apply universally, and may in any case be beneficial. Thus in the film of the Richard Bull Dance theatre (Bull, 1988) one of the works is "Artifact" (directed by Cynthia Novack, and using music of Steve Reich including "Clapping Music"). The dancers undertake improvised movements in slow cycles: these are out of tempo in relation to the musical score. At the same time they clap the (fast) rhythms of the piece, thus displaying both approximate and precise coordination at once.

In TimeDancesPeace, by Roger Dean and the ensemble Kinetic Energy (Dean, 1991), all performers work from the same score. This consists of the notations of mutlilayered musical rhythms which are gradually constructed in performance (see Figure 11). The performers are three musicians (1 saxophonist, 1 percussionist, and 1 keyboard player, using samples and sequences, percussive and otherwise) and two (or multiples of two) dancers. The work commences with improvised small non-demonstrative movements by the dancers (whose only referents are the rhythmic patterns to be delineated). The movements are subject at certain later stages to gradual expansion. In the tradition of previous dance improvisation, the dancers are each asked, if possible, to delineate two separate rhythmic patterns at once, within a common meter. Then the musicians join in gradually, synchronising with the dancers' meter. They too construct multiple layers of rhythms, and then everyone improvises together on the materials — mutually interacting so that a dancer can lead a rhythmic device, just as a musician can. It is suggested that both groups should introduce rhythmic pulse shifts, and these be developed in exactly the same ways as they might be by a group of sound improvisers. The piece goes through several cycles of this process, with different metres and levels of complexity of the contained rhythms. Between some cycles there is opportunity for freer, non-metrical improvising, and for very static moments, in which continued reciprocal exchange between the body and sound performers is sought.

The connotations of the work spring partly from the Balinese feel of many of the percussive rhythmic patterns; and partly from the Japanese impression that some of the small scale movements create, particularly at the outset. But these connotations are made more diverse by several superimpositions. For example, in some performances impressions of mechanisation were created through large but puppet-like movements; psychological detachment from the body was suggested by the juxtaposition of extreme stillness of the majority of the body with minute, but controlled, movements of a part. The connotations were sometimes overturned by devices such as rhythmic winking. Mobility between discontinuous rhythmic and continuous (non-rhythmic) movements was superimposed, making more ambiguous for the viewer the interpretation of discrete rhythms. The impression of sound as spatial movement is also enhanced in this piece.

Several other unusual features emerged from the process of this piece. One was the articulation of individual body movements into a wider range of rhythms than normal. It was also apparent, in considering the rhythmic structures of the two dancers together, that greater multiplicity of rhythmic discourse was occurring than is normal in dance. The work is also interesting because the body movements are articulated with much less precision than musical rhythms are by a percussionist. Thus the musicians can interpret the body rhythms before them in a range of ways, and possibly none of these would coincide with the dancer's rhythmic intention: the musicians can also respond more heterogeneously than they can to a musical rhythm. The range of rhythmic layers implied is enormous. The possibility of relating musical structure to transforming body shape also exists at several points in the piece.

This multiplicity of possibility indicates the potential of the improvisatory collaboration; and is another example of an improvisatory process enabling a degree of dissociation between a normal technical device (a body rhythmic movement) and its effect (c.f. Chapter 4). This is because the musicians may interpret the body movement as representing a different rhythm from that intended by the dancers. As we argue, such dislocations are one of the sources of stylistic transgression, and hence innovation. There is probably much further scope in such approaches, and in the exploration of the interaction between sound and body in improvising.

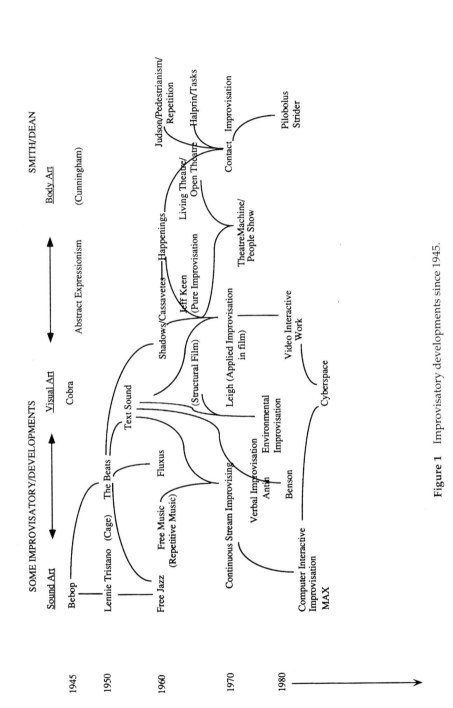

Figure 1 Improvisatory developments since 1945.

Figure legends are on pages 307–310.

155

1)

SCORE (for everyone) :	A	C	A	Z	A
RESULTS:					
Performer 1	A(n)	C(n)	A(n+1)	Z(n)	A(n+2)
Performer 2	A(n)	C(n)	A(n+1)	Z(n)	A(n+2)
Performer 3	A(n)	C(n)	A(n+1)	Z(n)	A(n+2)
...	A(n)	C(n)	A(n+1)	Z(n)	A(n+2)
Performer n	A(n)	C(n)	A(n+1)	Z(n)	A(n+2)

2)

SCORE for :					
Performer 1	A	C	A	Z	A
Performer 2	A	Z	A	C	A
Performer 3	Z	A	C	C	A
RESULTS:					
Performer 1	A(n)	C(n)	A(n+1)	Z(n)	A(n+2)
Performer 2	A(n)	Z(n)	A(n+1)	C(n)	A(n+2)
Performer 3	Z(n)	A(n)	C(n)	C(n+1)	A(n+1)

3)

SCORE for:					
Performer 1	A	C	C	A	Z	Z
Performer 2	A	S	NS	NS	S	S
Performer 3	A	A	A	C	S	NS

POSSIBLE RESULTS:						
Performer 1	A(n)	C(n)	C(n+1)	A(n+1)	Z(n)	Z(n+1)
Performer 2	A(n)	A(n+1)/ C(n)	A(n+2)/ C(n+1)/ X(n)	Y(n)	C(n)/Z(n)	Z(n+1)/ H(n)
Performer 3	A(n)	A(n+1)	A(n+2)	C(n)	Y(n)/ Z(n)	H(n)

Figure 2a Some scores for improvisors, and simple models of their possible results.

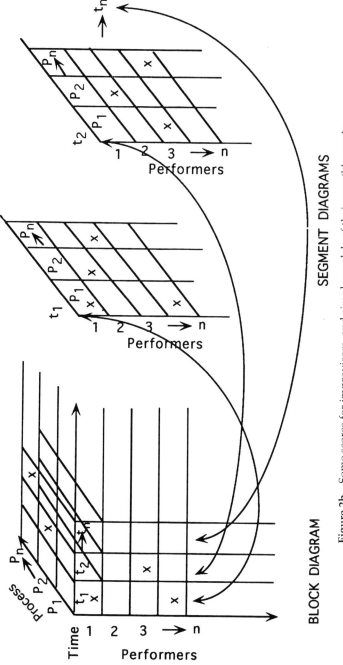

BLOCK DIAGRAM SEGMENT DIAGRAMS

Figure 2b Some scores for improvisors, and simple models of their possible results.

157

Cobra

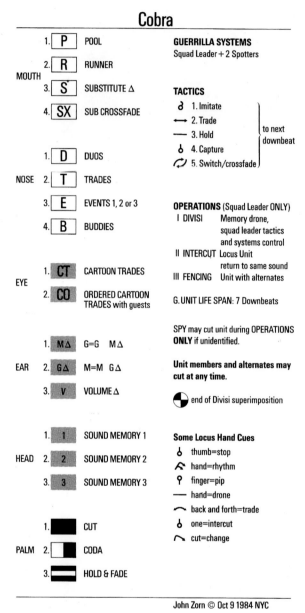

John Zorn © Oct 9 1984 NYC

Figure 3 Part of the score of John Zorn's *Cobra*.

what am i doing here?

since ive heard jerry before   i was prepared to ask myself
    a somewhat similar question   to the question *cokboy*
seems to have asked   which is   "what am i doing here?"
    the question has some funny aspects to it   one of them is
    i have no intention whatever   of reading   and   that
    would seem to put me   outside the general   scope of the
    genre   but maybe not   if im characterized by an odd
    futureness   science fiction like   which is a sort of funny
    pathetic position   the future   comes relatively
unequipped and bare   a dream of technology so to speak   so
    i came with a small tape recorder   and this is appropriate
    a tape recorder is probably more of a dream than anything else
    because they never work very well   but the point was
    that i was going to ask myself what i was doing here in several
senses   one of these senses is "what am i doing *here?*" in this
kind of ambience?   but what is "this kind of ambience"   i
    havent really wanted to be considered a poet   but i think that
takes refining to make clear what i mean   i dont want to be
    considered a poet   if a poet is someone   who adds art to
    talking   now i know there are several ways that people look at
    poetry   but there is a passage in bacon   where bacon says
    "if you talk about the manner of speaking that poetry is   its
just a mode of speech   and if you talk about its content   its

Figure 4   The opening of *what am i doing here?* by David Antin.

Steve Benson

1.

We'll go slowly starting out here
to get used to
the procedure.   We'll go slowly
                              starting out here, to get
I might quote from earlier works.   used to the procedure.
Stop to stub my toe.
Steve. Spelling?   Stop to stub my toe.
I might stop to appreciate   Steve! I return
the form of the line.   to myself. When I'm
I am easily hurt,   writing, -- spelling? --
but don't   I might stop.
cry easily. Change the words.   Appreciate the form of the line. . . .
Remind you of your part in this,   I am easily hurt.
now change the subject.   Don't cry.
Trees, for instance.   I don't cry easily.
"It's not a   I'm changing the words.
matter   I want to remind you that you
of necessity   have a part in this now. Each person changes
but of contingency," the text said.   the subject simultaneously.
                                    Trees, for
instance, balloons, cars driving too fast, over the
speed limit and in opposite directions, sharing the
          same lane. It's not a matter of necessity,
David says   but of contingency.
Steve is coming late winter or   Revolving over onto
early spring.   the other side of the page, into
In what

Figure 5   The opening of Steve Benson's *Back*.

Figure 6 Andy Goldsworthy's *Tossing Sticks in the Air* (1980).

■ BOB COBBING

Worm

rust	moth	fungus	mildew
dryrot	canker	maggot	WORM
wriggle	coil	roll curl	buckle
twine twirl	twist wind	spiral	WORM
hunt fish	ferret	root out	fathom
unearth	disinter	grub up	WORM
ingratiate	insinuate	intrude	invade
permeate	interpenetrate	infiltrate	WORM
crumbling	mouldering	rotted	blighted
decayed	corrupted	tainted	WORM
corpse	carcass	cadaver	carrion
dust earth	ashes	mummy	WORM

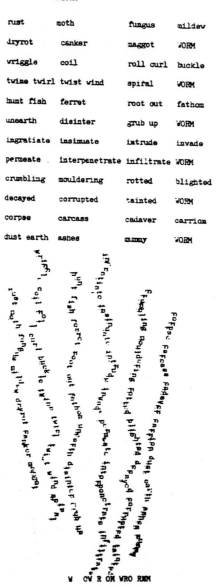

Figure 7 *Worm* by Bob Cobbing.

162

INTERRUPTED NAP

a verbal/pre-verbal landscape

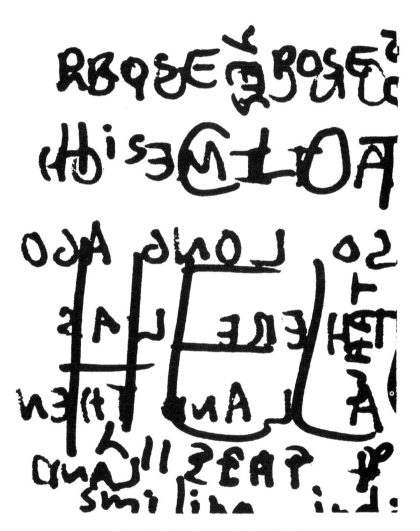

Figure 8 Part of a score by bp nichol.

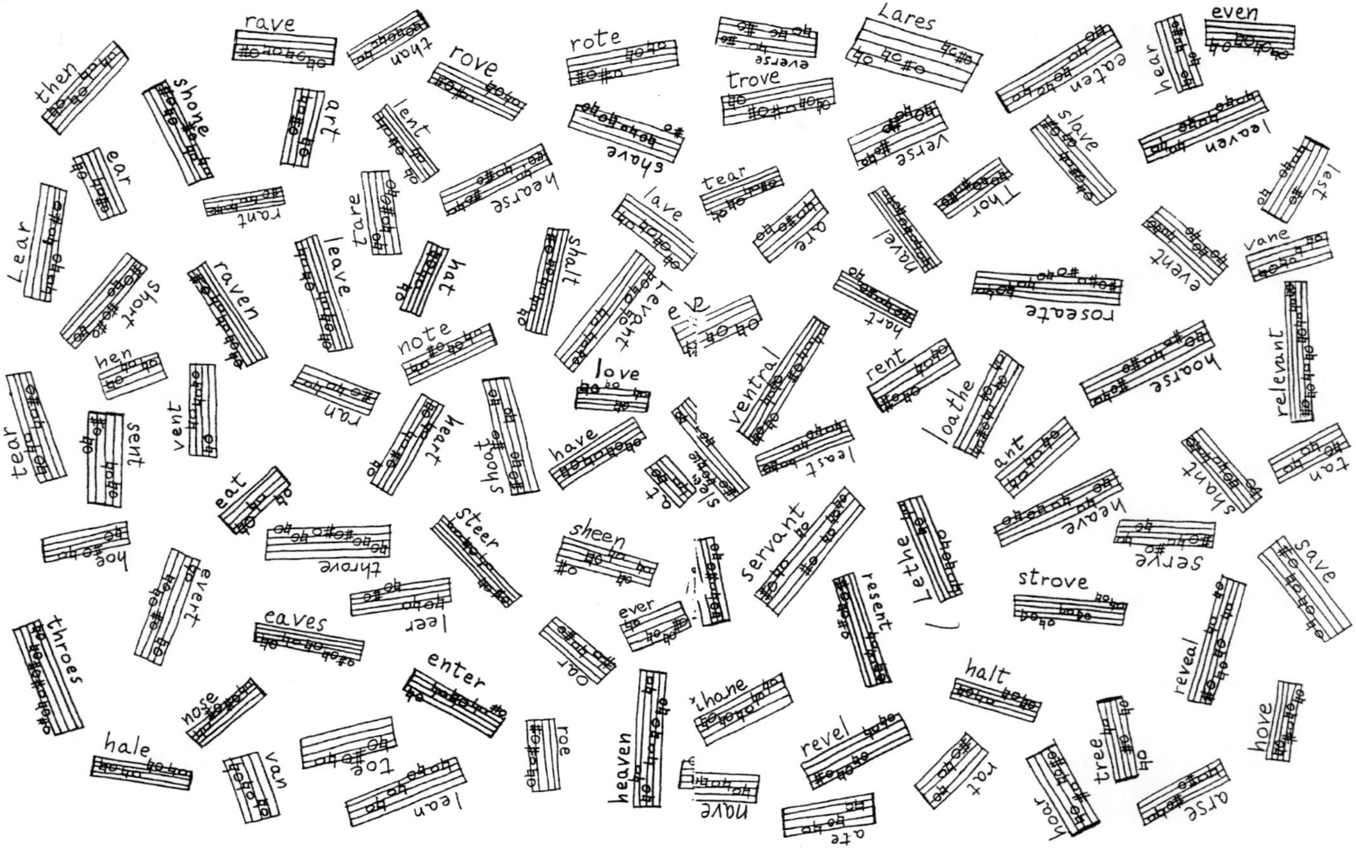

Figure 9 Part of Jackson Mac Low's *A Notated Vocabulary for Eve Rosenthal.* Copyright © 1978 by Jackson Mac Low – all rights reserved.

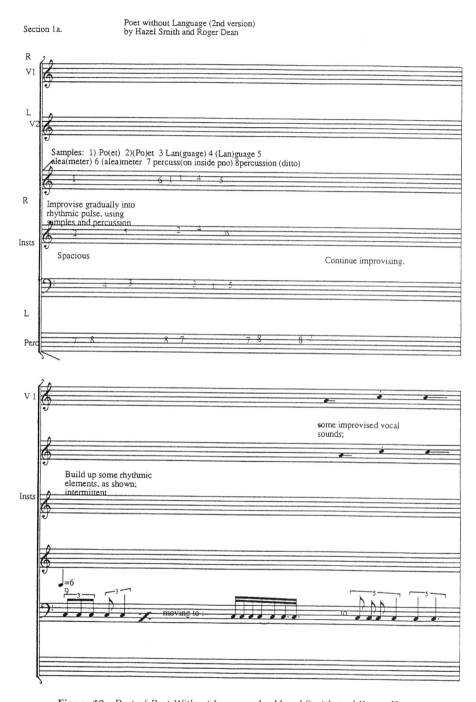

Figure 10 Part of *Poet Without Language* by Hazel Smith and Roger Dean.

This section could be performed faster, if wished: either crotchet 90 or 120, but just as strictly as at the slower tempo.

For Kinetic Energy and austraLYSIS. Commissioned by Kinetic Energy with funds from the Australia Council.

Figure 11 Part of *TimeDancesPeace* by Roger Dean.

166

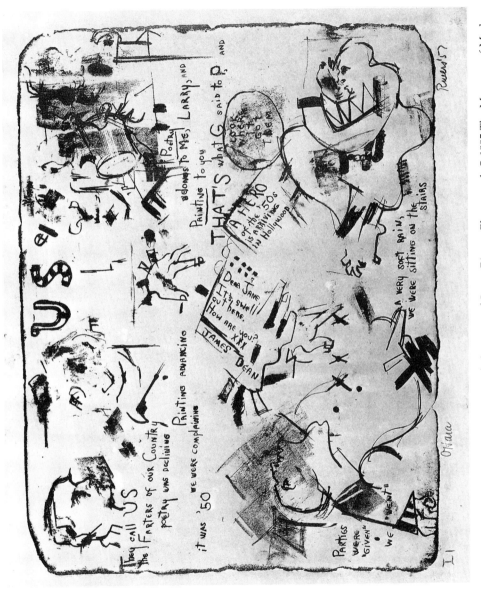

Figure 12 *US*, 1957, from *Stones*, by Frank O'Hara and Larry Rivers. Photograph © 1995 The Museum of Modern Art, New York.

Figure 13 Graham Jones wearing a *TranceFIGUREd Spirit* bodypiece by Sieglinde Karl.

Figure 14 Kinetic Energy in action (from *Who Lives?*, 1993). © Denise Davis.

Figure 15 cris cheek in performance in *Institutional Dim* (1993). Photo: Jim Harold.

Figure 16 *High Speed Gaz for Dave Curtis* by Jeff Keen.

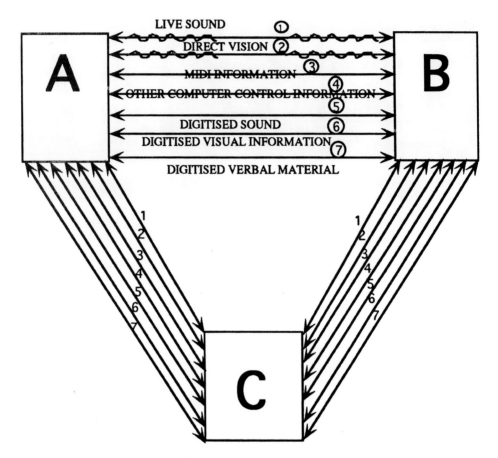

Figure 17   A hypothetical improvisors' network.

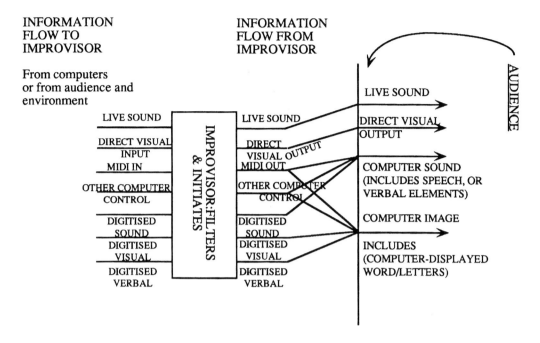

Figure 18 A solo improvisor at work.

IMPROVISATION IN BIMEDIA.
2: WORD/VISUAL; WORD/BODY; VISUAL/BODY

Word/Visual

Word/visual improvising exploits the differences and similarities between linguistic and visual systems by close interaction between artists participating in both fields. The previous summary of the properties of linguistic and visual systems will have given some idea of the possibilities this might suggest to artists coming together from different spheres. As we have seen, language is a system of discrete elements while a painting is not. Painting is richer in iconic signs (signs which resemble their referents), while language is richer in symbolic signs (signs which have no necessary relationship with their referent). But both systems are conventional: for example an iconic sign only resembles its referent, it is not identical with it. This means that both poetry and painting (or other forms of text and image) are mixed sign systems containing iconic and symbolic signs (Steiner, 1982). This balance between iconic and symbolic signs is not fixed within the particular medium, or fixed within individual art works. So there is the possibility of semiotic exchange between the two systems, of the balance of different signs changing between them, causing one to take on more overtly the characteristics of the other. This is particularly likely to happen in situations where two artists from different disciplines work in close proximity and fuse their efforts, in contrast to conventional illustration, where the image seeks to represent an already fixed text.

Another important aspect of the relationship between poetry and painting is that painting is usually considered a more spatial medium, and poetry a more temporal one. In this view, a painting manifests simultaneous relationships between elements within the painting surface, while the construction and perception of language is gradual in time. However, this opposition can be deconstructed: a painting is both painted and viewed in the temporal as well as the spatial dimension, since a complex configuration of signs cannot be simultaneously perceived in its entirety. On the other hand any creation or reception of a poem includes some simultaneous appreciation and consideration of its different elements. Word/visual improvising can extend this relationship between the spatial and the temporal by moving the creation of text-images between the two.

Word/visual improvising, therefore, opens up a special opportunity to explore the relationship between text and image, forcing each artist to enter an unfamiliar sphere. In working side by side and in immediate response to each other, visual artists and poets/writers are forced to confront the properties of the other medium in a way which is very different from direct illustration. Text and image improvising, in which poet and painter sit down together and work on a piece at the same time, is not particularly common. Yet it is a particularly effective way for poets and painters to collaborate. One possible advantage of improvising is that the relationships between the text and image do not necessarily become over determined; they remain relatively free-floating. The end result is often neither poem nor painting, nor an illustration of the poem by a painting. Instead it is a merging of the two, a new form in which the writing is often a short, pithy burst of words which exploits the spatial possibilities of writing.

Responding to an image or text as it arises, rather than responding to it in toto, also makes for greater interaction between the two media. The poet writes down a single word or phrase, (or parts of words or individual letters), the painter then associates from the word(s) or letters: alternatively the painter makes a gesture which becomes the basis for a verbal response. This is the synecdochal process we outlined in Chapter 2. Such a process allows for a complex juxtaposition of the elements, creating density and multiplicity of structure and meaning.

An important influence on text-image improvising after 1945 was the increased interest in collaboration between artists from the same and different media in the period. There were antecedents, such as the collaboration between Sonia Delaunay and Blaise Cendrars in 1913. Collaborations between artists of the same and different media were also common amongst the Dadaists, Surrealists and Futurists (see Chapter 5; and (McCabe, 1984)). Furthermore, collaboration was central to Cobra (Chapter 5) and their aesthetic of democratising art. The poet Dotremont collaborated with Jorn, Corneille, Appel, Alechinsky, Atlan and the Flemish writer-painter Hugo Claus, in text-image collaborations known as "word-pictures".

The Surrealists, Dadaists and Futurists were also significant influences on poet Frank O'Hara, and artists Larry Rivers and Norman Bluhm (known as second generation Abstract Expressionists or painters of the New York School). The close rapport of technical interests was important here as a basis for the collaborations, but so was the opportunity to extend social life into art. To O'Hara and Rivers, collaborating was part of a longstanding friendship, and an intermittent homosexual relationship. This developed into an artistic collaboration in 1957 when Tanya Grossman, who started a lithography studio, asked Rivers and O'Hara to create a set of lithographs for her. The result was "Stones": 13 lithographs printed in black from one stone (1957–1959). They are in the special collection of the Museum of Modern Art in New York, and some are reproduced in (Perloff, 1977; McCabe, 1984). These lithographs function as a set stylistically, but are not held together by any overall theme. Though the whole set took some time to make, individual lithographs are the result of particular occasions: brief, provisional, one-offs.

Similarly, the (non-sexual) friendship of Bluhm and O'Hara paved the way for their "Poem Paintings" which took place in New York in 1960 as a result of social meetings at Bluhm's studio on Sunday mornings. Bluhm claims that they were "not a serious art project" ((Perloff, 1977) p. 106), perhaps succumbing to the conventional idea that improvisation is not art. Shared social and artistic background was central to both the Bluhm/ and Rivers/ O'Hara collaborations, which are full of in-jokes and personal references. They exude a camp aesthetic typical of New York before the Stonewall Riots of 1969, characterised by exaggeration, ironising, trivialising the serious and making the serious trivial. They can also be aligned with "art as liberating play" which Sally Banes views as an integral part of the Sixties avant-garde:

> The artists aimed to restore to both work and play a prelapsarian, precapitalist, unalienated role in daily life, simultaneously cementing the bonds of community warmth and loosening whatever fetters were created by social structure. Furthermore, the artists proposed, it was through art that this unalienated vision could be realised — but an art that was playful rather than serious, in which public and private life were transposed or merged, and in which both work and play were freely chosen ((Banes, 1993) p. 140).

O'Hara, Bluhm and Rivers departed from the Dadaists, Futurists and Surrealists in their political ambivalence, which was a curious hybrid of anarchism, political indifference and liberalism, and in their postmodernist mixture of popular and high art subject matter.

Pop aesthetic and Dadaist experimentation also characterise the postmodern collaborations of Dieter Roth and Richard Hamilton in the seventies. In July 1974 an exhibition opened in the Galerea Cadaques entitled "Collaborations", which consisted of 74 paintings and drawings made jointly by the artists in Cadaques during the immediately preceding three weeks. These collaborations are different in kind from the others discussed here. They resulted in joint pictures and a subsequent joint literary component which emerged from dialoguing in response to the pictures: however, they do not combine text and image.

A more recent text-image collaboration was created very rapidly in 1982 at the Naropa poetry summer course by Karel Appel and Allen Ginsberg (Appel and Texts by P. Restany and A. Ginsberg, 1985). Appel drew, and then Ginsberg added words in a chosen colour, and the sequence was repeated. The process began humorously, cajolingly:

> Appel: 'Well just go ahead — any colour you think.' Ginsberg: 'I'm afraid'. Appel: 'It's all
> right, what you make is yours — even if you make mistakes it's okay, we can paint it up
> funny'. (Appel and Texts by P. Restany and A. Ginsberg, 1985).

But it took place in a spiritually committed context : this Naropa course was dedicated to Kerouac and his influence. This was obviously highly relevant to Ginsberg who then wrote "All yr graves are open"; referring to Kerouac's buried spontaneities returning to enlighten the world. The several resultant works were donated to Naropa.

There were several other contexts in which artists merged text and image. For example the concrete poetry movement (which arose around 1950) exploited the iconic properties of language, so that a signifier, such as "wave", was made to look like its signified (as in a work of that name by Ian Hamilton-Finlay). Many other possibilities of the relationship between text and image were explored in subsequent visual poetry (Wildman, 1969; Kostelanetz, 1979; Duke, 1981) or in the work of painters such as Colin McCahon (Gifkins, 1988) and Tom Phillips (Phillips, Bryars *et al.*, 1976), who used words as part of their paintings. The non-hierarchical relationship between text and image, which improvising can create, also contrasts with the juxtaposition of text and image in contemporary advertisement. Here the words are usually subordinated to the images, which have greater immediate impact (the progression in modern advertisements towards the predominance of the image has been well documented by Marjorie Perloff (Perloff, 1991)). However, both the O'Hara and Roth collaborations negotiate the relationship of high and low culture, but in a non-hierarchical relationship.

Processes and products

One of the most important features of text-image collaboration is the idea of immediately responding to what someone else is doing: Cobra often couched this in terms of an "automatic response". The method was a process of association which involved alternation between collaborators, and it took place as the poet and painter worked side by side. Corneille wrote to Constant in 1949 about his collaboration with Dotremont "Excellent work in Brussels with Dotremont. Blobs of colour I threw onto the paper sparked off a handwritten text for him (we each worked on separate sheets)" ((Lambert, 1984) p. 121). Dotremont recounted his collaborations with Jorn between 1947 and 1953:

Jorn and I had done a great deal of work over three days. We used small canvasses. Sometimes, I began to write words, then Jorn painted (all done automatically); sometimes it was the other way round. We wanted (automatically) to mix words and images...". ((Lambert, 1984), p. 95).

Likewise, Pierre Alechinsky recalled the process whereby Dotremont's and Atlan's "transforms" were made:

In my studio, Dotremont and Atlan would ask for a piece of paper — I had some grey stuff; with their colours, consisting of a schoolboy's box of gouaches, cracked saucers, a brush for each of them, some water, a rag, a lithographic pencil, they would sit down at the kitchen table. Without thinking, Atlan would trace out rough words in red, blue and black: 'If I get lost in the woods, it is only to find the forest.' (quoted in (Lambert, 1984) p. 95–96).

Photographs show O'Hara and Rivers working simultaneously on the stone, a process which Rivers described as being like jazz (Rivers, 1986). In documenting the process Rivers has also mentioned a number of features which suggest its improvisatory nature.

The title always came first. It was the only way we could get started. He'd write something, and with his charged breath on my neck to make something, I would think "What can I use in his words to continue?" I never entertained the idea of matching the mood of his words. It was always some specific object. Then he took what I did and either commented on it with his words or took it somewhere else in any way he felt like doing. If something in the drawing didn't please him, he could alter it by the quality of his words. Frank was almost as important as myself in the overall visual force of the print. ((Rivers and Brightman, 1979) p. 144).

Here Rivers describes the pressure which is generated by the collaborative process: "his charged breath on my neck"; and the interplay between collaborators: "What can I use in his words to continue?".

Collaboration, however, would have to be subordinated to the medium in which it took place and the difficulties it presented:

the lithograph stone surface is very smooth. The marks going on it are made with a rubbery, difficult-to-handle crayon or with a dark liquid called tusche. I had never seen any of this equipment before, and unless I was thinking about Picasso or Matisse, I thought of printmaking as the dull occupation of pipe-smoking, corduroy-jacket-type artisans. ((Rivers and Brightman, 1979) p. 115).

Rivers also points out the difficulty of revising on the stone:

Technically, it was a cumbersome task. Whatever you do on a stone comes out the opposite to the way you put it down. It is almost impossible to erase, one of my more important crutches. To change something, requires scraping it off the stone with a razor. One needed the patience of another age, but we kept doing it whenever my calendar of events and his fused into a free afternoon or evening. ((Rivers and Brightman, 1979) p. 115).

The Rivers/O'Hara collaborations seem to have been theme-referent based. According to Rivers:

> *Each time we got together, we would choose some very definite subject, and since there was nothing we had more access to than ourselves, the first stone was called US ((Rivers and Brightman, 1979) p. 115).*

"US" was used as a starting point, but the collaboration developed the many different aspects of the word US relevant to American society in the 1960s. It played on the idea of collaboration (the identities of the collaborators merge in the lithograph); it commented on the homosexual ethos in a homophobic society (artistic joining becomes sexual joining in the bottom right hand corner of the lithograph); and it suggested the United States (Figure 12). This was appropriately ambivalent: Rivers and O'Hara both felt alienated as artists and homosexuals from American society ("they call us the farters of our country") and yet identified with its rituals and icons (e.g. Hollywood, James Dean and partying).

In the case of the Roth-Hamilton collaborations the literary component was constructed using the paintings as a referent, but only in the sense of using elements of the paintings as multi-faceted metaphors in the stories. In "A Deserted Landscape", for example, the idea of the sausage returns in a number of different guises: as a sausage hat, a mammoth sausage, and as a "sausage appropriation" project. The whole is something of a spoof, turning the Don Quixote legend upside down and using a mundane object, the sausage, as symbol.

Some preparation took place in the case of the Roth-Hamilton collaborations. Hamilton, "anticipating a difference in pace", prepared some material in advance for Roth. The collaborations also took place in stages since the literary component emerged after the paintings. The stories resulted from improvised dialogue between Hamilton and Roth: they verbalised while looking at the transparencies projected in proper chronological sequence. A random (numerically determined) mix was made of the two versions for a final version which was revised only slightly, for the purposes of grammar and to make reading easier.

An important element of all these collaborations was their development away from the traditional text-image relationship, that is the image as an illustration of the text. For example, Norman Bluhm says of his collaboration with O'Hara:

> *we tried to keep the art as just a gesture (hence the decision to use only black paint) not as an illustration of the poem. The idea was to make the gesture relate, in an abstract way, to the idea of the poem. ((Perloff, 1977) p. 106–107).*

The result is sometimes an exchange of roles as described by Rivers:

> *We were fully aware by now that Frank with his limited means was almost as important as myself in the overall visual force of the print… Frank without realising it was being called upon to think of things outside poetry. Besides what they seemed to mean he was using his words as a visual element. The size of his letters, the density of the colour brought on by how hard or softly he pressed on the crayon, where it went on the stone (which many times was left up to him) were not things that remained separated from my scratches and smudges. (Rivers, 1963) p. 94–95).*

So improvised collaboration can merge text and image, setting up multiple relationships. In the Dotremont and Jorn collaboration "La Chevelure des Choses", words and images are less fragmented and less suggestive of simultaneous relationships than in the O'Hara and Rivers collaborations. But there are still several different points of contact between word and image. The words take the form of a brief but complex surrealist statement: "here the hair of things is coiffed with a finger of water", which is self-deconstructing. Reality is a hair, it can be styled with a finger alone, even a finger of water. The words are spaced and lineated within the fingers of the hand: "Ici/la chevelure/des choses/coiffée avec/un doigt/d'eau". They are written in bold black childish-looking handwriting, which becomes part of the visual effect. The fingers are partly abstracted into swirling wave like gestures, the blue background of the painting suggests water, and the brown colour of the hand could also suggest hair. There are several fingers not just one, and the whole suggests that reality is not singular or linear, but multi-faceted and elusive.

In the O'Hara/Rivers collaborations the interaction between text and image is taken even further. "US" not only ironically thematises the merging of poetry and painting ("Poetry belongs to me, Larry, and painting to you") but also involves their semiotic exchange. This takes place because of the exchange of symbolic and iconic signs, and spatial and temporal dimensions. Verbal and visual signs are pushed beyond their normal semiotic boundaries, posing the question: is this text or image? Visual icons of verbal signs abound such as the depiction of O'Hara in heroic pose which relates to the word "hero". There are metonymic links between the visual and the verbal, for example the image of O'Hara drinking could be seen to relate to "Parties were 'given' we 'went'". Text and image merge with, and e-merge from, each other in abstracted designs and smudges. Moreover, both text and image function symbolically and iconically. The words retain their (symbolic) referential capacities, but their iconicity is increased through emphasis upon their visual appearance. The use of handwriting, underlining, capital letters, blackened emphasis and smudging, strengthen their visual impact.

In addition the words take the form of brief, ideogrammatic insertions, which are more like visual messages than complete poems. Yet the images do not function as straightforward illustrations of the words because they are in part symbolic (i.e. abstracted). Many of the images, for example the triangular stripped flag-like object underneath "parties were 'given' we 'went'", have an ambiguous status as abstract gestures or represented objects, as iconic or symbolic sign, and are in fact a mixture of both. The visual and verbal meet and become identical in the sign "US". But this is both a symbolic sign (it refers to the collaborators and their country); a visual icon (the S resembles the US flag, and also a snake; the U might be a jug or an hour glass); and an abstract design resulting from the non-specific nature of the representations.

The lithograph also creates an exchange between the temporal and spatial dimensions of both systems. We tend to view the lithograph as a picture: the circular distribution of the images round the edge of the picture and the short terse nature of the text makes it easy to perceive the elements simultaneously. But the lithograph also demands to be read like a poem, though the order of succession is free and contributes to mobility of meaning. Text and image give the impression of being both still and in flux.

The lithograph ironises the relationship between text and image, popular culture and high art. Are poets and painters heroes in our society, or is James Dean the real hero because he is the king of popular culture? This is one of the thematic questions raised by the lithograph but it is also addressed at a formal level. The lithograph uses the techniques of high art, employing both portraiture and free gesture. Yet, in the manner of Pop Art, it seizes a format which suggests advertisements or comic strips, so that a postmodern montage is created by images and captions which do not seem to fit together. The tone of the whole is camp and ironic, yet has much profounder implications, raising the question whether it should be viewed as "serious" art or as light-hearted pop.

Finally, text-image collaborations can be public events involving improvisation by one or more of the participants. British poet and painter, Allen Fisher, on a few occasions painted live at the London Musicians Collective and Roebuck Pub while poets such as Bob Cobbing, Clive Fencott and cris cheek read their poetry. On one occasion Fisher collaborated with Paige Mitchell, in a painting with overlapping images which was a response to the poets' performances (Fisher, 1994). In a very different context the recent "food-paintings" of British performance artist Bobby Baker, in which she uses cooking ingredients to make paintings on the floor in conjunction with a monologue suggesting the restrictiveness of female domesticity, also turn the work of art into performance/event.

Word/Body and Visual/Body

> *...a piece becomes the story of the lives of the performers. So the context is changing and within that changing context, you see the life of a performer. We're not really working with any material except ourselves. Ruth Maleczech of Mabou Mines, (quoted in (Sayre, 1989), p. 79).*

Relatively little work has isolated these two combinations, word-body and visual-body, and thus they will be discussed together in the present brief section. While the category word/body is clear in the light of previous sections, it is necessary to outline the second combination a little more. What we consider under that heading are works which involve body performance, but which provide also a physically separable and dynamically changing visual element. Complex visual constructions such as film and video are considered elsewhere (Chapter 8, Polymedia). Overlaps are such that we will discuss a few truly polymedia works in this section, when they particularly illuminate word/body or visual/body relations as just defined.

Individual body-artists, at least those using dynamic movement, have usually found it very difficult to speak freely while performing, perhaps not surprisingly in view of the physical demands of the actions. Trisha Brown: "I could not keep track of my dancing while I was talking and vice versa" ((Sayre, 1989) p. 137). But the temptation to use word/body improvising to usurp the conventional position of music with body works (see Chapter 6), must have been obvious and strong. Thus Yvonne Rainer produced early word/body works (such as "Ordinary Dance" 1962, with an autobiographical narrative). In her work "Composite" (also known by other names: (Sayre, 1989)) she offered her "muciz", as a verbal "harangue against musical accompaniment" (to quote Sayre; p. 122). She herself argued: "I would like to say that I am a music-theatre. The only remaining meaningful form for muzeek in relation to dance is to be totally absent or to mock itself" ((Sayre, 1989) p. 123). Later, during the collaborative improvisatory phase of "Continuous Project" (see Chapter 6) she wrote "I want our speak stuff to be tertiary — someone else's material...... *as though* it is one's own..." (p. 123).

Verbal improvisatory processes, though limited, were a part of the performances of Rainer and others. One of Rainer's pieces "Some thoughts on Improvisation" (1964; Judson concert #14: (Banes, 1980)), also known as "Thoughts on Improvisation", comprised a conflicting monologue about "the free associative decision making process in performance", given while dancing. For Rainer "compositional ideas" had a purely "physical" (i.e. improvisatory movement) origin (Banes, 1993), and this was the focus of her monologue. On the other hand, in the UK, Mary Prestidge and her colleagues have used verbal discussion, apparently not heavily pre-arranged, and often about "feminist gymnastics" (Jordan, 1992), as in the piece "Rough Rhythms". The thrust of several of these works was highly humorous, but an improvised element was also triggered in the movement by the verbal component. The description "feminist gymnastics" implies the feminist but self-ironic stance that was often adopted.

Another improvisatory role for words in the context of body work (and sometimes theatre per se), springs from the use of constructed words, developed by Barba, and possibly originating in the Grotowski workshop (Goudsmit and Jones, 1994). Because of the dissociation between constructed "words" and the anticipation of verbal signifieds, it was possible to use these "words" with more varied and improvised nuance and emphasis. Related concerns were important in Peter Brook's work with his international company, leading to the "Orghast" and "The Ik" (Mitter, 1992). This work was undertaken by a group with members from many different countries, and hence with many different languages. Participants could retain some of their own linguistic identity while being forced to merge with the linguistic identity of other members of the group. Such hybrid languages have numerous implications; they can be seen as a return to pre-linguistic communication, or as the forging of a new "multiculturalism" which renegotiates national and racial linguistic differences in a language shared by, yet foreign to, all the participants. The idea of using a hybrid language, which was not initially understood by the audience, was a successful approach in several of Brook's rehearsal/development stages and in some performances (see for example: (Mitter, 1992)).

Another international theatre company, Kiss, originally based in Holland in the 1970s (Goudsmit and Jones, 1994), used languages which individual members hardly understood, to similar effect, for example in their work "Agamemnon". These performers found the dissociation of meaning from words quite acceptable, in a way which, for example, lieder singers might not.

Techniques for controlling word/body and visual/body improvisation

Kiss wanted to use multiple media, but the combination of body movement, verbal sound, and transformation of the space was central. In addition, they developed valuable procedures for controlling these improvised components. It is because of the emphasis on word/body and visual/body work, that we consider them further here, even though their work is truly polymedia in nature.

Kiss works often involved improvisation, almost always both in preparation and construction; and quite often in performance (Burnett, 1982). In performance, improvised segments were often based on pre-arranged referents, whether including verbal or sound elements or not, and the succession of these referents was triggered by verbal and visual cues. In the "Glass" series of works, these triggers might occur in any order, and the consequence was the necessity to develop all-round awareness of events, so that triggers could be immediately recognised by all participants. In this respect the procedure is markedly different from core contact improvisation, in which such all-round perception probably is and was unusual. Such broad sensory awareness is more commonly cultivated in sound improvising, as we discussed earlier. Most of the work was non-narrative, and in one case a video signal served as a trigger. Simultaneous multiplicity was a feature, even though some tasks were prearranged, and a perceived target was nevertheless "unification" (Goudsmit and Jones, 1994). Goudsmit, one of the members of Kiss, views this work as "live theatre", emphasising the complete distinction from video or other recorded forms.

Words themselves can readily be the vehicle for control of the succession of events in a body performance, or for audience interaction, as mentioned already (Chapter 6). Thus Maedee Dupree's 1977 work "Choice and Presence" invited audience comment, and this was used to trigger response. Trisha Brown's "Line Up" (1977) allowed instructions to flow from one dancer to the rest of the group, in determining the variation form, and also to discuss the progress of certain moves (Foster, 1986). And in her "Accumulations (1971) With Talking (1973) Plus Watermoor (1977)" she recited excerpts from two stories about an early performance of the solo she was then dancing, but the movement and story were disjunct, in a manner reminiscent of Rainer. As Brown said:

> *If you set yourself loose in an improvised form, you have to make solutions very quickly and you learn how. That is the excitement of improvisation...... if in the beginning you set a structure and decide to deal with X, Y and Z material.... that is an improvisation within set boundaries. That is the principle, for example, behind jazz. ((Banes, 1993) p. 211).*

Her ironic/instructional use of words, in improvised body and dance contexts, was also part of the work of Grand Union (formed 1970, and involving Rainer, Paxton etc), to which we will return in Chapter 8.

Richard Bull's "Radio Dances" (one performance shown in part in (Bull, Cornell *et al.*, 1988); another shown in full in (Bull, 1988)) has a recorded collaged text which controls the progress of the piece. The body work coheres rhythmically, using contact improvisation, call and response processes, body shaking, and hip-hop dance elements. The performers are dressed in colour and wear sneakers, giving a clearly postmodern appearance. One woman wears a dress and another is in shorts, so that their combination suggests both "feminine" and "anti-feminine" types of appearance. The tape collage is a mixture of snippets from radio programs, full of allusions to the mixture of dynamism, consumerism, violence, pollution, lack of communication, and neurosis which characterise American urban life. Beneath the surface energy, insecurity and sadness hover: a woman reveals her unhappiness with her husband's affair and his impatience with her jealousy. These anxieties are counterpointed with political complacency, a typical quotation from Ronald Reagan saying how humane he is. The tape is accompanied by frenetic body movements, contorted facial expressions, and frantic signalling, which complement, but do not "illustrate", the neurosis suggested by the tape. The tape collage is not unusual, but the combination of tape and movement is striking. At the end of a piece a musical quotation from classical ballet emerges, to which the dancers respond with a more balletic style, suggesting possibly another lost dimension, a nostalgic return to the past. Bull's improvising group sometimes invents text as well as body movements, for example in their ironic response to Tchaikovsky "Another Serenade".

The progress of a body improvisation is also controlled by text (in this case, rhythmically composed text), in "TranceFIGUREd Spirit", an installation performance piece by Hazel Smith, Sieglinde Karl and Graham Jones, first performed in Launceston, Tasmania in 1990 (Smith, Karl *et al.*, 1990). Although this was technically a polymedia work, we have chosen to discuss the texts and the improvised bodywork here. The texts, written and performed by Smith, were more like mosaics of words than conventional poems and were relatively fixed, though they were written in a way which emphasised semantic multiplicity. This meant that the movement performer, Jones, could easily respond to the possibilities of meaning differently in consecutive performances. Similarly the huge bodyworks worn by Jones and designed by Karl (made from unusual materials such as paper, bark, newspaper, and acacia and willow), were inscribed with words which could be activated in different ways each time. This was particularly the case in the first section of the piece "Signed Original Since", where the performer wore a voluminous bodywork made up of thin crinkly airmail paper from the "Guardian Weekly" of the time. The newspaper print referred to contemporaneous events such as the break up of Eastern Europe, but some words from the rhythmic text and freer visual gestures were also boldly superimposed in paint. The newspaper piece was moved into a swirling array of continuously changing patterns by Jones, making the prominence of particular painted words, and their relationship to the performed text, unpredictable (Figure 13). Jones could also choose to respond to, or ignore, the rhythmic propulsion of the text, which lurched between regular 3/4 and 4/4 rhythms and irregular 3/16 rhythms. The visual and verbal elements of the text create a tension between tribal and western culture, material and spiritual values, and past and present civilisations. This tension is set in motion by the movements which, both in themselves, and in the way they activate the words, produce new meanings each time.

Bill T. Jones has operated at the interface between the word/body and visual/body duo media. He has performed with texts, such as some of Jenny Holzer, and he has commented on the influence on him of "non-narrative filmmakers such as Mike Snow" (Banes and Blackwood, 1988). Accordingly, he has often controlled the interrelation between text and movement, and in several ways. His performance in the same "Studio Project" event as discussed earlier (Paxton and Jones, 1983) formed an interesting example. There he presented "Coffee", talking repetitively about how he "posted them there missiles on that hill", thereby possibly referring to US nuclear power, and anticipating a sexual drive. He then asked in an apparent dialogue : "Have you got somethin'? What? In case". This can be viewed as representing both gay and heterosexual events, in which the first questioner is concerned whether appropriate protection (against disease or procreation) will be available in the event of subsequent sexual activity. Jones' stance and movement reflect successively the disparate sexual attitudes his words embody. In the subsequent public discussion he indicated that this text had been improvised and also emphasised the influence of Afro-American culture and gayness, and his commitment to both.

His other performance on this occasion was "Excerpts to Brahms", a polymedia work which involved sound, body and visual elements and so could appear in Chapter 8. However, because the piece involved object manipulation, it is useful to discuss the piece here. During the performance Jones picked up and threw around a plaster head which suggested a Roman statue. This repeated classical reference was open to a variety of interpretations. It could represent the rejection of some classical ballet conventions, or equally Jones' position as a gay man, of necessary revolt against contemporary power structures. In agreement with this, Jones says articulately and convincingly on the film (Paxton and Jones, 1983) that he is "trying to deal with poetics" and to "transform himself and his targets" through "shamanistic" processes. He also wants to quote previous styles, and thus be a "modernist eclectic". His dancing suggests a post-contact improvisation return to the concept of "style", and the idea of the body as beautiful, in the context of the body as black and gay. His style incorporates Asian and African-suggestive movements with quotations from the balletic repertoire.

Shifting further towards the visual dimension, Robert Wilson's "Einstein on the Beach" (mid-seventies) involves a multiplicity of elements, including progressive and repetitive architectural construction of the chairs and other objects which are moved during the performance. These are combined with dance, theatrical and other visual elements. The dance component moves in a separate frame, in some ways conflicting with the architectural and visual elements, but involving a two fold repetition, the second of which includes substantial improvisation. According to Wilson "they break apart the space" (Obenhags, 1985). Thus the improvisation operates at least on the levels of movement of bodies, and alteration of the visual environment and its perception. This work is polymedia in nature, like most of Wilson's (and it includes Phil Glass' music). But it is important to consider here in relation to visual/body work, because it is an unusual example in which the body work is used partly to manipulate the visual environment improvisatorily.

Kinetic Energy, the Australian multimedia company which started in the early 1970s, has as its focus dance and theatre, through the varied backgrounds of its two core members (Graham Jones: The Place in London, Rambert Ballet, Cunningham, Trisler, Louis; Jepke Goudsmit: Grotowski, Kiss). One of their most remarkable performances, a section of the work "Eccentrics" created in 1987, involves an elaborate improvisation using an invalid wheel chair, which challenges the social construction of the disabled as helpless and immobile. This usage is in common with some previous contact improvisations, and particularly with the invalid contact improvisation movement (Novack, 1990). In Kinetic Energy's piece, the chair is made as integral to the visual structures as the body forms. The influence of Paxton and Pilobolus, is spread here to a further dimension of objects and constructions (Figure 14). In many performances in the early 80s, given in supermarkets and colleges, Kinetic Energy would collect visual "material" from people in queues, and manipulate it as they moved down escalator hand-grips, or across the upper areas of dining room spaces. They have also on occasion cunningly manipulated the audience role by offering both "hot" and "cold" spots in their loft performing space, The Edge, in Sydney. The audience members may find themselves actively involved at various levels in the performance, according to their choice of seating : for example, if they sit in seats which become a "park bench", they may enter the verbal dialogue; while sitting in other seats, they may be (gently) converted into performers. More important is that audience location can be controlled so that it contributes to the visual effect of the whole event and audience perception of it. Like others mentioned in this book, Kinetic Energy recognise the importance and impact of transferring to an audience the awareness that the performers are improvising (Goudsmit and Jones, 1994).

Visual objects can also be used as catalysts of audience participation. Maedee Dupree's "Overall White", performed at the Serpentine Gallery in London in 1977, involved images of "statues" which were given to the spectators. The audience was invited to throw objects onto the performing floor when Dupree formed a body image which corresponded to one of these "statues". Visual objects were also offered as part of Fenley's "Hemispheres": "portable decor" by Francesco Clemente, in the form of envelopes of cards, was given to the audience, who could use them as they wished. The cards depicted bound and mutilated bodies (Anderson, 1987).

The complex relations between word/body and visual/body improvising are of course central to many polymedia, and we will return to them in chapter 8.

8

IMPROVISATION IN POLYMEDIA

General Issues of Polymedia: Semiotics

In this section of the book we deal with polymedia, forms containing more than two media. We are using this term rather than multi-media because multi-media is now most commonly used to refer to commercial and educational materials, and sometimes to describe a particular type of avant-garde intermedia event. Polymedia include multi-media but also theatre and film. Improvisation in polymedia obviously involves an interaction between several of the semiotic systems such as the visual, linguistic, movement, gestural etc. that we have discussed earlier. There can also be interactions with other systems, such as lighting. Keir Elam has commented on the consequent "semiotic thickness" of the theatre ((Elam, 1980) p. 45) and has applied Christian Metz' description of the cinema, "Different, perfectly distinct systems intervene in the same message", to the theatre ((Elam, 1980) p. 44). By now it should be clear how these different semiotic systems can relate.

Polymedia are therefore characterised by their heterogeneity and density; their capacity for transformation of and exchange between semiotic systems; and their spatial and temporal complexity. Criticism has spawned many useful frameworks of analysis for artworks, and these all have to recognise the "thickness" of polymedia. For example, Foster has dissected dance into the following components: the frame; the mode of representation (by which she means largely how the work refers to the "world"); style; vocabulary; syntax (Foster, 1986). While this quite simple dissection is useful, and can be extended, improvisation tends to bring these components into dynamic interaction and exchange. In contrast, in some conventional polymedia there has been a continued assertion of a hierarchy in which the lead "actor" and his/her relevance to the action is heavily featured ((Elam, 1980) pp. 16–17).

Improvisation in the theatre to some extent predated a greater critical interest in the theatrical process. Elam has argued that some of the best theatre of the 1980s was "processural", that the attention in theatrical critical studies has shifted from the finished performance to the process of its making, and that there is now a strong interest in documentation of production (in (Fitzpatrick, 1989)). Obviously such theatre is more hospitable to improvisation than other kinds of theatre (in (Fitzpatrick, 1989) p. 70).

Real Environment Polymedia

Improvising in real environments has tended to grow out of a dissatisfaction with the limits of performance within a constructed environment, and with the connotations of an event involving time limits, a closed space, and separation between performer and audience. It is also symptomatic of a deeper dissatisfaction with art as special category, and a desire to fuse art and life while still maintaining something of the specialness of art. So real environments can be a means of precipitating the interaction between improvisation in art and in life.

Happenings

The term "Happening" seems to have been introduced in 1959 by Allan Kaprow, to describe work which was designed to draw theatrical performance and everyday life together and which minimised barriers between audience and performers, whose roles were merged. Some documentation of Happenings and related Fluxus events is available on film (Wirtschaffer, 1963). These events usually occurred in real environments, often out of doors. They had several direct antecedents: firstly, John Cage's 1952 Black Mountain College polymedia event, which involved sound, dance, painting and poetry, and its successors; secondly, the work of the Japanese Gutai, a group of painters who from 1955 onwards undertook real environment events, involving broad participation ((Popper, 1975; Kostelanetz, 1980)). Kaprow sought:

> more tangible reality than it was possible to suggest through painting alone. I wanted above all to be literally part of the work. I further desired something of my social world to be part of whatever art I did. Painting is far too abstract an art, even when it depicts recognizable images ((Kostelanetz, 1980) p. 107–108).

In a Happening, the performers were asked to perform actions which might not be different from actions which they would perform anyway, though sometimes there was a particular rule that had to be obeyed. In the Kaprow Happening "Self-Service" in 1967 forty-five events had to take place; nine might take place in Boston, ten in New York and twenty-six in Los Angeles.

One of the events was: "People stand on empty bridges, on street corners, watch cars pass. After two hundred red ones, they leave." ((Kaye, 1994) p. 36).

Kaprow has said that:

> *Intentionally performing everyday life is bound to create some curious kinds of awareness. Life's subject matter is almost too familiar to grasp, and life's formats (if they can be called that) are not familiar enough. Quoted in ((Kaye, 1994) p. 37).*

Kaprow used the Happening to defamiliarise normal events and make them a new point of focus. He was also committed to a different concept of the audience from that in conventional theatre; not an audience which pays to come and watch a specific series of events, but people who pass through the street during a Happening or participate in it. As Banes indicates, Kaprow moved from involving audiences to doing away with them, as participants became both performers and spectators (Banes, 1993).

Kaprow was dedicated to the idea of impermanence: he saw this as fundamental to the American outlook of renewal, which functions both at the economic and philosophical level ((Kostelanetz, 1980). This idea of impermanence is symbolised in the nature of some of the events, such as the later "Ice Happening", yet he was not averse to events which suggested permanence and resistance, such as the Masada Event in Israel (these two Happenings were filmed by Nam June Paik, together with comments by Kaprow: (Paik and Kubota, 1982)). There were also "compartmented Happenings", to use Kirby's phrase, in which unconnected Happenings took place simultaneously by design (Kirby, 1965).

Happenings took hold in many countries, and in 1966 in France Ben Vautier characterised them in a text called "Valid for the 13th April 1966". His five principal characteristics of "the extra-pictorial Happening" included "a series of unusual events whose basic framework is planned, though the details are improvised; a generally amateurish quality in the presentation". Vautier was also involved in the overlapping Fluxus movement. Fluxus events are not discussed in detail here because, like Happenings, they bear a limited relationship to improvisation. The movement was also highly diffused, and uncontrolled, in the sense that many associated themselves with it in performance for no specific reasons. Introductory information on Fluxus is available in (Banes, 1993) and one of its classic texts, containing performance pieces and background, is edited by La Monte Young (Young, 1962).

Happenings have a somewhat tangential connection with improvisation, in that they usually consist of instructions which must be carried out with only limited scope for innovation by the performer, and Kaprow himself has been reluctant to call them improvisations. Nevertheless, Happenings were related to improvisations in that they were unscripted and occurred in real-time: in addition Kaprow insisted that they should not be repeated. There was also considerable latitude for the participant in how any particular action was performed within the given rules. However, even an elaborate composition for improvisors almost always gives to them the opportunity to superimpose their own intentions, whereas the instructions for a Happening usually do not. Happenings, therefore, generally involve a restricted form of improvisation.

Grotowski: paratheatre

Jerzy Grotowski's whole career has been an exploration of what theatre can be, and improvisation has been one of his means. (We give some background information on him later in this Chapter, where theatre is discussed.) Grotowski's thinking has been strongly influenced by Eastern philosophies, and he has searched for a wholeness which avoids the division into mind/ body, and for a fuller sense of self than that provided by acting a role. However, Grotowski's paratheatrical work (from the early 70s onwards) was an expression of dissatisfaction with the theatrical environment, of his desire to break out of the confines of theatre altogether. As Grotowski's work evolved, "meetings", often in rural settings, replaced rehearsals and performances, and these meetings always implied improvisation in that there was no set script. The meetings involved isolation from normal living, walks, dances and physical exercises. They were likened by one of the participants, Ronald L. Grimes (who took part in the "Mountain" project) to a pilgrimage. Braun points out that paratheatre was controversial in Poland because it seemed to compete with organised religion, and particularly with pilgrimages, which have always been central to Polish culture and religion ((Braun, 1986) p. 238).

Kumiega (Kumiega, 1985) provides quite detailed information on one paratheatre piece, "Tree of People" (1979). This occupied seven days and nights, and sixty participants. There were areas for working, eating, and sleeping within the Wroclaw theatre building. Robert Findlay (an American participant) described the events:

> *The activities... were collective and improvisational, usually involving as few as 20 or as many as 60 people. It was not against the rules to sit and watch for a time. Grotowski... watched frequently from as unobtrusive a position as possible. ((Kumiega, 1985) p. 204).*

Grotowski Lab members first led, and later collaborated. Collective creations often lasted 1–2h. To quote Findlay again: it was like

> *improvised music created not only acoustically in time but kinetically in space… as jazz musicians are …we {seemed} capable of following one another not only melodically and contrapuntally but also through a progression of kinetic images. ((Kumiega, 1985) p. 206).*

Grotowski's paratheatre was quite different from Happenings, in that the participants were not given particular instructions which they had to fulfil, and there was much greater emphasis on individual creativity. In principle, paratheatre permitted the extremes of pure improvisation, and its influence was partly due to this possibility. Unfortunately, Grotowski was very reluctant to permit filming of either his repeatedly performed theatre pieces, or the infrequently essayed paratheatre events. So it is difficult to evaluate further the nature and extent of their achievement.

Other real environment polymedia

The "real" environment, as we have characterised it in Chapter 3, escapes from those spaces specifically constructed for performance, such as theatres. It provides a less restricted opportunity for spectator participation and improvisation than constructed environments. The Op Art movement of the 60s and 70s often produced outdoor works which were partly concerned with making two- and three-dimensional objects take on the appearance of movement. More important to our purpose here, it also initiated events, which encouraged greater audience participation than normal. For example, Mari and colleagues' "Percorso a Passagi Programmati" of 1968 (Popper, 1975) required all participants to walk a particular passageway, necessarily generating and observing a range of processes and events. Similarly the sound generating works of Harry Bertoia (some of which were constructed for real environments) may be activated by the audience in specific ways (Schaefer, 1990). The more complex, highly noisy, motile, and apparently self-destructive works of Tinguely can usually only be switched on and off, but are often to be found in outdoor environments.

Anna Halprin (discussed earlier in the sections on body work, and again later in that on dance) described the related concern of involving people with real environments in her "Lunch" of c. 1968. "I want to participate in events of supreme authenticity, to involve people with their environments so that life is lived whole" (quoted in (Popper, 1975)). The use of the term "authenticity" is revealing, since it confidently simplifies the issue of the relationship of art and life, while her work, like Kaprow's, was much more ambivalent about this. Halprin was thinking here of all the environments in which people live, real and constructed, outdoor and indoor. However, the Judson participants, Kinetic Energy, and many others have often concentrated on real environments, and taken their works out of galleries and lofts, and onto "rooftops, parking lots, or in successive locations, so that the audience had to move from place to place" (see for example (Foster, 1986) p. 119).

The constructed environment can also be challenged by using people from the "real" (as opposed to professional art) world, and having them "perform" in normal street clothes. This was the case, for example, with Steve Paxton's "Satisfyin' Lover" (1967). Untrained "dancers" in normal dress walked in apparently random patterns from one side of a space to another. This work was part of the emphasis of Paxton and Judson at large on normal (untrained) movements, such as the pedestrian ones, but the movement patterns were defined on a mathematical basis. Rainer's "We Shall Run" extended this control of pedestrian activity by producing multiple paths for running dancers, creating a rhythmic and spatial configuration, while Trisha Brown brought these ideas entirely back into the professional arena by making the dancers use the walls (Foster, 1986).

We have noted already that improvisation rarely uses the senses of smell and taste, and that the sense of touch is mostly used by the performer (as in contact improvisation or in the bodyworks of Parr, Brisley, and others). However, the audience-participant in many of the Happenings and Op Art events was able to use touch in an improvisatory way. A few improvisatory artists have tried, usually outdoors, to bring smell and taste into play in their works. Yves Klein's "Fire Sculpture" of 1970 uses them both in relation to heat, temperature and light, and the exciting performance works of the trio Bow Gamelan (1980s to present) add percussive sound, often derived from industrial objects in the unusual performance environments they choose (in and around warehouses, docks etc). More disturbing were some of the performances of Hermann Nitsch, involving disembowelling a lamb, which he described as his "area of lyricism" (Popper, 1975). These performances also had connotations of religious sacrifice. Nitsch' subsequent work with his "Orgy-Mystery Theatre" in part pursued related objectives. Such lethal work brings to mind the extremely distasteful genre of the snuff movie, in which the death of a powerless individual is not just enacted, but induced and recorded. In this, art and pornography are linked irretrievably. One can argue that ethical limits should apply to improvisation in the arts, as they must in other spheres.

In a major outdoor polymedia work "The Course of the Knife" (1975), artist Claes Oldenburg, writer Coosje van Bruggen and architect Frank O. Gehry vividly amalgamated many of the concerns we have outlined above. Oldenburg had been an active participant in early Happenings, for example with the Rutgers group. But this remarkable work, presented first on September 6, 1975 at Campo dell'Arsenale in Venice, was more focussed and aimed at a "dialogue between writing and sculpture, theatre and architecture, fiction and history" which produced "spectacular events, in which the arts come together to form a permanent weave" (from Celant's introduction to his book on this work (Celant, 1986)). Many of the set and costume components were related to the shape of the Swiss Army knife, which Oldenburg transformed into a plethora of images. This also formed the basis for a boat and its construction, and for many other components.

> *The knife became a visual metaphor designating the quality of activeness of both actors and objects. Through costume, it assumed human shape in the form of a souvenir vendor, Dr Coltello (performed by Oldenburg)... and by a dancer in his image... As a boat, it conquered the Arsenale canal. ((Celant, 1986) p. 21)*

In performance there was an outline script, which had been considerably filled in from the initial sketched time-line, but much improvisatory speech by key characters remained. Entries and exits of characters and objects were arranged, but the detailed actions were also improvised. Frankie Toronto (Frank Gehry) argued at the climax of the chaos of the work that

> *architecture does not consist in the disinterment of the ruins of the past, as the Postmoderns believe, but rather in the unsettling effect created by buildings that are born from "cutting and slicing"... For this reason... "real order is disorder". ((Celant, 1986) p. 26).*

One could even cynically argue that here the impact of improvisation is entombed: its chaos is the real order! We will return to the impact of improvisation on architecture, including the work of Frank Gehry, in Chapter 9. But as the protagonists point out in the book (Celant, 1986), this work was far more focussed and purposeful than Happenings in which they had participated in the 60s. Improvised disorder was harnessed in "Il Costello" to the generation of an array of non-stereotypic characters and their speeches.

Some community theatre work also takes place in the street, such as the work of the Death Defying Theatre in Sydney, which aims to create "socially responsible entertainment" and draws upon popular theatre traditions to devise works which are comic and examine Australian institutions critically ((Fotheringham, 1987) p. 154). While the group does perform in constructed environments such as universities, community centres and schools, it also performs in open air spaces such as showgrounds or shopping centres. Improvisation is largely applied, and follows a period of several weeks of research and discussion on a particular topic. But the performers do mould to the reactions of the audience: "this is a process-orientated theatre in which the community and the occasion can and should radically affect the work" ((Fotheringham, 1987) p. 156–157).

Polymedia Improvisation in Constructed Environments

Dance and performance art

> *One may write music and music but who will dance to it? The dance escapes but the music, the music — projects a dance over itself which the feet follow lazily if at all. So a dance is a thing in itself. It is the music that dances but if there are words then there are two dancers, the words pirouetting with the music. William Carlos Williams, Improvisations: Kora in Hell ((Williams, 1920) p. 51).*
> *Everyday the whole day from the minute you get up is potentially a dance. Deborah Hay, (from (Foster, 1986) p. 6)*

In spite of the movement towards polymedia forms, and the catalytic role of improvisation in this process, the generation of dance works involving improvisation in all the elements, sound, word and body seems to be very rare. As a result, the potential for using improvisation to create merging of, and exchange between, different media and their constituent semiotic streams has only been partly explored. We have in previous Chapters revealed these potentialities. We will mainly discuss here, by means of a limited selection of examples, the ways in which contemporary dance and performance has exploited improvisatory techniques in the component media we have analysed earlier. An early example relevant to virtually all these aspects of polymedia is the work filmed by Gene Friedman (1964) in which Judith Dunn improvises the section "Private" to music by John McDowell (Friedman, 1964). The other two sections of this work involved Steve Paxton and Robert Rauschenberg, together with public at MOMA, and the voice of Janet McCall. In addition, the film used time lapse, and overlaying.

We have alluded already to the improvisatory commitment of Ann(a) Halprin. Her 1967 filming of sections of "Procession" (Halprin and McCarty,) shows a remarkable fulfilment of this commitment in a polymedia form. She refers to the work as "total theatre", and it has composed and pre-recorded electronic music by Morton Subotnick, to which the performance moulds. As

Halprin says on the film, the elements of the piece are "equally important", even though slow movements often accompany dynamic music. The whole piece is an ongoing task, in which the costumed performers have to keep "moving forward", taking their environments (including large soft balls) with them. So they may become "movers of costumes" or painters or sculptors. They undertake walking through the "obstacles" of the set, of which the most important is a large piece of scaffolding. And as sculptors they may bring in pieces of new environment, which also become obstacles to be walked through. They try to make the process "visible", and the necessary slowness facilitates this (Halprin and McCarty, 1967).

Halprin's ideas in her works up to and including this piece are well outlined in an interview with Richard Kostelanetz ((Kostelanetz, 1980) p. 64–77). She indicates that the "tasks" in an earlier piece, "Five-legged Stool" (1962) were related to:

> *A concern for super-reality… This realism or blown-up naturalism, which grew out of the use of tasks, was not simply a literal translation of life. …What I mean is that each of us has an automatic stream of associating particular responses with certain actions seen or heard. …By blowing the lid on logical or habitual mental habits of responses, feelings of multiple dimensions became possible.*

Halprin says that she does not want the sound "to determine" or set up "rhythmic measures". Rather it should be an environment which permits a confrontation; the sound "crashes into" the performers just as they crash into the props they move and the scaffolding they surmount. Indeed the tape has at one point a pseudo-police car sound, implying confrontation, just as the screech and narration does on Miles Davis' "You're Under Arrest" (Davis, 1985). As Halprin says (Halprin and McCarty, 1967), "Procession" is a "journey" in the same way as the theatre is a place "to move through" not just "to enter". The whole suggests various types of biological, social and psychological adaption, in which past experience becomes a means of future problem solving, though only with effort and partial success. The piece anticipates contact improvisation in its body straining and body piles. Furthermore, the communal carrying of some objects can be seen as a technique in which people create mutual contact with the object as intermediate, and respond to each other through it. Similarly, several people wrap themselves up in a large cloth at various points, reminiscent of the wrapping and unwrapping of a car in Skolimowski's film "Barrier" earlier in the 60s, which conveys a related improvisatory impression.

Verbal control and meta-commentary were also important in improvised polymedia. The work of Grand Union concerned movement and visual elements, in such verbal contexts. Grand Union was formed in 1970, by Rainer, Paxton and others, and functioned mainly for the next six years, though its work and influence is also represented in some of Rainer's later film work. We have mentioned in the bimedia chapters the use of verbal instruction and commentary to guide body performance: Grand Union took this further. There were four roles in their work: characters, actors, choreographer/playwrights, and stage hands. But much was determined by last minute decisions, and real time improvisation, which sometimes resulted in body collisions, or periods of sustained inactivity. The audience members were "encouraged to compare {performers} decisions …with decisions they themselves might make in a similar situation" (Foster, 1986). Props were made to shift in identity, and there were requests between the performers, for example, to activate the music. The audience was placed in an ambivalent position as far as participation was concerned. The opportunity for participation definitely existed, and was utilised, but on some occasions the performers would ignore an audience member who tried to participate. Equally, the performers sometimes would ignore each other, so that improvisatory equality was asserted in this as in other ways.

Verbal meta-commentary has continued to be important in the 80s and 90s. The Richard Bull Company used narrative in its 1988 work "Another Serenade" with music by Tchaikovsky (Bull, 1988). This group developed 70s contact techniques further in the 80s, and remained committed to improvisation. Some of their work has been discussed in Chapter 7. The body work in their "Another Serenade" involves running wall to wall in the small loft space. There is also considerable "off-balance" work which exploits the role of a partner in contact improvisation in stabilising another individual's posture when it would otherwise be unstable. Foot pushing and body piles occur; however in general, direct body contact is much slighter than in the early days of contact, and individual floor work is emphasised instead. Towards the end, in a deconstructive and parodistic moment, Bull enters the performing floor from a seat in the audience area, and begins to discuss "his true feelings", "his feelings of the moment" and his wish to find out what he, a "happy person", is thinking.

Contact improvisation has continued to be widely influential within movement work in the 80s and 90s. As we have seen, it was initially presented more as activity than art work, in gymnasia rather than performance halls, and without sound. But some of the later participants in the process elaborated several aspects, for example, musical accompaniment became integral. Conversely, Steve Paxton and other former members of the Judson Group felt that the technical expertise needed for the fullest contact improvisations — in spite of the informality of their presentation — was already too great for an adventurous art, in part because of the hierarchy induced by an emphasis on technique. They continued to develop dance performances involving walking and running, in which a wide range of technical skill, from untrained to cultivated, could be used. Quite often audience members participated in group actions, which were inevitably largely improvised at the level of detail, and often beyond.

Contact improvisation was also incorporated into the vernacular of contemporary dance. For example, there is a regular exercise in contact improvisation in which a dancer throws herself into the awaiting arms of another, who catches her and transforms the momentum into a new movement, usually resulting in one or both parties reaching the floor. Sometimes the jumping person can land stably in the arms of the other, sometimes on their arms and shoulders. This procedure has become a feature of the choreography of many companies, a clear instance of the influence of improvising procedures on the general grammar of the form. Thus one can see Bill T. Jones on film repeatedly jumping into a stable horizontal position on the arms and shoulder of a somewhat larger, almost impassive narrator (Banes and Blackwood, 1988).

Events outside the US exploited this contact improvisatory influence too. For example, several pieces performed by UK dance companies used intermittent improvisation, with sectionalisation determined by simple devices such as banging a gong. They permitted freedom of style to the performers, so much so that the results were very heterogeneous even within an individual performance. For example, in conversation with us, Graham Jones mentioned several 70s works performed within Ballet Rambert which showed the influence of contact improvisation (the works were lead by Chesworth, Tetley, Sokolow and himself (Goudsmit and Jones, 1994)). His own later work with Kinetic Energy in Australia is discussed elsewhere in this book. The UK company Strider received the input of Mary Fulkerson, an American contact improviser mentioned already. Strider presented a series of "events" modelled on Cunningham events (Jordan, 1992). One (1974, Akademie der Kunst, Berlin) involved ten bursts of Richard Alston's "Rainbow Bandit" (based on the Charles Amirkhanian sound piece "Just"). Every five minutes, a visual signal was given for a "crossing" between improvisations (and other music involving improvisation was provided by Stephen Montague and Jim Fulkerson).

Contact improvisation with more than two participants was troubled and difficult, for the reasons discussed in Chapter 5, but could generate interesting asymmetric body-piles and pyramids. This became a feature of the work of several successful companies, perhaps most notably "Pilobolus", formed in 1971 by Moses Pendleton and Jonathan Wolken. They were Dartmouth undergraduates who met in the class of Alison Chase, who herself joined the company in 1973. Later in 1971 they were joined by Robby Barnett, who remains, with Chase and Wolken, one of the artistic directors at the time of writing. From the outset, Pilobolus used improvisatory and collaborative methods to develop its work, and the improvisations clearly sprang in part from the contact improvisation movement, since the catches, contact and body piles and pyramids were, and still are, a central feature.

The 1990 work "The Particle Zoo" exemplifies these ideas. It creates ironic relationships with some of the tenets of contact improvisation, such as the development of mutual sensitivity, recognition of body-weight-focus and equilibrium, and centrally of collective trust. The core idea of this work is that a group of friends treat an outsider to a sequence of small scale betrayals, eventually culminating in acceptance of mutual trust. The dance was choreographed by Barnett, Wolken and Michael Tracy, in collaboration with Jack Arnold, Adam Battelstein, Kent Lindemer and John-Mario Sevilla. In a 1994 season in San Francisco, the performers were the last three named, together with Darryl Thomas, who had not participated in the development of the work and was the newest member of the company. Movements which had been developed by improvisation and collaboration were by then fairly reproducibly fixed, and could be learnt by a newcomer. It is consistent with this that Pilobolus' works are in the repertoires of many other companies.

During the piece, the outsider tries repeatedly to join the three other male dancers in their activities. He is frequently rebuffed, often by the betrayal of his confidence when he starts a jump which demands a catch, but is simply left to fall, though the potential catcher(s) first make(s) as if to act. In contrast, the three friends catch each other frequently, and this often results in the jumper being at a stable horizontal equilibrium on the shoulders of a catcher, who then rotates him. At one point in the piece, when the outsider has at last been caught rather than dropped, two of the dancers are rotated at different speeds, one holding onto his catcher forcefully, the other hardly at all. This contrast of rhythmic speed epitomises the relationship of the dance to the very rhythmic music of John Abercrombie, David Darling and Terje Rypdal, Jean-Luc Ponty, Jan Garbarek and others: the sound and the dance rhythms proceed with no metrical coordination and in quite different frames, even though the dance rhythms are motoric and coordinated loosely with the progression of the music. The final event in the piece is the complete acceptance of the responsibility and trust the initial outsider requests: he falls from the ceiling in a horizontal position, and happily, is caught.

The visual environments of Pilobolus and some other contemporary companies are rich and luxurious, and offer the affluent attraction most audiences, even those unused to avant-garde events, can enjoy. Elaborate costumes, subtle and frequently varied lighting diffused by cloths and surfaces, and sometimes sets, are used. These components are rarely improvised, though again Pilobolus can be exceptional. The work "Rejoyce" (1993), a collaborative piece by Barnett, Tracy and Wolken together with 6 company members, uses balloons (eventually very large ones) as props which are propelled around the stage. A nice moment occurs near the end where one of the large balloons is projected into the audience. In one San Francisco performance (1994) the audience were entranced by it, and continued to propel it around the auditorium for some minutes after the work had ended and all curtain calls had been taken. This was a remarkably successful transference of the performers' improvisatory momentum to the audience.

The potential of improvisatory inputs and their massive influence on what have now become composed works, or compositional processes, is obvious from the above. The relative lack of improvisation in current full scale dance performance, in which sound, set, costume and bodywork is involved, is not a denial of this. Rather it may be a reflection of the need for dance performances to be extravagant in order to ensure high level financial support. For such performances, even the minimum feasible financial outlay becomes very large, since music, sound projection, construction, stage management etc are all considered essential. The reconciliation of these commercial pressures with the open-ended self-challenging nature of improvisation is very difficult, as Bill T. Jones discussed with Steve Paxton (Paxton and Jones, 1983). Jones also pointed out that the relatively slight financial demands of contact improvisation performances had coincided (in the 70s) with relatively easy access to funding, whereas the more expensive work of the 80s was occurring while funds were more difficult to obtain, and hence needed to negotiate with commercial pressures more seriously. But, as Jones also implied, the continuing influence of improvisation on many of the works displayed since the 80s is fundamental.

In other types of performance art, the works often escape these considerations of affluent style and associated high finance. We have discussed many examples of performance art in the preceding chapters, and here we focus on a few which are truly polymedia. Much performance art is not substantially improvised, and the field has attracted very considerable historical documentation (Loeffler and Tong, 1980; Goldberg, 1988; Sayre, 1989; Forte, 1990; Marsh, 1993). Thus a few more examples must suffice here to reveal the points of polymedia interest, paralleling those in the dance polymedia works we have just discussed. In addition, we have mainly chosen examples in which improvisation is used within all of the constituent media.

Such a piece is Mike Parr's (1974) "Rules and Displacement Activities Part II", which is available on film (Parr, 1974). Parr's work is discussed in detail in (Bromfield, 1991; Marsh, 1993). "Rules... " involves polymedia activity, including a tirade about "personal liberation", the "abolition of Sunday school" and the "bullshit of modernism". Decoration with ice, chocolate sauce, fish, and a jelly-like fluid with floating particles, is improvised on the bodies of four people lying on the floor. Parr presents himself almost as a group "guru", certainly as the leader of the event. As the event progresses he becomes active, and then (when he inflicts cuts on himself until he bleeds), the subject of the action. In common with Nitsch he undertakes the killing of a rooster, though rather inefficiently so that blood spatters on him and elsewhere. The relation between performer and film-recorder roles is emphasised by the fact that the sound man is also one of the group seen nude in earlier scenes. This work thus breaks some of the boundaries between performance and film, in ways related to those we will discuss later. It illustrates that film is not necessarily an unreal recreation of a real environment, although it has such potentials. The piece is strongly influenced by the anarchistic and revolutionary mentalities of the 60s. It suggests that an individual in a position of leadership can reflect and induce the whole range of psychologies of the individuals in the society of which he or she is a part.

Improvisation in all of the component media is also a feature of chris cheek's works, which are probably the most outstanding examples of performances with a sophisticated improvised verbal component. cheek's performances are usually solo, and include slides, manipulation of lighting (by himself), and the use of bodily gesture (Figure 15). This produces a subtle interweaving of elements, though the verbal aspect is still dominant. cheek, who was very active in sound poetry in the seventies, has been an important figure on the English poetry scene (see (Allnutt, Aguiar *et al.*, 1988; Sheppard and Clarke, 1991)). A vocalist, musician, photographer, film and videomaker, he has also composed for and worked with dancers. He is an almost exact contemporary of Steve Benson, with whom he has performed and recorded (Benson and cheek, 1979), and with whom he shares the particular involvement with verbal improvisation. Since the 1970s he has been eliding the line between poetry and performance with

> Instant Compositions made while walking on streets, riding in cars or on buses and trains (I might add as much as possible undemonstrably and without imposition, it might be performance but is not A Performance) and also those pieces generated in my home alone. ((cheek, 1985) p. 73).

Since 1991 cheek has used a dictaphone for recording these instant compositions (cheek, 1994).

cheek says that he that he "balances composition and improvisation." He also regards creativity as "fairly normal" and practices improvisation and composition in "cooking and gardening and shopping and looking and listening to the everyday." His improvisations are political in that they relate to "consciousness, critique, communication, engagement" (cheek, 1994).

cheek's performance pieces evolve over a period of time, and often start from an idea found through improvisation in performance. He sometimes records the performance and develops some of the material in subsequent performances which "cross-pollinate" each other. These pieces are subtle mixes of prepared and improvised material. Sometimes cheek writes down material improvised in performance and memorises it; thus some passages of text and complex linguistic constructions may be delivered without fundamental change. Alternatively, he may "ditch" the memorised passage in performance, "stripping it down to its essence in front of people", and he regularly enlarges or edits material in the performance situation, or transforms it through vocal delivery. He always encourages new material to emerge, sometimes through unexpected transitions between known materials. cheek says that he has a repertoire of moods, materials and activities, and that different aspect of these materials are brought into play at different times. He likens his processes to that of a jazz musician — he seems to be here referring to the idea of recombining and transforming "personal cliches" which we mentioned earlier — but he also assembles material which he draws on for a series of performances, and which is then abandoned. A series of performances is sometimes documented in a "final text", and there is forthcoming video of those performances discussed here. The final text is an amalgamation of previous performances, and though cheek does not rule out the possibility of returning to the material in subsequent work, it is unlikely that he would (cheek, 1994).

The three 1992 events discussed here are a performance at Brooklands College (South London) called "Skin Upon Skin"; another at the Cafe Gallery, Bow, East London, in a piece called "The Jitters"; and a third at the Holborn Centre, London, untitled. The stimulus for the pieces arose out of a radio program cheek heard in the early eighties, which featured the alleged voice of a twelve year old girl at a poltergeist gathering. He was struck by the strange quality of the voice and improvised some texts in response to this. Later when he was working for a literary agent he was sent a manuscript by Colin Wilson called "Poltergeist", which alluded to the same incident, and cheek was struck by some similarities between his own texts and Wilson's (cheek, 1994).

The three performances "cross pollinate" (cheek, 1994) so that material from one is recycled in another; we have already noted recycling in the performances of Steve Benson and David Antin in Chapter 4. The Holborn Centre performance, in particular, feeds on and grows out of the others. All the performances have certain features in common: for example one is strongly reminded of Shakespearian text and acting (with which the performances bear ironic relationships, as they all share allusions to England's guilt ridden historical past); and phrases, such as "king upon king, dust upon dust" or "the mark of a man's naked foot on the ground", recur. But material is constantly permuted in different ways. For instance, while both the Holborn and Brooklands performances include a sustained section where cheek jams on the word "gust", combining it with other words — and in one case with a slide image of the word — the combinations are different in each case. Again, in all three performances a standard lamp is used as part of the improvisation, sometimes free-standing, sometimes carried and swung around in swirling gestures. This creates various torch-like and lantern-like impressions (again there are shades of Shakespearian England). However, the use of the lamp is freely devised within the performance, and the moving of the light is most extensive in "The Jitters."

cheek's performances have strong shamanistic overtones, which are amplified by vocalisation, and which contrast with the Shakespearian projection. Indeed, he says that he has sometimes been called a "postmodern shaman" (cheek, 1994). The performances are very intense, and often suggest a mind pushed to the edge of sanity, while at the same time humorously debunking that intensity. The dynamic of the performances hinges on projecting a theatrical self, for example through narrative possibilities and theatrical allusion, and dispersing that theatrical self in multiple contradictory selves, linguistic play and fragmentation, and gestural and lighting effects.

The performance "Skin Upon Skin" is a rewriting or "respeaking" of the Robinson Crusoe story, and cheek created a score for the performance consisting entirely of words taken from Crusoe in chronological order. These constitute a pool of words on which cheek draws and to which he largely restricts himself (cheek, 1994). However, many of the combinations of words are improvised. The basis for "Skin Upon Skin" is Britain's colonial and class-ridden past, in which the black man is subjugated by his white master and made to speak his language. While an impression of character intermittently emerges, cheek breaks down any unified impression by projecting into the simultaneously multiple selves of oppressor and oppressed which overlap in himself. The narrative in which this character is engaged is also constantly broken up by other possible narratives and by a wealth of linguistic devices. These linguistic devices have special relevance because they represent the alienation of the black man from the language of the white man, and its concomitant syntactical conventions.

These verbal developments, which move between metonymy and complete dissociation, and between syntactical and non-syntactical combination, are also of considerable interest with regard to improvising techniques. For example, cheek sometimes disrupts the verbal flow by repeating a word with multiple juxtapositions, such as the jamming on "gust" mentioned above. He also takes up words and develops them by association through sound: this is graphically demonstrated in a passage where he plays on the word "lamp", permuting it and combining it with words such as "lump" and "light" which are connected in sound, so that it is repeated over and over successively with numerous alternatives. In addition he builds rhythmic structures which, though quite simple, are very effective in producing linguistic and sonic intensification. He uses repetition as a structural device, bringing back phrases such as "king upon king/skin upon skin" at various points in the performance to give continuity and to reinstate the narrative possibility. He also uses an exceptionally wide range of vocal delivery, from Shakespearian declamation to the free vocalising central to much text-sound improvising.

In "Skin Upon Skin", striking slides made by British poet and artist Ulli Freer accompany the verbal monologue: these are collage-based though some use improvised computer drawings. They were made in response to one of cheek's textual "versions" but sometimes they have no obviously direct connection with the words, though it is always possible for the spectator to forge one. Lighting is used to create enlarged shadows on the slides and wall of cheek's body, suggesting "the other" in various threatening or awe-inspiring guises, and creating new visual patterns. Body movements are extensive and provide fluidity. At other times, for example when there are repeated arm movements, they act as a form of intensification. The relationship between shadow, body, slide, word and gesture is a constantly shifting mesh of forms.

cheek's performances, therefore, demonstrate a remarkable convergence of improvisation in several different semiotic streams: verbal, gesture, lighting and visual objects. They are very different in this and other respects from earlier examples of performance art. Most significantly they are verbally and vocally based, while in much earlier performance art of the 60s and 70s verbal material was slight and verbal improvising rare. This was partly because many performance artists were reacting against the notion of theatrical dialogue and wanted to find other expressive means, and partly because the participants in earlier performance pieces were visual artists. cheek arises out of a different context, regarding himself primarily as a poet, and his performances mark a partial return to the idea of theatre, while simultaneously interrogating its norms of role and character, through parody of the theatrical tradition. They also reinstate narrative, though in an extremely fragmented way, and tread the line between high seriousness and self-debunking. cheek's ideological concerns (epitomised in the "respeaking" of the Crusoe story) also seem characteristic of predominant issues in the eighties and the nineties: the obsession with England's colonial, class-ridden past, with racial difference and the imperial enforcement of standard English.

Improvisation in the theatre

Improvising in theatre has taken place within both realistic and non-realistic forms, but it has a special relationship to avant-garde theatre. It can problematise the relationship between the actor and his role by eliding the two, as in the work of Joseph Chaikin and The Living Theatre, discussed below. This is part of the complex relationship in avant-garde theatre between sign and referent. According to Pavis "The avant-garde distrusts and tries to free itself from the sign, but always succumbs to it in the end" ((Pavis, 1982) p. 182). Improvisation can elude "the constraint of re-petition and re-presentation", as exemplified in the Living Theatre's wish to avoid playing roles ((Pavis, 1982) p. 182). Improvisation can also create a structure whereby one event initiates or transforms into the next, rather than one where events are subordinated to a particular plot structure. It may create complex relationships between semiotic systems, and may make the focus of the theatrical experience the relationships between the systems themselves, rather than an external referent (as in realistic theatre). It can break up the hierarchies within performance, for instance the subordination we find in traditional theatre of the other actors to the lead actor, and of action to the well-shaped plot.

However, breaking down conventional genre has not always been central to theatrical improvisation. Improvisation can work within the conventions of realistic theatre (and sometimes has, for example in the cinema and theatre of Mike Leigh, as we discuss later in this chapter). In this kind of theatre it may introduce more subtleties and detail into the portrayal of characters and their relationship to the plot. It may also permit a more creative role for actors, subtly changing their relationship with the role (they have more investment in it). In the same way it has played an important part in community theatre and in the international development of theatresports, in which improvisation becomes a competitive game.

While real time improvisation seems to suggest the most exciting and radical possibilities, theatrical improvisation has largely been applied improvisation. This has been part of the work of directors as diverse as Peter Brook, Charles Marowitz, Mike Leigh, Grotowski, the research theatre group Kiss and many others. Here the input of improvisation is vital for the development of the play, which may then become fully scripted. Improvisation in performance has been much less common. Frost and Yarrow point out that

"...in virtually all cases, as *production work* begins to become the priority, improvisation gets relegated to the 'back burner'" (Frost and Yarrow, 1990, p. 35). This is partly political: the need to produce a commodity in the theatre means that it is difficult to justify the time needed to develop works through prolonged applied improvisation. There is also a genuine fear of failure: the need to be a success means that people are not prepared to take the risk, and as Keith Johnstone points out, fear of failure is inculcated at an early age in our culture (Johnstone, 1979).

Nevertheless, real-time improvisation has occurred in the performances, for example of the British theatre group Theatre Machine, and of Kinetic Energy. Some plays allow for its partial inclusion, even where there is a largely pre-arranged script. While improvisation in performance opens up many exciting possibilities, improvising in rehearsal is also crucial because it means that the performer can intervene in the final script and co-author it, and that performer/performer interaction can contribute at every moment of the film/play or performance's development.

Theatre improvisation since 1945 and its accompanying ideas

One of the remarkable aspects of improvisation in the theatre after 1945 is the way it has evolved in so many different directions, from satire and comedy, through both realism and non-realism. There were many antecedents to this, well described by Frost and Yarrow (Frost and Yarrow, 1990). Although Stanislavsky's early teaching was not improvisatory he gradually became convinced that a director should be interested in the actor's process, and that the actor should use improvisation to attempt to penetrate the nature of his character. This became the basis of the American "Method" Acting taught by Strasberg and others. It was Copeau (1879–1949) who decided to abandon texts, and to engage with a twentieth century revitalisation of the improvisatory commedia dell'arte (see Chapter 1), believing that "improvisation is an art which has to be learned" ((Frost and Yarrow, 1990) p. 25).

In Poland Grotowski's early works such as "The Constant Prince" and "Akropolis" were mainly based on interpreting a script with considerable flexibility. However, "Apocalypsis Cum Figuris" marked a turning point where the actor's investigation of the subject matter became more central ((Kumiega, 1985) p. 155). Grotowski was guarded about the use of the term improvisation, but in fact improvisatory exploration was central to his work. In America the avant-garde groups the Open Theatre, Living Theatre and the Wooster Group emerged in late 1960's and early 1970's on off-off Broadway, at a time when the anti-Vietnam movement and the counter culture were at their most forceful. All these groups rejected the traditional relationship between director, playwright and actor, and espoused the contrary approach in which a script (like the Living Theatre's "Paradise Now" (Malina and Beck, 1971)), evolves out of rehearsal rather than the other way round.

During the late sixties and early seventies improvisation was connected in the avant-garde with a particular philosophical and ethical outlook. Improvisation was seen to be attractive because it involved a collective democratic approach to the theatre. As Paul Sills said "Improvisational theatre is (also) the closest thing you'll find to democracy in the theatre" ((Sweet, 1978) p. 20).

The Living Theatre, under the leadership of Julian Beck and Judith Malina, was influenced by a sixties ethos of gestalt therapy, mysticism, sexual liberation and improvised jazz, but most significantly by radical socialism, and the desire for social and cultural revolution (Beck, 1972; Rochlin and Harris, 1983). Beck and Malina were not dedicated to improvisation as a formal technique, and the group's texts (usually arrived at by improvisation) were not complex on a formal level. In addition, the texts remain quite similar in successive performances of the same work, as evidenced by the several excerpts of different performances of "Paradise Now", and one complete performance, available on video (Rochlin, 1970; Rochlin and Harris, 1983). However, they did see improvisation as an important political tool: they were keen to provide ways of encouraging the audience to engage with them as part of their program, which was the journey towards revolution and the establishment of collective, non-competitive endeavour. As a member says on the film "Emergency" (Brown, 1968), "there've been a lot of great solos — we're trying to make an orchestra". Consistent with this, in segments of "Paradise Now" there are body-piles reminiscent of those of contact improvisation, and of Pilobolus, but arrived at as an expression of collectivity, rather than of acrobatics. These masses sometimes incorporated audience members who joined with the group in shamanistic chant, body manipulation, and body carrying. In the complete film of "Paradise Now" (made in Brussels) the audience actively interrogate the group, and seriously question their ideas and awareness of political reality.

The desire for freedom in performance was part of a desire to liberate man from a closed capitalist society, and to show that the individual is not powerless. Working always on a very tight budget they rejected the idea of the theatre as a pursuit of fame and fortune. They were fiercely oppositional to the US government which they saw as completely repressive. In "Signals Through the Flames" (Rochlin and Harris, 1983) Beck and Malina discuss their work, and reveal the sources of more of their ideas. For example, talking of Jack Gelber's "The Connection", they mention how influenced they were by the jazz musicians, and their commitment to improvisation. They also allude to the role of Paul Goodman (psychotherapist, writer, Artaudian playwright etc), whose ideas influenced them, and of whom Malina was a client for two years. The psychotherapeutic component is even more predominant in their later work such as "Mad House Play" (1982), a participatory piece with sung drones, in which psychiatric clients are taken out into the street. Though they were persecuted for their ideas in the 50s to 70s, their attitudes and performances now seem pure idealism.

The Open Theatre was also strongly politically motivated. Joseph Chaikin, the director, reacted strongly against the idea of theatre as commercial enterprise. (Chaikin, 1972). He also sought, like Malina and Beck, to make the company as egalitarian as possible and to relate the work to contemporary political issues. The company opposed itself to the ideals of bourgeois theatre: for example, one actor comments (Rochlin, 1970) that he does not want to address "middle America" because he has no "empathy" with it. Chaikin was equally interested in innovation in the theatre and rethought many of the basic theatrical conventions. He rejected the idea of playing a role: "When we as actors are performing, we as persons are also present and the performance is a testimony of ourselves" ((Chaikin, 1972) p. 6). The actor should cease "putting on a disguise" ((Chaikin, 1972) p. 6). "An old idea of acting is that you make believe you care about things which you don't care about... Ideally, acting questions have to do with giving form to what one *does* care about" (pp. 10–11).

Improvisation was likewise seen by some other Open Theatre participants as a way of opening up the self:

> to express the fragmentation and multiplicity of experience, and the inconsistency of internal and external "truth" about character or events... to break down the actor's reliance upon rational choices, mundane social realism and watered-down Freud, and to release his unconscious through non-rational, spontaneous action celebrating the actor's own perceptions about modern life. (Peter Feldman in (Croyden, 1974) p. 174–5).

Chaikin also rejected the idea of the theatre as a reproduction of life. "The theatre, in so far as people are serious in it, seems to be looking for a place where is not a duplication of life" ((Chaikin, 1972) p. 25). Instead improvisation meant absolute alertness in both mind and body to the present moment. He emphasised exploration rather than pre-set ideals:

> Julian Beck said that an actor has to be like Columbus: he has to go out and discover something, and come back and report on what he discovers. Voyages have to be taken, but there has to be a place to come back to, and this place has to be different from the established theatre. It is not likely to be a business place. ((Chaikin, 1972) p. 54).

Chaikin wanted the actors to interact with each other and with the environment as much as possible, rather than to imitate an external reality.

In England, a number of theatre groups used improvisation in rehearsal or performance. The People Show (Rees, 1992), specialised in improvised surrealism and audience intervention. They included improvising musicians such as George Khan, and as their long-term member Mark Long says, in the early days they used "very free jazz" improvisation within the pieces (in (Rees, 1992)). Kershaw aligns the People Show with "the idea of carnival and the carnivalesque, the symbolic overthrow of the hierarchic socio-political order in a wild frenzy of excessive anti-structural celebration" ((Kershaw, 1992) p. 68) and photographs and other documentation of their work are in (Craig, 1980). Collective playmaking involving improvisation was carried out by groups such as Joint Stock, Hull Truck etc.

Improvisation also arose in a more comic, popular type of theatrical event, such as the performances of Theatre Machine. This company was founded in 1967 by Keith Johnstone as director, with Ben Benison, Roddy Maude-Roxby, Ric Morgan and John Muirhead, though the group had already worked together at the Royal Court Theatre in London. Keith Johnstone said that the immediate inspiration for one of their productions "Clowning" was the English music hall and that the group was "essentially concerned with making people laugh" ((Frost and Yarrow, 1990) pp. 56–57).

Similarly, in Chicago the group Compass was launched in 1955 by Paul Sills (son of the theorist and teacher of theatre improvisation, Viola Spolin) and David Shepherd. Compass was satirical, mainly ridiculing middle class values by scenario-based improvising. Each week they took new scenarios "rehearsing through the days" and performing at nights to (initially) packed and enthusiastic houses (Sweet, 1978). Before each scenario they created a "living newspaper", and sometimes they acted scenarios proposed by the audience after a short discussion gap. Once "a 3 scene play involving a mercy killing was plotted in about 20 minutes and staged immediately". Later they performed more fixed pieces. Although Paul Sills' aims were avowedly about entertainment, he also had the "highest" ideals since "mere entertainment is not crucial". He tried to merge these ideals with the work:

> ...*Improvised theatre... is part of the oral tradition... connected with story-telling... When you truly tell a story, there is self-discovery. ((Sweet, 1978) p. 23).*

And Sills again:

> *True improvisation is a dialogue between people. Not just on the level of what the scene is about but also a dialogue from the being — something that has never been said before that now comes up... It's not what I know and what you know; its something that happens between us*

that's a discovery. As I say, you can't make this discovery alone. There is always the other. ((Sweet, 1978) p. 23).

Paul Sills also stresses the openness of impro:

I'm not interested in improvisational theatre per se. *I'm interested in the establishment of these free spaces where people can do their own work, and I'm interested in the forms which begin to emerge in these free spaces... Finding the forms involves a combination between the spiritual and the earthly. It's an exploration into the unknown, into a world that one can't enter alone. ((Sweet, 1978) p. 19).*

Like the American political theatre mentioned above, improvisation has also played a part in left wing theatre in England. An early innovator was Joan Greenwood, whose Theatre Workshop, in the fifties and sixties, was a reaction against mainstream English Theatre and was viewed with suspicion because it was a group theatre. Theatre Workshop received no subsidy until 1957, and even then the Art Council's support was low compared with that to many more conservative peer groups (Goorney, 1981). In 1971 the formation of the Arts Council's Fringe and Experimental Drama Committee meant that more money was injected into alternative theatre, but it remained on a small scale.

Improvisation has also been important in community drama (Kershaw, 1992). John Arden's and Margaretta D'Arcy's "The Business of Good Government" was a one-act version of the nativity story which was performed by the villagers of Brent Knoll village in Somerset, UK, in 1960. Improvisation was used to develop the play which was notable for its informality and ordinary language spoken by mythical characters. Similarly in their "Ars Longa, Vita Brevis" (which was staged within one year by both the RSC and the Company of Kirkbymoorside Girl Guides), the play grew out of improvisations, and Arden and D'Arcy threw out their own original dialogue. Applied improvisation has also been taken up by the realistic theatre in the work of Mike Leigh (who has also worked in TV) and of other playwrights such as Phil Young, where it is mainly used as a way of building character.

Since the seventies improvisation has reached a wider public through theatresports, in which improvisation becomes a spectator sport for entertainment. In theatresports teams of players act out scenes, sometimes in response to audience suggestions and within time limits. The scenes are judged by a panel of judges and the team with the highest score wins. Theatresports originated from the work of Keith Johnstone (discussed below) at the University of Calgary, and is now played in many countries and languages in Europe, the US, Canada and Australasia. Certain principles underlie theatresports wherever they are played. In Australia, where theatresports has been active since 1985, these are known as the "ten commandments". They include provisions to make the improvisation focussed and yet flexible: "Thou shalt not block" and "Thou shalt always retain focus" ((Pierse, 1993) p. 8). The ten commandments also foster ideals of equality: "Thou shalt not shine above thy team-mates"; interactivity: "Thou shalt always be changed by what is said to you"; and attempts to break down self-consciousness about giving a good performance: "To wimp is to show thy true self". The techniques and approaches used by participants, and the principles to which they adhere, are largely based on those of Keith Johnstone elucidated below. These approaches have contributed directly to popular tv programs such as "Whose line is it, anyway?", and also to performances of artists such as Canadian Robert LePage (Gravel and Lavergne, 1987).

In the eighties and nineties improvisation has been appropriated by feminist groups, such as the nuclear protest group, Common Ground, originating at Greenham Common in the UK. Such feminist groups have often used improvisation as part of their collaborative practices, and it has also become widely disseminated as a theatrical practice among mixed sex groups such as The Sydney Front, and the community-based Death Defying Theatre, also based in Sydney. Since the 1980s feminist theatre has sometimes used improvisation as a political weapon against male theatrical practice. While there are no means of production which are exclusive to feminist theatre, there are creative processes and working methods including improvisation which tend to be used because they are more acceptable politically. Feminist playwrights who have worked this way include Caryl Churchill, Elaine Feinstein and the groups Trouble and Strife and Common Ground. This demonstrates that improvisational techniques tend to reappear in social contexts in which egalitarianism is stressed.

The status of the actor remained an important issue throughout the period: a number of the companies did not differentiate absolutely between professionals and amateurs; some also appreciated that the professional could be impeded by too much specialisation (e.g. Kiss: (Goudsmit and Jones, 1994)). Similarly, Ariane Mnouchkine's Théâtre Du Soleil in France sought an equation between theatre and life, and therefore initially used only amateurs. Later, in major works such as "1789", they attempted to involve all present at performances in their presentation.

Developing improvisational techniques in the theatre

A wide range of techniques have been developed for theatrical improvising and it is not our aim to detail them all here. Looking at the work of any improvisor or director in terms of the exercises they favoured is inevitably reductive; nevertheless, exercises were used (and still are) as a way of developing improvisational skills. Readers are referred to a number of books which deal with theatrical improvisational techniques (such as (Spolin, 1963; Johnstone, 1979)). Some techniques which are not discussed here are discussed extensively elsewhere (e.g. masks (Johnstone, 1979)). However, it is useful to outline some techniques displayed in the works of the key protagonists of improvisational practice in the theatre. We will note some additional approaches covered elsewhere as we discuss these key figures. Many of the exercises can be categorised in terms of the improvisational processes outlined in Chapter 2, such as transformational, sensory or referent-based.

Techniques in non-verbal sound
Vocal exercises such as the "chord" have been used in various different forms by the Living Theatre, the Open Theatre and Kiss, and other companies. Here the actors (in an exercise which is sensory in the terms outlined by us Chapter 2) coordinate breathing, droning and humming, to create a total sound and physical ambience within which individual sound and breathing becomes subordinate. Chaikin also used singing exercises and sometimes used a conductor to orchestrate the dynamics and intensity of a song ((Blumenthal, 1984) p. 81).

Non-verbal techniques: body interaction
These exercises are used as a way of encouraging actors to explore the expressive potential of their bodies and their relationship to other bodies. Chaikin's early "wattage" exercises explored the gradation between total withdrawal and involvement. An actor would start to do something in a state of minimal awareness, gradually increase the intensity, and then let it recede. The Open Theatre also improvised scenes in which characters switched on and off, both in mundane and in more highly charged situations.

Chaikin evolved many different exercises, borrowing from both Viola Spolin and Grotowski. Some exploited more fully the interactiveness of the actors, and these included trust exercises (now widely incorporated into improvisational workshops) where actors touched and explored each others' bodies and fell against and caught each other. These were done both with open and closed eyes, and were clearly connected with contact improvisation. "Mirror" exercises were also used by Chaikin and Peter Brook (Brook, 1968), as were machine exercises in which each actor becomes part of an organic machine (originating from some of Viola Spolin's exercises). Jamming (the term borrowed from jazz) was used by the Open Theatre to help the actors

in a representational genre, through improvisation (e.g. (Martin and Vallins, 1972; Martin and Vallins, 1973)).

Applied improvising as a means of exploring a script

Improvisation has sometimes been used in the theatre as a way of exploring and deepening the actors' understanding of a particular script, for example Peter Brook's exploration of Shakespearean plays. The film of Brook rehearsing "The Tempest" (Brook, 1968) shows that improvisation helps him to explore the play's enigmatic qualities. He uses such exercises as the "mirror" to help the actors work more effectively as a group, and "improvising a monster", whereby each actor reveals his own subconscious, his own monster (Brook, 1968).

Similarly Joan Greenwood rarely started to rehearse a play with the words of the script. In the case of a new play the script was usually modified during rehearsals. The actors would exchange parts and would be made to experience the situations they were trying to portray, thereby closing the gap between actor and role. In preparation for Brendan Behan's "The Quare Fellow", the prisoners improvised upon the dreariness of prison life. In rehearsals for Shelagh Delaney's "A Taste of Honey" the actresses dragged heavy suitcases round the stage and down dark imaginary tunnels, so they could experience the same exhaustion as the characters they were portraying. Sometimes Littlewood would make the actors improvise a situation which extended the characters they were playing and generated dialogue. This dialogue could be incorporated into the script or could provide the author with ideas and stimulus (Goorney, 1981). More intensive applied improvisation, developing empathy with the (pre-existent) parts in the script, was used by the Living Theatre in preparing Kenneth Brown's "The Brig" (Brown, 1965). This emphasised the moronic automaton-like nature of the behaviour required of the prisoners by the screws (the officers). Rehearsal periods were conducted entirely within an agreed set of highly restrictive behaviour codes, for hours at a time; though actors were allowed to call a rehearsal break when they felt it was essential. Judith Malina, who directed, has discussed in detail this rehearsal process and the huge psychological pressures it produced (Brown, 1965).

Applied improvising as a means of devising a play

Applied improvising has been used by many groups as part of the collective endeavour of making a play: it may be one element in a mixture of research, improvisation and collective writing. Grotowski's Lab Theatre frequently used improvisation in these ways. In preparing "Hamlet" (1964) they improvised whole scenes, according to Flaszen, their literary director who was in many ways co-equal with Grotowski (Kumiega, 1985). Similarly, "Apocalypsis cum Figuris" was developed by improvisation and only fixed after a long rehearsal period. Flaszen says that Grotowski had to learn to discard "expectation" which lead to "overmanipulation"; so that he could sit "silently, waiting, hour after hour".

Actor Zbigniew Cynkutis says:

> *I remember that he selected from improvisation points that weren't even important to me... he recalled... positions of my body or the place I was in — not* how *I did something but* where *I was and* what *I did... and when I tried to repeat it... I {had to} improvise again. ((Kumiega, 1985) p. 137).*

The Open Theatre's play "Terminal" (Open Theatre, 1970), constructed by the whole company but with words by Susan Yankowitz, was a piece about death based on the idea of accepting mortality rather than ignoring it. The company started with the idea of confronting the dread of dying. They also wanted to explore the way in which our society distracts us from death and disguises the natural process of dying ((Chaikin, 1972) p. 31–32). Preparation included discussions with an embalmer, and talking to Joseph Campbell about the mythology of passing from the living to the dead ((Chaikin, 1972) p. 29–33).

Improvisation was often used by the Open Theatre as a process of trial and error whereby ideas were discovered and explored, though the basis for the improvisations might be quite specific (Blumenthal, 1984). In collective work which preceded "Terminal", numerous improvisations were tried out on the ideas of calling up the dead and the notion of the pregnant dying, though some of the ideas were ultimately discarded ((Chaikin, 1972) p. 29–33). In the case of "The Serpent", a combination of improvisations and research resulted in the choice of the "Book of Genesis" as a topic which explored feelings of loss, shame and regret, and had a metaphorical connection with American contemporary violence. Once the subject had been chosen improvisations were conducted on specific scenes connected with Genesis. Open Theatre exercises (as discussed above) were often the basis for these improvisations. For example, when creating the animals in the garden of Eden, the actors used a form of the exercise "inside out" and tried to investigate outward shapes for internal aspects of themselves. From a wide range of improvisations a few animals were chosen: improvisation was therefore subject to a selective procedure.

Sometimes improvisations would be superimposed on each other, so a series of improvisations resulted in the amalgamation of the serpent and the tree of life, two central images in the play. The actors formed a writhing mass but also held apples, catching both the movement of the serpent and the swaying of the tree in the wind. At other times different actors would attempt their own versions of improvising on a particular theme. In the case of Eve eating the apple, each actress copied what the previous one had done and then created her own version, rather like the sound and movement exercise. Sometimes improvisations began by one person chanting or making repetitious movements, and then others joining in. As one of the actors says, somebody makes an offer and the others respond to it. This can be seen on the video of the "Serpent" where the company are shown improvising for the production of "Terminal", and also discussing it (Open Theatre, 1972). Shami Chaikin tells a story about how she thought one of the actors was dead: she starts chanting "I thought he was dead" and other actors join in with chanting and movement (Open Theatre, 1972).

The effects of the non-verbal exercises and improvisations are very evident in the final Open Theatre productions, which stress the rhythmic musical aspects of performance, the expressive possibilities of the body, and transformational imagery. In "The Serpent" (Open Theatre, 1972) there is much non-verbal sound, chanting and body combinations. These combinations include the writhing arms and vertical body-masses which make up the serpent image. Similarly, "Terminal" is a mixture of musical elements: the actors strike simple but strong rhythms with sticks or hit sticks on the table, and there is repetitious chanting. Phrases such as "we call upon the dying" or "the judgement of your life is your life" are repeated and broken up with expressive gestures, often involving considerable distortion of the mouth and eyes. Parodistic scenes are interwoven, such as the sections in the beauty parlour where we are told that the most attractive models "avoid wrinkles by restricting grimaces and smiles to an absolute minimum". Or the scene where bodies are embalmed to make them agreeable to the living, and the lips are sewn up to give a more "natural expression". These parodies are conducted in the style of the mass media; for example the embalming scene is accompanied by a voice-over commentary.

The transformational element can be seen in the way ideas and images are repeated in different forms, so that their significance is mobile. In "Terminal" the white boards on which dead are embalmed are also used as drums for rhythmic beating, while one of them becomes the backcloth to a Hassidic chant by a woman. The sticks used to beat time are also employed in the section entitled "The Interview" to strike a victim and make him produce the right answer, though it is not apparent what that would be. Similarly, the rhythmic aspect of the play is sometimes ritualistic, sometimes militaristic. Even specific references (e.g. to the holocaust) are not followed through in a narrative fashion but are transformed in relation to the theme of death.

Throughout, the actors engage in simultaneous but not necessarily unrelated actions. The result is a web of motives which reappear in a mixture of representational and abstract forms creating multiplicity of meaning. The polymedia aspect of the production also helps to catch subliminal aspects of the experience of guilt and violence. The play is about death in living (this state being closely linked with modern capitalistic America) and living in death. However, often the living do not want the dead to live, and this is symbolised by the corpse who struggles against being embalmed.

The weakest part of the productions often seems to be the verbal element, and perhaps this is because of the stress on non-verbalised experience. This was a necessary feature of such stylistically revolutionary work, because non-verbalised expression had previously been neglected in the theatre. Partly because of this emphasis on non-verbal expression, there were some disparities of opinion about the "authorship" of some Open Theatre works, especially as they sometimes worked in collaboration with writers such as Jean-Claude van Itallie. In the published text of "The Serpent" ((van Itallie, 1978) p. 5), the work is described as "created by the Open Theatre under the direction of Joseph Chaikin, assisted by Roberta Sklar, words and structure by Jean-Claude Van Itallie". In the introduction to the published play, Chaikin asserts the desirability of other performers using the improvisatory opportunities which are made explicit in the printed text. He wanted to encourage applied improvisation (more than pure improvisation) as a means of penetrating the text. Chaikin says that the "Serpent" is a "ceremony reflecting the minds and lives of the people performing it", ((van Itallie, 1978) p. 8–10) which is consistent with this view. Open Theatre performances were mainly predetermined (as a result of the construction process), but sometimes included pure improvisation and certainly evolved with time. However, distinctly conflicting, writer-centred views are expressed by van Itallie in the same volume. He states that actors "should not improvise in performance", and even goes as far as to suggest:

> *Actors are not poets… Their concentration had better not be on the invention of words while they are performing. If it is then the words are at very best, trite, and the performances suffer. ((van Itallie, 1978) p. 11).*

Problems of authorship were linked to more general problems of notation created by the non-verbal element. Indeed, one member commented on the impossibility of notating the works (Open Theatre, 1972). In fact the videorecordings of the "Serpent" and "Terminal" represent the work of the Open Theatre much more effectively than the written text.

Improvising on specific material is also an important part of the work of the Wooster Group, which collaborated from about 1974, and took on its name in 1980. In the beginning of its work the group, directed by Elizabeth LeCompte, would sometimes improvise freely without a referent. At the same time Spalding Gray, one of the members, was exploring non-verbal work through improvisation with collaborators of Robert Wilson. He explains that when he began working with LeCompte and the other performers in the spring of 1974 he "had no conscious objective themes or ideas from which to work" (Savran, 1986). He would bring props into the empty rehearsal space and perform certain silent associative actions with them. The others would join in one at a time, while LeCompte observed, made notes, and commented. "Sakonnet Point" developed without any particular set of material as its base. However, as the work of the group developed, improvisations often started from found objects, such as previously written dramatic material or pre-recorded sound, film and video, or personal interviews. LeCompte has said in discussing a more recent work "LSD" (1985) that almost any type of material could be used as the basis of a play. She also felt that if an improvisation fell out in a particular way it should stay like that : "I cannot stray from that text. As someone else would use the lines of a playwright, I use that action as the baseline" ((Savran, 1986) p. 51).

In preparing "Rumstick Road" (1977; the second part of the Rhode Island trilogy, Sakonnet Point, Rumstick Road and Nayatt School: (Gray, 1978a; Gray, LeCompte *et al.*, 1978b) and on film in (Wooster Group, 1980)) the Wooster group worked with material collected by Spalding Gray concerning his life, particularly the suicide of his mother. The outcome was a multi-media event including slides, tapes and visual imagery. It was begun partly because of Gray's own obsession with this element of his past life and his fear of inheriting his mother's manic-depressive illness. Found material was used as the basis of the play, mainly tape recordings of Gray's mother's psychiatrists and his grandmothers. These tapes were also used as a basis for improvisations.

The improvisations seem to have been important in developing non-verbal aspects of the play and therefore extra layers of suggestiveness. The play evokes a variety of levels on which the mother's suicide might be understood and even celebrated. It consists of certain narrative elements and some more abstract movements and images, such as the mother repeatedly shaking her head down to her knees, which raise the narrative to a symbolic level. For example, the final letter from his father to Gray describes how, on the night his Gray's mother died, a partridge came through the window breaking the glass and he and Gray's grandmother ate the bird. In the context of the play this takes on sacrificial, mystical overtones, suggesting the idea that the mother's madness and death may have had a spiritual significance.

These symbolic overtones are present in the letter itself, but are heightened by the other imagery in the play. The improvisations also seem to have been important in extending and objectifying the relevance of Gray's personal material, while still keeping the same sense of personal immediacy. Rumstick Road is on one level a personal quest by Spalding Gray into the meaning of his mother's death and the possible causes of her madness (which are never resolved). However, the development of the original material results in a play which has a number of additional areas of concern. It is an investigation of society's wish to marginalise madness: to the medical profession, for example, it is simply a matter of chemical imbalance, while to the family the visions are simply hallucinations. There is a clear parallel here with the psychoanalytic work in the sixties and seventies of R. D. Laing and Thomas S. Szasz, in which madness was seen to be largely a social construct.

Rumstick Road is also an open-ended exploration of the possible spiritual significance of madness. It explores the complex web of multiple cause and effect which surround any particular incident such as a breakdown. As Gray says:

> *I don't think there's any one reason for my mother's suicide. And there was no one reason for my collapse after India. It was a collision of events, including diet, that sometimes happens in peoples' lives. ((Savran, 1986) p. 71).*

Mike Leigh and applied improvisation in realistic theatre and film: improvisation as a means of building character

The British playwright Mike Leigh has written a large number of plays (and TV scripts and films) since 1965 by improvisatory collaboration with actors in rehearsal, and the earlier part of this work has been well detailed by Clements (Clements, 1983). In conversation (Leigh, 1994), Leigh commented on the danger of "codifying, quantifying" his approach and emphasised that it should not be viewed as a reproducible "method", or one which could be learnt or followed (indeed he is now "unprepared" to discuss certain aspects of his own processes).

Leigh's playwriting and film-making accentuates the input of the actors, allowing them to partially create their own roles. But this is kept within controlled limits: the objective has to be a realistic character. The actors have to make suggestions as to possible characters they could explore and give Leigh lists of these characters. Each character is to be based on someone the actor knows, and Leigh's wish is that

> *the character whom the actor will create will be drawn from 'a specific placeable, social, educational, economic, cultural environment'. ((Clements, 1983) p. 22).*

Leigh has been preoccupied with working class environments, and with the plight of the working class, though his work has adapted to the changing social environment of the 80s and 90s. He is part of the strong socially committed strain in British theatre and film, which includes the work of Edward Bond, Howard Brenton, Ken Loach and others. Despite the freedom Leigh gives to the actors these social concerns always predominate, and this to some degree influences his choice of actors. His actors sometimes develop characters who have very dissimilar backgrounds to their own (Leigh, 1994), but actors from working class backgrounds tend to know "the territory" which Leigh wishes to inhabit.

The stage of deciding on a character is known as the pre-rehearsal stage, then, after an extensive discussion period, actual events in the character's life are explored through improvisation. The actors also engage in research which explores the culture, social and physical environments of the characters. At some point in the process Leigh chooses characters from those suggested by the actors; sometimes his choice of character is guided by the possibilities of interaction. The divergent character improvisations can then be brought together by Leigh, and it is significant that he asks the actors initially not to discuss characters with each other, nor to accommodate to each other.

Next the actors begin to improvise together in their characters. All the action is based on the characters' motivations, and at the beginning of this phase the actors should not know the motivations of each other's characters. Research still continues: sometimes actors not involved in a particular rehearsal will engage in research for another. During the filming of "High Hopes", a scene in Highgate cemetery (home of Karl Marx) arose as a result of the actors' decision to visit it.

After the pre-rehearsal phase Leigh draws up a rough scenario, but the structure and details are still further developed through improvisation. Leigh also uses more abstract exercises, such as the exploration of a situation using hands only, to dislodge the actors from their normal perspective on the character and to remind them they are creating a fiction (Clements, 1983). Interestingly, Leigh detects sometimes a shamanistic "high" in his improvising actors, but resists such a state himself while he observes and distils (Leigh, 1994).

In Leigh's work, then, improvisation is used as a way of generating ideas for the playwright and widening his net, and this certainly challenges the idea of creative work as individual perception. On the other hand the work is not entirely collaborative either, since in the early stages Leigh interviews the actors alone and does not allow them to interact with each other. He also retains the final decision about which material goes into the play. Thus some hierarchy is maintained but his approach offers the actor much wider scope than most.

The results of these methods are plays notable for their detailed and relatively slow-moving surface, in which repetitious mannerisms, sentence construction, phraseology, and small scale actions of the characters, often act as a key to the tensions between them. Mannerisms are used a form of articulation when the character has limited verbal skills, as in the case of Trevor's repeated giggling in "Kiss of Death" (Leigh, 1977). Event and action are often minimal but there is sometimes a sudden "freak-out" in the midst of repressed feelings: for instance the uncontrolled, grotesque behaviour of Beverley which accompanies the death of Laurence in "Abigail's Party" ((Leigh, 1977; Leigh, 1979)) or Keith's emotional outburst because a fellow camper lights a fire in "Nuts in May" (Leigh, 1976). Although the plays are "realistic" they are in many way at odds with the norms of realistic theatre.

Many of Leigh's plays were TV plays and more recently Leigh's work has been almost entirely directed towards producing film. In his interview with us Leigh commented on the encouragement he first received from his BBC producer Tony Garnett, who was, at the same time, fostering improvisation in the work of Ken Loach. Leigh also mentioned the inspiration he found in "Shadows" ((Cassavetes, 1960); which is discussed later), and the stimulus from the UK improvised film from the 60s, "Four in the Morning". He views the performance attitudes of theatre and film as similar, and hence feels unhappy with the idea of pure improvisation in the final work, though he conceded that many small scale examples of it exist in his films. This is true of some moments in "Hard Labour", for example the scene in the market, and that with the bookseller.

Leigh's recent film work shows some interesting developments, particularly with regard to the relationship between dialogue and "freak out" mentioned above. Leigh argued (Leigh, 1994) that the improvisation has to be "open-ended", but the constraints which exist by the time the improvisation starts in each pre-rehearsal and rehearsal session are substantial, such that the improvising can hardly be "free" (see Chapter 4). Nevertheless, David Thewlis performs a virtual monologue in an empty office block in "Naked" (with brief interjections from the friendly security guard) which seems to go further towards free improvisation than any other speech in Leigh's work. The reason that most text in his works seems constrained is that it reflects characters with limited verbal worlds, who cannot readily articulate ideas. In contrast, Johnny (Thewlis' character) is highly intelligent and verbal, very interested in ideas and their form of expression, and makes a stream of subtle puns about complex issues. In the monologue he discusses the nature of the universe, time, numerology, biblical events, and their implications for personal outlook, objectives and commitment. This speech can be viewed as more autonomously generative, hardly character-based, because of its flux of logically irreconcilable concepts, and thus seems quite like the product of a free improvisation. However, if taken seriously, Johnny's statements about the world and its transience, together with his pessimistic position, are entirely predictive of his final rejection of commitment to his long-standing lover. The speech therefore can still be seen as a direct result of character improvisation, since the character base is complex, and since its logical conclusions are followed through in the subsequent actions of the character, the rejection. Consistent with this latter analysis, Leigh does see this film as the product of his normal character-improvisation process (Leigh, 1994).

Leigh's favours "the language of real life" and regards himself as a "storyteller" who prefers "showbiz" to "experimental" theatre. But it is notable that his "realism" became more complex and varied, even more expressionistic, in "Naked". There are scenes of a metaphorical underground hell in London, and Thewlis' monologue, mentioned above, is presented in a changing environment rather than a fixed domestic one. It often exploits an expressionistic, darkened background with Thewlis, shadowy, at the front. Consistent with this, Leigh supports a distinction between naturalism and realism based on the view that the former is surface phenomenon, while the latter concerns essentials, and may sometimes tend towards exaggeration, even allegory. He has very recently filmed a murder story bordering on fantasy, Jim Broadbent's "A Sense of History". Its script, the monologue of an evil English country landowner, was first improvised by Broadbent, who is a long time colleague of Leigh and has appeared in several of his works. While certainly not naturalistic, this film retains elements of realism, in Leigh's sense.

Leigh's plays and films eventually often become embodied in published scripts like those of any other dramatist, but this can present difficulties because of the reliance on non-verbal expression. He particularly likes "Ecstasy", but anticipates a problem with publishing "Naked", presumably because of its very high density of visual and other non-verbal expression. The published play-texts are available for performance by other groups in exactly the same way as composed texts, but clearly the difficulty of expressing appropriately the non-verbal components remains. The interpreting group has to forge its own path through these challenges, either choosing to imitate components of previous Leigh theatre, or film productions of the piece, or choosing a distinct approach. To us the latter approach seems more valuable. Leigh expressed a typical writer's ambivalence about the outcome of such performances.

Leigh agreed that to engage with improvised theatre when he commenced was in itself a political gesture within the theatrical scene, and he commented on the lack of improvising experience in drama school graduates at that time: happily now he finds much more experience and sympathy for improvisation in the newer graduates. One can envisage pre-rehearsal applied improvisation being used for the generation of works with other kinds of conventions than those used by Mike Leigh, or even for some which show "unreal life".

Some other applied improvisors in theatre

Applied improvising was often used by the group Joint Stock, which had much in common with Leigh. In their construction of "The Ragged-Trousered Philanthropists" (1978) non-referent improvisations were mixed with quite specific improvisations based on the book by Robert Tressell of the same name (Craig, 1980). The improvisation often explored the relationship between character and social circumstances, for example investigating the way capitalism has a negative effect on working standards, and the influence of social status beyond the immediate work environment ((Craig, 1980) p. 110–114).

Mike Leigh's work has also influenced a number of other British playwrights who have written plays as a result of improvised work. An example of this is Phil Young's "Crystal Clear" (Young, 1983) created through improvisations with Anthony Allen, Diana Barrett and Philomena McDonagh, but then taking form as a fully scripted play. The play is about the social perception of blindness, and within a realistic framework plays metaphorically on the idea of blindness and insight. Here an aid was used to promote improvising in a specific way: special lenses were used to block out the sight of the actors in order to simulate blindness.

Like Leigh, South African playwright Athol Fugard used improvisations by actors in making plays with a strong social-political basis, though this is an approach which he no longer adopts. Fugard was very influenced by Grotowski and was of necessity adopting a "poor theatre". He said that he had "absolutely no reverence for words on paper, texts", though the lack of a text was also useful for escaping political censorship ((Vandenbroucke, 1982) p. 37). In Fugard's case the collaboration of John Kani and Winston Ntshona helped him to partially overcome the difficulty of his position as a white writer dealing with the black experience of apartheid, although one might still feel that the work projects a white middle-class perspective. Furthermore, when the plays were commodified for non-South African audiences they were published as "by Athol Fugard" rather than as collective efforts, therefore undermining their mixed racial authorship.

Pure improvising in the theatre

So far we have mainly considered applied improvisation in the theatre. But some theatre groups have attempted pure improvisation, as in the case of Rachel Rosenthal's work in Los Angeles in the 1960s, in which "Instant Theatre" was created involving improvised costumes, sets, lights and texts in many languages (Nachmanovitch, 1990). More commonly, real time (pure) improvising in the theatre usually involves a score. Interesting examples of scores for performance are Kenneth Koch's "Easter", "Mexico City" and "Coil Supreme" (Kostelanetz, 1980). Here the scores themselves make interesting reading and are full of humorous and ironic ambiguities. "Easter" requires a number of different improvisations on the subject of Easter, each "scene" having its own set of instructions. Throughout there is multiplicity of viewpoint and unexpected juxtapositions. So the improvisation where the Easter rabbits "discourse on the pleasures and burdens of Easter from the rabbits' point of view" is followed by a scene which "ends with very thunderous music, probably from Berlioz". There is no binding or sequential narrative (this leaves flexibility for the actors) but there are sudden spurts of narrative improvisation: for example, a murder is committed. Altogether the whole is an entertaining springboard for improvisation which both controls and contains the action. The piece gives scope for creativity, suggests a surreal dimension, and questions religious values and certainties in a light-hearted way.

"Coil Supreme" lasts thirty minutes, and suggests that eight or ten actors speak; that every sentence they utter should contain the words "coil supreme"; that they may distort the language in any way they wish; and that the play "should end on a note of unbearable suspense". It is a sophisticated word game requiring extreme verbal dexterity and a sense of theatrical shape.

Theatre Machine, the British theatre group mentioned above, sometimes used an improvising referent such as a routine involving a deck of cards with a sentence of dialogue on each card (Jencks and Silver, 1972). After shuffling, several people read the cards in turn, making "sense" of them by constructing linking speech. Johnstone, director of the group, could also direct the progress of the improvisations, from a sitting position on stage, by telling them to use a range of props.

In Compass performances the lines were also never written out; there was a story skeleton and a floor plan, but the details changed from performance to performance. The verbal humour of Mike Nichols and Elaine May was central to the group: their technique was built on fast repartee. Nichols claims that Elaine was more inventive but that he was more concerned with the shape of the improvisations (Sweet, 1978). They both had considerable experience of psychoanalysis, and the language, the subject matter and the free-associational patterns of therapy were all improvisational tools they could share. Mike Nichols took these tools into tv and commercial film.

The relationship between the verbal and movement component of pure improvisations has sometimes been very important. Theatre Machine often dissociated the verbal and movement components of their improvisations by means of a conductor, who controlled the movements of each of the verbal improvisors as if they were puppets. As argued before, an advantage of this could be that it permitted the verbal improviser more time to achieve continuity, but in addition the actors commonly found it amusing to delay their movements in relation to those implied by the speech. In another approach, two performers would mime something in slow motion, with a third providing a counterpoint commentary, which could build scene and relationship. Some entertaining photographs of the group at work are available, including one with "magazine photograph masks in bed", looking quite deceptively like people (Jencks and Silver, 1972).

Pure improvisors can also adopt roles and strategies as a basis for play generation. Poets Allen Fisher, Steve Benson and cris cheek improvised a play together called "Assumptions Table" in the early 80s. They practised in private often making up rules and strategies such as interrupting each other or misunderstanding each other. The play was performed at Chisenhale Dance Space, in East London.

Improvising and audience interaction

Improvising theatre groups, whether applied or pure, have often encouraged audience participation. The Living Theatre usually devised a rudimentary script of their productions in rehearsal. However, they often left considerable latitude for the audience to intervene and change the micro-structure if not the macro-structure of the performance. In spite of the slowness of their performances, the Living Theatre do show remarkable skill at engaging the audience and interpolating audience comments into the event of the play, while still keeping a grip on the play's overall direction. Their work

"Paradise Now" announces itself in the written version as "a vertical ascent towards Permanent Revolution" and fuses ideas from the Kabbalah, Tantric and Hassidic teaching, the I Ching and other sources (this is elaborately documented in the later published text (Malina and Beck, 1971)). In the film of "Paradise Now" in Berlin in 1970 (Rochlin, 1970) the actors mingle with the audience with remarks designed to provoke, such as:

> *I am not allowed to travel without a passport, I don't know how to stop the wars, you can't live if you don't have money, I'm not allowed to smoke marijuana.*

The actor keeps to his phrase but listens to the spectators' responses. The way that the actors control the audience response while coercing it is shown in a subsequent passage, as documented in the printed version:

> *As the actors speak the lines of the Text, they break up the formation of the letters of the word PARADISE and move to various positions in the theatre.*
> *They then wait at least sixty seconds for the public to initiate the action. If the public begins any sort of enactment or initiates any movement, speech or dialogue, the actors then join with the spectators in giving support to the scene that the spectators are playing. If this digresses from the revolutionary theme or from the plateau to which we have been brought by the Rite and the Vision, the actors then try to guide the scene back to the meaning of the Rung. If the public is extremely passive and unresponsive, the actors will initiate spontaneous/ improvised action. Having initiated an action, they will again wait for the public to take it up. ((Malina and Beck, 1971) p. 45)*

Sometimes the response to these kind of cues from the actors was quite verbose: in one instance an audience member broke out into a heated tirade accusing the group of political naivety (Rochlin, 1970). In another interjection they were labelled "The Dead Theatre" (Brown, 1968). Sometimes in "Paradise Now" the audience responded to the invitation by taking off their clothes and/or by making contact with the actors in a physical way. During the same video of the performance, Julian Beck can be seen discussing with one actor how to deal with an intervention by a spectator which is taking too long, and how to integrate the incident into the performance structure.

Audience participation of the type initiated by the Living Theatre is designed to shake the audience members from their passivity and complacency, to confront them with the unexpected, and in some cases to break social taboos. Similarly, in a People Show performance in 1969 performers invited members of the public into a nearby telephone booth, to see some "dirty" photos. Once inside photos were not produced but rather alternatives, such as two sugar lumps coloured with red ink or a bra stuffed with baked beans. These ways of inducing audience participation can be means of exploring and controlling power relationships. At the end of the Sydney Front piece "Don Juan" (1991–3) the audience was invited/exhorted to provide a volunteer to undress for money.

Even further in the direction of using audience participation to political ends is Augusto Boal's Theatre of the Oppressed. Boal was the artistic director of the Arena Theatre in Sao Paulo in Brazil between 1964 and 1971. He wanted to find a "poetics of the oppressed" for which he proposed a "forum theatre" in which spectators can challenge the roles of the actors and themselves change the course of the action (Norden, 1991). Boal rejected the "poor theatre" of Grotowski, which he saw as elitist and based on the idea of the sacred actor. He moved to France in 1978 where he directed for more than a decade the Paris-based Centre du Théâtre de l'Opprimée. The actors employed by the theatre still work with anti-racist, feminist, ecological, or otherwise politically committed groups. In Europe Boal found he had to fight more subtle types of oppression, what he called "the cop in the head", than in Brazil. He returned intermittently in the 1980s to Brazil where he recommenced his participation in social and political struggle, but since then he has rejected the help of multi-national companies in Brazil, who would invest money but expect political complicity in return. Boal uses improvisation as a way of helping people to break out of their oppression; for instance he encourages people to improvise different behaviours in different situations and then asks them to switch behaviours in response to spectator suggestion. The objective of this is make the subject feel

> that some rituals of our daily life impose upon us masks of behaviour that we don't want to have, but sometimes we can change the mask and break the ritual. (Norden, 1991)

Polymedia Improvisation in Film and Virtual Environments

> There's no such thing as a "good actor". {Acting} is an extension of life. How you're capable of performing in your life, that's how you're capable of performing on the screen. John Cassavetes (quoted in (Carney, 1985) p. 57).

We discuss here some improvised film/video works which involve dialogue. We exclude non-verbal videos and interactive visual works such as discussed in Chapters 5, 6, 7, 10. A key example of the use of applied improvisation in film, the works of Mike Leigh, has been discussed in the previous section of this Chapter. Most films which are relevant are primarily examples of the influence of improvisation, rather than being strictly improvised. However, films usually contain at least limited improvised elements in the performances by the actors. In this respect, they are similar to the other performing arts where even compositions involve some flexibility. For example, dance may include small scale improvisation during every performance or rehearsal, and this may make a significant contribution to the resultant work.

An implication of Cassavetes' remark above is that amateur actors inevitably largely improvise. The degree to which actors' performances in film can be dictated by script and direction partly depends on the background of the actors: amateurs have to behave as they do outside film, and hence their actions are not "acted" but simply used by the director. Thus there is a continuity between the behaviour of amateur film actors seen in many works by Bresson, and in some recent Asian films such as "The Scent of the Green Papaya" (Hung, 1993); and the more cultivated improvising in some films by Cassavetes, Nilsson and others which we will discuss briefly here.

If Cassavetes' idea, that performing in a film is like performing in life, is to be taken seriously, then it is not surprising that the amateur actor can be effective, as is clearly the case in many Bresson and Italian Neo-realist films. That the amateur might give the impression of cinema verité (i.e. the recording of events) is an initial extrapolation which does not properly allow for the director's and filmographer's influence. The question we address here is, does the improvisatory impulse (in amateur or professional actors) have any contribution to make in directed verbal film/video? According to Cassavetes the question is circular, since the improvisatory impulse is not separable from that of life. However, most viewers and critics recognise that a few of his films, notoriously his "Shadows", give the impression of improvisation.

The Cassavetes quotation also reflects his central objective of obtaining living, not acted, performances on the screen, usually by professionals. This objective is closely related to that of Chaikin and others discussed earlier in this Chapter: overcoming the separation between actor and role. Cassevetes also shared Chaikin's distaste for commercial practices, particularly Hollywood's mass production of films which enact "the syndrome of the isolated, atomic self and the noninteracting interaction" for middle class audiences ((Carney, 1994) p. 24). "Shadows" was filmed in 1957–8, and involved the production of thirty hours of film before the first (sixty minute) version was released in 1958. There was a very poor response, except from Jonas Mekas and a few of the film coterie of New York. Cassavetes viewed the director and cameramen as "recorder" and "slaves" (Carney, 1985), because the film concerned "real lives" and "real people". The film credits indicate that the film was improvised, but actually it springs from applied improvisation in a drama workshop. Most of the parts were taken by "friends or relatives willing to work for little or nothing", and the film was financed by Cassavetes' own efforts, including his very successful work as a commercial "method" film actor. Cassavetes was much removed from the "Visionary" film of the then avant-garde such as Kenneth Anger and Jack Smith, for he was concerned to represent reality as closely as he could. This is the reason his films exhibit the slowness, awkwardness, and banality of everyday existence.

Then he further revised "Shadows", recording a new sound track (because the original was too poor in quality), and a further twenty hours of film, so as to produce the present eighty-seven minute version. This version of the film has music by Charles Mingus, the bassist hero of the bebop jazz era, and solos by Shafi Hadi (saxophone). After this release he was reviled even by his previous supporters such as Mekas: according to Carney, Mekas had realised by then that the film did not fit within the dogma of Visionary film which he was supporting avidly. Mekas' opinion was paralleled by (and may have been related to) the changed opinion of the actors in the film. They felt betrayed by the revision of the film, about which they had not been consulted. Their negative reaction may have been partly because many of them were playing themselves: they had accepted one vision of themselves and hence could not readily accept a new one. Even some of the key participants, such as the lead actor Ben Carruthers, felt betrayed. At the same time they admired the expression of their own complex feelings. This successful expression resulted from the slowness and awkwardness mentioned above.

In the film, Ben is a trumpeter and a Bird (Charlie Parker) addict: he is a "rendition of a member of the Beat Generation" (Carney, 1985). Since Cassavetes was producing "improvisations not of actors acting but characters living", and at the same time, as Carney puts it, "attracted to moments when conventional... codes of behaviours break down", it was apparent that an actor might be alienated by the "representation". Character development is not central, and there are essentially no mature persons ("adults") in the film: as Cassavetes says "there is no problem that is not overcome and replaced by other problems". In fact as Carney points out the metaphor of the mask is central to the film and it involves "a comparison of the 'masks' we wear in public with the 'faces' we hide beneath them" ((Carney, 1994) p. 36). The idea of stripping away the mask is also central to Cassevetes concept of film-making.

The film concerns the discrimination, both gross and subtle, faced by contemporaneous blacks, and the portrayal of this is possibly strengthened by the improvisatory input of the actors, who "play themselves". Particularly strong is the expressive performance of Lelia Goldoni, which results in an important feminist dimension to the story. At the same time, these performances are mediated by the direction of Cassavetes, such as the choice of relatively white skinned actors to play Lelia and her brother Ben. As Carney points out, the fact that Lelia and Ben are relatively white means that the viewer goes through a quite slow process of discovering their racial background in the film, analogous to that of Tony, Lelia's unconvinced lover ((Carney, 1994) p. 48). This not only means that the viewer is forced to share Tony's point of view more fully, but also that Cassavetes uses the improvisations to reassess the conventional representation of black people.

The film depicts the jazz milieu, but the film also uses some techniques which are analogous to that of the jazz musician. Lelia's black brother Hughie (an aspiring jazz singer) is highly protective towards his sister, particularly when she becomes briefly involved with Tony, an exploitative and racist white lover. A climactic scene involves Hughie in almost violent expulsion of the lover from a party, and the tension in this scene is developed largely through a repetitious "jamming" in the party itself. Cassavetes' choice of a jazz milieu for his first film is entirely in keeping with his commitment to revealing real life, in part by using applied improvisation to construct the work. More generally, the use of collaborative development, which seems to continue through his work though later in a different form, allowed him to penetrate characters and situations, rather than directing them from outside.

Although improvising was integral to the development of this film, the refilming used scripting i.e. recomposition, based on the original improvised scenes. Yet Cassavetes emphasised that "at no point was there a written script". Carney points out the problem of defining improvisation, but does not go far towards indicating its gradations, with which we introduced this book. He does mention that complete improvisation occurs during the work of directors such as Hawks and Capra; but that more strikingly, Cassavetes continued to give the impression to his audience that "Shadows", and most of his subsequent work, involved improvisation. In fact, all his subsequent work had elaborate scripts. For example, "Faces" was based on a three hundred and nineteen page script, which was only revealed after the critics had discussed at length its improvised nature. The film speech involves hardly any changes from the script; yet it does convey an impression quite unlike that of most films, an improvisatory one. The key element of this is probably the prolongation of scenes and timings, to approximate life's timing rather than condensed edited film timings; and equally to retain the inconsistencies, and the trivialities of many life events. An improvised spirit influences all of his work, even when he adapts scripts of others, as in "Love Streams", as Viera has also argued (Viera, 1990). This is not achieved by applied improvisation during development of the script, which is largely worked out by Cassavetes himself or by another writer. Rather, it is achieved by extensive improvisation of gesture, timing and other non-verbal elements, on the set during the filming of the pre-arranged scenes. Many photographs of the work illustrate this quite clearly (Carney, 1985; Carney, 1994). The improvisors in this work were not only the actors, many of whom like Gene Rowlands (Cassavetes' wife) had a profound influence, but also Cassavetes himself, who would frequently "block" (that is, run through all the actions of) the scenes, and develop new ways of presenting them.

A more recent filmmaker with a special reputation for improvisation is the Cassavetes follower Rob Nilsson. But his reputation, unlike Cassavetes', reflects the reality of his production methods, which are substantially improvised at most levels. Several of his films, for example "Signal 7", include a credit line indicating that improvisation was central in the film (Nilsson, c. 1970). Fittingly, this features out-of-work actors who drive cabs in San Francisco, and their efforts to rejoin, and fantasies about, the acting profession. Another work, "Heat and Sunlight" (Nilsson, 1988) shows the end of a love affair. Nilsson says

> It's a way to get access to more complex personal emotions… people have done improvisatory cinema before; they've rehearsed for months and shot 360 degree lighting before (all key elements of Heat and Sunlight's production), but to do all these things together is, I think the revolutionary thing.

A particularly impressive achievement of the improvisation in this film is the climatic love scene. The male character has had to seek his departed lover, and in the subsequent love scene, his anger and violence slowly converts into physical intimacy. This is performed like a heterosexual contact improvisation which exploits rather than neutralises its eroticism. In this it contrasts with the movement in contact improvisation we discussed earlier. This scene has strikingly more impact and conviction than most sexual scenes in film.

Prolonged and somewhat banal scenes are a feature of Nilsson's work, as of Cassavetes', but are less pronounced in his more commercial and conventional films, some documentary (Nilsson, 1978). Such scenes are also found in the work of Jon Jost, often involving fixed camera positions filming extended slow, largely improvised, actions. Thus "Slow Moves" is exactly as its title implies, a chance meeting on a bridge which progresses very slowly; but it is not without realistic impact. Several other Jost works are constructed this way. They also exploit a structural film device, the controlling of the duration of film segments independently of what is represented on them. These segments, nevertheless, show improvised actions which stem from detectable motives, revealing that the actors are improvising in relation to each other, rather than independently, as they do in the early stages of Mike Leigh's construction process.

Some other contemporary films involved pseudo-improvisation, for example, Robert Frank and Alfred Leslie's "Pull My Daisy" of 1959, and Shirley Clarke's "The Connection". The first of these was a beat film about a day in the domestic life of a group of poets. It was scripted by Kerouac, and featured poets Ginsberg, Corso and Orlovsky as themselves, while painter and jazz musician Larry Rivers, musician David Amram and actress Delphine Seyrig played fictional parts. Though celebrated at the time as an improvised documentary, Leslie later debunked the idea that his was an improvised work ((Leslie, 1986); see for example, (Banes, 1993)). "The Connection" was a Jack Gelber play produced by the Living Theatre in the early 1960s and then filmed by Clarke (Clarke, 1961). In it, a fictional author, Jaybird (referring again to Charlie "Bird" Parker), keeps telling the audience that the play is improvised, although in fact his "spontaneous" interventions are scripted. "Is your name going to be on this film?" he is asked at one point. The only improvisation on the film, which is a sordid celebration of the New York drug culture of the time, is that of the musicians Jackie McLean and the Freddie Redd Quartet. However, the preceding Living Theatre stage production depended on considerable applied improvisation. As Judith Malina said: "we found suddenly... in... the true improvisation of 'The Connection'... an atmosphere of freedom in the performance", and this promoted a "truthfulness, startling in performance, which we had not so thoroughly produced before" (quoted in (Banes, 1993) p. 157).

Shirley Clarke's later film "Cool World" (1963) is improvised to a very limited extent, and it uses both actors and neighbourhood New York kids to depict street drug dealers and gang violence. It is characterised by abrupt cuts, fragmented narrative and nervous energy, all of which have been interpreted as showing "jazz structure" (Banes, 1993). But the idea of "jazz" behind this attribution is one of naive spontaneity. It is also based on limited understanding of the contemporaneous idiom of hard bop (the music heard and seen on "The Connection" and heard on "Cool World"), since this does not involve "abrupt cuts", rather extended solos on repetitive defined structures. Equally it is not a "fragmented" form, but one developed by additive means, and by a process of intensification. Neither was free jazz of the period characterised by such features, though it took on some in the 1970s onwards (see Chapter 4; (Dean, 1992)).

Improvisation is also often important for film scriptwriters such as Paul Mazursky. Mazursky was interested in improvisation, having been an associate of the Compass school of improvised theatre, and used its mother figure, Viola Spolin, as Donald Sutherland's mother in his "Alex in Wonderland". In an interview he says:

Improvisation is a wonderful tool. I used it as a writer. Larry (Tudor) and I wrote "Bob and Carol and Ted and Alice" and I think we improvised 75% of it in 5 days in Palm Springs. We rented a place and went down there and I played one character and he played another and we just put it down on tape. I haven't worked that way since.

His use of improvisation in other respects seems very limited : he states that he does not use improvisation when he directs "as much as some people think" ((Sweet, 1978) pp. 250–1).

Documentation of improvisation during film production is limited. Some idea of its omnipresence can be gained from the film of Buster Keaton at work on "The Railrodder", in his later life (Keaton, 1965). Here we see improvisation of facial and physical guise, within the then well known Keaton style, but also the construction of a comic scene involving a railroad tunnel and Italian workers. Similarly, film actor B. Henry (Henry, 1993) has detailed several cases in which dialogue was improvised. He comments that many European films involve the verbal improvisation of text which is then not used, since overdubbing is involved, and the actor may not speak the final language of the film. An alternative approach, still permitting the final text to be overdubbed, was adopted by Fellini. According to Henry, he often asked his actors simply to count up to ten instead of speaking lines. This dissociation of speech from gesture may allow greater improvisatory control of gesture in film acting than elsewhere. We have discussed the related dissociation of speech from gesture in theatre. Kiss' actors spoke text which they hardly understood because it was in a language they did not speak, and this also increased the emphasis on gesture.

Henry appeared in Forman's "Taking Off" (1971), and commented that improvisation was important since the script, though produced by many writers, was never seen by the actors. Indeed, Forman was not fluent in English at the time, and seemed to seek dialogue which was without conscious significance. Henry also comments that in Cassavetes' filming:

the more oddball the dialogue, the more the script supervisor cleared her throat and rolled her eyes, and the more Cassavetes nodded happily, and smiled his odd, slightly pained, smile.

These are clearly examples of directors attempting to encourage unconventional speech in their improvising performers.

Some experimental film makers make the improvisatory elements rather obvious, by appearing in their own films and deconstructing their role as creator. For example, George Kuchar (b. 1942: see (Zippay, 1991)), director of "Hold Me While I'm Naked", talks about the filming as it progresses, and makes other self-referential asides, while leaving the camera apparently running to record whatever happens. He eventually wraps himself up in the film stock in this particular film. Of course artifice and genuine improvisation overlap and may become indistinguishable in such processes. Jean-Luc Godard does not star in his "Pierrot le Fou", but it too has self-reflexive elements. Its "narrative" is remarkably haphazard, if at the same time somewhat shamanistic, romantically cleansing Pierrot and his lover of their frustrations. "Pierrot le Fou" reflexively refers to the idea that a work cannot be finished, as Clark Coolidge has suggested (Foster, 1994). Godard was influenced by the French tradition of using improvisation in production initiated by Renoir, and followed occasionally by other adherents of the Nouvelle Vague, for example Eric Rohmer in his "Summer" (1992).

Many directors, from Makavejev to Norman Mailer, like to make improvised scenes which they can then use as material in the editing room. Mailer mentions the case of "Maidstone" as a general example: he says that the "film was made out of the materials of its making, a movie which had almost no existence in plans or on drawing boards." An attempted assassination was outlined by Mailer for one scene, together with the utensil (hammer) which should be used, but the who and when of the incident was left unspecified before the actors worked on the scene (Mailer, 1971).

Improvisation with the film stock material, and with the filming process, are perhaps the most fundamentally film-specific uses of improvisation. Michael Snow is active in this respect, for he normally uses out-of-date film stock, and improvises with chemicals, temperatures and processing times in developing them (Snow, 1994). Processing is regularly done by one person, and several different film stocks are used at once, heightening the unpredictability. In contrast, for his still photographic work, Snow uses a single conventional commercial lab, with predictable outcome. Nam June Paik has produced a huge oeuvre of video/film works using every kind of analogue and digital/computerised filming and editing technology available. His works are visually exciting and diverse, and combine the most representational images with the most abstracted, often in incredibly rapid flux. Quite frequently his videos contain improvisation by those who appear in them. For example, his "Spring/Fall Pt II" (Paik, 1987) shows Joseph Beuys improvising at the piano, together with bursts of Laurie Anderson, and others. Similarly, he arranged the filming of the improvised Fluxus two piano performance he and Beuys gave: "In Memoriam G. Maciunas" (Paik, 1978), which is also available on L. P. Paik's "Global Groove" ((Paik and Godfrey, 1973) shows Ginsberg in action, intoning mantras and exploiting his belly resonance; and Charlotte Moorman improvising on the TV-cello (mentioned above). Moorman also interprets Saint-Saens' "The Swan" (a conventional cello party-piece) on the TV-cello, with hilarious effects. At the same time as playing the TV-Cello, she intermittently improvises discussion of the "chocolate cello", thereby dripping extra layers of sweetness. This film also includes sections of the Living Theatre's "Paradise Now" accompanied by music by Stockhausen. Very often these images are modified by computer grabbing of the edges of objects, and by rippling the digitising effect across the screen. In most cases the intercutting is very fast also. With all these effects and personal sympathies one cannot avoid detecting the vast influence of improvisation on Paik's work. But the degree to which improvisation takes place within the filming itself, as opposed to within the events being filmed or the editing, seems quite limited. The editing process is commonly improvisatory, and Paik's work makes this seem the more evident because of the improvisatory flux at other levels of his productions.

Pure improvisation is central to the experimental film work of the British pioneer, Jeff Keen, who has been producing films for thirty years (Curtis, 1975). He often films with two standard 8 cameras, reversal stock, and 6–8 performers, usually mainly friends (and indeed faces reappear regularly in his works) (Figure 16). A film, such as "Day of the Arcane Light", would be based on a "jazz head arrangement" (Keen, 1994), and developed by improvisation. The "head arrangement" in jazz is simply the format by which the first few choruses of a standard tune or blues will be played by the group: it determines who will play the tune, the harmony, the counterline etc. But the analogy thereafter is better related to free jazz than to conventional jazz, since the subsequent filming is virtually free improvisation and free jazz pieces often did commence with a "head".

The group of participants then went to a location on the edge of Brighton, where Keen lives, and spent a day filming. The cameras were passed around the participants, and there were multiple exposures of the film. Superimposition was appropriate for the medium of standard 8, because this has to be run through: hence real time superimposition, without clear knowledge of where one is on the film, is feasible. Besides superimposing further action, Keen might paint on the stock, or more commonly film "animations" which he constructed and improvised himself in his flat. To make these animations, he used multiple drawings, cut-ups (sometimes from comic books, often from his own drawings) and a variety of other materials. The superimposition might also be images of the multiple idiosyncratic dolls, soldiers, tanks, toy machines etc which adorn Keen's flat. He rapidly shuffled and rearranged his stock of these visual objects while filming on top of the pre-existent action. In interview he mentioned the influence of the slightly more conventional animation techniques of Borowcyk and Lenica on his work. Thus for him the action becomes the narrative; film is "kinetic not dreamtime" (Keen, 1994). Indeed, Keen was worried on one occasion when a participant asked "Why didn't you direct us?", until he realised that the frame is limiting, and "things must swell out of it" (Keen, 1994). The humour which emerges depends partly on the spirit of the 70s — when many of his films, in which friends would "innocently" play together, were made — and partly on the wish for abstraction rather than for an "ideas approach". Keen described himself as having "been through" Marxism, though his current work was becoming more overtly political again (Keen, 1994). His work is a fascinating example of pure improvisation, and of the widest interest. Unfortunately, it is not yet well known, in part because of his self-effacing approach and quiet existence in provincial Brighton.

Keen's work, because of its "kinetic" multiplicity, seems to transmute some of the dolls, model soldiers and animated objects which it uses into futuristic fantasies. This effect is enhanced by the fact that frequently the performers wear costumes which are similarly space age in appearance. Quite often the impression is of the space age as it was imagined in the 60s and 70s, rather than as we might imagine it now, just as for example, the Archigram architects drawings of the same period sometimes look dated (see Chapter 9). But, like Archigram, some of Keen's images seem parts of a dateless fantasy, or at least one which is still undated, even 15–20 years after its production.

Keen's films already fulfil some of the futuristic potentials of the virtual reality which film can now exploit quite easily. "Jurassic Park" is one of the first major commercial films using virtual reality and its computer-related ideas. Improvising film makers will have wonderful opportunities using this medium, if they can tailor their technological need to their budgetary resources. As computing power continues to become cheaper daily, so this will become easier. We return to these future computer-based possibilities in the Chapter 10.

9

IMPROVISATION AND POSTMODERNISM IN ARCHITECTURE

About fifty of us were at a driftwood beach on the seacoast. My husband {Lawrence Halprin, the architect} planted a stick in the sand and gave a simple direction. "Use only driftwood as your material and build a structure for yourself to use. Stay within a 150-foot radius of this centre." Some people chose to work by themselves, some in teams, or couples. In each instance a unique statement evolved — a personal and imaginative driftwood structure. As the momentum and energy of the work process built up more and more connections between structures were made. Finally, in only three hours, a city was built. ...The city that took form evolved as a natural flow of the process, and the result was a configuration, a structure by itself independent of the many independent individual parts within. ...There was constant discovery, change and flux; performers and audience were the same. The main idea which impressed me was that the working process was both a life process and an art process, the two being interchangeable. (Ann Halprin, in (Kostelanetz, 1980) p. 76).

Most improvisation occurs inside constructed environments, as we have pointed out already. But what relevance does improvisation have to constructed environments themselves? It is pertinent from the point of view of both the architect and the users. Architecture, the production of constructed environments, is a practical as well as artistic activity. So it is worth discussing the procedures in its production, and their relevance. Note also that in Appendix 1 we propose and investigate the possible construction of environments specifically intended for the use of improvisors: this does not seem to have been attempted to date.

Architecture can be distinguished from art in providing long-term protection and shelter to humans. The scale of architectural building is often (but not always) greater than that of artworks. Because architecture is a complex and protracted process from conception to completion of a building, it is unlikely to be entirely improvised. But it can often have improvisatory components which reveal the positive influences of that process, and we will thus briefly discuss some. To quote the architectural critic Rory Spence: "The architect has built-in fellow improvisors in the form of unpredictable clients, briefs, site conditions and other powerful external factors which demand a response" (Spence, 1994).

There are two kinds of performers involved with architecture, the producers, and the users; both may well utilise improvisatory strategies in interacting with it. Amongst the producers are some "amateurs" who produce for themselves, often building directly; and others who produce for clients. The production process involves at least two stages at which different kinds of improvisatory impact can readily occur: that of conception/design/drawing; and that of construction. The two processes are inevitably intertwined in our discussion.

An important approach to considering architecture generally involves the idea of "adhocism", proposed by Jencks and Silver (Jencks and Silver, 1972). They have emphasised that for the designer-builder (professional or otherwise), an element of adhocism often rules. An ad hoc process is one which proceeds even though its normal means are not available, exploiting whatever comes to hand. Thus Jencks and Silver illustrate many intriguing examples of homes made from "the leftovers of a consumer society" (e.g. p. 22) and they embellish these houses with the term "drop city home" (pp. 111, 159). A slogan they quote is "Everything can always become something else" (p. 23), and this process is apparent in many hippie constructions, aboriginal buildings in Australia, and self-build housing in developing countries. They distinguish between successful and unsuccessful adhocism, their criterion being whether there are considered relations between the parts (p. 24). They extend the concept very widely to refer to the arts, the practical and commercial world including everyday objects, and the social and political process. For example, they argue that many political decisions are taken simply on the basis of conveniently available information and solutions, rather than fundamental ones. Clearly, such adhocism can be disadvantageous, though in the main they view it as creative.

"Improvisation" is mentioned very sparsely and loosely: e.g. p. 108 when referring to an "improvised cart", and the usage is not defined, even though the word is part of their book title. It is apparent that adhocism is not synonymous with improvisation, but is a process which can on occasion be harnessed to improvisation. In so far as improvisation sometimes involves solving new problems, there is no normal method, and so it can only use "available" materials or ideas and fulfils the definition of adhocism (see Chapter 1).

However, the idea that an adhoc, often improvisatory, approach influences the design of buildings is well established by the numerous intriguing and often appealing examples they give. Many are "add-ons" (additions to pre-existent buildings) which give rise to pluralist outputs. They give particular emphasis to the work of Bruce Goff, both before our period and within it. For example, his "Star-Bar", according to Goff (quoted on p. 85) was *improvised off backstage for the entertainment of entertainers. It had to be done for a low budget... Grocery string was used for spatial decorative lines. The white wire cone had an electric fan in the floor to... activate colored balloons inside the cone — a balloon fountain.*

This particular "building" was constructed quickly, and in a truly improvisatory fashion. In summing up his work, Jencks and Silver say "...Only such {adhoc} articulation is equal to the pluralism, delightful heterogeneity and complexity of modern life."

Spence discusses the *construction* process as follows:

Where contract conditions allow, architects sometimes respond in a somewhat improvisatory manner to accidents, mistakes or simply unpredicted effects that occur in the process of construction. Some architects eg. Richard Leplastrier {Australian architect, on whom Spence is researching}, deliberately do not resolve all details before starting on site, so that they can take advantage of exactly this situation... The classic case of this improvisatory way of working during construction, but nevertheless based on very sophisticated overall plans and structural ideas, was Antonio Gaudi — the detailed design of the Sagrada Familia church in Barcelona, for example, was continually modified as work progressed and I believe that this was a largely intuitive and improvisatory process, even though the results of the improvisatory thinking have to be very deliberately and laboriously turned into actual constructed form. (Spence, 1994).

The adhoc spirit is also evident in the construction of many art works, and one might indicate the "readymade" such as Duchamp's 1913 "Bicycle Wheel" as an early application of this. Allan Kaprow's Happening, "Yard" (1961), comprising tyres, is another archetype. Similarly, there is a striking relation between Jencks and Silver's Figure 33, "Four ways of seeing the corkscrew" (as soldier at attention, as a hold-up, as a traffic policeman, or as a rocket on a launching pad), and the uses to which Claes Oldenburg has put the image of the Swiss Army knife (for example in the collaboration with Frank Gehry, "Il Costello", discussed in Chapter 8). Jencks' own "Madonna of the Future" (p. 49) is "made up from one Belling heater, one headless mannequin, thirty feet of cord, one oval flange, and the book of Henry James". The idea of application of adhoc materials to the development of sound-generating instruments has been mentioned before, and is a common trait amongst sound improvisors, as analysed in detail by Hugh Davies, Ernie Althoff and others (Althoff, 1986; Davies, 1987; Althoff and Dean, 1991).

Jencks theory of adhocism has further implications because it is an antecedent of his seminal theories of postmodernism. According to Jencks, postmodernist architecture is a necessary reaction against the unity, autonomy, and functionalism of modernist architecture: Jencks develops this into a general theory of postmodernism which has specific implications in individual media. Such a postmodernism courts fragmentation, dislocation, transience, quotation, parody, pastiche, representation and pluralism. The idea of adhocism is retained in Jenck's theory of postmodernism but linked with hybridity and eclecticism. (Jencks, 1992). We have already argued in Chapter 1 that improvisation was amongst the important impulses in postmodernism, that it is a process which embodies post-modernist attitudes and values. We have also shown that this often results in works which are complex, fragmented and multiple; which challenge the distinction between art and life, and between the artist and any other individual. We can here see a related line of thinking in the idea of adhocism, which is more relevant to architecture than the more performance-based concept of improvisation, but includes some of the same elements of recycling, transformation, and adaptation of inventiveness to the present challenge.

The spirit of this "postmodernist adhocism" is even more important in many unrealised architects' and city-planners' designs. The example of the "Electric Mobile Home", a concept generated by the British Archigram group (1966) is striking (see (Jencks and Silver, 1972) p. 52; (Crompton, 1994)), and its larger scale counterpart (on paper and in mind) was the "plug-in city" of mobile elements, whose forms were mostly chosen ad hoc from then available domestic items such as the electric plug. In the concept of "L'Architecture Mobile" of Yona Friedman (1957), the inhabitants even more completely determine the form of the buildings. As Constant (of Cobra) said "architecture will be reborn when it is created by all — each for himself, and in collaboration with the others for the tasks held in common" (quoted in (Popper, 1975) p. 62).

In a classic work on fantasy in architecture (Conrads, Sperlich *et al.*, 1962), the concept of improvisation, again not defined clearly, is relegated solely to the discussion of designs, mostly unrealised. The implicit argument is that the architect can be free to "improvise" by having a conceptual referent, and disregarding the future necessities of its uses; this freedom is enhanced by the fact that the work is to be produced only in the form of a model, which does not have to meet the structural constraints of a real building. These referents are often geometric, for example stars, triangles and circles. Whether such improvisatory freedom was at the origin of Buckminster Fuller's long term work with the geodesic structure is unclear. The geodesic concept itself is not primarily improvisatory, but rather based on the search for an ideal structure "which with every stress is deformed equally and simultaneously in all its parts" (Conrads, Sperlich *et al.*, 1962). It is interesting, however, that portable spaces sometimes used by improvising groups are usually based on the geodesic structure (such as that used by the English music group Domus in the early 1980s).

Such ideals are taken to extremes in the concept of architectural utopias, of which clearly none have taken a definitive solid form. However, the design of such potential buildings is perhaps the most fertile field for conceptual improvisation in architecture. Conrads defines "a structural utopia" as a design "which for the time being can only be carried out theoretically, and which is always positively constructive and logically consistent within itself". Even such an arbitrary definition as this would not elude the possibilities of liquid cyberspace, discussed in Chapter 10.

Improvisation in this often "extraterrestrial" sphere has a long and fascinating history (Conrads, Sperlich *et al.*, 1962). More terrestrially, Frederick Kiesler's "Endless House" (1937), a remarkable cave-like structure, exists only in model form; and the concept and detailed shape of the surfaces relate to the idea of "continuous tension", in which concrete can be moulded extensively ((Conrads, Sperlich *et al.*, 1962) p. 70, a.o.). They also relate to the "oblique space/line of greatest slope" concepts of Claude Parent, applied in designing performing spaces, and their immediate surrounds (Popper, 1975). These concepts emphasise the use of non-horizontal surfaces within the spaces, and their articulation by asymmetric contrasting slopes. Bruce Goff has also offered stimulating irregularly shaped designs, such as his projected glass house for a musician in Urbana (1952: (Conrads, Sperlich *et al.*, 1962) p. 58).

Returning to the conceptual processes in *realised* architecture, one can legitimately ask whether improvisation is at all relevant. The Viennese "Coop Himmelblau" architects state repeatedly during an interview that they conceive the structure of buildings "very rapidly", so much so that the client can be a little frustrated by the speed and lack of exchange of ideas (Himmelblau, 1988). But the exchange between the two Coop Himmelblau themselves apparently operates largely on a non-verbalised level, of swapping drawings, adding on materials and so on. The work process is a collaborative improvisatory one, and the schematic drawings in Blaubox are exactly what this might be expected to produce; yet they become the basis for highly professional meticulous design plans done by the Coop team, and then their successful realisation in remarkable buildings (Himmelblau, 1988).

Spence concurs:

> *...the initial overall compositional idea for a building often comes, I believe, in the form of a somewhat improvisatory, intuitive response to the particular requirements, restrictions and opportunities, of the brief, built context and general site conditions. Architecture is with a few exceptions almost inevitably situation specific and involves a direct response, not unlike the environmental artist working with a specific site. ...I would say that architects generally prepare for this kind of improvisation by being open to the role of chance or unpredictable occurrences in the design process — though some architects actually create conditions for*

> *improvisatory response by various techniques: eg. Alvar Aalto used to leave all the practical*
> *and deliberate compositional issues aside and then draw freely in order to allow an intuitive*
> *response to the design problem to emerge from the unconscious or semi-conscious faculties;*
> *similarly Coop Himmelblau and Will Alsop use free sketching techniques to develop free*
> *gestures than can then be used as a stimulus for new ideas about form which can be wedded*
> *to the building program and site. (Spence, 1994)*

Frank Gehry's work (Foster, 1987; Grillet, 1991), unlike shanty houses, does not involve ad hoc materials, nor collaborative processes. However, often he has worked with Claes Oldenburg, producing fleeting designs of an improvisatory nature, and the irregular geometry reflects this. He has provided stage sets also, such as for the Lucinda Childs/John Adams work "Available Light" (1983; (Anderson, 1987)). His collaboration on "Il Costello" is probably his most substantial example of improvisation (see Chapter 8).

Those architects who are concerned to relate their buildings to the surrounding environment, particularly a natural environment, also necessarily improvise as they strive to form connections with it. These connections may be obvious if they choose to form direct physical links between the building and the environs, or to create interpenetration i.e. a lack of separation between the building interior and the environmental exterior. This lack of separation can facilitate the dwellers' activities and improvisation in the interfacial zone. The trend towards forming flexible and open building/environment articulations has a long tradition (for example in Japan), and in some mild climates such as Australia has been pursued to considerable lengths (for example in works of Leplastrier: see (Carter, 1990)).

This interpenetration is of course the domain of the user:

> *...many architects have deliberately designed for improvisation in the sense that they have*
> *seen that buildings are inevitably adapted over time to suit changing needs and desires and so*
> *have tried to enable this improvisatory nature of everyday life to occur more easily. They have*
> *designed spaces that are flexible due to their non-specific nature (the Georgian house has long*
> *been admired for this flexibility); or flexible due to movable screens, walls, floors, roofs, etc —*
> *though this has often led to cumbersome elements that are awkward and therefore seldom used,*
> *and when involving sophisticated technology they become expensive and provide many*
> *opportunities for technical failure, etc. The traditional Japanese house was extraordinary*
> *flexible, as commonly, all its walls could be slid away and no room had a sole specific function,*
> *so improvisation by the occupants was the name of the game. (Spence, 1994)*

The concerns of Jean Nouvel and his colleagues that the user should be able to transform the space and its situation, follow the earlier ideas of adaptable architecture of the Dutch architects Nicholaas Habraken, Aldo van Eyck, and Hermann Hertzberger. Eyck's idea of a "polyvalent space" is closely related to Nouvel's wish to devolve control to the improvising user, absolutely in parallel with that permitted by the composer to the sound improvisor, as discussed earlier in the book. It is striking that Nouvel collaborated considerably with the scenographer Jacques Le Marquet, though their initial plan for a theatre was not fulfilled. However, their later plan for updating Belfort Theatre was completed, thereby "opening one of its faces onto the city" (Boissiere, 1992).

By the 80s, Nouvel was at war with the "autonomy of architecture" ((Boissiere, 1992) p. 9), and wanting to make the user more important, and architecture more socially relevant, was one of the battles. To quote Nouvel: "Architecture means introducing values of culture and civilisation into the built". And his friend Le Marquet said, in a complementary fashion: "Architects should cultivate fiction so as to approach reality better" ((Boissiere, 1992) p. 20). He shares these ideas with Jencks and the postmodern movement more generally. Nouvel has indicated his taste for cinema, and he clearly uses cinematographic visual processes, such as "framing, panoramics, zooming, high and low angle shooting" (Boissiere, 1992). Here he has in mind the user, who can choose the positioning (of chairs, tables, implements), and hence how the environment will be viewed. In so doing users improvise their experience of the environment, and sometimes actually change it. Within Nouvel's council flats at Nimes there is ready scope for inhabitant-improvisors to change the environment.

Such scope is even greater within some of the artificial environments we will discuss in the next chapter, as are their potential applications in improvisation in general.

10

COMPUTERS AND IMPROVISATION

Computers can be both tools of improvisation, and provide the environment (with)in which improvising takes place. They are central to the concepts of virtual space, virtual reality and hypermedia. In this chapter, we will discuss some of the powers of these spaces and processes, some achieved and some as yet unfulfilled.

Computers create a new kind of improvisation for the 90s and the next century, by facilitating improvisation with a machine, and between computer-improvisors who may not be immediately present to each other. They permit multidimensionality and non-linearity and also allow for new levels and facilities for controlling the processes of improvisation. They create a different concept of the audience, since the improvisor is no longer in direct contact with the audience: in this way the improvisor's activity may move into a private situation quite like that of the composer. Alternatively, the improvisor may be viewed as a member of the (dispersed) audience who also manipulates the work. Computers also permit the possibility of creating multi-media objects which cannot be transcribed in any other form, and they can be programmed to hinder or facilitate the effect of personal choice. The avoidance of what we have called "personal cliches" is one possible application of this.

It is useful to summarise briefly the historical background of computer improvising. The first computer occupied a whole room (an IBM machine) and was proudly unveiled in the 1950s. So called "main-frame" computers were predominant until the 70s, as they still are for large scale activities, and were generally insufficiently accessible for significant use by artistic improvisors. A very few exceptional uses for image and sound generation existed, but the improvisatory components were very limited. It was only after the 70s, when the microcomputer began to appear on office and home desks, that artists could usefully involve themselves in improvisation with computers. The translation of main frame programs into an accessible form which runs at a reasonable speed on a microcomputer, then permitted their conversion into real-time programs with which improvisation was possible. The computer interactive sound work of

Rosenboom (e.g. (Rosenboom, 1976)), Teitelbaum, Lewis, and others was pioneering, and mainly based in University departments, since these provided the financial resources necessary. The development of the programming environment MAX was equally important, and was also largely undertaken in a research/education institution, IRCAM, in Paris. Comparable developments in visual improvisation lead to programs such as the AARON generative drawing program of Harold Cohen (Boden, 1990), and the academic environment was important for such developments too, though the Fairlight Computer Visual Instrument of the 80s was a commercial development corresponding to their earlier Computer Music Instrument. Specialised programs for applications such as designing choreography have also been produced. Merce Cunningham currently uses a program called "Life Forms", for this purpose, but it is clearly not primarily improvisatory (Jacobson, 1992). The present broader potentials of polymedia application and video are clear in work such as that of Ritter and others.

The computerisation of our society may mean that improvisatory skills generally become more widely disseminated. Already much technopop music is produced by applied improvisation on home computers; and there is a techno-MUD on the Internet, as mentioned earlier. Much of the improvisatory thrust of the arts in the 60s sprang from the power of improvised music, and many who improvised in other spheres were induced to do so because of this. Computers may have a comparable effect in the future, and this will be equally spread through the visual and aural arts, and perhaps through body-work. Many computer users do and will become aware of the possibilities of improvising, without necessarily thinking of it as such; thus the frequency of improvising abilities in our society will probably increase, and as we argue in Appendix 2 this will be widely advantageous, both within and outside the arts.

The Improvisor-computer Interface

The improvisor frequently uses a computer as the base of the work, be it visual, sonic or even verbal. Some of the specific programs which are in use are summarised in Appendix 3. Here we point out some of the general features. There are probably two main uses: i) to provide rapid processing of some activity entirely dictated by the improvisor, such as reordering some visual elements, or undertaking a calculation and using the result; and ii) providing an algorithmic counterpoint to the input of the improvisor, so that the computer generates continuously material of comparable complexity and range to that supplied by the improvisor.

The interface is the feature which dictates the utility to improvisors of a particular medium. For example, a musician will usually be happy with a music-keyboard interface, and because of its similarity, perhaps also with a computer keyboard interface. On the other hand, a body improvisor will not want to use a keyboard, but will perhaps be happy with a light or acoustic detector to interpret improvised movements, and transmute them into acoustic or visual signals which can be part of the performance. Alternatively, the body improvisor might like using a computer "glove" which can be controlled fully by the hand, and which contains a range of pressure or tension sensors to transmit movement or position messages to a computer, again for the purpose of their conversion into new signals, visual, verbal etc. By 1995, such devices were routinely used in popular contexts by artists such as Laurie Anderson.

By now, almost anything, including almost any body part, can be interfaced to, or provide signals to, a computer, either by a directly attached or a distant unattached sensor. Sometimes the detection is still imprecise and/or slow (as in the case of certain pitch or timbral ranges of sound, such as some low pitches on the double bass). But the possibility of quite subtle control of the computer output by the improvisor still remains.

Many examples of these kinds of improvisor-computer interaction have been mentioned already. They include the work of George Lewis, Richard Teitelbaum, Jon Rose, and many other sound improvisors who have developed a variety of interfaces, sometimes quite personalised, for their purposes. And they encompass installation environments in which audience or performer is encouraged to "dance" and thus trigger audio or visual output through detectors: for example the spaces of Rolf Gelhaar (shown in London, 1980s), and many others (see for example (Loeffler and Tong, 1980)).

What sort of output can these interactions trigger? In the 60s, relatively simple noises were triggered by "biofeedback", where sensors attached to the body usually activated the sounds. David Rosenboom developed this approach to a high level of sophistication, so that the sound output was influenced by quite subtle features of the body actions being detected (Rosenboom, 1976). These might be, for example, electrical patterns in the brain, detected by surface electrodes and then transduced into relatively complex synthesised sounds, using information extracted from the patterns by computers or simpler "microprocessor" antecedents. Gelhaar and many others used distant detectors of body movements to interact with sound and light generating and controlling systems of variable complexity. For example, a computer generated sound process using MAX (see Appendix 3) might take an input from the sensors, and use it for small or large scale change. An example of a small scale change might be modulating an ongoing process, and a larger scale change might occur when a new choice of process (unit x of material instead of unit y) is made. Unusual uses of triggering to influence verbal display occur in some works by American/Australian artist Bill Seaman (see for example (Seaman, 1994)). More often triggering has been used to control sound and light.

It is more difficult to use computers to trigger other sensory stimuli, but especially in virtual reality which we discuss below, this is perfectly feasible. It is amusing that the Europa Times of July 1994 quoted from the Hollywood Insider that cinemas had begun to install "Smellivision". This produces odors from devices installed in cinema seats which "are particularly effective in replicating food smells during advertisements". No doubt these are activated by remote computers; perhaps they are as undesirable as the "shittyville" to which Johnny refers in Mike Leigh's "Naked".

However, all of the real space uses of computers we have just mentioned have counterparts, exploited or not, in the virtual worlds within the computer and the Internet — the highway of cyberspace — and these will be cleaner. We will turn to these later in this chapter.

Computers and Inter-improvisor Interaction

One of the difficulties (and also the advantages) of group improvisation is that individuals often cannot directly indicate how they would like the improvisation to progress, or transform. For example, a dance improvisation may involve a group of individuals all moving quite separately within the space. How does one of them suddenly induce a group change if desired? This is akin to the question of identification of transition point, which we discussed in Chapters 2 and 4, and showed was complex and unreliable even in retrospect. The Grand Union and other groups sometimes dealt with this problem by incorporating spoken instructions to which the other members would respond. But such an approach would not coincide with the aesthetic of many improvisors, and has not been common. Similarly, in music or sound generally, such levels of control decided within performance are rare. They are confined to the jazz group indicating the next improvising soloist, while the accompanying rhythm section continues, and to comparably simple processes within other conventionalised formats (e.g. Indian music). In many media, such control is very difficult to envisage. The aesthetic problem for many improvisors would be that they do not wish the control process itself to be identifiable as such to the audience, nor even to be part of the detectable performance. This is quite a different issue from that mentioned earlier, of whether an audience can detect that the work being performed is being improvised. As noted, many improvisors like their work to be seen to be improvised, because they feel that it enhances audience response and appreciation. But many of these improvisors would also prefer that those elements of the improvisation which constitute purely control mechanisms, and which are not *necessary* components of the presented work, should not be displayed. For example, many sound improvisors using instrumental or computer sound do not like to interrupt the flow of such sounds by a verbal control command, though they might like better access to such controls.

Computer interactions offer a multitude of ways of effecting such controls without making the control process necessarily known to the audience. Thus performers can be networked to each other, by using computer keyboards (which might be suitable for a sound performance). Or they can be networked using radio emitters and detectors, together with miniaturised keyboard or other interfaces which the performers can carry and use while moving. Such networks are quite well developed for sound work, and have been exploited by several groups, notably the San Francisco based group "The Hub". Much of their work is improvised, and they use computer nodes of a network connected primarily by MIDI, a specialised interface designed particularly for transmission of information which can control synthesisers or other electronic keyboards to generate sound. This constitutes flow of control information only, rather than of sound. They have also interacted with poets, who offered verbal cues to the Hub via the Internet during a performance, as we discussed in Chapter 6. A higher performance facility for performing these data flows is the commercial Miditap system (Jacobson, 1992). This permits such flow (of MIDI and also digitised sound or visual information) between a local group of performers, using fibre-optic cable to permit very fast data transfer by means of light encoding. This system is faster and less susceptible to corruption than the present Internet.

Figure 17 offers an idealised diagram of a network for an improvising group. In the future, when data transmission rate (i.e. "bandwidth") is sufficient, this could be local or widespread. The putative group uses all those forms of sensory component which can be expressed in digital form; presently including visual, verbal, sound and musical elements, to refer to the categories we established earlier. In principle, taste, touch and smell might be transmitted, through a virtual world component, but this is discussed in the next section. Many significant developments towards permitting such an improvising network are underway, such as the ZIPI protocol initiated at University of California at Berkeley with commercial collaboration. The future of such improvising is one of continuing expansion and wonderful possibility.

ZIPI involves collaboration with the Californian company ZETA, and Doc Rosenberg has a comment on this ((Rose and Linz, 1992) pp. 170–174):

The Virtual Violin
Veta Music Systems

> *Violin music has undergone little change since Antonio Stradivari and Giuseppe Guarneri, But the world of violin music continUes to evolve at supersonic speeds. sYnthesisers create nearly eVery sound imaginable; digital samplers record and playback Every sound ThAt can Be heard; personal compUters assist in the preparation and composition of complex music scores.*
> *Now, from Veta Music sYstems comes the Virtual violin....*

and finally, several pages later

> *Eh, you might Be interested to know that all the violin mUsic You heard, before it crashed, was extrapolated out of white noise by the use of a quite sophisticated filter program — eh. A sort of "Waves of History" approach to music, if you'll allow the term. Eh, I can see on my watch that there is still a little time to go — of course you could just turn IT off. Well, that winds it up for today — oh I see you didn't do it. Well, I cn stay here as long as you, fella. If you don't turn it off. NOW, I' m going to have to...*

Cyberspace and Improvisation

In alluding to the Internet and to virtual worlds above and in Chapter 3, we have already touched on the concept of cyberspace. Cyberspace is the world-wide web of computer networks, and all the spaces it can conjure in visual or audible form on any of the computer terminals attached to it, or in other forms of sensory input to persons interfaced with it. This web is continually humming with vast fluxes of data across the world, and it contains immense and expanding resources which are continually available to any who wish to interrogate them, often free of charge. The available resources range from library catalogues, to visual objects, games, and sound resources. There are even some resources relevant to the study of improvisation, besides the library and other bibliographic sources; for example, there is presently a discourse in action on the subject of Sun Ra, the Afro-American sound improvisor-composer.

An exciting book on Cyberspace has been edited by Michael Benedikt, mentioned earlier as theoretician of architecture (Benedikt, 1991). He offers some stimulating descriptions of cyberspace:

A common mental geography, built, in turn by consensus and revolution, canon and experiment, ...a million voices in... a... concert of enquiry, dealmaking, dreamsharing, and simple beholding. (p. 2)

For our present purposes, the interest of cyberspace is again two fold: as large scale network communication device (whose potentials we have already discussed, since they are similar to those of local networks); and as source and vehicle of artificial environments of various kinds, which may provide sites for improvisation. An artificial environment can equally be generated on a free-standing computer. But because of their psychological separation from the physical real space, even such free-standing artificial environments are still normally considered as cyberspace, whether or not they involve the distant network.

To quote Benedikt again:

...language-bound descriptions and semantic games will no longer be required to communicate personal viewpoints, historical events, or technical information. Rather, direct — if "virtual" — demonstration and interactive experience of the "original" material will prevail, or at least be a universal possibility. (p. 12).

Benedikt points out calmly that such a cyberspace, a "heavenly city", does not yet exist.

The artificial environments in cyberspace can lack most of the physical constraints of real space: as William Gibson ((Gibson, 1984) envisaged, one can travel through them instantaneously. As Gibson suggests: "Ride music beams back to base" (Gibson in (Benedikt, 1991)). On the other hand these environments can also represent a virtual reality through which one can move while gaining an impression of a real space which is being represented. It is necessary here to separate some of the categories of these artificial environments, and to explain some of the confusing nomenclature which we have avoided elsewhere in the book. "Virtual space" has been used to refer to computer environments which can be made visible on a screen, in which people or objects which are present in separate, often distant real spaces, can be superimposed visually. When people can move around in their real space this is reflected in the visible virtual space, and thus they can interact with each other, though obviously without physically touching. However, the visible interaction with each other, which they can observe, creates psychological restraint, in that they feel at least discouraged by politeness from apparently touching.

An "artificial reality" is one which "creates an experience that we treat as a real one, whether or not we're wearing data goggles, gloves or other computer clothing" (Krueger, in (Jacobson, 1992) p. 246). The originator of the term, Krueger, was and is particularly concerned that the computer which generates the reality should be

> *perceiving a participant's action in terms of the body's relationship to a graphic world, and {generating} responses that maintain the illusion that his or her actions are taking place within that world.*

In other words, Krueger wants the participant to be able to behave normally in respect to body movements, without computer gloves, and still to be able to interact with the computer artificial reality in a believable way. Less emphasis has been placed on these forms of artificial reality, than on the more familiar "virtual realities", which usually involve gloves etc.

"Virtual reality" is a subcategory of this general concept of artificial reality. Virtual reality is a "computer generated multisensory representation of data" and creates a "simulated experience" ((Jacobson, 1992) p. 272) using a variety of participant bi- and mono-directional interfaces. The term simulated is added because often virtual reality is attempting to recreate aspects of real space. But this is not a necessary feature, and as mentioned already, the virtual reality can have novel, quite unreal, unphysical properties, of which the participant can gain an "experience". Since it cannot be accessed any other way, the experience can be said to be real, not "simulated". Such a space (unreal only in the sense of being non-existent beyond the computer interface) can be distinguished as a hyperspace (c.f. Chapter 3), and may be multidimensional and instantly traversable. As mentioned above, virtual reality is taken to be part of cyberspace, though cyberspace does not necessarily involve the invoking of a virtual reality.

The improvisor (or any other participant) may interact with a virtual reality using a variety of transducers, such as computer gloves, or goggles. These may transmit to the computer information about movements; and thus they share the possibilities mentioned earlier in the section on the improvisor-computer interface. But they may also be vehicle for the return of sensory data to the participant. For example, the goggles may be used to present the desired virtual reality visual components to the participant; the gloves to give physical tensions, or even mild electrical impulses, and so on. The possibilities for improvisation using these realities are thus immense. Indeed, the sense in which the inhabitant of an building improvises its use (Chapter 8) is also a sense in which the traveller through virtual reality necessarily improvises. But the possibilities go far beyond that, and they have only begun to be explored.

For example, the computer screen image, and the other digital messages it is relaying, such as sound, word etc, can be controlled by the participant in almost any way one can envisage. The reality software simply has to be set up to permit the interpretation of the particular signals concerned; and may be set up to provide any kind of response, at least within the sense ranges currently available. As mentioned already, virtual reality is efficient in transmitting visual and sonic elements, but not highly advanced as yet with regard to touch, taste or smell. But these remain possibilities.

Interactive video is a small subcategory of these possibilities in which significant improvisation has already been produced. The components of the video images are often both objects and people in the same space as the video; computerised transformations of them; and computer-generated images transformed in turn by signals dictated by movements of the people present. The people thus interact with the digital processes to control the video images. Such work is mostly closer to the concept of artificial reality than to virtual reality, in that usually no special body-attached interfaces (such as the gloves) are used to send information to or from the computer. The humanising of the digital images by this process creates a fascinating hybrid of the computer abstract image, and the virtual space mentioned at the beginning of the section. It illustrates the immense potential of interaction with artificial reality, and the fact that its application is only in its early stages.

Hypermedia: Computers and Multidirectional Improvisation

Hypermedia are computer programs such as Hypercard which permit non-linear access from any point to almost any other. They are sometimes termed "multidimensional", as opposed to both the linear (essentially, one dimensional) printed book, and the two dimensional surface of a computer screen. An alternative description of hypermedia is "multidirectional and direct access". Thus from any point in the program, one can jump almost instantaneously to any other, rather as one can move through virtual reality. There is no need for the two points to be in any physical sense adjacent, though they usually need to have some notional connection. For example a word or icon may lead to a whole new dimension of information about it, even though appearing in the middle of a dense screen. This is the current common use of hypermedia, to provide information access, and the possibility for the user to interrogate any aspect of the information presented to gain more information about it, if available in the system. CD-Rom encyclopedias are a common example of this, and so are many other teaching materials, and popular cd-roms such as "Myst".

But hypermedia such as this offer the artist a way of presenting an entity through which the audience has to navigate actively. These hypermedia embody the concept that the audience is at least co-creator of the work.

Members of the audience have to make their own choices, and because they will not be able to grasp in advance the implication of every choice they make, they will have to improvise with the material.

Perhaps the best examples so far of such artworks are those generated within Storyspace (see Appendix 3) such as Michael Joyce' "Afternoon" (Joyce, 1990). Rather than a linear book, these are multidimensional arrays of computer screens, many of whose words can be interrogated to provide non-linear access to further aspects: a fascinating new mode of operation for the reader, open to creative use on both the writer's and the reader's side. Such artworks take to their logical extreme the experiments in narrative choice and flexibility of such writers as Robert Coover, Marguerite Duras, John Fowles and B. S. Johnson, where the reader is given a variety of narrative choices rather than one storyline. In such programs the characters, storyline (and in consequence the possible implications of these) will change according to the navigator's choices. Many visual art works have been constructed in such interactive multimedia, and they can permit a similar improvisatory approach by the "reader". In some cases, the reader's choice can lead to such unpredictable results, because of random elements within the program, that a repeatable reading could never be generated. In others, perhaps where words articulate somewhat logically with other sections, it might be possible to learn a series of choices so as to read the work reproducibly; but it would not be necessary or even desirable. As we indicate at the very outset of the book, the concepts of improvisation and composition form a continuum. Hypermedia help to blur this as much for the audience as it has long been blurred for the producer.

Finally, the idea of developing hypermedia programs specifically for the use of improvisors in their creative work has not yet been exploited, but is a logical outcrop from the above. Interactive programs exist, such as MAX (see Appendix 3) but commercial hypermedia improvising programs have yet to appear in substantial form. The range of possibility can be glimpsed as shown in Figure 18 which for simplicity represents a solo improvisor at work. The improvisor might be marshalling sound, word, and visual elements. As sound improvising proceeds, the computer would receive the sound input, either as MIDI information or as digitised sound; and similarly for the other elements. In relation to each component, sound, word and visual object, the program might permit multidimensional interactions, so that one sound component could trigger the program to jump to a "remote" node of its actions. This node might then initiate a different way of processing the incoming sound, or a new sound output from the computer itself, or from an associated MIDI or digital instrument. The same kinds of interactions would be possible within the verbal and visual worlds. But in addition, information from the visual might influence the verbal or other components. And similarly the performer would be able to interact directly with the program by means of another interface(s) which does not involve the generation or sensing of verbal, sound or visual elements per se: for example, it might be the conventional computer keyboard. This would then permit the performer, in a multidimensional, multidirectional manner characteristic of hypermedia, to dictate the new direction of the program's actions in relation to any or all of the elements being generated. The audience might be given access to any combination of the sensory elements, and of the hypermedia interaction processes. They might also be allowed to interact with them via computers....

The whole process might occur in cyberspace, across the virtual galaxies. The potentials are expansive if not infinite.

Appendix 1

A SPACE FOR IMPROVISORS

The reform of the theatrical space, for architecture, has long been the imputation of the reform of the world stage. (Sorkin, in (Himmelblau, 1988)).
The theatre is dead. …We are not working for new theatres. …We are working for the theatre that has survived the theatre. (Kiesler, quoted by Sorkin in (Himmelblau, 1988)).
…building the giant experimental theatres with video cameras gliding like sharks through a sea of information… (Benedikt in (Benedikt, 1991) p. 14).

No real space has so far been designed specifically for the artistic improvisor, as far as we know. Yet we have shown, in many ways, that it is not safe to assume that conditions or products of composing are congruent with those of improvising. Some of the features of the improvising arts could be supported more fully by appropriate spaces for their production. We propose here a space of extreme flexibility, which might fulfil this need; at the same time it would be likely to be an appropriate space for most art presentations.

The architect Craig Hodgetts ((Lacy and deMenil, 1992), p. 26) has written about the ways that architecture and environment can aid "expanding and amplifying the human condition". In discussing his sketches "Studies of Skinner's Room", he refers to a story by William Gibson, the pioneer of cyberspace writing, which is the stimulus for the design. However, the "Studies" are intended for a

time when …consumption and… development have all but exhausted the natural resources and human spirit…. It is the reality of soft tech, dead tech, no tech.

Striking and flexible though these images are, we need an improvising space which will enhance the human spirit: this could be a "hypertech" in which every technology could interact with every other directly.

By now the reader of this book can probably deduce many of the features, or at least opportunities, we would encourage in such a space. In essence, these include flexibility, mutability, multiplicity, and continuity; and all these features should be open to control by the improvisors themselves. They should also be arranged such that there is no necessary division of function between audience and performer, so that performers can choose the degree of control they permit the audience.

Concepts which might be brought to bear on designing such a space are those discussed in the earlier section on improvisation in architecture, particularly those of flexibility and mutability. Relevant spaces include Jacob's Pillow (dance centre) in Massachusetts, where the rear of the conventional stage has a window which looks out onto an attractive natural environment, and this can be opened to create direct continuity between space and environment. Some of Frank Gehry's performance buildings have similarly continuity, such as the Merriweather Post Pavilion of Music in Columbia, Maryland (1966–7). This is trapezoidal, and has two canopies, an acoustical and a 'firestage' canopy which extends 30ft out over the audience and is open-sided. The house can be tuned acoustically by movable baffles; and amplification is not used within the pavilion, but is available for those seated outside on the grass. Gehry's crater-shaped Concord Pavilion, Concord, California (1973–5) has a related open construction, and is in a crater so as to minimise the road noise from nearby. These two buildings are described in Futagawa (Futagawa, 1993). The works of several other architects have fostered such direct continuities and flexibilities, as in the case of the Dutch Forum Group, often considered "structuralists".

Spence also mentions that

> ...more recently, the so-called "High Tech" architects have been interested in flexible, adaptable spaces and have actually built some — for example, Norman Foster, Richard Rogers and Renzo Piano. (Spence, 1994)

Another possible source of influence is the communal "holding area" of the Hajj Terminal at King Abdul Aziz International Airport, Jeddah, which provides open protection for travellers to Mecca for the religious festivities there. It was designed by the large US firm Skidmore Owings and Merrill in the 1980s. Likewise, Joseph Paxton's Crystal Palace (built in 1851 for the International Exposition in London) and Mies van der Rohe's Convention Hall Chicago — particularly in the design form before the installation of roof and walls — are antecedents to the openness of form we would seek (illustrated, for example in (Conrads, Sperlich *et al.*, 1962)). The small work of Giacometti "The Palace at 4:00 a.m." (1932–3, Collection of the Museum of Modern Art, New York) is also relevant: constructed of wood, wire, glass and string and only 25 X 28 1/4 X 15 3/4 inches, this is a model for the openness and clamberability which we seek in the description below.

The multilayered surfaces of Claude Parent's "oblique space" or "line of greatest slope", an exhibition space built in 1970, anticipate some of the floor and general surface flexibility we advocate (discussed in (Popper, 1975)). On a larger scale, The Ronacher Theatre, by Coop Himmelblau, was clearly related to Moreno's ideas for a performing space (as Sorkin points out (Sorkin, 1991)). Its multilayered roof conjures an impression of movement from one layer to another, anticipating our demand that the users be able to move across "roof" surfaces just as they can across other surfaces (see later). Related impressions are conveyed by their "Open House" (1983), to which Kiesler's 1937 "Endless house" (Popper, 1975)) is a relevant antecedent. Similarly, the Coop Himmelblau designs for the town of Melun-Senart (1987) indicate a rare combination of the sociofugal and sociopetal. The Russian group Dvizjenije, involving Lev Nusberg, produced an "artificial area" (1970) which was 660 metres square, and 6 metres high. It contained lights, kinetic objects and sound, and had a floor but no ceiling or walls. The floor was broken up into different coloured horizontal segments. The user ("audience") could participate in the space, using stop/go pedals, and activating photoelectric detectors, to influence the kinetic elements of the piece. This is one of the works most relevant to the kind of improvisors' space we envisage.

Many possible influences on the realisation of our proposal operate as much on the level of ideas as on achieved buildings, since many fascinating projects in architecture are not realised. Yona Friedman's concept (c. 1957) of "L'Architecture Mobile", in which the inhabitants determine form, has direct bearing. Similarly, Archigram proposed the "plug-in city", in which mobile elements, often modular, could be organised at will; such would also be a component of the improvising space we propose. Constant, one of the initiators of the Cobra group discussed earlier, summarises these ideals (quoted in Popper, p. 62):

> *Architecture will be reborn when it is created by all — each for himself, and in collaboration with the others for the tasks held in common.*

Michael Benedikt (Benedikt, 1987) offers some additional ideas about how a space may engage its users. He argues for a "high realism" in which buildings "capture us by their presence, significance, materiality and emptiness" (p. 66) and indicates that

> *presence... means something... analogous to the "presence" attributed to certain people — stage presence in an actor, for instance — or to "presence of mind". Implied is a certain... attentiveness... (p. 34).*

He also suggests that "when we feel the pull of an empty room for us to enter and dwell there, when we see in something incomplete the chance of continuation or find in things closed a gate...... there is *emptiness*".

The two features that Benedikt describes, presence and emptiness, are intended to attract people into the spaces, so that they contribute their presence. In that improvising may seek to involve everybody, we could hope that both improvisation and the spaces in which it operates might fulfil these aims.

The Improvising Space

The key features of a valuable improvising space, permitting the opportunities we have mentioned, seem to be: first, that there should be few immutable barriers in space, horizontally or vertically; second, that the space should be larger than can be surveyed completely by any single audience member at any instant (so that it is possible for there to be events (s)he does not perceive); and third, that most mutable aspects of the space can be controlled by the improvisors, as well as by any specialised "space-managers".

There has to be a constructed area somewhere in the space, which besides protection from the elements, provides a site for basic functions, hygienic, sheltering, and financial, required by performers and audience. This construct should also provide locales for performance components. This space will be termed the protective space, in what follows, since it need not be central, and need not be used in the performance. However, often it will function as the central performing space, like a conventional theatre.

The protective space should have floors which can be moved in three dimensions, to create changing articulations. It should have vertical divisions which can be moved, so that the vertical constructs necessary for the stability of the building are minimised, and potential for rearranging access between different areas within the protective space, is maximised. Similarly, while there will need to be roof-like structures for protection, these need to be movable and multiple. They should also provide a potential path (i.e. some kind of 'ladder') along which a performer or audience member can move, out of the lower level ('floor'), on to the 'roof' and back to the floor. In other words, as far as possible, all components of the structure should not simply be protective, but also surfaces on which people can move. Sophisticated theatres contain machinery for moving elements of the stage horizontally and vertically: this protective space should also contain such devices. But most critically, they should be accessible to performers and audience alike, and not solely to space-managers. This degree of flexibility will permit the construction of an audience 'pen' whenever it is actually required. It should also be possible to move these 'floors' into the surroundings, creating further connections between the two, or creating new floors (protected or not) in the surroundings.

While there will inevitably still be some discontinuities between the protective space and its surroundings, these should be minimised and be flexible. Thus every wall should be openable, so that movement in any direction in and out of the protective space is possible. Similarly, movement over the external edge of the protective space into the surroundings should be possible at times. Objects need to be wheel-movable within the protective space, and the surroundings, though, of course, there they may meet natural insurmountable objects.

What of the peripheral space? It might be appropriate for this to contain both a constructed and fixed, yet external and unprotected component; and a natural, unmodified one. The constructed component, like a garden, would provide some geometric elements, and some controlled and marshalled growth forms; while the unmodified component would be natural proliferation of vegetation and animals, including trees. This unmodified area would need to be sufficiently soil-based to allow for construction of earthworks, and movement of elements such as rocks, for or in performance. Such a peripheral space would permit all the improvising continuities and possibilities we have discussed earlier.

What of communications, and environmental features such as sound, light, odour? It would be important to forge computer links throughout the space, but in the natural area at least, for these not to be hard-wired. Instead they should be passed by radio devices, which could be movable, and either carried by audience or performer, or transiently installed. These links would be needed for the transfer of control information, which might act on lighting etc; for the transfer of verbal information; and for the transfer of digitally encoded sound and visual elements, which could then be displayed or projected. Any of these elements could be directed only to selected recipients or could be made widely available. All the potential features of computer improvisation we discussed earlier should be available.

If there is decor, i.e. visual objects which are not intrinsic to the space, then it should be movable. Lighting facilities might need to be extensible into the 'garden' and beyond to the natural spaces, but should be mutable, rather than fixed, otherwise they would limit the potential of those spaces for improvisation. Likewise, sound diffusion can be achieved with movable speakers. In addition, the input, detection and redirection of both improvisors' sounds, audience sounds, and natural environmental sounds, needs to be controllable. This can be achieved through the use of moveable and placeable radio microphones, without irrevocable alteration of any of the environments. The radio links should permit both local control (by the performer or audience-participant) and central control, perhaps by other improvisors or by the space-managers.

Such a space for improvisors would have almost "unreal" potential. Indeed, it would be continuous with the potentials for improvisation of virtual space. At present, the control of odour diffusion and its digital transfer is limited, but the path forward is apparent, partly originating in the polysensorial improvisations of Hermann Nitsch (Chapter 8). The path will no doubt be pursued. Let us hope that the future of improvisation includes such a polysensorial range of opportunities.

Appendix 2

OTHER USES OF IMPROVISATION

It is easy, if rather trivial, to suggest, as many have done, that every aspect of life is improvisation. This grossly underestimates the control possible in improvisation, as we have revealed. In contrast, we have two very simple purposes in this appendix: to point to some of the areas in which improvisation, usually applied improvisation, is valuable in a learning or self-enhancing process; and to mention some examples of cultivated performance in every-day existence, in which improvisatory skills may be valuable. These examples imply a belief that such skills would be valuable to everyone, and that their directed development in the education process would have wide benefits. Improvisation is, of course, one particular kind of creative process and arguably a component of any kind of creative process. To develop these ideas fully would require another book, and so we will not attempt an elaborate presentation.

Improvisation in Self Development

There is a substantial literature on improvisation in education, but in most cases it concerns using improvisation to develop a particular *limited* skill. For example, it encourages children to play percussion instruments in an improvisatory manner in order to teach them essentials of rhythmic structure, or group texture. Or again, using improvised stories and group interactions to show the essentials of the dramatic process. These are very valuable approaches, which need to be encouraged. But the lack of emphasis in the education of musicians on even these limited skills, particularly at tertiary level, has serious negative consequences for both the psychological adaptation and the creativity of performing musicians (Jenkin, 1991). And as mentioned in Chapter 8, Mike Leigh has similarly negative experiences of the lack of improvisation study in tertiary drama college in the past, though the situation seems to have improved much more than it has in music. Improvisation is sometimes introduced in creative writing courses at tertiary level, in, for example, the guise of "freewriting". But this is not usually accompanied by training in the kind of linguistic techniques which might assist the generation of an improvisation, and students are usually encouraged to see such work as only preliminary. The development of oral improvising techniques on such courses is rare.

However, there is another level on which the development of improvisatory abilities in everyone would facilitate *fundamental* creative, analytical and practical work in most professions and circumstances. This is probably the most important reason for including the study of improvisation in any educational system.

It is not just the limited idea that "life is improvisation". It is rather that analytical and creative solutions to any problem require starting points, and techniques to find and exploit them. How does one arrive at a new starting point for tackling an intransigent problem? Does this involve the famous "lateral thinking" or another of its commercialised friends? More fundamentally, it is probably the ability to improvise, and thus to be able rapidly to try out and to assess new approaches. This improvisation would concern the practical issues at hand, but the training for it could be in part training in artistic, non-practical, improvising. The solutions to a practical problem which are generated by improvisation can be assessed against objective criteria. But the capacity to assess even artistic improvisation against objective criteria exists: the degree of precision with which the improvisatory artistic task is defined dictates the degree of objectivity with which its fulfilment can be assessed (see for example (Hodgson, 1967)). Thus artistic improvising offers a way to train the mind to practical as well as open-ended artistic improvisation, and to assess the development of the improvisatory capacity.

The development of this facility in artistic areas should be a necessary component of the educational process, and it should be complemented by subsequent teaching of improvisatory approaches to more practical, scientific, and business-oriented problems. A few courses in universities are beginning to address such ideas (e.g. one at Macquarie University in Sydney run by Richard Vella), but they need to be developed much earlier within our educational systems.

The potential of improvisation for other aspects of mental development is highly esteemed in some professions, or at least in some parts of those professions. Psychotherapy, used in its most general sense, has traditionally been rooted in schisms, such as that between the psychoanalysts and the non-analytic therapists. For a valuable sub-group of these professionals, improvisation is a central tool, and it is interesting that Keeney, one of the main writers on the subject, has developed a notational procedure for describing and understanding the improvisations he experiences (Keeney, 1991). This notational system has some aspects in common with Laban dance notation, and is admitted also to share serious limitations. A fascinating historical antecedent to current improvisatory psychotherapy is the therapeutic theatre of Moreno, described in his highly imaginative books (Moreno, 1973; Moreno, 1977). They show the use of improvisation in theatre, which he commenced certainly by the 1930s, and its application to personal development or sometimes rectification. Many current artists are aware of these relationships and, particularly since the 60s, have sought through the meditative or physically immersive components of their work to help themselves and others. For example, this has been a dynamic within contact improvisation, the work of Anna Halprin (particularly recently) and Augusto Boal, and also in the sound-body explorations of the Living Theatre and the Open Theatre. Similarly, many of these artists have been drawn to psychological and psychotherapeutic subjects in their work, as in the case of Kinetic Energy's "Who Dies?" and "Who Lives?" (see Chapter 8).

There is little doubt that educational and psychotherapeutic improvisation can help prepare the individual to solve problems, and so can benefit their achievement and well being in many contexts. We hope to see an expansion of the awareness and exploitation of these possibilities.

Improvisation in Everyday Activity

While we do not wish in the least to equate life with improvisation, there is a case for pointing out one example (from the many possible) of a professional activity outside the arts which can exploit improvisatory skills in obvious ways. This may serve to underpin at a simpler level the more fundamental claims made in the previous section.

The auctioneer's work is such an example. It is an amusing one, because the objectives of this commercial exchange are, of course, far removed from the political ideals of many of the improvisors we have discussed. The auctioneer is engaged in a dialogue with an interactive audience. The scope of the interaction is limited, but essential to the success of the activity: selling an object for a good price. The auctioneer commonly has a regular patter of phrases which follow a bid, and help to elicit the next. The whole activity is one of performance, but the element of improvisation is in sensing the length of patter which is acceptable, and the speed and pitch which will induce excitement. The patter is not usually simply description of the object for sale and its virtues, it is also timbral and rhythmic excitation of the audience, and sensitivity to the degree of audience enthusiasm, the rate of increase in the bid values and so on. The auctioneer has to learn to improvise beyond the level of simply filling the gaps in trade, to a level at which the improvisation actually induces response and higher bids. Many auctioneers also have a reward-like phrase with which they terminate the transaction, such as "Very well bought!" by which they hope to mean, "Very well sold".

 This example is a simple one, in which the activity has the rapidity of sensory-generative responses characteristic of much improvisation, and in which the generative aspect is quite restricted, though possibly subtle. Without falling into the trap of seeing everything as improvisatory, one can nevertheless appreciate the potential importance of having control of such improvisatory skills in many aspects of professional and social existence.

Appendix 3

SOME SOFTWARE FOR IMPROVISORS

In considering software for artistic improvising, we may, for the sake of simplicity, view computers as producing visual objects, words, or sounds (be it directly or indirectly). They can also trigger any electrical or mechanical device. Computer programs permitting drawing, visual object processing and word display are probably at least as helpful to the improvisor in these media as the traditional means of undertaking these activities. In addition, they can permit algorithmic processing of any of the objects, allowing rapid access to permutations and any other systematic or random variation which one might want to use as a source of developing ideas.

Thus computers clearly can facilitate many kinds of improvisation, and so some programs have been developed which have particular interest for the improvisor. Since the improvisor at a computer is simply a specialised example of computer interaction, it is not surprising that programs have been produced which facilitate interaction with artistic objects by individuals who may equally be "audience", "participants" or "creators". Here we discuss two examples of such programs which are commercially available. The program called "MAX" (distributed by Opcode) is directed towards the improvising (or composing) creator, mainly orientated towards sound generation. "Storyspace" (Eastgate Systems), on the other hand, is intended both as the base for a creative production primarily in the verbal domain, and also as part of the interactive interface which can permit the "reader" of the work to navigate it and hence·modify its impact, progression, nature and content.

MAX is named after one of the pioneers of computer music, Max Mathews, and was developed by Miller Puckette at IRCAM, and released commercially after further work by David Zicarelli (Puckette and Zicarelli, 1990). It is an object-orientated programming environment rather than simply a program: in other words the users build their own programs using MAX. It exploits the MIDI (Musical Instrument Digital Interface) protocol, in that it sends information to digital sound generating modules such as keyboards using this procedure. MIDI is designed to permit ready specification and transfer of information about pitch, velocity (that is intensity or loudness) and duration. It has possibilities, and also some limitations, in relation to transmitting other features of complex musical sound, such as continuous timbral variation of individual sounds with time. These technical details of the information being transmitted need not overly concern us. More to the point are the potentials the program offers for improvisation, and the degree to which these realise the theoretically desirable possibilities of improvising software.

As we have argued, one can usefully distinguish at least the following components of improvisation: systematic manipulation of material; random generation of material; systematic response to external input; and memory functions which can be accessed at any time. MAX permits the computer to perform any of these functions in real time, and thus to participate in a pure or applied improvisation (or in a composition) by means of processes at least analogous to those used by the improvisors themselves. The systematic manipulation must be built into the program devised by the user, though its parameters dictating the modification and response elements can be varied by the performer in real time, as can the data to which it responds directly. Experienced improvisors find MAX both a stimulus and occasionally a restriction or even irritation. Most of the restrictions stem from the limitations of MIDI itself, and the possibility of overloading the computer with data, such that it lags behind, or cannot respond and perhaps crashes. Such problems can mostly be avoided by more controlled programming, so that events which are unnecessary, or which exceed the system's flux capacity, are filtered out.

For the performer who uses a keyboard instrument habitually, translation of notes into MIDI is not a problem, and hence they may gain most from MAX, as is the experience of Roger Dean. On the other hand, keyboard improvisors such as Richard Teitelbaum have still found it desirable to use their own software, perhaps through historical tradition (they were writing it before MAX was available) or perhaps because they have needs not fulfilled by MAX. Robert Rowe, primarily a composer rather than improvisor, has also developed his own software, Cypher, which he discusses together with MAX and related issues in a valuable book (Rowe, 1993). Non-keyboard players have needed their own software even more, so that components of their input sound, beyond those readily encoded in MIDI, can affect the software. For example, George Lewis has developed software specially for interacting with his trombone playing (as revealed on his cd "Voyager" (Lewis, 1994)). Another factor is portability, and Jon Rose has his interactive microprocessor systems (the "virtual violin" (Rose and Linz, 1992)) usually in small boxes, such that they are easy to carry around and relatively simple to set up for performance.

MAX was designed for sound generation, but readily permits manipulation of screen images, and of video material. In a recent work "The Silence of Eyes", commissioned by our ensemble austraLYSIS, Greg White used MAX to control both sound generators and also the display of words which were coordinated with words spoken by one of the performers. Equally MAX can be used to drive mechanically activated devices of any kind. It is also an attractive idea to use it to coordinate the sounding of computer generated words and their fragments with visual displays.

Of course, coordinated display of visual and verbal material is a feature of most multimedia software including Hypercard. The issue is the degree to which real time, and therefore improvisatory, interaction is possible. Macromedia's "Director" is such a multimedia generation platform which permits the interactive use of the product by the viewer. However, the scope for interaction by the participant viewer is largely limited to directing the program between different pre-existent multimedia elements. In principle the possibility for controlling the generation of such elements is present, though not foregrounded.

Particularly in the case of verbal elements, Storyspace brings forward the possibility of multilayered interactivity. The software is not intended as an improvising vehicle, though it does permit some such work. It is intended more as a computer platform on which a verbal (and possibly visual) work can be constructed in such a way that the viewer/participant can substantially modify its progress in time, and thus be an active player. As with Director, Storyspace is not primarily intended to permit player generation of material, but rather to permit player specification of direction through pre-existing material. The multiplicity of meaning intrinsic in most works is thus brought to the fore by the multiple viewer-paths, and the viewer can certainly improvise these paths in the sense of systematic response to material. The viewer can point with the computer mouse-arrow to areas of the text or image which are particularly appealing, and the software can then generate a response which is a new screen image, in some way articulating with that selected area. The viewer usually cannot *determine* that the next events will be random, nor systematically manipulate them. But the viewer does have some control.

Some video artists have wished to emphasise the possibility of controlling the generation and transformation of visual objects (often obtained from immediately recorded images) in a way which no commercial software seems to do. Don Ritter and other video/multimedia artists have developed various pieces of real time software for this purpose. These extend beyond the possibilities of the Fairlight Computer Video Instrument (a later development of the pioneering computer music instrument company) and related machines. Ritter's software is not readily available, so one has to rely on the information offered in his writings (Ritter, 1993), and discussed by Rowe (Rowe, 1993). From a concern with real time visual response to ongoing visual events, Ritter has developed a chain in which a video image of the event is the subject of transformation, control information, and other aspects of software operation on computer generated or transmitted images. In other words the video image might be the source of the computer generation of a fresh image, or the computer processing of that image itself, or of modification of a previously digitised real image. Ritter has worked a good deal with musicians, and so he has developed means for using sound information as controlling data within his software (Ritter, 1993). Ritter seems to believe that sound has power beyond visual image, and therefore that he should harness the sound to control the image:

> I have concluded that musical media — especially improvised music — are expressions of life, while visual media, such as painting, drawing and sculpture, are expressions of death. The difference becomes obvious in comparing the experience of visual media with the experience of live music. In a museum or gallery, for example, visitors calmly observe inanimate objects, rarely speaking and never clapping or cheering in approval. These viewers are like the bereaved at a wake, paying respect to a friend who will later be entombed in a storage room....
> I have attempted to overcome these usual limitations of the visual arts by creating a visual medium that contains the living qualities found in music performance. Through events of interactive video controlled by improvised music, my collaborators and I create works entirely before an audience. The technological interaction is the music controlling the video, while the musicians' improvised playing is affected by the images. (Ritter, 1993).

The principles at work here are only limited by the digitising and transmission protocols (e.g. MIDI), the speed of the software and computer, and the availability of labile, rapidly accessible memory for event information. Only some of the minimal desirable criteria of improvisation, which we mentioned in Chapter 2, are fulfilled by any of these programs, as their generators would be the first to mention. Their present possibilities are immense, yet their futures are probably unimaginable.

Appendix 4

THE QUESTIONNAIRE AND INTERVIEWS

Our research included interviews with practitioners, and sending a questionnaire to both practitioners and critics. More than forty people were interviewed, or gave personal communications in conversation. Questionnaires were sent to about one hundred and forty people, of whom seven were critics or theorists, about twenty were both artists and writers on the arts, while the remainder were artists. The artists chosen included many declared improvisors, but also many who would usually be considered composers. The questionnaire to the artists is reproduced below, together with the information which accompanied it. As discussed in the methodology section of the book, this questionnaire was designed not to give our opinions, definitions or frameworks, but to elicit as far as possible the unaltered opinions of the responders. A modified version of the questionnaire was used for critics/theorists and for artist-writers, in which some critical concepts were mentioned and some greater indication of our stance was revealed.

The following list indicates those who responded to the questionnaire (R), and those who were interviewed or were the source of other verbal personal communications, not necessarily formal interviews (I). The latter normally did not receive the questionnaire, with the exceptions noted, and we attempted firstly to seek their opinions in their own terms, before pursuing some issues in our own. One person responded to the questionnaire by means of a tape.

Interviewees and Questionnaire Responders

Ernie Althoff (R)
David Antin (I)
Michael Atherton (R)
Richard Barrett (R)
Steve Benson (I)
John Bischoff (I)

David Bromige (I)
Chris Brown (I)
Paul Buck (R)
Tony Buck (I)
Joanne Burns (R)
cris cheek (I and R)
Harold Cohen (I)
Graham Collier (I and R)
Lyell Cresswell (R)
Simone de Haan (I)
Paul Dutton (I)
Sandy Evans (I)
Philip George (R)
Peter Gidal (R)
Jepke Goudsmit (I)
Neville Hall (R)
Carla Harryman (I)
Philip Hayward (R)
Lyn Hejinian (I)
Liam Hudson (R)
Graham Jones (I)
Allan Kaprow (I)
Sieglinde Karl (R)
Jeff Keen (I)
Mike Leigh (I)
George Lewis (I)
Peter Lyssiotis (R)
Jackson Mac Low (I)
Larry Ochs (I)
John Oswald (R)
Daryl Pratt (I)
Jeff Pressing (R)
Jon Rose (I)
Jerome Rothenberg (I)
Rik Rue (I)
Ian Shanahan (I)
Michael Snow (I)
Rory Spence (R)
Larry Wendt (R)
David Wessel (I)
Frans Widerberg (I and R)

Some Features of the Responses

As we expected, the proportional response rate to the questionnaire was low (about 15%), and so no secure *general* conclusions can be drawn. But a few impressions conveyed by the responses and interviews were interesting. Firstly, there seemed to be a quite widespread awareness that improvisation and composition form a continuum, but that they nevertheless permit distinct outputs. For example. Richard Barrett, sound composer-improvisor, observes that he finds it "increasingly difficult" to distinguish the two approaches, and continues:

> *In as much as one can speak of two distinct activities here, each is able to generate musical results which are closed or unidiomatic to the other. (Barrett, 1994).*

Barrett finds that in his own work composition and improvisation converge upon a concern with the "tactile" in sound, as we mention in Chapter 4, and indicates how such an approach often stems from improvisation.

We argue that such specific influences of improvisation continue to be productive within composition. Indeed, another common feature of the responses was a very optimistic view of the possibilities of improvisation. Of course, such is the response one might expect when one focuses questions on improvisation. But it was also noticeable that the composers (in whichever art) generally viewed improvisation as important, and felt that it had a role in their own work.

The opinions about the political import of improvised art were interesting. Hardly anyone indicated that their work was unconnected with political issues, but those who did were mainly sound-workers, and at the same time they usually indicated, quite clearly, that they themselves held strong political views, even though they did not feel these were important in their works. Some recognised separately the political significance of adopting improvisation rather than composition.

The requested lists of "interesting" improvisors were also striking in their diversity. Even within a particular art form, the responders' lists rarely overlapped by more than 10%. And in some cases, they listed a few improvisors with whose work we were not familiar at the time, though we rectified this subsequently. Similarly, it is notable that Frost and Yarrow in their excellent book (Frost and Yarrow, 1990) do not consider several of the theatre improvisors we discuss or mention, (Chaikin, People Show, Open Theatre, Marowitz, Wooster Group, Kantor). This diversity probably indicates the healthy breadth of aesthetic approach intrinsic in contemporary improvisation, springing in part from the radical nature of its process.

The Questionnaire

The questionnaire was sent in early 1994 with a letter of invitation to respond, a partial list of recipients of the questionnaire, and brief biographies of ourselves, to indicate our involvement in both the improvised arts and in critical work:

Brief Biographies of Hazel Smith and Roger Dean:

Hazel Smith, *who lived in England until she moved to Australia in 1989, works in the area of experimental poetry, text-sound and performance work and has published in numerous international poetry magazines. Her volume* **Threely** *was published by the Spectacular Diseases Imprint in 1986, and her volume* **Abstractly Represented: Poems and Performance Texts 1982–90** *was published by Butterfly Books in 1991. Some of her work was included in the 1991 Anthology* **Floating Capital: new poets from London**, *Potes and Poets Press, U.S.A.*

She has given poetry performances in many countries including Australia, Great Britain, USA, Belgium and New Zealand, and also on the ABC, BBC and US radio. She appeared at the Tasmanian Poetry Festival *in 1989 and in the series* Writers in Recital *at the Art Gallery of New South Wales, Sydney in 1990. In 1990 she collaborated on the installation-performance piece TranceFIGUREd Spirit, which was supported by the Australia Council. In 1992 and 1993 she gave poetry performances in San Francisco, San Diego, Auckland, Brisbane, Perth, Auckland and in New South Wales. She has collaborated on several pieces with Roger Dean and their* Poet without Language, Silent Waves, Caged John UnCaged *have featured on the ABC programs* The Listening Room, Jazztracks *and* Returning the Compliment: A tribute to John Cage *respectively. Their work has also been broadcast recently on Radio France, and on New Zealand radio.* Poet without Language *was nominated for the Prix Italia in 1993.*

Hazel Smith has a PhD in contemporary American poetry and is a lecturer in the School of English at the University of New South Wales. Her research has concerned the poetry of Frank O'Hara; technology, improvisation and real-time text performance; and many aspects of poetics. She is also an internationally active violinist and currently leader of the contemporary music group austraLYSIS. She has performed solos and chamber music in many parts of the world including Australia, Belgium, Denmark, Great Britain, Hong Kong, India, Indonesia, New Zealand, Norway and the Philippines and she has featured as soloist on several gramophone records including two of works by Milhaud.

Roger Dean, *composer and sound-artist, is involved with improvisation and composition. He has composed more than 60 works for chamber and improvisation groups, and has more than 30 works available on commercial recordings. He has performed in more than 30 countries, both as double bass player (for whom many works have been written) and as keyboardist. His works have been broadcast in more than 50 countries. Recent compositions have included computer music works, such as* Silent Nuraghi, *as well as instrumental works, such as the recent* Elektra Pulses *for the Elektra String Quartet and computer sounds on tape. His works are published in print by the Open University Press (UK/USA) in his two books on musical improvisation (Creative Improvisation; and New Structures in Jazz and Improvised Music), by Red House Press and La Trobe University Press (Melbourne), and by Sounds Australian. They are available on disc on the European labels* Mosaic *and* Soma; *the Australian label,*

Tall Poppies; and in the immediate future, on Aerial, and other US and UK labels. He is also the Director and founder of the international contemporary sound arts ensemble, austraLYSIS. His research particularly concerns improvisation in the arts; though he is also a professional scientist, and directs the Heart Research Institute in Sydney.

v4/0194.

Questionnaire to artworkers from Hazel Smith and Roger Dean, concerning 'Improvisation and Realtime Manipulation in the Arts since 1945', to be used in a book we are preparing on this subject (Publisher: Harwood Academic).

1) Is your work improvisation? If not, do you improvise within your work? Is improvisation important within it? Is improvisation part of your performances (if any) or your working sessions? Or does improvisation precede your performances (if any) or working sessions? (How) do you prepare for improvisation? Is your improvisation distinct from composition? Does it permit you access to unique kinds of creativity?

2) Does your improvisation take place in realtime; i.e. continuously from start to finish of the creation of an artistic object, be it in performance or private? Or does it take place within a restricted time frame, though not necessarily continuously? If so, roughly how long does it take?

3) Does improvisation allow any dislocation of your mind from its normal procedures? Is your improvisation spontaneous; or ritualised; or shamanistic? Do other people influence your improvisations as they proceed? Do you participate in group improvisations? If so, how do you interact with your fellow improvisors? Does the audience improvise in response to your work? Do environmental factors interact with your improvising as it proceeds? Do you revise your improvisations? Do your improvisations permit transformation of material? Does your improvisation permit inter-media interactions?

4) What is your conception of the idea, improvisation? Do you think improvisation closely related to other creative processes which you or anyone else might use? Would you say that improvisation is important in the arts viewed as a worldwide endeavour? Why? Do you think improvisation is of lesser importance in the arts which are not primarily performance based (e.g. painting, photography)? Is improvisation important in your art-form(s)? Why? Please name some improvisors who you find of interest within your artform(s) or other artforms? (a) From your own country; b) From other countries.)

5) If you are female, do you consider your improvised work in any sense 'feminist' or 'gender specific'? Does your improvisation have a political

intent? Do you consider improvisation a 'political' strategy? How are these questions relevant if you are male?

6) Do you use computers or microprocessors for your work? Do you use them to permit you to improvise? Do you think that computer devices can improvise themselves? Can they interact with your improvising?

7) Would you care to offer a definition of 'improvisation'? Would you like to make any other comments on : improvisation outside the arts; improvisation within the arts; or any other issues?

Would you like to be **interviewed** by us on these matters, and on how your work relates to them? We have interviewed several practitioners and plan further visits to USA and Europe for more interviews gathering material to be used in our book. These will be between April and July 1994. We can also interview by telephone.

REFERENCES

Bibliography and References

Abrioux, Y. (1985) *Ian Hamilton Finlay. A Visual Primer*. Edinburgh, Reaktion.

Adair, C. (1992) *Women and Dance. Sylphs and Sirens*. London, Macmillan.

Adshead-Lansdale, J. and J. Layson (eds) (1994) *Dance History. An Introduction. (2nd Edition)*. London, Routledge.

Allen, D. (ed) (1979) *The Collected Poems of Frank O'Hara*. New York, Knopf.

Allen, D. (ed) (1980) *Composed on the Tongue*. Bolinas, Grey Fox.

Allnutt, G., F. Aguiar, K. Edwards and E. Mottram (eds) (1988) *The New British Poetry*. London, Paladin.

Althoff, E. (1986) Ernie Althoff: low budget composer. Melbourne, Melbourne College of Advanced Education. Film/video.

Althoff, E. (1994) Response to questionnaire.

Althoff, E. and R. Dean (1991) Extending the hardware. *Sounds Australian*, **32**, 38–40.

Altieri, C. (1986) The postmodernism of David Antin's Tuning, *College English*, **48**, 9–26.

Amankulor, N. (1991) Jerzy Grotowski's "Divination Consultation": objective drama seminar at U.C. Irvine. *The Drama Review*, **35**, 155–164.

AMM (1968) The Crypt. Matchless MR5. Sound recording.

AMM (1982) Generative Themes. Matchless MR6. Sound recording.

AMM (1987) The Inexhaustible Document. Matchless MR 13. Sound recording.

Anderson, J. (1987) *Choreography Observed*. Iowa City, Iowa University Press.

Anderson, P. (1988) *Contemporary Jewellery: The Australian Experience 1977–1987*. Sydney, Millennium Books.

Andrews, B. and C. Bernstein (eds) (1984) *The L=A=N=G=U=A=G=E Book*. Carbondale, Illinois, Southern Illinois University Press.

Anfam, D. (1990) *Abstract Expressionism*. London, Thames and Hudson.

Anonymous (1991) *Dance Film and Video Guide*. Princeton, NJ, Dance Horizons.

Antin, D. (1976) *Talking at the Boundaries*. New York, New Directions.

Antin, D. (1984) *Tuning*. New York, New Directions.

Antin, D. (1992) The Other. San Francisco, Carroll's Books. Performance talk.

Antonio, E. D. (1972) Painters Painting: The New York Art Scene 1940–1970. New York, Film/video.

Appel, K. and Texts by P. Restany and A. Ginsberg (1985) *Street Art, Wood Relief, Tapestries, Murals, Villa El Salvador*. New York, Abbeville.

Archer, M. and W. Furlong (1983) Bruce McLean in Conversation with William Furlong. London, Audio Arts.

AREA (1990) Artists Representing Environmental Art. Environmental Art: Working with the elements (Air, Earth, Fire, Water). Hofstra, Hofstra University. Video.

Ashcroft, B., G. Griffiths and H. Tiffin (1989) *The Empire Writes Back*. London, Routledge.

Association of Improvising Musicians (1984) *Improvisation – History, Directions, Practice*. London, Association of Improvising Musicians.

Aston, E. and G. Savona (1991) *Theatre as Sign-System*. London, Routledge.

Atherton, M. (1994) Response to questionnaire.

Auslander, P. (1989) *The New York School Poets as Playwrights. O'Hara, Ashbery, Koch, Schuyler and the Visual Arts*. New York, Peter Lang.

austraLYSIS (1991) Moving the Landscapes. Sydney, Tall Poppies TP007. Sound recording.

austraLYSIS (1994) The Next Room. Sydney, Tall Poppies, 1st CD of double CD TP050. Sound recording.

austraLYSIS (1994) Solid as An Age. Sydney, Tall Poppies, 2nd CD of double CD 'The Next Room', TP 050. Sound recording.

Ayers, R., M. Mollison, I. Stocks and J. Tumeth (1992) *Guide to Video Production*. Sydney, AFTRS.

Bailey, D. (1980) *Improvisation: Its Nature and Practice in Music*. Ashbourne, Moorland (republished Prentice Hall; and revised edition, British Library). This book also formed the basis of a series of British Broadcasting Corporation films "On the Edge" (1991), directed by J. Marre.

Baker, D. N. (ed) (1990) *New Perspectives on Jazz (Proceedings of a conference held 1986)*. Washington, Smithsonian Institution Press.

Banes, S. (1980) *Democracy's Body: Judson Dance Theatre 1962–4*. Ann Arbor, UMI Research Press.

Banes, S. (1980) *Terpsichore in Sneakers: Post-modern Dance*. Boston, Houghton Miflin.

Banes, S. (1993) *Greenwich Village 1963*. Durham, N.C., Duke University Press.

Banes, S. and M. D. Blackwood (1988) Retracing Steps: American Dance Since Postmodernism. Cologne, WDR. Film/video.

Barrett, M. and A. Phillips (1992) *Destabilizing Theory: Contemporary Feminist Debates*. Cambridge, Polity Press.

Barrett, R. (1994) Response to questionnaire.

Barthes, R. (1977) *Image-Music-Text*. London, Fontana.

Baskervill, C. R. (1929) *The Elizabethan Jig and Related Song Drama*. Chicago, University of Chicago Press.

Beardsley, J. (1989) *Earthworks and Beyond: Contemporary Art in the Landscape.* New York, Abbeville Press.

Beck, J. (1972) *The Life of the Theatre. The Relation of the Artist to the Struggle of the People. (Reprinted 1986, with foreword by Judith Malina).* San Francisco, City Lights.

Becket, F. (1991) Language beyond the lexicon. The sound poetry of Bob Cobbing. *Performance,* **64**, 37–46.

Beckett, T. (ed) (1994) *Interruptions.* Kent, Ohio, Beckett.

Beeman, W. O. (1981) Why do they laugh? An interactional approach to humour in traditional Iranian Improvised theatre. *J. American Folklore,* **94**, 506–526.

Benedikt, M. (1987) *For an Architecture of Reality.* New York, Lumen Books.

Benedikt, M. (ed) (1991) *Cyberspace: First Steps.* Cambridge, Mass., MIT Press.

Benson, S. (1981) *Blindspots.* Cambridge, Mass., Whale Cloth Press.

Benson, S. (1983) About the Subject. San Francisco, San Francisco State University. Film/video of performance.

Benson, S. (1988) *Blue Book.* The Figures/Roof.

Benson, S. (1989) *Reverse Order.* Elmwood, Potes and Poets Press Inc.

Benson, S. (1994) Interview with Hazel Smith.

Benson, S. and c. cheek (1979) The Other Side of Steve Benson. Baltimore, Wide Mouth. Sound recording.

Berendt, J. (1983) *The World is Sound. Nada Brahma.* Rochester, Vermont, Destiny Books (English vn, 1991).

Berk, E. and J. Devlin (1991) *Hypertext/Hypermedia Handbook.* New York, McGraw-Hill.

Berkson, B. and J. LeSueur (1980) *Homage to Frank O'Hara.* Bolinas, California, Creative Arts Book Company.

Berliner, P. F. (1994) *Thinking in Jazz. The Infinite Art of Improvisation.* Chicago, University of Chicago Press.

Best, S. and D. Kellner (1991) *Postmodern Theory. Critical Interrogations.* London, Macmillan.

Bilder, E. and J. Malina (eds) (1992) *Theandric: Julian Beck's Last Notebooks.* Living Theatre Archive Section. Chur, Harwood Academic.

BirdYak (1988) Aberration. London, New River Music, Kunder Zoundz KZ 8801. Sound recording.

BirdYak (1988) Green Computer. London, Kunder Zoundz KZ8805. Sound recording.

Bischoff, J. (1994) Interview with Roger Dean.

Blom, L. A. and L. T. Chaplin (1988) *The Moment of Movement. Dance Improvisation.* Pittsburgh, University of Pittsburgh Press.

Blumenthal, E. (1984) *Joseph Chaikin: Exploring at the Boundaries of Theater.* Cambridge, UK, Cambridge University Press.

Boal, A. (1979) *Theater of the Oppressed*. London, Pluto Press.

Boden, M. A. (1990) *The Creative Mind: Myths and Mechanisms*. New York, Basic Books.

Boissiere, O. (1992) *Jean Nouvel. Jean Nouvel, Emmanuel Cattani and Associates*. Zurich, Artemis.

Braun, K. (1986) Where is Grotowski? *The Drama Review*, **30**, 226–240.

Braxton, A. (1989) Seven Compositions (Trio) 1989. Therwil, hat ART Records CD 6025.

Brecht, S. (1988) *Peter Schumann's Bread and Puppet Theatre*. London, Methuen.

Brind, S. and B. Catling (eds) (1994) *Breathing Form*. Oxford, Southern Arts.

Bristol, M. D. (1985) *Carnival and Theatre: Plebeian Culture and the Structure of Authority in Renaissance England*. New York and London, Methuen.

Bromfield, D. (1991) *Identities. A Critical Study of the Work of Mike Parr 1970–1990*. Perth, University of Western Australia Press.

Bromige, D. (1994) Interview with Hazel Smith and Roger Dean.

Brook, P. (1968) The Tempest. Paris, Saga Films. Film/video.

Brook, P. (1991) Grotowski, art as a vehicle. *The Drama Review*, **35**, 92–94.

Brook, P. and J. Kalman (1992) Any event stems from combustion: actors, audiences and theatrical energy (interview with P. Brook). *New Theatre Quarterly*, **8**, 107–112.

Brown, A. C. (1993) Conversation with Roger Dean.

Brown, C. (1989) Snakecharmer. Berkeley, Artifact ART 1001. Sound recording.

Brown, C. (1994) Interview with Roger Dean, Mills College, Oakland, California.

Brown, G. (1968) Emergency. New York, Mystic Fire Video. Film/video.

Brown, K. H. (1965) *The Brig*. New York, Hill and Wang.

Bruce, L. (1991) The Lenny Bruce Originals Vol 1. Berkeley, Fantasy records FCD 60-0231. Sound recording.

Buck, P. (1980) Improvisations. *Spanner*, **2**, 165–186.

Buck, P. (1994) Response to questionnaire.

Buck, T. (1992) Conversation with Roger Dean.

Buckminster Fuller, R. (1970) *I Seem to be a Verb*. New York, Bantam.

Bull, R. (1988) Warren St. Loft, May 19, 1988. New York, Improvised Arts Inc. Dance performance.

Bull, R., H. Cornell and L. Vanaver (1988) Eye on Dance: Improvisation around Musical Forms. New York, ARC VideoDance. Film.

Bunker (1988) Bunker. Toronto, Underwhich. Sound recording.

Bürger, P. (1984) *The Theory of the Avant-Garde*. Minneapolis, University of Minnesota Press.

Burnett, J. (ed) (1982) *Theatre Research Book. Kiss*. Amstelveen, Holland, Boekmakerij.

Burns, J. (1994) Response to questionnaire.

Burwell, P. and D. Toop (1976) Radical structure. *Studio International*, **192**, 319–325.

Busignani, A. (1971) *Pollock*. London, Hamlyn.

Cairns, C. (1988) *The Commedia Dell'Arte: From the Renaissance to Dario Fo*. London, Edwin Mellen Press, UK.

Cardew, C. (1968–1970 (3rd edition 1984)) The Great Learning. The First Chapter of the Confucian Classic with Music in 7 Paragraphs by Cornelius Cardew. London, Cornelius Cardew Committee. Performance score.

Cardew, C. (1971) *Treatise Handbook*. London, Peters.

Cardew, C. (1976) Wiggly lines and wobbly music. *Studio International*, **192**, 249–255.

Carney, R. (1985) *American Dreaming. The Films of John Cassavetes and the American Experience*. Berkeley, University of California Press.

Carney, R. (1994) *The Films of John Cassavetes: Pragmatism, Modernism, and the Movies*. Cambridge, Cambridge University Press.

Carter, A. (1990) Leplastrier. *Arkitekten*, **92**, 2–11.

Cassavetes, J. (1960) Shadows. (Released on video 1992). Los Angeles, Touchstone. Film/video.

Cassavetes, J. (1968) Faces. (Released on video 1992). Los Angeles, Touchstone. Film/video.

CCMC (1985) *Decade. The First Ten Years of the Music Gallery (by Members of the Canadian Contemporary Musicians' Collective)*. Toronto, Music Gallery Editions.

CCMC (1994) Decisive Moments. Toronto, Track and Light Recordings; TLR 02.

Celant, G. (1986) *The Course of the Knife. Claes Oldenburg, Coosje van Bruggen and Frank O. Gehry*. Milano, Edizioni Electa (English translation 1987, Rizzoli, New York).

Chaikin, J. (1972) *The Presence of the Actor. Notes on the Open Theater, Disguises, Acting and Repression*. NYC, Atheneum.

Cheang, S. L. (1994) Fresh Kill. USA, Airwaves Project. Film.

cheek, c. (1985) No title; in Symposium on narrative: what is the status of narrative in your work? *Poetics Journal*, **5**, 71–75.

cheek, c. (1994) Interview with Hazel Smith.

cheek, c. (1994) Response to questionnaire.

Cheeseman, P. (1977) *Fight for Shelton Bar*. London, Methuen.

Childs, B. and C. Hobbs (eds) (1982/3) Forum: Improvisation. *Perspectives of New Music*, 26–111.

Chopin, H. (1983) Henri Chopin. Paris, Cassette A. 102.

Circle (1970) Live In Paris. Berlin, ECM 1018/19. Sound recording.

Cixous, H. and C. Clément (1986) *The Newly Born Woman (translated by Betsy Wing)*. Manchester, Manchester University Press.

Clark, B. (1971) *Group Theatre*. London, Pitman.

Clarke, S. (1961) The Connection. Mystic Fire Video. Film.

Clements, P. (1983) *The Improvised Play: The Work of Mike Leigh*. London, Methuen.

Cobbing, B. (1990) *bob jubile: selected texts of bob cobbing 1944–1990*. London, New River Project.

Cobbing, B. and B. Griffiths (1992) *verbi visi voco: a performance of poetry*. London, Writers Forum.

Coleman, J. (1990) *The Compass. The Improvisational Theatre that Revolutionized American Comedy*. Chicago, University of Chicago Press.

Coleman, O. (1960) Free Jazz. Los Angeles, Atlantic Records ATL 1364. Sound recording.

Collier, J. G. (1994) Response to questionnaire.

Coltrane, J. (1965) Ascension. New York, Impulse Records AS 95. Sound recording.

Coltrane, J. (1967) Expression. New York, Impulse S-9120. Sound recording.

Coltrane, J. (1967) Interstellar Space. New York, Impulse ASD 9277. Sound recording.

Conrads, U., H. G. Sperlich and C. C. a. C. (Translated by Collins, R.) (1962) *The Architecture of Fantasy*. New York, Praeger.

Cotton, B. and R. Oliver (1993) *Understanding Hypermedia. From Multimedia to Virtual Reality*. London, Phaidon.

Couani, A. and P. Lyssiotis (1989) *The Harbour Breathes*. Sydney, Sea Cruise Books.

Craig, S. (ed) (1980) *Dreams and Deconstructions: Alternative Theatre in Britain*. Ambergate, Derbyshire, Amber Lane Press.

Cresswell, L. (1994) Response to questionnaire.

Crohn Schmitt, N. (1990) *Actors and Onlookers: Theater and Twentieth Century Scientific Views of Nature*. Evanston, Illinois, North Western University Press.

Crohn Schmitt, N. (1990) Theorising about performance; why now? *New Theatre Quarterly*, **6**, 231–234.

Crompton, D. (ed) (1994) *A Guide to Archigram 1961–74*. London, Academy editions.

Croyden, M. (1974) *Lunatics, Lovers and Poets: The Contemporary Experimental Theatre*. New York, McGraw-Hill.

Cunningham, M. (1985) *The Dancer and the Dance. In Conversation with Jacqueline Lesschaeve*. London and New York, Marion Boyars.

Curran, A. (1991) Maritime Rites. Sydney, ABC Listening Room; producers Andrew McLennan and Roz Cheney. Symphony for ships' horns.

Curtis, D. (1975) English avant-garde film. *Studio International*, **190**, 176–182.

Daniels, B. (ed) (1990) *Joseph Chaikin and Sam Shepard: Letters and Texts, 1972–1984*. New York, Plume, Penguin.

Davie, A. (1958) *Alan Davie (Catalogue of an exhibition of paintings and drawings from 1936–1958 held at the Whitechapel Art Gallery, London June–August 1958)*. London, Whitechapel Art Gallery.

Davie, A. (1963) *Catalogue of Exhibition at Kunsthalle Bern*. Bern, Kunsthalle Bern.

Davie, A. (1969) *Watercolours and small oils*. London, Gimpel Fils.

Davie, A. (1980–3) Conversations with Hazel Smith and Roger Dean.

Davie, A. (1987) *Alan Davie: Major Works of the Fifties*. London, Gimpel Fils.

Davies, A. (1987) *Other Theatres. The Development of Alternative and Experimental Theatre in Britain*. London, Macmillan.

Davies, H. (1987) A survey of new instruments and sound sculpture. *Echo*. P. Panhuysen (ed), Eindhoven, Het Apollohuis.

Davis, M. (1985) You're Under Arrest. New York, CBS. cd.

de Haan, S. (1991) Improvising the listener: the listener improvises. *Sounds Australian*, **32**, 45–51.

de Quincey, T. (1992–3) Square of Infinity. Lake Mungo, and Performance Space, Sydney, Australia, Body/landscape work.

Dean, R. T. (1977) Jazz vibes: bebop and after. *Jazz Journal*, **30**, 4–7.

Dean, R. T. (1988) Barry Guy. *New Grove Dictionary of Jazz*. B. Kernfeld (ed). London, Macmillan.

Dean, R. T. (1988) Derek Bailey. *New Grove Dictionary of Jazz*. B. Kernfeld (ed). London, Macmillan.

Dean, R. T. (1989) *Creative Improvisation: Jazz, Contemporary Music and Beyond*. Milton Keynes, Open University Press.

Dean, R. T. (1991) TimeDancesPeace. Sydney, Australian Music Centre. Score of sound/body work; also private video.

Dean, R. T. (ed) (1992) *Eleven Views of Music Improvisation*. Sounds Australian (Volume 32). Sydney, Australian Music Centre.

Dean, R. T. (1992) *New Structures in Jazz and Improvised Music since 1960*. Milton Keynes, Open University Press.

Dean, R. T. (1993) It Gets Complicated; in *Australian Piano Miniatures*. Melbourne, Red House Publications. Sound work for speaking pianist.

Dean, R. T. and H. A. Smith (1991) Digesting the message: a view of texts for interpretation, reconstruction and improvisation. *Sounds Australian*, **29**, 38–40.

Dean, R. T. and I. Wilcox (1993) Possible atherogenic effects of hypoxia during obstructive sleep apnoea. *Sleep*, **16**, S15–S22.

Delany, P. and G. P. Landow (eds) (1991) *Hypermedia and Literary Studies*. Boston, MIT Press.

Denley, J. (1991–2) Improvisation : the entanglement of awareness and physicality. *Sounds Australian*, **32**, 25–29.

Denley, J. (1992) Dark Matter. Sydney, Tall Poppies TP008. Sound recording.

Dennis, B. (1970) *Experimental Music in Schools*. Oxford, Oxford University Press.

Denny, P. (1992) Farther in to basic sound. *Musicworks*, **54**, 24–27.

Derrida, J. (1972) Structure sign and play in the discourse of the human sciences. *The Structuralist Controversy*. R. Macksey and E. Donato (eds), Baltimore, John Hopkins University Press.

Dolphy, E. (1964) Last Date. New York, Limelight LS 86013 (and reissues). Sound recording.

Duchartre, P.-L. (1928) *The Italian Comedy: the Improvisation, Scenarios, Lives, Attributes, Portraits, and Masks of the Illustrious. (Reprinted 1966)*. New York, Dover Publications.

Duke, J. H. (ed) (1981) *Missing Forms*. Melbourne, Collective Effort.

Duke, J. H. (1989) Jas H. Duke. Melbourne, NMA Publications. Sound recording.

Duke, J. H. (Undated (1988 or earlier)) *War and Peace*. Melbourne, Collective Effort Press.

Dupuy, J. (1980) *Collective Consciousness: Art Performances in the Seventies*. New York, Performing Arts Journal Publications.

Dutton, P. (1992) Beyond doo-wop or how I came to realise that Hank Williams is avant-garde. *Musicworks*, **54**, 8–19.

Dutton, P. (1994) Informal conversation with Paul Dutton in Toronto.

Eastgate Systems (1990–3) Storyspace. Cambridge, MA, Eastgate Systems. Software.

Elam, K. (1980) *The Semiotics of Theatre and Drama*. London, Methuen.

Erven, E. V. (1992) *The Playful Revolution*. Indiana University Press.

Evans, S. (1994) Conversations with Hazel Smith and Roger Dean.

Feinstein, E. (1985) *Bessie Smith. Empress of the Blues*. London, Penguin.

Féral, J. (1989) Mnouchkine's Workshop at the Soleil: A Lesson in Theatre, *The Drama Review*, **33**, 77–87.

Findlay, R. and H. Filipowicz (1986) Grotowski's laboratory theatre: dissolution and diaspora. *The Drama Review*, **30**, 201–225.

Finley, K. and R. Schechner (1988) A constant state of becoming. *Drama Rev.*, **32**, 154.

Fisher, A. (ed) (1977–80) *Spanual Two*. London, Spanner.

Fisher, A. (1994) Telephone conversation with Hazel Smith.

Fisher, J. (1992) *The Theatre of Yesterday and Tomorrow: Commedia Dell'Arte and the Modern Stage*. Lewiston, Queenstown, Lampeter, Edwin Mellen Press.

Fitzpatrick, T. (ed) (1989) *Altro Polo. Performance: from Product to Process*. Sydney, Frederick May Foundation for Italian Studies.

Fitzpatrick, T. (1991) *Exporting advanced production techniques to Europe: The Commedia dell'Arte and its impact*. Unpublished conference proceedings.

Forte, J. (1990) Women's performance art: feminism and postmodernism. *Performing Feminisms: Feminist Critical Theory and Theatre*. S. E. Case (ed), Baltimore, John Hopkins University Press.

Foster, E. (1994) *Postmodern Poetry: The Talisman Interviews*. Hoboken, NJ, Talisman House.

Foster, K. (1987) Improvisations on location: Kurt Foster on Gehry's architecture. *Architectural Review*, **182**, 65–66.

Foster, S. L. (1986) *Reading Dancing: Bodies and Subjects in Contemporary American Dance*. Berkeley, University of California Press.

Fotheringham, R. (ed) (1987) *Community Theatre in Australia*. Sydney, Currency.

Frascina, F. (1985) *Pollock and After: The Critical Debate*. London, Harper and Row.

Fredman, S. (1990) *Poet's Prose. The Crisis in American Verse*. Cambridge, Cambridge University Press.

Fried, M. (1968) Art and Objecthood. *Minimal Art: A Critical Anthology*. G. Battcock (ed). New York, E. P. Dutton.

Friedman, G. (1964) Three Dances 1964. New York, Film.

Friedman, T. and A. Goldsworthy (eds) (1990) *Hand to Earth. Andy Goldsworthy Sculpture 1976–1990*. New York, H. N. Abrams.

Friedman, V. (1994) Navel Gazing and the Biological Clock. *New York Times*, 21.

Frith, S. (ed) (1989) *World Music, Politics and Social Change*. Manchester, Manchester University Press.

Frost, A. and R. Yarrow (1990) *Improvisation in Drama*. London, Macmillan.

Futagawa, Y. (ed) (1993) *Frank O. Gehry*. Tokyo, A. D. A. Edita.

George, P. and R. Wayment (1994) Mnemonic Notations I. CD-rom interactive.

Gibson, W. (1984) *Neuromancer*. New York, Bantam.

Gidal, P. (1975) Theory and definition of structural/materialist film. *Studio International*, **190**, 189–196.

Gidal, P. (1994) Response to questionnaire.

Gifkins, M. (ed) (1988) *Colin McCahon: Gates and Journeys*. Auckland, Auckland City Art Gallery.

Gill, J. (1995) *Queer Noises*. London, Cassell.

Gillespie, L. (1991) Literacy, orality and the Parry-Lord formula: improvisation and the Afro-American jazz tradition. *Int. Rev. Aesthet. Sociol. Music*, **22**, 147–164.

Ginsberg, A. (1956) *Howl and Other Poems*. San Francisco, City Lights Books.

Ginsberg, A. (1971) *Improvised Poetics*. San Francisco, Anonym Press.

Gioia, T. (1988) *The Imperfect Art*. New York, Oxford University Press.

Gioia, T. (1992) *West Coast Jazz. Modern Jazz in California 1945–1960*. New York, Oxford University Press.

Giroud, D. (ed) (1977) *20th Century Polish Avant Garde Drama*. Ithaca, Cornell University Press.

Goldberg, A. (1991) *Improvised Comedy*. Hollywood, S. French.

Goldberg, R. (1988) *Performance Art: From Futurism to the Present*. London, Thames and Hudson.

Goldsworthy, A. (1990) *Andy Goldsworthy*, London, Viking.

Goldsworthy, A. (1994) Public talk, San Francisco, May.

Gooding, M. (1982) *Bruce McLean*. Oxford and New York, Phaidon.

Goodman, L. (1993) *Contemporary Feminist Theatres: To Each Her Own*. London and New York, Routledge.

Goorney, H. (1981) *The Theatre Workshop Story*. London, Methuen.

Goudsmit, J. and G. Jones (1994) Interview with Hazel Smith and Roger Dean.

Gravel, R. and J.-M. Lavergne (1987) *Impro. Réflexions et Analyses*. Ottawa, Bibliotheque Nationale.

Gray, S. (1978) Playwright's Notes. *Performing Arts Journal*, **3**, 87–91.

Gray, S. (1987) *Swimming to Cambodia: The Collected Works of Spalding Gray*. London, Picador.

Gray, S. (1990) Monster in a Box. New York, Film/video.

Gray, S., E. LeCompte and The Wooster Group (1978) Rumstick Road. *Performing Arts Journal*, **3**, 92–115.

Greenberg, C. (1966) *Art and Culture*. Boston, Beacon.

Grillet, T. (ed) (1991) *Frank Gehry: Projets en Europe*. Paris, Pompidou Centre.

Grooms, R. (1961) The Unwelcome Guests. Film.

Grotowski, J. (1971) Akropolis. New York, Arthur Cantor Films.

Grotowski, J. (1991) *Towards a Poor Theatre. (First published 1968)*. London, Methuen.

Group, P. (1970) *Dionysus in 69*. New York, Farrar, Straus and Giroux.

Grundberg, A. and K. M. Gauss (1987) *Photography and Art: Interactions Since 1946*. Abbeville Press.

Hall, D. and S. J. Fifer (eds) (1990) *Illuminating Video. An Essential Guide to Video Art*. San Francisco, Aperture/Bay Area Video Coalition.

Hall, F. (1985) Improvisation and fixed composition in clogging. *J. Anthropological Study of Human Movement*, **3**, 200–217.

Hall, N. (1994) Response to questionnaire.

Halprin, A. (1974) *Collected Writings*. San Francisco, Dancers' Workshop.

Halprin, A. (Undated) Working with the unconscious series. Berkeley, Thinking Allowed Productions. Film/video.

Halprin, A. and M. D. McCarty (1967) Procession: Contemporary Directions in American Dance. Berkeley, University of California Extension Media Centre. Film.

Hamilton, R. and D. Roth (Undated) *Collaborations of Ch. Rotham*. Hamburg, Hansjörg Mayer/Galleria Cadaqués.

Hammons, D. (1994) *San Francisco Musem of Modern Art Exhibition Catalogue*. San Francisco, MOMA.

Hargreaves, D. J., C. A. Cork and T. Setton (1991) Cognitive strategies in jazz improvisation: an exploratory study. *Can. J. Res. Music Education*, **33**, 47–54.

Harris, C. (ed) (1993) *The Leonardo Almanac. International Resources in Art, Science, and Technology*. Cambridge, Mass, MIT Press.

Harryman, C. (1994) Conversation with Hazel Smith.

Hartigan, G. (1986) Interview with Hazel Smith.

Hartman, C. O. (1991) *Jazz Text. Voice and Improvisation in Poetry, Jazz and Song*. Princeton, Princeton University Press.

Hassan, I. (1980) The question of postmodernism. *Bucknell Review*, **25**, 117–26.

Hattendorf, R. L. (1993) The visual pen: instances of intermedia slippage in Henri Michaux's Meidosems. *Word and Image*, **9**, 133–139.

Hayward, P. (1994) Response to questionnaire.

Hejinian, L. (1994) Conversation with Hazel Smith.

Henry, B. (1993) Talking the talk (Film and improvised dialogue). *Film Comment*, **29**, 39–39.

Hetu, J., D. P. Roger and D. Tremblay (1992) Quand les femmes se melent d'improvisation. *Musicworks*, **54**, 20–23.

Higby, S. S. (1989) Is the body obsolete? (A forum). *Whole Earth Review*, **63**, 47.

Higgins, D. (1984) *Horizons: The Poetics and Theory of the Intermedia*. Carbondale, Southern Illinois University Press.

Himmelblau, C. (1988) *Blaubox*. London, Architectural Association.

Hodgson, J. (1967) Improvised Drama — An Enquiry into its Value. London, BBC. Film/video.

Hodgson, J. and E. Richards (1966) *Improvisation. (revised edition 1974)*. London.

Horn, D. T. (1991) *Comedy Improvisation: Exercises and Techniques for Young Actors*. Colorado Springs, Meriwether Publishing.

Horsemen (1988) 2 Nights. Toronto, Underwhich Editions.

Horsemen, F. (1983) Performance Scores. Toronto, Underwhich Editions.

Howell, J. (1992) *Laurie Anderson*. New York, Thunder's Mouth Press.

Hudson, L. (1990) The Photographic Image. *Imagery*. P. J. Hampson, *et al.* (ed.). London, Routledge: 223–246.

Hudson, L. (1994) Response to questionnaire.

Hudson, L. and B. Jacot (1991) *The Way Men think. Intellect, Intimacy and the Erotic Imagination*. New Haven, Yale University Press.

Hung, T. A. (1993) The Scent of the Green Papaya. Film/video.

Jackman, C. C. (1992) *Some Sociological Issues of Live Music Performances*. Brunel, The University of West London, PhD Thesis.

Jacobson, L. (ed) (1992) *Cyberarts: Exploring Art and Technology*. San Francisco, Miller Freeman.

Jameson, F. (1984) Postmodernism or the cultural logic of late capitalism. *New Left Review*, **146**, 53–92.

Januszczak, W. (1983) *Alan Davie: Village Myths and Other Works*. London, Gimpel Fils.

Jencks, C. (1986) Essay on the battle of the labels: late-modernism vs post-modernism. *Architecture and Urbanism*, January: Charles Jencks Issue, 209–36.

Jencks, C. (1992) *The Post-Modern Reader*. London, Academy Editions.

Jencks, C. and N. Silver (1972) *Adhocism. The Case for Improvisation*. New York, Doubleday.

Jenkin, P. (1991) Improvisation and today's classical performer; or, the neophyte improvisor. *Sounds Australian*, **32**, 34–35.

Johnson, B. (1993) Hear me talkin' to ya: problems of jazz discourse. *Popular Music*, **12**, 1–12.

Johnson, K. and C. Paulenich (1991) *Beneath a Single Moon: Buddhism in Contemporary American Poetry*. Boston and London, Shambhala.

Johnstone, K. (1979) *Impro: Improvisation and the Theatre*. London and Boston, Faber and Faber.

Jones, D. R. (1986) *Great Directors at Work. Stanislavsky, Brecht, Kazan, Brook*. Berkeley, University of California Press.

Jones, L. (1966) *Blues People: Negro Music in White America. (First published 1963)*. London, McGibbon and Kee.

Jordan, S. (1992) *Striding Out. Aspects of Contemporary and New Dance in Britain*. London, Dance Books.

Jost, E. (1974) *Free Jazz (English Edition)*. Graz, Universal.

Joyce, M. (1990) Afternoon: A Story. Boston, Eastgate Systems.

Judson (1980–2) The project tapes. Bennington, VT, Bennington College. 13 Videos, 2–83 minutes each.

Kaeppler, A. (1987) Spontaneous choreography: Polynesian dance. *Yearbook for Traditional Music*, **19**, 13–22.

Kaldor, J. (ed) (1984) *An Australian Accent*. New York, P.S.1.

Kantor, T. (1979) *Le opere di T. Kantor – I pittori di Cricot 2 – Il teatro Cricot 2*. Milano, Palazzo Reale.

Kantor, T. (1986) The Writings of Tadeusz Kantor 1956–1985. Translated by Michael Kobialka. *The Drama Review*, **30**, 114–176.

Kantor, T. (1990) *wielopole, wielopole*. London and New York, Marion Boyars.

Karl, S. (1994) Letter to Hazel Smith and Roger Dean.

Kaye, N. (1994) *Postmodernism and Performance*. London, Macmillan.

Keaton, B. (1965) Buster Keaton Rides Again. Ontario, Canada, National Film Board of Canada. Film/video.

Keen, J. (1970) Meatdaze. Brighton, Film/video.

Keen, J. (1972) White Dust. Brighton, Film/video.

Keen, J. (1977) *Iron Man: Twelve Poems*. Brighton, Paysden.

Keen, J. (1994) Interview with Hazel Smith and Roger Dean.

Keen, J. (c. 1965) *Zippzapp: in Praise of True Love Comics, Monster Fan and the B Feature*. Brighton, Future City.

Keen, J. (c. 1960) Cine Blatz. Brighton, Keen. Film/video.

Keen, J. (c. 1960) White Lite. Brighton, Film/video.

Keen, J. (undated) *The Theatre of Dr Gaz (book of the film)*. Brighton.

Keen, J. (undated) *White Dust (the book of the film)*. Brighton, Family Star Productions.

Keeney, B. P. (1991) *Improvisational Therapy: A Practical Guide for Creative Clinical Strategies*. New York, Guilford Press.

Kennedy, H. (1991) Mike Leigh about his stuff. *Film Comment*, **27**, September/October.

Kerouac, J. (1959) *Mexico City Blues*. New York, Grove Press.

Kerouac, J. (1962) *Big Sur*. New York, McGraw-Hill.

Kerouac, J. (1990) The Jack Kerouac Collection. Santa Monica, Rhino Records R-70339. Sound recording.

Kerouac, J. (1992) *Visions of Cody. (First published in part 1960)*. London, Flamingo Books.

Kershaw, B. (1992) *The Politics of Performance: Radical Theatre as Cultural Intervention*. London and New York, Routledge.

Keyssar, H. (1984) *Feminist Theatre*. London, Macmillan.

King, W. and R. Milner (eds) (1971) *Black Drama Anthology*. New York, Signet.

Kirby, M. (1965) *Happenings. An Illustrated Anthology*. New York, E. P. Dutton.

Klossowicz, T. (1986) Tadeusz Kantor's journey. *The Drama Review*, **30**, 98–113.

Kobialka, M. (1986) Let the artists die? An interview with Tadeusz Kantor. *The Drama Review*, **30**, 177–184.

Koch, K. (1986) Interview with Hazel Smith.

Kofsky, F. (1970) *Black Nationalism and the Revolution in Music*. New York, Pathfinder.

Kostelanetz, R. (1979) *Visual Literature Criticism*. Southern Illinois University Press.

Kostelanetz, R. (1980) *Scenarios*. New York, Assembling Press.

Kostelanetz, R. (1980) *Text-Sound-Texts*. New York, Morrow.

Kostelanetz, R. (1980) *The Theatre of Mixed-Means*. New York, RK Editions.

Kostelanetz, R. (1989) *On Innovative Musicians*. New York, Limelight.

Kostelanetz, R. and S. Scobie (eds) (1981) *Precisely: Ten Eleven Twelve. Aural Literature Criticism*. New York, RK Editions.

Kraft, W. B. (1989) Improvisation in Hungarian ethnic dancing. *Oral Tradition*, **4**, 273–315.

Kumiega, J. (1985) *The Theatre of Grotowski*. London, Methuen.

Lacy, B. and S. deMenil (eds) (1992) *Angels and Franciscans. Innovative Architecture from Los Angeles and San Francisco*. New York, Rizzoli.

Lambert, J.-C. (1984) *Cobra*. New York, Abbeville Press.

Landau, E. (1989) *Jackson Pollock*. London, Thames and Hudson.

Lange, A. and N. Mackey (eds) (1993) *Moment's Notice. Jazz in Poetry and Prose*. Minneapolis, Coffee House Press.

Lask, U. P. (1982) Lask. Munich, ECM disc 1217. Sound recording.

Leclerc, D. (1993) Frank Gehry and his collaboration with artists. *Architecture d'Aujourdhui*, **286**, 78–87.

Leigh, M. (1969) An account of the development of my improvised plays, 1965–1969. An application for the George Devine Award, 1969.

Leigh, M. (1971) Bleak Moments. London, Autumn Productions/BFI. Film.

Leigh, M. (1976) Nuts in May. BBC TV.

Leigh, M. (1977) Abigail's Party. London, Film/video.

Leigh, M. (1977) The Kiss of Death. BBC TV. Film/video.

Leigh, M. (1979) *Abigail's Party*. London, Samuel French.

Leigh, M. (1982) *Goose-Pimples: A play devised by Mike Leigh*. London, Samuel French.

Leigh, M. (1982) Mike Leigh Making Plays. London, BBC. BBC TV Arena documentary; Producer Alan Yentob.

Leigh, M. (1983) Meantime. London, Film/video.

Leigh, M. (1994) Interview with Hazel Smith and Roger Dean.

Leja, M. (1993) *Reframing Abstract Expressionism: Subjectivity and Painting in the 1940s*. New Haven and London, Yale University Press.

Lendra, I. W. (1991) Bali and Grotowski: some parallels in the training process. *The Drama Review*, **35**, 113–139.

Leslie, A. (1986) Interview with Hazel Smith.

Levy, M. (1993) *Technicians of Ecstasy*. Connecticut.

Lewis, G. (1992) Conversation with Roger Dean and Hazel Smith.

Lewis, G. (1994) Voyager. Sound recording.

Lewis, J. (1972) So what do you want from your music — security? *Time Out*, 14 December, 38–40.

Lippard, L. R. (1973) *Six Years: The Dematerialisation of the Art Object from 1966 to 1972*. New York, Praeger.

Litweiler, J. (1992) *Ornette Coleman: The Harmolodic Life*. London, Quartet.

Lock, G. (1988) *Forces in Motion. Anthony Braxton and the Meta-reality of Creative Music*. London, Quartet.

Loeffler, C. E. and D. Tong (1980) *Performance Anthology: Source Book for a Decade of California Performance Art*. San Francisco, Contemporary Arts Press.

Long, R. (1991) *Walking in Circles*. London, South Bank Centre.

Long, R. (Undated) Stones and Flies. Richard Long in the Sahara. London, Arts Council (UK). Film/video.

Lorch, J. (1989) Pirandello, Commedia dell'Arte and Improvisation. *The Commedia dell'Arte*. C. Cairns (ed), Lewiston, Edwin Mellen Press: 297–314.

Lyons, L. and R. Storr (1987) *Chuck Close*. New York, Rizzoli.

Lyotard, J. (1984) *The Postmodern Condition: A Report on Knowledge*. Manchester, Manchester University Press.

Lysis (1984) Music in our Time Recording, BBC. London, BBC. Sound recording.

Lysis (1985) Performance of "A Notated Vocabulary for Eve Rosenthal" by Jackson Mac Low, at Logos Foundation. Ghent, Logos. Sound tape.

Lysis (1987) Superimpositions. London, Soma Recordings, SOMA 783. Sound recording.

Lyssiotis, P. (1994) Response to questionnaire.

Mac Low, J. (1986) *Representative Works; 1938–1985*. New York, Roof Books.

Mac Low, J. (1992) Interview with Hazel Smith and Roger Dean.

MacDonald, S. (1993) *Avant-Garde Film. Motion Studies*. Cambridge, Cambridge University Press.

Machine for Making Sense (1993) Machine for Making Sense. Santa Fe, Aerial. Sound recording.

Mackie, A. (1989) *Art/Talk:Theory and Practice in Abstract Expressionism*. New York, Columbia University Press.

Mailer, N. (1971) A course in film making. *New American Rev.*, **12**, 225–230.

Malina, J. (1984) *The Diaries of Judith Malina*. New York, Grove.

Malina, J. and J. Beck (1971) *Paradise Now. Collective Creation of the Living Theatre*. New York, Random House.

Malloy, J. (1992) Electronic Storytelling in the 21st Century. *Visions of the Future. Art Technology and Computing in the Twenty First Century*. C. A. Pickover (ed). New York, St Martin's Press: 137–145.

Mandeles, C. (1981) Jackson Pollock and jazz: structural parallels. *Arts Magazine*, **56**, 139–141.

Mann, R. (1982) Poetry in Motion. New York, Giorno Systems. Film/video.

Mann, R. (1992) Poetry in Motion. New York, Publisher. CD-ROM (a 2nd edition of Mann, 1982).

Marowitz, C. (1978) *The Act of Being. Toward a Theory of Acting*. New York, Taplinger Publishing Company.

Marranca, B. (ed) (1977) *The Theatre of Images*. New York, Drama Book Specialists.

Marranca, B. and G. Dasgupta (1981) *American Playwrights. A Critical Survey, Vol. 1*. New York, Drama Book Specialists.

Marsh, A. (1993) *Body and Self. Performance Art in Australia 1969–92*. Melbourne, Oxford University Press Australia.

Martin, W. and G. Vallins (1972) *Drama Work One*. London, Evans Brothers.

Martin, W. and G. Vallins (1973) *Drama Work Two*. London, Evans Brothers.

McCabe, C. J. (1984) *Artistic Collaboration in the 20th Century*. Washington, D.C., Smithsonian Institution Press.

McCaffery, S. and b. p. Nichol (eds) (1978) *Sound Poetry: A Catalogue for the Eleventh International Sound Poetry Festival, Toronto, Canada. October 14th to 21st, 1978*. Toronto, Underwhich Editions.

McCormick, J. and H. Sky (1993/4) Under the Sky. Hong Kong (1993) Sydney (1994), Dance/computer interactive performance.

McPhee, C. (1949) The five-tone gamelan music of Bali. *Musical Quarterly*, **35**, 250.

Mekas, J. and A. Mekas (c. 1985) The Brig; by Kenneth Brown (originally released 1964). New York, Mystic Fire Video. Film/video.

Meyer, L. B. (1956) *Emotion and Meaning in Music*. Chicago, University of Chicago Press.

Meyer, L. B. (1965) *Music, the Arts, and Ideas*. Chicago, University of Chicago Press.

Middlemiss, J. (1992) *Guide to Film and Television Research*. Sydney, Allen and Unwin.

Middleton, R. (1990) *Studying Popular Music*. Buckingham, Open University Press.

Minton, P. and R. Turner (1993) Dada da. London, Leo Records CD LR192. Sound recording.

Mitter, S. (1992) *Systems of Rehearsal*. London, Routledge.

Monson, I. (1994) Doubleness and jazz improvisation: irony, parody and ethnomusicology. *Critical Enquiry*, **20**, 283–313.

Moore, R. (1966) U.S.A. Poetry: Frank O'Hara and Ed Saunders. San Francisco, KQED-TV. Film.

Moore, R. (1992) The decline of improvisation in western art music: an interpretation of change. *Int. Rev. Aesthet. Sociol. Music*, **23**, 61–84.

Moreno, J. L. (1973) *The Theatre of Spontaneity*. Boston, Beacon House.

Moreno, J. L. (1977) *Psychodrama*. Boston, Beacon House.

Morgenroth, J. (1987) *Dance Improvisations*. Pittsburgh, University of Pittsburgh Press.

Morrow, B. (ed) (1991) *Conjunctions. The Music Issue.* New York, Bard College.

Moss, D. (1988) The Dense Band: Live In Europe. Berlin, Ear-Rational Records ECD 1004. Sound recording.

Nachmanovitch, S. (1990) *Free Play. Improvisation in Life and Arts.* Los Angeles, J. P. Tarcher.

Namuth, H. and P. Falkenberg (1951) Jackson Pollock. New York, Film.

Necks (1989) Sex. Sydney, Spiral Scratch. Sound recording.

Nettl, B. (1974) Thoughts on improvisation: a comparative approach. *Musical Quarterly,* **LX**, 1–19.

Nettl, B. (1991) New Perspectives on Improvisation (edited by Nettl). *World of Music,* **33**, 3–91.

nichol, b. p. (1982) Ear Rational: Sound Poems 1970–80. Wisconsin, Membrane Press. Sound tape.

nichol, b. p. (1987) Ten sound poets on the poetics of sound. *Musicworks,* **38**, 9–17.

nichol, b. p. (1990) *A Book of Contexts.* Tucson, Chax Press.

Nikolais, A. and M. Louis (1988) Improvisation: the spice of life. New York, ARC Videodance.

Nilsson, R. (1978) Northern Lights. (Video 1989). Los Angeles, New World Video.

Nilsson, R. (1988) Heat and Sunlight. Film.

Nilsson, R. (c. 1970) Signal 7. London, Virgin. Film.

Norden, B. (1991) Forum for freedom. Augusto Boal's Theatre of the Oppressed. *Performance,* **64**, 48–53.

Novack, C. J. (1988) Contact improvisation: a photo essay and summary movement analysis. *The Drama Review,* **32**, 120–133.

Novack, C. J. (1988) Looking at movement as culture: contact improvisation to disco. *The Drama Review,* **32**, 102–119.

Novack, C. J. (1990) *Sharing the Dance. Contact improvisation and American Culture.* Wisconsin, University of Wisconsin Press.

Nunn, T. (1988) Electroacoustic percussion boards: sculptured musical instruments for improvisation. *Leonardo,* **21**, 261–265.

O'Hara, F. (1983) *Standing Still and Walking in New York.* San Francisco, Grey Fox Press. (Edited by Donald Allen).

Obenhags, M. (1985) Einstein on the Beach: The Changing Image of Opera. New York, Public Broadcasting Services. Film.

Ochs, L. (1994) Interview with Roger Dean.

Oliveros, P. (1962) Sonic Meditations. Baltimore, Smith Publishing.

Olson, C. (1973) Projective Verse. *The Poetics of The New American Poetry.* D. Allen and W. Tallman (ed). New York Grove Press: 147–181.

Ong, W. (1982) *Orality and Literacy: The Technologizing of the Word.* London, Routledge.

Open Theatre (1970) Terminal. New York, Camera 3 TV. Film/video.

Open Theatre (1972) The Serpent. New York, Arthur Cantor Presents TV Programme. Film/video.

Osiński, Z. (1991) Grotowski blazes the trails: from objective drama to ritual arts. *The Drama Review*, **35**, 95–112.

Oswald, J. (1994) Response to questionnaire.

Overall, M. J. (1991) Stelarc: an event. Australia, VHS.

Paik, N. J. (1978) In Memoriam G. Maciunas. New York.

Paik, N. J. (1987) Spring/Fall Pt II. New York, Film/video.

Paik, N. J. (1989) Living with the Living Theatre. Pompidou Centre, Paris. Film/video.

Paik, N. J. and J. Godfrey (1973) Global Groove. Boston, WNET. Film.

Paik, N. J. and S. Kubota (1982) Allan n' Allen's Complaint. San Francisco, Send Video Arts. Film/video.

Paik, N. J. and J. Yalkut (1971) Electronic Fables. New York, Film/video.

Panhuysen, P. (ed) (1987) *Echo: The Images of Sound*. Eindhoven, Het Apollohuis.

Parker, E. (1978) Monoceros. London, Incus 27. Sound recording.

Parr, M. (1974) Rules and Displacement Activities Part II. Sydney, Film.

Pasolli, R. (1970) *A Book on the Open Theatre*. Indianapolis, Bobbs-Merrill.

Pavis, P. (1982) *Languages of the Stage: Essays in the Semiology of the Theatre*. New York, Performing Arts Journal Publications.

Paxton, S. (1988) Filmed Conversation with Nancy-Stark Smith. Bennington College. Film/video.

Paxton, S. and B. T. Jones (1983) The Studio Project. New York, Video.

Perkis, T. and J. Bischoff (1989) Artifical Horizon. Berkeley, Artifact Recordings ART 1003. Sound recording.

Perloff, M. (1977) *Frank O'Hara: Poet Among Painters*. Austin, University of Texas Press.

Perloff, M. (1991) *Radical Artifice: Writing Poetry in the Age of Media*. Chicago, University of Chicago Press.

Phillips, T. (1975) *Tom Phillips. Works. Texts. To 1974*. Stuttgart, Hansjorg Mayer.

Phillips, T. (1980) *A Humument. A Treated Victorian Novel*. London, Thames and Hudson.

Phillips, T., G. Bryars and F. Orton (1976) Tom Phillips: Interview. *Studio International*, **192**, 290–296.

Pickover, C. A. (ed) (1992) *Visions of the Future. Art Technology and Computing in the Twenty-First Century*. New York, St Martin's Press.

Pierse, L. (1993) *Theatresports. Down Under*. Sydney, Improcorp.

Placksin, S. (1982) *American Women in Jazz, 1900 to Present*. New York, Wideview Books.

Poole, R. (1985) The origins of the Mahlidingaviser. *Scandinavian Studies*, **57**, 244–285.

Popper, F. (1975) *Art-Action and Participation*. New York, New York University Press.

Poster, M. (ed) (1988) *Jean Baudrillard: Selected Writings*. Cambridge, Polity Press.

Pressing, J. (1988) Improvisation: methods and models. *Generative Processes in Music. The Psychology of Performance, Improvisation and Composition*. J. Sloboda (ed). Oxford, Clarendon Press: 298–345.

Pressing, J. (1992) *Synthesiser Performance and Real-Time Techniques*. Madison, A-R Editions, Inc.

Pressing, J. (ed) (1994) *Compositions for Improvisers: An Australian Perspective*. Melbourne, La Trobe University Press.

Pressing, J. (1994) Response to questionnaire.

Puckette, M. and D. Zicarelli (1990) MAX – an interactive graphic programming environment. Menlo Park, Opcode Systems. Software.

Quinn, W. A. and A. S. Hall (1982) *Jongleur: A Modified Theory of Oral Improvisation and its Effects on the Performance and Transmission of Middle English Romance*. Washington, D.C., University Presses of America.

Rabinow, P. (ed) (1984) *The Foucault Reader*. London, Penguin.

Radano, R. M. (1993) *New Musical Figurations. Anthony Braxton's Cultural Critique*. Chicago, University of Chicago Press.

Rainer, Y. (1974) *Work: 1961–1973*. Halifax, Press of the Nova Scotia College of Art and Design.

Rainer, Y. (1980) Film about a Woman who —. New York, Zeitgest Films. Film/video.

Rainer, Y. (1989) *The Films of Yvonne Rainer*. Bloomington, Indiana University Press.

Rees, R. (1992) *Fringe First: Pioneers of Fringe Theatre on Record*. London, Oberon Books.

Reichardt, J. (1968) Cybernetic Serendipity. *Studio International*, special issue.

Reid, D., P. Monk and L. Dompierre (1994) *The Michael Snow Project: Visual Art*. Toronto, Art Gallery of Ontario.

Reid, D., P. Monk and L. Dompierre (1994) *Visual Art 1951–1993. The Michael Snow Project*. Toronto, Art Gallery of Ontario.

Restany, P. (1982) *Yves Klein*. New York, Harry N. Abrams.

Richards, K. and L. Richards (1990) *The Commedia Dell'Arte: A Documentary History*. Oxford, Basil Blackwell.

Ritchie, M. (1992) Electronic Manipulation. *J. Electroacoustic Mus*, **6**, 11–12.

Ritter, D. (1993) Interactive Video as a Way of Life, Video controlled by live improvised music. *Musicworks*, **56**, 48–54.

Rivers, L. (1963) Life among the stones. *Location*, **1**, 90–98.

Rivers, L. (1986) Interview with Hazel Smith.

Rivers, L. (1992) *What Did I Do?* New York, Harper Collins.

Rivers, L. and C. Brightman (1979) *Drawings and Digressions*. New York, Clarkson N. Potter Inc.

Rochlin, S. (1970) Paradise Now. New York, Mystic Fire Videos. Film/video.

Rochlin, S. and M. Harris (1983) Signals Through the Flames. New York, Mystic Fire Video. Film/video.

Room (1989) Room. Backnang, Sound Aspects CD 1028. Sound recording.

Roose-Evans, J. (1970) *Experimental Theatre: From Stanislavsky to Today*. New York, Avon Books.

Rose, B. (ed) (1975) *Readings in American Art 1900–1975*. New York, Praeger.

Rose, J. (1994) Interview with Roger Dean.

Rose, J. and R. Linz (1992) *The Pink Violin. A Portrait of an Australian Musical Dynasty*. Melbourne, NMA Publications.

Rose, M. (1991) *The Post-Modern and the Post-Industrial*. Cambridge, Cambridge University Press.

Rose, T. (1994) *Black Noise: Rap Music and Black Culture in Contemporary America*. Hanover, USA, University Press of New England.

Rosemont, F. (ed) (1978) *What is Surrealism? Andre Breton Selected Writings*. London, Pluto Press.

Rosenboom, D. (ed) (1976) *Biofeedback and the Arts: Results of Early Experiments*. Aesthetic Research Centre of Canada.

Rosenthal, R. (1993) Filename: Futurfax. Sydney, Performance.

Ross, C. (ed) (1990) *Abstract Expressionism: Creators and Critics. An Anthology*. New York, Harry N. Abrams, Inc.

Rostagno, A., J. Beck and M. Judith (1970) *We, The Living Theatre*. New York, Ballantine Books.

Roth, M. (ed) (1983) *The Amazing Decade. Women and Performance Art in America 1970–1980*. Los Angeles, Astro Artz.

Rothenberg, A. (1990) *Creativity and Madness. New Findings and Old Stereotypes*. Baltimore, Johns Hopkins University Press.

Rothenberg, J. and D. Rothenberg (eds) (1983) *Symposium of the Whole*. Berkeley, CA, University of California Press.

Rova (1989) This Time We are Both. San Francisco, New Albion NA 41. Sound recording.

Rowe, R. (1993) *Interactive Music Systems. Machine Listening and Composing*. Cambridge, MA, MIT Press.

Rue, R. (1991) Assembling...... improvising. Rik Rue in conversation with Roger Dean. *Sounds Australian*, **32**, 29–35.

Rue, R. (1993) Ocean Flows. Sydney, Tall Poppies Records TP 036. Sound recording.

Sandler, I. (1970) *The Triumph of American Painting: A History of Abstract Expressionism*. New York, Harper and Row.

Savran, D. (1986) *The Wooster Group, 1976–1985: Breaking the Rules*. Ann Arbor, Michigan, UMI Press.

Sayre, H. M. (1989) *The Object of Performance. The American Avant-Garde Since 1970*. Chicago, University of Chicago Press.

Sbait, D. H. (1993) Debate in the improvised-sung poetry of the Palestinians. *Asian Folklore Studies*, **52**, 93–117.

Schaefer, J. (1990) *New Sounds. The Virgin Guide to New Music. (Published US 1987)*. London, W. H. Allen and Co.

Schafer, M. (1967) *Ear Cleaning*. Scarborough, Berandol.

Schechner, R. (1973) *Environmental Theatre*. New York, Hawthorn Books.

Schechner, R. (1988) *Performance Theory*. London, Routledge.

Schimmel, P. (ed) (1984) *Action Precision. The New Direction in New York 1955–60*. Newport Beach, Newport Harbor Art Museum.

Schmitt, N. C. (1990) *Actors and Onlookers. Theater and Twentieth-Century Scientific Views of Nature*. Evanston, Illinois, Northwestern University Press.

Scholz, C. (1989) *Untersuchungen zur Geschichte und Typologie der Lautpoesie. Teil 11 Bibliographie*. Obermichelbach, Gertraud Scholz Verlag.

Schuller, G. (1968) *Early Jazz*. Oxford, Oxford University Press.

Seaman, B. (1994) Exquisite Mechanisms of Shivers. Sydney, Binocular. Sound recording.

Shank, T. (1982) *American Alternative Theatre*. London, Macmillan.

Sharp, D. (1989) Performance. *Arch. Review (edited section)*, **185**, 23–85.

Sheppard, R. and A. Clarke (eds) (1991) *Floating Capital: New Poets from London*. Elmwood, Connecticut, Potes and Poets Press.

Silverstein, M. (1991) "Body-presence," Cixous's phenomenology of theatre. *Theatre Journal*, **43**, 507–516.

Sloboda, J. A. (ed) (1988) *Generative Processes in Music: the Cognitive Psychology of Music*. Oxford, Clarendon.

Small, C., A. Durant and E. Prevost (1984) *Improvisation: History, Directions, Practice*. London, Association of Improvising Musicians.

Smith, G. (1983) *Homer, Gregory and Bill Evans? The Theory of Formulaic Composition in the Context of Jazz Piano Improvisation*. Harvard, Boston, PhD Thesis.

Smith, H. (1988) *The Sense of Neurotic Coherence: Structural Reversals in the Poetry of Frank O'Hara*. Nottingham, PhD Thesis.

Smith, H. (1991) *Abstractly Represented: Poems and Performance Texts 1982–1990*. Sydney, Butterfly Books.

Smith, H. (1991) The verbal improvisor. *Sounds Australian*, **32**, 36–38.

Smith, H. (1993) Performance, improvisation and technology: American contemporary avant-garde poetry. *Australasian Journal of American Studies*, **12**, 15–31.

Smith, H. (1994) Poet Without Language. Sydney, Rufus Records, RF 005. Sound recording.

Smith, H. (1994) Simultaneity; in *Australian Compositions for Improvisors* (ed. Pressing, J.). Melbourne, La Trobe University Press. Performance score.

Smith, H. (1994) The transformation of the word: text and performance in the work of Ania Walwicz and Amanda Stewart. *Representation, Discourse and Desire: Contemporary Australian Culture and Critical Theory*. P. Fuery (ed). Melbourne, Longman Chesire.

Smith, H., S. Karl and G. Jones (1990) *TranceFIGUREd Spirit*. Sydney/London, Soma.

Smith, H. A. (1989) Image, text and performance: inter-artistic relationships in contemporary poetry. *Literary Theory and Poetry: Extending the Canon*. D. Murray (ed). London, Batsford: 149–166, 206–208 and 211–213.

Smith, H. A. and R. T. Dean (1991) Poet Without Language. Sydney, Australian Music Centre. Sound Score.

Smith, H. A., R. T. Dean and D. Antin (1993) Talking and Thinking: David Antin in conversation with Hazel Smith and Roger Dean. *Postmodern Culture: An Electronic Journal of Interdisciplinary Criticism*, **3**.

Snow, M. (1964) New York Eye and Ear Control. New York, Film Makers Coop. Film/video.

Snow, M. (1994) Interview with Hazel Smith and Roger Dean. Toronto, Canada.

Snow, M. (ed) (1994) *Music/Sound 1948–1993. The Performed and Recorded Music/Sound of Michael Snow, Solo and with Various Ensembles, his Sound-Films and Sound Installations*. Toronto, Art Gallery of Ontario.

Snow, M. (ed) (1994) *Visual Art 1951–1993. The Michael Snow Project*. Toronto, Art Gallery of Ontario.

Sorkin, M. (1991) *Exquisite Corpse. Writing on Buildings*. London, Verso.

Spence, T. R. (1994) Response to questionnaire.

Spolin, V. (1963) *Improvisation for the Theater. A Handbook of Teaching and Directing Techniques. (updated 1983)*. Evanston, Northwestern University Press.

Steiner, W. (1982) *The Colours of Rhetoric: Problems in the Relation between Modern Literature and Painting*. Chicago, Chicago University Press.

Stewart, A. (1993) ≠. Cambridge, ISAST. Sound recording on Leonardo Music Journal CD Volume 3.

Stokvis, W. (1987) *Cobra: An International Movement in Art after the Second World War*. New York, Rizzoli.

Sweet, J. (1978) *Something Wonderful Right Away: An Oral History of The Second City and The Compass Players*. New York, Avon Books.

Taylor, C. (1958) Coltrane Time. New York, Solid State SS18.o25, disc.

The Hub (1994) Wreckin' Ball. Berkeley, Artifact Recordings. Sound recording.

Thonell, J. (ed) (1994) *Poles Apart. The Music of Roger Smalley*. Perth, Evos Music.

Treitler, L. (1991) Medieval improvisation. *World of Music*, **33**, 29–52.

Tucker, M. (1992) *Dreaming with Open Eyes. The Shamanic Spirit in Twentieth Century Arts and Culture*. London, Aquarian.

Tucker, M. (1992) Music Man's Dream. *Alan Davie: with Essays by Douglas Hall and Michael Tucker*. M. Tucker (ed). London, Lund Humphries.

Tucker, M. (ed) (1993) *Alan Davie: The Quest for the Miraculous*. London, Lund Humphries.

Tufnell, M. and C. Crickmay (1990) *Body Space Image: Notes towards Improvisation and Performance*. London, Virago.

Turner, P. (ed) (1985) *American Images. Photography 1945–80*. London, Penguin.

Tytell, J. (1986) *Naked Angels: The Lives and Literature of the Beat Generation*. New York, Grove Press.

Unruh, V. (1989) Eluding the censor: from script to improvisation in Patética. *Modern Drama*, **XXXII**, 345–356.

van Erven, E. (1988) *Radical Political Theatre*. Indianapolis, Indiana University Press.

van Erven, E. (1992) *The Playful Revolution*. Indiana, Indiana U. Press.

van Itallie, J.-C. (1978) *America Hurrah and Other Plays*. New York, Grove Press.

Vandenbroucke, R. (1982) Athol Fugard: the director collaborates with his actors. *Theater*, **14**, 32–40.

Vandenbroucke, R. (1984) In dialogue with himself: Athol Fugard's notebooks. *Theater*, **16**, 43–48.

Viera, M. (1990) The work of John Cassavetes. Script, performance style and improvisation. *J. Film and Video*, **42**, 34–40.

Vincent, S. and E. Zweig (eds) (1981) *The Poetry Reading. A Contemporary Compendium on Language and Performance*. San Francisco, Momo's Press.

von Flemming, V. (1984) Tarn-name A. R. Penck. Hamburg, NDR. video.

Vostell, W. and D. Higgins (eds) (c. 1973) *Fantastic Architecture*. West Glover, VT, Something Else Press.

Vowinckel, A. (1981) *Natur-Skulptur*. Stuttgart, Wurttembergischer Kunstverein.

Wallace, J. (1995) In the game I make of sense: the poetry of Hazel Smith. *Pages*, volumes are unnumbered, 295–300; expanded version in *Southerly*, **55**, 136–146.

Wallenstein, B. (1979–80) The Jazz-Poetry connection. *Performing Arts Journal*, **11/12**, 142–151; 122–134.

Ward, G. (1993) *Statutes of Liberty*. New York, St. Martin's Press.

Weinreich, R. (1987) *The Spontaneous Poetics of Jack Kerouac*. Carbondale and Edwardsville, Southern Illinois University Press.

Weintraub, L. (1984) *Land Marks. New Site Proposals by Twenty-two Original Pioneers of Environmental Art*. Annandale on Hudson, Bard College.

Weisberg, R. W. (1993) *Creativity: Beyond the Myth of Genius*. New York, W. H. Freeman and Company.

Wendt, L. (1993) Vocal Neighborhoods. A collection from the Post-Sound Poetry Landscape (edited by L. Wendt). Cambridge, ISAST. Sound recording; Leonardo Music Journal CD Volume 3.

Wendt, L. (1993) Vocal neighborhoods: a walk through the post-sound poetry landscape. *Leonardo Music Journal*, **3**, 65–71.

Wendt, L. (1994) Response to questionnaire.

Wessel, D. (1994) Conversation with Roger Dean, Berkeley, California.

Widerberg, F. (1994) Reponse to questionnaire.

Wigley, M. (1993) *The Architecture of Deconstruction: Derrida's Haunt*. Cambridge, USA, MIT Press.

Wildman, E. (ed) (1969) *Anthology of Concretism*. Chicago, Swallow Press.

Wiles, D. (1987) *Shakespeare's Clown: Actor and Text in the Elizabethan Playhouse*. Cambridge, New York, Cambridge University Press.

Williams, R. (1977) *Marxism and Literature*. Oxford, Oxford University Press.

Williams, W. C. (1920) *Kora in Hell: Improvisations*. Boston, The Four Seas Company.

Wilmer, H. (ed) (1991) *Creativity: Paradoxes and Reflections*. Wilmette, Chiron.

Wilmer, V. (1977) *As Serious as Your Life*. London, Alison and Busby.

Winterbottom, P. (1991) Two years before the master. *The Drama Review*, **35**, 140–154.

Wirtschaffer, B. (1963) What's Happening. New York, Film Makers' Coop. Film/video.

Wodiczko, K. (1985) Spalding Gray: the Performing Garage. *Art Forum*, **13**, 99–99.

Wolford, L. (1991) Subjective Reflections on Objective Work: Grotowsi in Irvine. *The Drama Review*, **35**, 165–180.

Wooster Group (1980) Rumstick Road. New York. Film/video.

Yentob, A. (1982) Mike Leigh Making Plays. London, BBC TV. Arena Documentary Film.

Young, L. M. (ed) (1962) *An Anthology. (2nd edn 1970)*. New York, Heiner Friedrich.

Young, P. (1983) *Crystal Clear*. London, Penguin.

Yuan, Z. (1993) Beijing Bastards. China/Hong Kong, Fortissimo Film Sales. Film.

Zimmer, E. and S. Quasha (eds) (1989) *Body against Body: the dance and other collaborations of Bill T. Jones and Arnie Zane*. Barrytown, NY, Station Hill.

Zippay, L. (ed) (1991) *Artists' Video*. New York, Electronic Arts Intermix, Abbeville Press.

Zorn, J. (1985) Cobra. Hat Art CD 2-6040 (2 CDs). Sound recording; 2 performances.

Zorn, J. (1991) Memory and Immorality in Musical Composition. *Poetics Journal*, **9**, 101–105.

Zumthor, P. (1990) *Oral Poetry. An Introduction*. Minneapolis, University of Minnesota Press.

Zurbrugg, N. (1982) Futurism and after: Marinetti, Boccioni and electroacoustic literature. *Comparative Criticism*, **4**, 193–211.

Zurbrugg, N. (1988) Post-modernity, métaphore manquée and the myth of the 'trans-avant-garde'. *Leonardo*, **21**, 61–70.

Zurbrugg, N. (1989) Sound art, radio art, and post-radio performance in Australia. *Continuum: An Australian Journal of the Media*, **2**, 16–49.

Zurbrugg, N. (ed) (1994) *Electronic Arts in Australia. An edited volume of Continuum, Vol. 8, No. 1*. Murdoch, Continuum.

FIGURE LEGENDS

Figure 1. Some Improvisatory Developments since 1945. The figure attempts to indicate in a highly simplified way some of the fluxes between different improvisatory activities, and the continuities between sound, visual and body art. Some individual artists, such as Cage and Cunningham, are shown in brackets, to indicate that they were not primarily improvisors.

Figure 2a. Some scores for improvisors, and simple models of their possible results.

Score 1 is shared by all performers; and it is indicated that there might be from 1 to n performers. Scores 2 and 3 are each for three performers, who have different score instructions, but the principles implied can be used for any number of performers. Score 2, like 1, is based on the idea of discrete kinds of material (action, words, sounds) being used as the basis of the improvisation.

The scores are in sections and are read successively from left to right. In each Score, A, B, C —> Z, correspond to different types of material to be used as the basis for improvising. A(1) —> A(n) —> A(n + 1) —> A(n + 2) —> etc. forms an associative chain as a result of successive improvisations on material A; and similarly for B(1) —>B(n) and so on. For each type of material, for example A, A(n) is the generic term, but each performer would probably have different versions of A(n). At any point a performer might move from A(n) to A(n – 1), or A(n ± any number) rather than A(n + 1), but these possibilities are neglected for clarity.

Score 3 adds to this the concept of process instruction in the score. Here A to Z are different kinds of improvisatory process (for example, rhythmic improvising; or expanding or contracting a movement or phrase) rather than specified material. In addition, S and NS refer to the sensory and non-sensory modes of improvisatory generation, discussed in the text of Chapter 2. A multiplicity of possible results exist, and only a limited selection are indicated. For example, performer 2, in the second section, has the instruction S, i.e. sensory, indicating that the performer should concentrate on sensing all the surrounding events, and on responding to them. Thus possible outputs from this performer include A(n + 1), relating to the preceding section; or C(n), relating to the ongoing process of performer 1. In the third section, performer 2 has NS, and thus possible outputs include

A(n + 2) or C(n + 1). These outputs would continue the preceding process, and be independent of any changes in the processes of performers 1 and 3, though as indicated in the results description, this might well *coincide* with the processes adopted by performers 1 and 3. The main alternative possibility for performer 2 is a new, unconnected process, indicated as X(n). In section 4, the single result shown for performer 2 is such an unconnected process Y(n), though of course many alternatives would be possible at this point. Finally, consider the role of performer 2 in the last section, where the score indicates process S. Because performer 3 has a non-sensory process here, we have indicated the commencement of H(n). Performer 2 might then make a positive sensory generative response, giving rise to another H(n), though alternatives such as Z(n + 1), a positive response to performer 1, might also occur.

Figure 2b. The performance matrix for a small group of free improvisors.
         This is a highly simplified representation of the succession of events as performers 1 to n improvise through a succession of freely chosen states (t1 to tn) in which they pursue processes (P1 to Pn). Xs indicate the status of each performer at a particular time; and the segment diagrams reveal the process instruction each player has, some of which are obscured in the block diagram. The segmentation into time units t1 —> tn in this case might be determined by at least one improvisor making a change of process type. However, some improvisors might continue "unperturbed" across such a time unit interface. Each time unit would nevertheless constitute a "transition" point as discussed in the text, so some works might involve only a few time units, although lasting many minutes.

Figure 3. Part of the score of John Zorn's "Cobra". Reproduced from the CD sleeve notes with acknowledgments to hat ART recordings (hat ART CD 2-6040; 1991).

Figure 4. The opening of " what am i doing here" by David Antin. Reproduced with thanks from his "talking at the boundaries", New Directions Books, New York, 1976.

Figure 5. The opening of Steve Benson's "Back". Reproduced with thanks from a manuscript provided by the author.

Figure 6. Andy Goldsworthy's "Tossing Sticks in the Air" (1980), by kind permission of the artist. Another in this series of tossing events is illustrated in "Earthworks and Beyond", (Beardsley, 1989), p. 53.

Figure 7. "Worm" by Bob Cobbing. Reproduced by kind permission of the author.

Figure 8. Part of a score by bp nichol. Reproduced with thanks to Chax Press, Tucson, from "A Book of Contexts" (bp nichol, 1990).

Figure 9. Part of "A Notated Vocabulary for Eve Rosenthal" by Jackson Mac Low, reproduced by kind permission of the author.

Figure 10. A score page of "Poet Without Language" by Hazel Smith and Roger Dean (1993), by courtesy of the Australian Music Centre and the Australian Broadcasting Corporation.

Figure 11. Part of "TimeDancesPeace" by Roger Dean (1991), by courtesy of the Australian Music Centre.

Figure 12. "US" by Larry Rivers and Frank O'Hara (by permission of the Museum of Modern Art, New York).

Figure 13. Kinetic Energy in action (from "Who Lives?", 1993). By kind permission of Kinetic Energy.

Figure 14. Graham Jones wearing a "TranceFIGUREd Spirit" body piece by Sieglinde Karl. By kind permission of Sieglinde Karl and Rufus Records.

Figure 15. cris cheek in performance in "Institutional Dim" (1993). This performance was part of "Breathing Form", a series of events in Oxford, UK, and is documented in the booklet of the same name (Brind and Catling, 1994).

Figure 16. High Speed Gaz for Dave Curtis, by Jeff Keen, from his pamphlet, The Theatre of Dr Gaz (undated). Reproduced by kind permission of the film-maker.

Figure 17. A hypothetical improvisors' network. A, B, and C are three improvisors, shown communicating reciprocally with each other in 7 different ways. Solid lines indicate electronic connections, while wavy lines indicate connection by the human senses. Any or all of the electronic signals might be presented to the audience directly, or after modification by a receiving improvisor. Not shown are 7 connections from each of A, B and C to a central computer which could be running software such as MAX, or an artificial intelligence program to produce responsive information, sound, image and other outputs.

Figure 18. A solo improvisor at work. The diagram attempts to illustrate the multiplicity of receiving, initiating and filtering processes which an improvisor might undertake in projecting a work to an audience, in collaboration with computer and real inputs. These are some of the processes which the three improvisors shown in Figure 17 might be simultaneously undertaking.

INDEX